P9-EDS-624

WAGNER'S
RING
OF THE NIBELUNG

'Mark well my new poem –
it contains the world's beginning
and its end.'

Wagner to Liszt,
11 February 1853

WAGNER'S RING

OF THE NIBELUNG

A Companion

The full German text
with the acclaimed English translation by Stewart Spencer
and commentaries by Barry Millington,
Elizabeth Magee, Roger Hollinrake and Warren Darcy

Edited by Stewart Spencer
and Barry Millington

 Thames & Hudson

© 1993 Stewart Spencer, Barry Millington,
Roger Hollinrake, Elizabeth Magee
and Warren Darcy

All Rights Reserved. No part of this publication may be
reproduced or transmitted in any form or by any means,
electronic or mechanical, including photocopy, recording
or any other information storage and retrieval system,
without prior permission in writing from the publisher.

First published in hardcover in the United States of
America in 1993 by Thames & Hudson Inc.,
500 Fifth Avenue, New York, New York 10110

thamesandhudsonusa.com

First paperback edition 2000
Reprinted 2010

Library of Congress Catalog Card Number 93-60196

ISBN 978-0-500-28194-9

Printed in Slovenia by DZS-Grafik d.o.o

Contents

Introduction

STEWART SPENCER

WITH THE UNPRECEDENTED EXPLOSION in the popularity of opera in recent years and an increase in scholarly interest in the libretto as a genre there has come a need for reliable editions of the texts in question. Of no opera is this more true than Wagner's *Der Ring des Nibelungen*, a work described by Gerhart Hauptmann as 'perhaps the most mystifying work of art of the last few thousand years' (Hauptmann 1942: XVII,307). The present volume is an attempt at partial demystification and, to that end, offers an authoritative edition of the German text, a literal translation of the poem and a series of introductory essays designed to complement one another and to throw light on the musical, philosophical and literary background of the work as well as on its performance and recording history.

Surprisingly, perhaps, no reliable edition of Wagner's libretto exists. The edition which the composer himself superintended in the early 1870s and which was published in volumes 5 and 6 of his *Collected Writings* cannot be regarded as his final word on the subject. Not only was he still working on the musical setting of the words (the full score of *Götterdämmerung* was not completed until after these volumes had already appeared), he was evidently reluctant to introduce changes to the earlier parts of the poem lest they reveal chinks in the theoretically indissoluble unity of words and music which had been an article of Wagnerian faith at the time of the work's conception. In consequence, any modern editor has to take a number of critical decisions in establishing a working text. The present editor decided to use the layout of the *Collected Writings* and, perhaps more controversially, to retain Wagner's 19th-century orthography, since it seemed to him that this is as integral a part of the text as the grammatical and semantic archaisms which it contains and that there is no logical reason why *Nothung* should be modernized as *Notung*, while *frug* is left as *frug* rather than altered to *fragte*. The wording of the poem was then revised in the light of the full score,* so that the text reflects what the reader might expect to hear in the opera house or on record. Where the variants of the full score seem questionable, a note has been included to that effect. The stage-directions are those which appear in the full score. (In keeping with Anglo-American theatrical usage, Wagner's 'stage right' becomes 'stage left' in the translation.)

The translation aims to be as literal as possible. Total literalness is undesirable if one wants to avoid the 'Go and bite your bottom, son of a silly person' school of translating (Chapman and others 1977: 10). Equally, English and German differ in

---

*In the case of *Die Walküre* and *Siegfried* the first editions of 1874 and 1875 respectively were used. For *Das Rheingold* and *Götterdämmerung* the new critical editions of Egon Voss and Hartmut Fladt, published as part of the ongoing *Sämtliche Werke* (Mainz 1970–), were preferred. Most of the vocal and full scores in circulation contain variant readings, but the present edition makes no attempt to take account of all these later aberrations.

a number of important respects: German, for example, can happily use adjectives as nouns, and although generations of opera-goers have made do with (for example) 'Stop, you greedy one', the present translator preferred something less literal and more idiomatic. Furthermore, it was hoped that, by means of a judicious choice of words and sentence structure, something of the poetic flavour of Wagner's original could be recaptured, so that, even if they disagree with Thomas Mann's dictum that 'it has always seemed to me absurd to question Wagner's poetic gifts' (Mann 1985: 190), audiences unfamiliar with German may none the less be able to appreciate why Mann felt able to advance this claim.

Neither the annotation nor the bibliography is intended to be comprehensive: they are merely designed to draw attention to problematical aspects of the work and invite the reader to study the work in greater depth.

The translator is grateful to all the contributors – Warren Darcy, Roger Hollinrake, Elizabeth Magee and Barry Millington – for their authoritative essays and would like to record his particular indebtedness to Barry Millington for co-editing the volume and for rescuing him from some of his more risible attempts to outdo Alfred Forman's pioneering translation of the poem.

The following abbreviations are used in the introductory essays and annotation:

BB   *Das Braune Buch: Tagebuchaufzeichnungen 1865–1882*, ed. Joachim Bergfeld (Zurich and Freiberg, 1975); trans. George Bird as *The Diary of Richard Wagner: The Brown Book* (London, 1980)
CT   *Cosima Wagner: Die Tagebücher 1869–1883*, 2 vols, ed. Martin Gregor-Dellin and Dietrich Mack (Munich and Zurich, 1976–7); trans. Geoffrey Skelton as *Cosima Wagner's Diaries* (London and New York, 1978–80)
GS   Richard Wagner, *Gesammelte Schriften und Dichtungen*, 10 vols, 4th edn (Leipzig, 1907)
MHG   Middle High German
ML   Richard Wagner, *Mein Leben*, ed. Martin Gregor-Dellin (Munich, 1976); trans. Andrew Gray as *My Life* (Cambridge, 1983)
NHG   New High German
OE   Old English
OHG   Old High German
ON   Old Norse
PW   *Richard Wagner's Prose Works*, 8 vols, ed. and trans. William Ashton Ellis (London, 1892–9, R/1972)
SS   Richard Wagner, *Sämtliche Schriften und Dichtungen*, 16 vols (Leipzig, [1911–16])
SW   Richard Wagner, *Sämtliche Werke*, 31 vols, ed. Carl Dahlhaus and Egon Voss (Mainz, 1970—)
WWV   *Wagner Werk-Verzeichnis: Verzeichnis der musikalischen Werke Richard Wagners und ihrer Quellen*, ed. John Deathridge, Martin Geck and Egon Voss (Mainz, 1986)

Chronology

1813	22 May	Wilhelm Richard Wagner born in Leipzig
1839–42		Wagner in Paris
1842–9		Wagner in Dresden
1842	20 October	First performance of *Rienzi*
1843	2 January	First performance of *Der fliegende Holländer*
	after 19 July	According to *My Life*, Wagner first reads Grimm's *Teutonic Mythology*
1844	17 January	Starts borrowing Nibelung material from Royal Library at Dresden
1845	19 October	First performance of *Tannhäuser*
1848	1 April	Eduard Devrient reports Wagner's plan to write a Siegfried opera
	2 June	Wagner informs Schumann of his plan
	4 October	Completes *The Nibelung Legend (Myth)*
	20 October	Completes prose draft of *Siegfried's Tod*
	before 12 Nov	Completes prose draft of prelude
	12–28 November	Verse draft of *Siegfried's Tod*
	before 18 Dec [?]	Revises ending of *Siegfried's Tod*
1849	before 22 Feb	Completes *The Wibelungs*
	March	Plans *Achilles* drama
	March/April	Plans *Jesus of Nazareth*
	May	Abortive Dresden Uprising: Wagner flees to Switzerland
	late July	Completes *Art and Revolution*
	4 November	Completes *The Art-Work of the Future*
1849–58		Wagner in Zurich
1850	January–March	Drafts *Wieland the Smith*
	August	Musical sketches for *Siegfried's Tod*
	before 22 August	Completes *Judaism in Music*
	28 August	Weimar première of *Lohengrin*
	14 September	First mention of a festival theatre for a performance of *Siegfried's Tod*
1851	10 January	Completes *Opera and Drama*
	3–10 May	Prose sketch of *Der junge Siegfried*
	21 May – 1 June	Prose draft of *Der junge Siegfried*
	3–24 June	Verse draft of *Der junge Siegfried*
	July/August	*A Communication to my Friends*
	Oct/Nov	Prose sketches of *Das Rheingold* and *Die Walküre*
1852	23–31 March	Prose draft of *Das Rheingold*

	17–26 May	Prose draft of *Die Walküre*
	1 June – 1 July	Verse draft of *Die Walküre*
	15 Sept–3 Nov	Verse draft of *Das Rheingold*
	before 15 Dec	Revises *Der junge Siegfried* and *Siegfried's Tod* for private publication of poem in February 1853
1853	1 November	Begins first composition draft of *Das Rheingold* (fair copy of full score completed on 26 September 1854)
1854	28 June	Begins first composition draft of *Die Walküre* (fair copy of full score completed on 23 March 1856)
	October	Reads Schopenhauer's *The World as Will and Representation* ('Only now did I understand my own Wotan')
1856	16 May	Drafts prose sketch for a Buddhist drama, *The Victors*, and conceives a new ending for *Siegfried's Tod*
	before 22 Sept	Begins first composition draft of *Siegfried* (fair copy of full score completed on 5 February 1871)
1857	9 August	Finishes second complete draft of *Siegfried* Act II before laying the work aside to concentrate on *Tristan und Isolde* and *Die Meistersinger von Nürnberg*
1858–64		Wagner leads an unsettled existence, living in Venice, Lucerne, Paris, Vienna and Biebrich
1864	12 March	Ludwig II accedes to the Bavarian throne and assures Wagner's material existence
	22 December	Wagner resumes work on first full score of Act II of *Siegfried* (completed on 2 December 1865)
1865	10 June	First performance of *Tristan und Isolde* in Munich
1866–72		Wagner lives at Tribschen on Lake Lucerne
1868	21 June	First performance of *Die Meistersinger von Nürnberg* in Munich
1869	1 March	Begins first complete draft of Act III of *Siegfried* (full score completed on 5 February 1871)
	22 September	First performance of *Das Rheingold* in Munich
	2 October	Begins first complete draft of *Götterdämmerung* (full score of Act III completed on 21 November 1874)
1870	26 June	First performance of *Die Walküre* in Munich
1872–82		Wagner in Bayreuth
1876	13–17 August	First complete performance of the *Ring* in the Bayreuth Festspielhaus
1882	26 July	First performance of *Parsifal* in Bayreuth
1883	13 February	Wagner dies in Venice

'Or Strike at Me Now as I Strangle thy Knee': A note on the text and translation

STEWART SPENCER

WAGNER'S DECISION TO TACKLE AN OPERA on the Nibelung legend appears to have been prompted by a series of articles in the *Neue Zeitschrift für Musik* inviting composers to write a 'national opera' based on the late 12th-century *Nibelungenlied*, a work which, since its rediscovery in 1755, had been hailed as a 'German *Iliad*' and which, by the early years of the 19th century, had come to be seen as the epitome of national aspirations. Other composers, including Mendelssohn, Schumann and Liszt, toyed with the idea of writing a Nibelung opera, although in no case have any musical sketches survived.

For a long time Wagner seems to have been alternately encouraged and discouraged by the evident historicity of the *Nibelungenlied*. As long as his interest was historicist, as it had been in *Tannhäuser* and *Lohengrin* (set, respectively, in 13th-century Thuringia and 10th-century Brabant), the medieval epic clearly had operatic potential; but its appeal must have started to wane once the composer began to develop anarchical leanings and to turn to myth as the expression of a process of necessary revolutionary change. Reluctant Hegelian that he was, Wagner could not use history to predicate the future: myth alone could embody the cosmic struggle between the forces of reaction and a more human and enlightened regime. It was in order to excavate the mythic substratum of the material that Wagner started to delve more deeply into the Scandinavian versions of the legend, versions which, in keeping with the scholarly thinking of the time, he regarded as more archaic and, therefore, more prototypically Germanic. And it was here, too, that he found the verse form of the *Ring*, a form of alliterative metre which is perhaps the work's most striking and notorious linguistic feature.

Wagner's decision to abandon Romantic prosody appears to have been taken in the light of Ludwig Ettmüller's *Die Lieder der Edda von den Nibelungen* (Zurich, 1837). Although other dramatists – including Fouqué, Rückert, Goethe and Bürger – had used alliteration in their stage plays, Wagner was the first to employ *Stabreim* in an operatic libretto. Eduard Devrient, whom Wagner regularly regaled with readings from his latest works, was sufficiently impressed to note in his diary: 'The fellow's a poet through and through. A beautiful piece of work. Alliteration, as used by him, is a real find for opera poems; it ought to be raised to the level of a general principle.' (Conversely, Devrient was frankly alarmed at the 'socialist pretensions' of the 1848 scenario, *The Nibelung Legend*.)

Ettmüller was alone among early 19th-century Germanists in realizing that the alliterative verse forms of Old Norse, Old High German and Old English poetry were fundamentally different from Romance metres and that little was to be gained from parsing them in terms of spondees, trochees, dactyls and the like. Instead, he analysed the lines in terms of *Hebungen* (lifts) and *Senkungen* (dips), noting that there are typically two, occasionally three, lifts or heavily accented syllables per line, with a variable number of dips or weakly stressed syllables dividing them. In consequence, the number of syllables per line may vary from two to nine or more, as in the following example from the end of *Das Rheingold*, where the lifts are marked by an oblique stroke (/) and the weakly stressed syllables by a cross (x). (Lines with two lifts are distinguished typographically from those with three.)

   /   /
*R*heingold!
  / x   /
*R*eines Gold!
x   / xx /
O *l*euchtete noch
x x / x x   / x /
in der *T*iefe dein *l*aut'rer *T*and!

(The present translation attempts to adhere to this arrangement of lifts and dips, and although many of the lines have had to be expanded to accommodate the sense of the original, so that they now contain four or sometimes even five lifts, it is hoped that they will still be read as multiples of two and three and thus give a flavour of the metrical flow of Wagner's German.)

In his translation of the Eddic poems, Ettmüller noted that lines of two lifts each are linked together alliteratively in pairs: the main stave (German *Stab*, hence *Stabreim*) is located on the first lift of the second line of each pair (technically described as a half-line), while the two lifts in the preceding half-line are treated as supporting staves, one or both of which must alliterate with the main stave. In the case of lines with three lifts, any two of the staves may alliterate with each other. (As the above example shows, Wagner also interlaces the two systems, with the third and fourth lines linked by the *l* of *leuchtete* and *laut'rer*.) For the purposes of alliteration, all vowels and diphthongs may rhyme with one another (Erb' und Eigen, / ein' und all'), while initial *h* is ignored, as are weakly stressed prefixes (wie mein *Bl*ick dich verzehrt, / er*bl*indest du nicht?). Wagner also adheres to the rule that consonantal clusters should be treated as discrete sounds: *str* can alliterate only with *str*, not with *st* or *s*, and so on. No translator can hope to work within these constraints without sacrificing the sense of the original, with the result that the present translator has included alliteration only when the demands of literalness and metre have already been met.

In one sense the poem of the *Ring* is untranslatable, since it manifests a degree of linguistic purity which no other language can hope to match. Of all his translators, only Alfred Forman attempted to follow Wagner in eliminating all non-Germanic roots, but the result is sadly unedifying and makes sense only to a reader already familiar with the original (Or strike at me now, / as I strangle thy knee, / thy darling mangle, / to dust with thy maid, / but not fiercely unfence / her here to a nameless harm). At the same time, the elaborate puns (as in the lines quoted above, where the *Rhi*negold is described as *rein* or pure) defy translation altogether, although the translator may occasionally be able to smuggle in other examples of paronomasia in a desperate attempt to reproduce this particular aspect of Wagner's German.

In the winter of 1850/51, in his major aesthetic treatise, *Opera and Drama*, Wagner set out to provide a theoretical justification for his use of *Stabreim*. Adopting an essentially Romantic argument that can be traced back to writers such as Herder, he asserts that the earliest language and most direct expression of human emotion is music. Heightened emotion is said to have been vented in the form of a vocalic melody, while accompanying gestures imbued the utterance with a sense of rhythm. The addition of consonants enabled early man (and woman) to distinguish between objects in the world of physical phenomena, while initial rhyme or alliteration was used to point up relationships between cognate roots. As language developed, it moved further away from its poetic origins and towards a form of speech which, adept at expressing concepts, was no longer capable of expressing emotions. By recreating the language of the heart, as spoken by the 'folk', Wagner hoped to appeal directly to the stultified hearts of his 19th-century listeners and rekindle the human emotions which he felt had been extinguished by modern civilization: the right *sound*, in phonological and musical terms, would evoke a spontaneous resonance in the audience without the need for the intermediary of rational thought processes.

Like his contemporaries, Wagner believed that the *Poetic Edda* was a spontaneous product of the *Volk* (modern scholarship sees it as a highly conscious artefact) and that by recreating its 'natural' diction, he would be instantly understood: the more insistent the *Stabreim* and the more archaic the language, the more 'authentic' the language of the *Ring* would be as an expression of 'purely human' emotions. But by transferring an essentially lyric form to an epic drama and by mistaking the densely allusive and highly elaborate artistry of the Eddic poems for the intuitive outpourings of the popular spirit, Wagner has counterfeited a style which all too often proves an obstacle to our understanding of the poem. Whether or not there is any truth in the anecdote that Wieland Wagner used to insist that his singers translate the text of the *Ring* into German before beginning work on the stage production, the story has a certain poetic truth to it.

Finally, even Wagner himself seems to have admitted that in itself the poem was not instantly communicable: 'To a certain extent it is a matter of indifference to me whether people understand my verses, since they will certainly understand my dramatic action,' he told his second wife, Cosima, on 22 January 1871; and, discussing the scene between Alberich and Hagen in Act II of *Götterdämmerung*, he argued, 'It will have the effect of two strange animals conversing together – one understands nothing of it, but it is all interesting' (CT, 27 December 1873). These are the words of a Schopenhauerian convert who believed in music's ability to express the 'essence' of things without the intermediacy of words. Even for the Wagner of the 1850s the words in themselves could not tell the whole story, of course; yet without a close study of them and the background against which they were written, we shall not come any closer to an understanding of the *Ring*.

Wagner's revolutionary musical reforms

BARRY MILLINGTON

WITH THE COMPOSITION OF THE *RING* and the other great music dramas of his maturity – *Tristan und Isolde*, *Die Meistersinger von Nürnberg* and *Parsifal* – Wagner changed the course of operatic history. The revolution was one both of intent (the 'art-work of the future', unlike conventional opera, was no longer to be mindless entertainment for the privileged) and of construction (new forms had to be evolved to accommodate the new requirements). Central to this revolution was the innovative musical language developed by Wagner with which to articulate his new ideas.

One of Wagner's primary concerns in the *Ring* was that the all-important text should be projected intelligibly. To that end he developed a new kind of vocal line that faithfully reflected the verbal accentuations, poetic meaning and emotional content of the text. The musical setting was no longer to be dictated by regularly phrased melodies (as, say, in Bellini or Meyerbeer) but tailored to the demands of the text. Wagner therefore abandoned (at least in principle – the prescriptions of his theoretical essays were not always strictly adhered to) the traditional modes of recitative and aria, and had his characters declaim to a new, hybrid mode of arioso. In *Das Rheingold*, especially Scenes 2 and 4, there are passages that revert to an old-fashioned *recitativo* style, with abrupt and sustained chords alternating in the orchestra in the traditional manner.

The rigorous matching of poetic shape with musical phrase also resulted, in *Das Rheingold*, in some admittedly pedestrian melodic ideas. By Act I of *Die Walküre*, however, Wagner had brought this new 'musico-poetic synthesis' to a peak of perfection. Here the text is set with natural word stresses and to a melodic line that registers every nuance while remaining musically interesting in its own right. A passage such as 'Traurig saß ich' (Sadly I sat there), from Sieglinde's narration in the third scene, is replete with felicitous examples: the falling semitone from 'Traurig' (sadly) to 'saß' (sat) and the implied appoggiatura on 'während' (while) suggesting Sieglinde's sadness; the low-lying notes, all on a level, at 'tief hing ihm der Hut' (his hat hung so low), depicting the sinister low brim of the Wanderer's hat; the arpeggio figure at 'als ein Schwert in Händen er schwang' (as he brandished a sword in his hands), imitating the swinging of the sword, and so on.

In Acts II and III of *Die Walküre* there are already perceptible signs of Wagner's subsequent shift away from absolute equality of poetry and music. The encounter, at this very time, with the philosophy of Schopenhauer – who elevated music above all other forms of art – may well have been largely responsible for the shift. In *Siegfried* and *Götterdämmerung*, Wagner's adherence to his theoretical prescriptions was far less rigorous. Both works draw on heightened arioso in powerfully conceived vocal lines, but often in Act I of *Siegfried* song-like forms with a more or less regular phrase structure are also in evidence. The conventional divisions into aria, duet, trio, chorus and so forth were abjured in *Das Rheingold* and *Die Walküre*, as in the theoretical writings, but begin to reappear, at least in vestigial form, in *Siegfried* and *Götterdämmerung*.

It has often been noted that *Götterdämmerung*, in particular, represents something of a stylistic regression: the trio of the conspirators (Hagen, Gunther and Brünnhilde) in Act II, for example, with its verbal duplications, ensemble singing and its mode of declamation in general, is often likened to the gestures of traditional grand opera. The paradox can be accounted for, in part, by the fact that the libretto for *Götterdämmerung* was written more than twenty years before the music, at a time when the theories of the music drama had not yet been formulated.

Similarly regressive is the chorus of the vassals in Act II, Scene 2: a C major ensemble (though with augmented-triad coloration under the baleful influence of Hagen) in a somewhat old-fashioned style. It is undeniably rousing in the theatre, however, and it evidently made a forceful impression on the young Schoenberg, for it is alluded to extensively in his *Gurrelieder*. For all its backward-looking tendencies, the stylistic integrity of *Götterdämmerung* is scarcely compromised. The disparate elements are welded together with a technical skill and a dramaturgical conviction that sweep petty criticisms aside.

The word-setting and structural divisions of the 'art-work of the future' may represent the most fundamental of Wagner's innovations, but undoubtedly the most prominent aspect of the *Ring* scores – and the one that for decades attracted most attention from commentators – is the use of leitmotifs: those short, pithy themes associated with specific people (the giants, Loge), objects (sword, ring), emotions or ideas (love and the curse on it). The temptation to assign a label to each motif, as was done with great industry by Hans von Wolzogen in 1876 and subsequently by many others, should be resisted. The dramatic conditions that call forth a motif are rarely uncomplicated; they are subtle complexes of psychological impulses, and an identical psychological situation will never occur.

The motifs assembled in the Thematic Guide on pp. 17–24 are therefore given only a number, except in cases where the association appears incontrovertible. Motifs [10b] and [36] are denied their traditional, and misleading, names of 'Flight' and 'Redemption', since they are more accurately identified with 'love' and 'Brünnhilde' respectively. The Thematic Guide makes no attempt to be comprehensive: the density of motifs in *Götterdämmerung*, in particular, precludes any such possibility. Only the most characteristic motifs, and those repeated frequently, are listed, and generally only their first appearance. (Sometimes, it should be noted, a motif appears in inverted form or in the process of transformation.)

Debussy's jibe, with reference to the system of leitmotifs, about characters leaving their calling-cards, is misplaced. In general, motifs recall not simply a character, but attributes of that character. Thus [9] serves to identify Wotan's spear and the contracts engraved on it (hence his authority and the responsibilities that go with it), while [15] represents not merely the Nibelungs but more generally their industry and, in *Siegfried*, the 'wearisome labour' of Mime.

But the leitmotif principle at its most subtle and dramatically effective is less patent still. In Act I, Scene 1 of *Götterdämmerung*, at the words 'Brächte Siegfried die Braut dir heim' (If Siegfried brought the bride back home), the sounding of the Tarnhelm motif [16] hints at Hagen's plan for winning the bride for Gunther, long before the magic tarnhelm itself is mentioned. Another telling example – instances can be multiplied indefinitely – occurs in *Siegfried*, Act II, Scene 3, where the song of the Woodbird [48] alerts us, and Siegfried, to the murderous intentions behind Mime's blabbering.

A motif which has suffered considerably from unwise labelling is [34]. Often simply called the 'Fate' motif, this one actually has a very specific identity in *Die Walküre* and *Siegfried*, at least. In the Annunciation of Death Scene (*Die Walküre*, Act II, Scene 4) it is heard to the words 'Look on me!', as Brünnhilde appears before Siegmund. In the last scene of *Siegfried* it is heard as Siegfried gazes on the sleeping Brünnhilde. The concept it represents here, then, is the Hegelian one of 'mutual recognition': the notion that the individual recognizes, and therefore attains fulfilment for, him- or herself in the love object. Thus [34] is heard as Brünnhilde tells Siegfried 'What *you* don't know, I know for you', and this gaining of insight also lies behind its appearance at Siegfried's 'stunned, I cannot understand'. Such examples demonstrate the eloquence with which the orchestral voice commentates on the action, or the text, adding a dimension of which the characters themselves are only subconsciously aware.

One further aspect of the leitmotif is worth mentioning: the extent to which it is elevated, in the *Ring*, to a structural principle. Where, in *Lohengrin* and the earlier operas, motifs have generally only a referential function – in other words, they appear when a particular person or idea is alluded to – in the *Ring* they also serve as a means of advancing and articulating the flow of the musical argument. Wagner's process of motivic transformation can be seen throughout the *Ring*: notable examples include the quasi-symphonic development of prominent motifs in the transition passage linking Scenes 3 and 4 of *Das Rheingold*, or that launching the great Wanderer/Erda confrontation of *Siegfried*, Act III, Scene 1.

Some motifs are associated with specific tonalities – the curse with B minor, the tarnhelm with B minor, Valhalla with D flat major (later also with E major), the sword with C major (later also D major) – and although each motif can also be heard in other keys, it is notable how often Wagner steers the music round to a certain key to accommodate one of these motifs. The modulations are always effortless, the manoeuvring skilful. Moreover, the tonality of a large-scale unit may be determined by such a harmonic switch: as Siegfried appears in Gunther's form (*Götterdämmerung*, Act I, Scene 3), the Tarnhelm motif establishes B minor, the key in which the scene and the act will end.

Groups of characters are also identified with a particular tonality: the valkyries with B minor, the Nibelungs with B flat minor. In all four scenes in the *Ring* that feature the Nibelungs and their racial characteristics, B flat minor is predominant and may even be regarded as the tonic key.

The principle of the leitmotif, which Wagner developed and refined in the *Ring*, was perfectly geared to the intricate web of allusions and psychological associations of which the cycle is constructed. It was a principle that was to leave an indelible mark on the operas of subsequent generations of composers – Debussy included. And as with Wagner's other musical reforms mentioned above – the musico–poetic synthesis, the supersession of conventional formal structures – it was irreversibly to change the very nature of opera.

Thematic Guide

[8] Valhalla

[9] Wotan's Spear and Contracts

[10]

[11]Fasolt and Fafner

[12]

[13] Freia's Golden Apples

[14a] Loge

18   *Thematic Guide*

[14b] Loge

[15] Nibelungs and Mining of Gold

[16] Tarnhelm

[17]

[18] Dragon

[19] Curse

[20] cf. [1b]

[21]

[22]

[23] Sword

[24]

[25]

[26] cf. [10b]

[27]

[28] Hunding

[29] Wälsungs

[30] Valkyries

[31] Valkyries' Warcry

[32a]

[32b]

[33]

[34]

[35]

[36]

[37]

[38] Magic Sleep

[39]

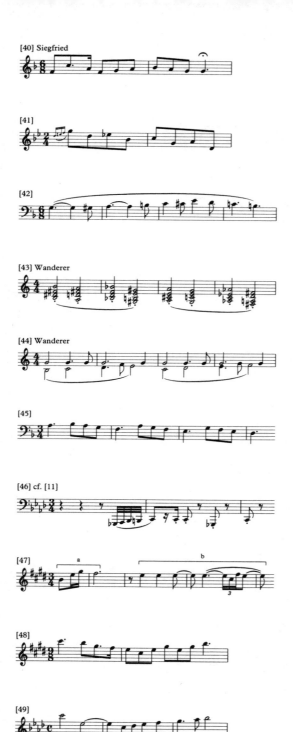

[50]

[51]

[52]

[53] World Ash-Tree cf. [8]

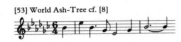

[54] cf. [9] and [20]

[55] cf. [40]

[56]

[57]

[58]

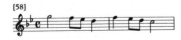

[59]

[60] Gunther

[61] Gutrune

[62] Blood-Brotherhood

[63] Blood-Brotherhood

[64]

[65]

[66]

[67]

'What shall we do for a Ring?'

BARRY MILLINGTON

THE DECADES SINCE THE END OF World War II have seen nothing less than a revolution in the stage representation of opera, with increasingly radical, 'interventionist' directors gradually supplanting those of a more traditional persuasion. With no composer's works has this trend been more pronounced than with those of Wagner. Indeed, the unique challenge presented by the aesthetic and logistical demands of the *Ring* has meant that time and again in the history of staging it is productions of this work that have blazed a trail. The postwar 'New Bayreuth' has, in particular, been a powerhouse of dramaturgical development.

The sets for the first *Ring* at Bayreuth in 1876 were made by the Brückner brothers after designs by Josef Hoffmann, a landscape artist rather than a conventional scene-painter. Hoffmann's drawings, which are all that remain, suggest a Romanticized view of nature à la Caspar David Friedrich. Inevitably, perhaps, these works of the imagination suffered in their transposition to the stage, and Wagner was deeply disappointed with the results. 19th-century stage technology was unable to cope with Wagner's transformations from rivers to mountain tops to subterranean caverns and back, and his determination to attempt, in his own inaugural staging, a literal dragon and ram-drawn chariot – against the advice of his artistic collaborators Carl Brandt and Richard Fricke – consolidated the naturalistic mode of production that was to dominate Bayreuth for decades.

In terms of stage movement, on the other hand, the 'natural' gestures and expressions fostered by Wagner represented something of an advance, in that they superseded the traditional mode of histrionics. Singers were encouraged to ignore the audience and respond only to fellow performers on the stage; strong emphasis was also placed on the role of improvisation and inspiration in stage blocking.

After Wagner's death, control of the festival passed to his widow, Cosima, who attempted to reproduce the naturalistic style of acting which she had witnessed at the first festivals. In her determination to replicate the style fostered by Wagner himself, Cosima succeeded in turning a progressive tendency into an over-prescriptive, reactionary one. The so-called 'Bayreuth style' (both of stagecraft and *mise-en-scène*) held sway at the Festspielhaus until the 1930s and provided a model for other houses too, for example the Metropolitan, New York, where the pre-World War I sets of the Kautsky brothers continued to be used right up until 1939.

For the time being, one had to look elsewhere for radical developments – to the Swiss designer Adolphe Appia. Appia's intention was to penetrate to the essence of Wagner's music dramas by approaching them in a new, anti-naturalistic way: the action was to be simplified and stylized, and colour and light accorded a primary role. Appia's aim of interiorizing the dramas, in order to reveal their symbolic content, was a revolutionary one in the 1890s, when he was developing his theories. Even in the 1920s, when Appia was able to put his theories to the test in stage productions of *Das Rheingold* and *Die Walküre* at Basel (1924–5), he was decades ahead of his time. The hostile public response prevented the cycle from being completed, and it was not until the productions of Wagner's grandson Wieland in the 1950s that the principles of Appia gained widespread approval.

Appia's theories, expounded in a series of essays, were nevertheless influential, at least outside Bayreuth, in the years preceding and following World War I, being reflected in the work of such directors as Gustav Wunderwald in Berlin, Alfred Roller in Vienna, Hans Wildermann in Cologne, Dortmund and Düsseldorf and Ludwig Sievert in several German cities. Other experimental stagings of the 1920s included those by Saladin Schmitt and Johannes Schröder in Duisburg (1922–3) and by Franz Ludwig Hörth and the designer Emil Pirchan in Berlin (1928–9) – the latter making use of film and other expressionist techniques.

Meanwhile, at Bayreuth, Wagner's son Siegfried had succeeded Cosima, and in the years between 1924, when the festival reopened after the war, and his death in 1930, he made a sustained attempt to introduce solid three-dimensional sets and other cautious innovations more in tune with the times. Such 'conservative experimentation', to borrow Mike Ashman's apt phrase, was continued at Bayreuth after the deaths of Cosima and Siegfried in 1930, under the new régime of Heinz Tietjen (artistic director) and Emil Preetorius (scenic designer). The conflicting demands of Bayreuth orthodoxy and a desire for moderate reform are all too evident in the confused argumentation of Preetorius' essay *Wagner: Bild und Vision* (Wagner: Stage Picture and Vision). Preetorius here calls simultaneously for on the one hand a faithful, even reverential recreation of the many natural effects in Wagner's works, which, he said, 'must be rendered clearly and with complete illusion', and on the other for a recognition that the works were conceived essentially as allegories. The latter insight justified his own use of symbolism, reflecting that of the composer himself, and like Appia he favoured the reduction of stage props and the imaginative use of lighting.

Adolf Hitler's unfortunate enthusiasm for Wagner's works may have done little for the composer's reputation, but it had at least two positive consequences. The signing of the Non-Aggression Pact between Germany and Russia in 1939 prompted Stalin, as a friendly gesture to Hitler, to stage *Die Walküre* at the Bolshoy in Moscow. The director chosen was the film-maker Sergey Eisenstein, who attempted to render Wagner's highly pictorial music in an innovatory way. Sieglinde's Act I narration was played out in pantomime by a 'mimic chorus', a group of extras, the latter also being used to shadow the singers in the Ride of the Valkyries. Eisenstein's enacting of the events of the Prelude has subsequently become something of a commonplace, as has his idea of having Hunding accompanied by a gang of henchmen.

The other positive consequence of Hitler's enthusiasm was the determination of Wagner's grandsons, when the Festspielhaus reopened after the war, to make a clean break with all the traditions and ideology with which the works had become associated. Wieland Wagner's 1951 production of the *Ring*, for example, stripped the work of its naturalistic trappings – the forests, the rivers, the mountains and rocky ravines – reducing his sets to the barest essentials. A disc, representing the world and of course the ring, provided the basic set for the whole action, and the symbolism of the sets was enhanced by subtly impressionistic lighting.

Wieland's aim was to reveal the cycle's 'purely human element, stripped of all convention'. When challenged about his abandonment of Wagner's stage directions, he drew a distinction between the stage directions, which remained bound to contemporary 19th-century theatre, and the timeless ideas of the works themselves, which demand constantly new representations. The stage directions, in other words, he regarded as inner visions rather than practical demands.

Wieland Wagner's ideas dominated the European stage throughout the 1950s and 60s. When Ralph Koltai was commissioned to design a *Ring* for the Sadler's Wells (later English National) Opera in the early 1970s, he too contrived to exploit the power of abstract symbolism, evoking a world beyond ordinary human dimensions. There were two important differences, however: one was that Koltai's conception entailed a modest and modified return to naturalism, albeit a naturalism transmuted through the imagination of a creative designer. Forests and rocks were thus present, but represented by shiny bluish-silver metallic planks and spheres. The other difference was that Koltai's designs had a futuristic tendency: this was a *Ring* for the Space Age.

Those for whom the ideal opera production is unobtrusive, passing almost unnoticed, were able to reconcile themselves to the futuristic aspects of this production, because there were few, if any, extraneous elements in terms of the action on stage. Indeed, it is no coincidence that the production is often remembered as 'Ralph Koltai's *Ring*' rather than that of John Blatchley and Glen Byam Shaw, the directors. Certainly, it was a model of constraint compared with the next *Ring* production to be seen in London: the first of Götz Friedrich's, staged at Covent Garden between 1974 and 1982. Friedrich, in common with other followers of the great Walter Felsenstein, fused the latter's principles of psychological and social realism, and his emphasis on role identification, with the quite contrary ones of Brechtian theory to establish the fundamentals of an approach that succeeded Wieland Wagner's as the predominant one throughout the 1970s and 80s. Brecht's so-called 'alienation effect' was used conspicuously by Friedrich by bringing his characters, notably Loge, Alberich and Wotan, to the front of the stage to address the audience directly.

According to Friedrich, the action of the *Ring* takes place not in 13th-century Scandinavia, nor in 19th-century Germany, but here and now in whichever theatre we are currently located. Consequently he believed that first and foremost he was producing not a myth, but a piece of *Welttheater*, i.e., a piece of theatre which holds up a mirror to the world. He believed that the ancient myths interested Wagner primarily as a means of portraying the power struggles of his own period. Yet Friedrich wished to avoid restricting his representation to the 19th century, preferring to emphasize its contemporary and universal relevance.

Another Felsenstein protégé was Joachim Herz, whose socially critical Leipzig *Ring* of 1973–6 set a number of trends. Beginning the second act of *Die Walküre* inside Valhalla instead of on the rocky pass was to become a popular idea, for example. Herz's intention in setting the action in a bourgeois palatial home was presumably to remind the audience that Wotan's dilemma arises from the conflict between natural instincts and materialist society. A historically significant *Ring* production of the same period that should not be overlooked is that of Ulrich Melchinger, mounted at Kassel from 1970. Its *Star Wars* images and Pop Art references, unintegrated into any coherent unity, set the action not in the present but in some timeless sphere.

A landmark in the history of Wagner staging was reached with Patrice Chéreau's *Ring* at Bayreuth in 1976. Chéreau's demythologization of the tetralogy entailed an anti-heroic view of the work, as essayed by Wieland Wagner, Friedrich and Herz, and his setting of the action in an industrialized society, with a hydroelectric dam taking the place of the free-flowing Rhine, along with occasional 20th-century costumes and props, suggested a continuity between Wagner's time and our own. Chéreau's production was no less ground-breaking in its sheer theatricality: scene after scene was recreated in a series of powerful images that have lingered in the memory, and which have been echoed, but rarely surpassed, in subsequent stagings.

Other directors too have emphasized the relevance of the *Ring* to the world of the late 20th century. The ecological aspect was forcefully engaged by Harry Kupfer in his 1988 production at Bayreuth, the entire action taking place in a world already ravaged by a catastrophe, presumably nuclear. Kupfer's reading highlighted the message of the *Ring* that the abandonment of love and humanity's finer sensibilities in favour of territorial aggrandizement and enhanced material possessions leads to the despoliation of nature and ultimately global extinction.

Nikolaus Lehnhoff's 1987 production of the *Ring* for Munich similarly concerned itself with the 'immorality and perversion of human values' engendered by the pursuit of political power and ambition. Erich Wonder's designs, though visually striking, were outstripped by those of Axel Manthey for Ruth Berghaus's *Ring* in Frankfurt (1985–7), in which a constant succession of bizarre, shocking images and of references and gestures from the Theatre of the Absurd overturned all expectations based on the tradition of naturalism. Such references have also informed the work of the younger generation of directors, notably Richard Jones, whose witty, imaginative *Rheingold* of 1989 initiated a *Ring* for Scottish Opera, which, like Appia's, was aborted after *Die Walküre* – though there are now plans for its completion at the Royal Opera House. Herbert Wernicke's production for La Monnaie in Brussels (1991) was equally provocative in the audacity of its visual imagery: a grand piano, representing the primacy of music, on stage throughout; Fricka's rams and Brünnhilde's horse Grane represented as besuited extras with animal heads; Wagner's stage directions projected as flickering silent-film titles. Here the message was not a political one, however; rather that the death of God requires humanity to take control of its destiny.

Each of these radical visions in turn, like that of Wagner himself, has been subjected to uncomprehending ridicule in some quarters. A parallel conservative tradition has thus continued to find a certain degree of support. Peter Hall's naive fairy-tale representation (Bayreuth, 1983) and Otto Schenk's picture-postcard exercise in nostalgia (Metropolitan, 1986–8) are the most notable, or notorious, examples of this tendency.

The continued capacity of Wagner's *Ring* to engage audiences and interpreters, and to excite interest and passionate controversy, is striking confirmation of the work's universal and timeless significance.

In pursuit of the purely human: the 'Ring' and its medieval sources

ELIZABETH MAGEE

ANYONE FAMILIAR WITH THE *RING* who reads the medieval *Nibelungenlied* will be aware that the relationship between Wagner's Nibelung drama and its literary sources is not a simple one. The *Nibelungenlied*, written probably in present-day Austria, is the earliest, greatest and most widely-known German literary version of the native Nibelung saga, itself the fusion of two: one dealing with the historical slaughter of the Rhineland Burgundians by the Huns in 436 and another, of disputed origin, telling of the dragon-slayer Siegfried and his death at the hands of his treacherous in-laws. A popular, well-travelled saga, it eventually made a second home for itself in Scandinavia.

Around the year 1200 the saga crystallized into the *Nibelungenlied*. Its unknown poet evidently relished the courtly ceremonial of his day, for he describes in joyous detail the processions, banquets, costumes and customs which mark the major events of his tale. Carefully reared by royal parents, his hero, Sîvrit, determines to win Kriemhilt, sister of the Burgundian kings at Worms, and performs many services for his future in-laws to secure his bride. A potent mixture of motives ensures Sîvrit's downfall – fear of his power, anger at some injury to Gunther's honour and Prünhilt's reputation, and an acquisitive interest in his celebrated hoard. Out on a hunting expedition across the Rhine, Sîvrit is stabbed in the back by Hagen as he drinks innocently and unsuspectingly from a stream.

For the *Nibelungenlied* poet, Sîvrit is the flower of chivalric convention, so much so that certain well-attested saga events sit uneasily in his poem. The rumbustious episodes where Sîvrit gives Gunther invisible assistance with the wooing and taming of Prünhilt read like interpolations in less elevated taste. The fanciful exploits of Sîvrit's youth – meeting the heirs of Nibelunc's treasure, combating its whip-wielding, tarnhelm-bearing guardian dwarf Alberich, conquering Nibelungenland, slaying a dragon and bathing in its blood – are relegated to Hagen's narration. With Sîvrit laid low among the flowers, the poet moves to his main business, the annihilation of the swashbuckling Burgundians, now themselves called Nibelungs, at Etzel's court.

Little was remembered of the *Nibelungenlied* after the Middle Ages until the early years of the nineteenth century. Then, with Romanticism in its heyday and national awareness stirring under the Napoleonic yoke, the German reading public awoke to its national epic. New editions were published by the dozen, in both original and modernized language, accompanied by intended study aids. The *Nibelungenlied* was taught in schools and lectured on in universities. Leading artists illustrated it. In the 1830s and 1840s, there were calls for a German national opera to be made from it.

The *Nibelungenlied* was the first of the literary sources to come to public attention and probably also the first to come to Wagner's. In the autumn of 1843 Wagner, now resident in Dresden as Court Kapellmeister, settled into an apartment in the Ostra-Allee and straightway laid in a substantial library. It included four editions of the *Nibelungenlied* to complement the Cornelius title-page print which hung over his desk. By January 1844 Wagner was borrowing from Dresden's Royal Library Friedrich Heinrich von der Hagen's *Die Nibelungen* and a year later he took out two further *Nibelungenlied* editions.

A comparison between Wagner's drama and the Middle High German poem shows how strikingly little the two Nibelung works have in common. Only in *Götterdämmerung*, in the encounters with the Rhinedaughters and at Siegfried's elegiac death on the banks of the Rhine, does Wagner approach the events or the mood of the *Nibelungenlied*. He may have responded to the call for a Nibelung opera, but not for a *Nibelungenlied* opera. He later acknowledged as much, confessing that the possibility of making Siegfried the hero of a drama 'had never occurred to me so long as I knew him only from the medieval *Nibelungenlied*' (GS IV,312; PW I,358–9). Wagner's quest for the 'purely human', in accordance with his developing concept of music drama, demanded a hero stripped of courtly veneer and free from the trappings of historical time and place.

Fortunately, the saga had produced other literary sources, some decidedly less courtly, and these were by then also available to the German reading public. Among his sources Wagner mentions the *Thidreks saga*, a wide-ranging work compiled in Norway around 1250 using German material. The comic element of the Siegfried saga which we detected in the *Nibelungenlied* was evidently well-rooted in the German tradition, for it appears again in the *Thidreks saga*. Dispensing with a royal upbringing, the *Thidreks saga* introduces instead the forest foundling motif. The orphaned Sigurð is suckled by a hind until discovered and adopted by the smith Mimir. As a boy, Sigurð displays considerable strength and corresponding nuisance value: he scuffles with the apprentices and, when called upon to turn his hand to useful work, his first blow demolishes the anvil. Mimir sends him into the forest in the hope that his brother, the dragon Regin, will dispose of him; but Sigurð kills first Regin, then Mimir. His assistance at Gunnar's wedding goes beyond his performance in the *Nibelungenlied* and by the time he hands her back to her lord, Brynhild's maidenhead is no more.

Siegfried in the smithy features again in *Das Lied vom hürnen Seyfrid*, written probably in the fifteenth century and printed in the sixteenth. Here there is no Brünnhilde; the action centres on the release of Krimhilt from her dragon captor and exhibits down-trodden dwarfs suffering under the twin oppression of dragon and giant. Hans Sachs, Wagner's revered mastersinger, included a similar smithy scene in his play *Der hürnen Seufrid* of 1557, and in 1726 the *Volksbuch vom gehörnten Sigfrid* provided a prose version. So popular was the smithy scene that it continued in oral tradition and when the Grimm brothers compiled their collection of *Kinder- und Hausmärchen* – the 'fairy tales' – they thought they could point to at least one tale, 'The Young Giant', which continued the smithy-scene tradition of the Siegfried saga.

Wagner's library in the Ostra-Allee boasted the Grimms' fairy tales and three separate works entitled *Das Heldenbuch* – medleys of heroic poems – each containing *Das Lied vom hürnen Seyfrid*. While there is no evidence that he ever read the *Volksbuch* version, Wagner did possess Hans Sachs's play.

In Scandinavia the saga had gone its own way. A prologue to the saga tells of the gods' riverside adventure, when Oðin (Wagner's Wotan) and Loki, accompanied by Hoenir, kill an otter but find he is Fafnir's and Regin's brother. As wergeld they must fill and cover the otterskin with gold. Loki is sent to capture the dwarf

Andvari and demand his hoard as ransom; but as he takes the dwarf's ring, Andvari curses it. The curse is soon seen in action: Fafnir and Regin first kill their father, then brother turns on brother. Regin is forced to flee and Fafnir, now a dragon, guards the hoard.

The scene changes to Hjalprek's court, where Sigurð, son of the late Sigmund, is being reared by Regin, now a smith. Sigurð demands a sword to avenge his father's death. Regin eventually delivers one which withstands Sigurð's exacting tests, but his price is the slaying of Fafnir.

As Sigurð sits roasting Fafnir's heart, he tastes the juices and understands the birds singing of Regin's intended treachery and of the flame-surrounded valkyrie. He despatches Regin, wakes the valkyrie and eventually arrives with Andvari's treasure at Gjuki's court. Here he is induced, with or without the aid of a magic potion, to marry Guðrún, sister of Gunnar and Högni (Hagen).

Disguised as Gunnar, Sigurð wins Brynhild for his brother-in-law. But Brynhild wants only Sigurð. Denied her choice and provoked by Guðrún, she schemes his death. Reluctantly Gunnar and Högni agree. A third brother, Gutthorm, kills Sigurð in bed. Now that her jealousy is appeased, Brynhild declares Sigurð's innocence and joins him on the funeral pyre. The saga continues with the valiant deaths of Gunnar and Högni, the Niflungar, at Atli's hands.

The Scandinavian saga survives in three major literary works. By 1241 Snorri Sturluson had produced his book of poetics, the *Snorra Edda*. This includes stories of the Norse gods and a brief outline of the Niflung/Nibelung saga.

The same saga and some of what went before feature again in the collection of mythological and heroic poems known as the *Poetic Edda*, first compiled in the same period as the *Snorra Edda* and containing poems of varying antiquity, written in alliterative verse. The mythological section employs dialogue and prophecy, didactic verse and knowledge contests, seasoned with a good helping of comedy, to tell of the creation of the cosmos, its ultimate destruction by battle, fire and flood, and the doings of the gods. Most of the heroic section is devoted to Sigurð and the Niflungar. It is inspiring poetry, but the *Poetic Edda* has its drawbacks. A missing section in the only major manuscript leaves a gap between the waking of the valkyrie and the death plots. Matters are not helped by different poems giving varying, sometimes conflicting testimony. Telling a connected story was in any case not the function of many Eddic poems, but rather the evoking of moods and interactive tensions.

The *Volsunga saga*, completed by about 1270, suffers sometimes from trying to fit in too much information but it does give the fullest and completest version. It is the *Volsunga saga* which traces Sigurð's ancestors back to the god Oðin and, through the figure of the one-eyed stranger, shows the god's sustained interest in the family's fortunes. Only the *Volsunga saga* gives the full life story of Sigmund, embracing the incestuous union with his twin sister, the enmity of his brother-in-law, his death at the hands of a rival and Oðin's conferral and withdrawal of the sword-gift.

Wagner had great trouble locating the *Volsunga saga* but eventually ran it to earth in October 1848 in the Royal Library. His own library contained two translations of the *Snorra Edda*; a handful of Eddic mythological poems, including the renowned prophecy *Völuspá*; and the heroic poems as far as Sigurð's death. Over the summer of 1848 he borrowed further volumes of Eddic poems from the Royal Library, although a complete translation of the *Poetic Edda* was not available until 1851.

Wagner had the full range of source material at his disposal; and what a wide range it was. From north to south across the spectrum he found versions of events which tallied nowhere except for Siegfried slaying the dragon, winning a hoard and marrying Gunther's sister. Even the manner of his death and the identity of his murderer were not agreed, let alone the mode of his upbringing. What was Wagner to make of a hero who appears now as valiant champion, now as superman, now as a kinsman of Dennis the Menace and Desperate Dan? What of the Nibelungs: princes, dwarfs or hoard-owners? inhabitants of Nibelungenland? the Burgundian kings themselves and their retinue? – or even, as the *Nibelungenlied* obscurely indicates, something of all these?

Wagner's first move was to cast his net still further. He read the *Heimskringla* of Snorri Sturluson and found there a skaldic poem which possibly inspired the Death Annunciation scene in *Die Walküre*. He adopted another of the Grimms' fairy tales, 'The Tale of the Youth Who Left Home to Learn Fear', and worked it into *Siegfried*. A version of Puss-in-Boots by Ludwig Tieck helped with the capture of Alberich in *Das Rheingold*. Karl Simrock's *Amelungenlied* showed a fresh way of treating the smithy scene; so, too, probably did the Nibelung trilogy by a friend of Wagner's uncle, Friedrich Heinrich de la Motte Fouqué. The list could continue.

For the welding of this material into shape Wagner's most inspiring assistance, best in line with his own artistic instincts, came strangely enough from the scholars. According to the wisdom of the day, the Nibelung saga was One, and what could not be fitted into a cohesive story line might be rationalized away. Karl Lachmann and Wilhelm Grimm, leading scholars both, each produced an 'essential' version of the saga and their methods, if not their results, were not lost on Wagner. Even more so, the urge to see quantities of jostling information in some way unified and brought within one system, typified by Ludwig Frauer's work on the valkyries and, especially, by Jacob Grimm's *Teutonic Mythology*, led among other things to the rich psychological complexity of Wagner's Wotan portrait.

Looking back, we can see how the *Eddas* supplied most of *Das Rheingold*, aided by a view of Nibelungs taken from *Das Lied vom hürnen Seyfrid*. The *Volsunga saga*, supplemented by skaldic poetry, dominates *Die Walküre*. *Siegfried* retains the Wanderer from the *Volsunga saga* and introduces the *Thidreks saga* boyhood tale into an *Edda*-based scenario. In *Götterdämmerung* Wagner blends *Edda* and *Volsunga saga* material until finally, at Siegfried's death, the German *Nibelungenlied* is allowed to come into its own. The perishing gods of the epilogue and the purging by fire and flood bring us back to the *Snorra Edda* and the *Völuspá*.

All the major literary sources, then, and many minor ones reappear in freely varied and liberally tailored form in Wagner's *Ring*. Their influence extends beyond the plot and characters, affecting mood and style; the poetry of the *Edda*, for example, contributed not just alliteration to the *Ring* but also such items as the riddle-contest format in *Siegfried* and Brünnhilde's awakening paean. Finally, the deeper view of the saga Wagner gained from his wider reading and the hints he found there on managing the material helped him produce a dramatic tetralogy rich in complexity, subtlety and significance.

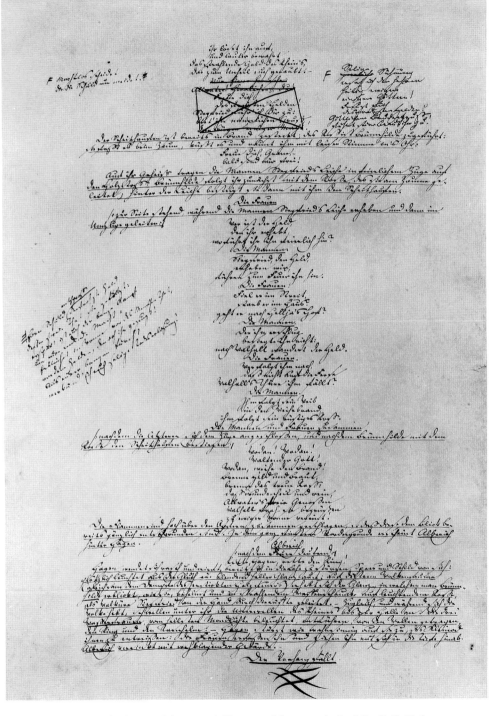

1 The final page of the second fair copy of the verse draft of *Siegfried's Tod*,
November/December 1848. (Private collection)

2 The orchestra pit at Bayreuth. This photograph, taken in the 1920s, shows Siegfried Wagner preparing to conduct.

3 The final page of the manuscript score of *Götterdämmerung*, finished and dated 21 November 1874.

4 A sketch by Adolf von Menzel, showing Wagner on the stage of the Festspielhaus, Bayreuth, during rehearsals in 1875.

5   View from backstage of *Das Rheingold*, Scene 1, at the Metropolitan Opera,
New York, in 1889.

6   Josef Hoffmann's design for *Götterdämmerung*, Act III, Bayreuth, 1876.

7   *Siegfried*, Act III: Emil Preetorius's designs, Bayreuth, 1933–42.

8   *Siegfried*, Act III: Wieland Wagner's production, Bayreuth, 1951–58.

9   *Das Rheingold*, Scene 2: Götz Friedrich's production,
     Royal Opera House, Covent Garden, 1974–82.

10   *Götterdämmerung*, Act II: Joachim Herz's production, Leipzig, 1976.

11   *Götterdämmerung*, Act III: Patrice Chéreau's production, Bayreuth, 1976–80.

12   *Götterdämmerung*, Act III: Peter Hall's production, Bayreuth, 1983–86.

13 *Siegfried*, Act II: Harry Kupfer's production, Bayreuth, 1988-92.

14 *Siegfried*, Act II: Alberich and the Wanderer in Ruth Berghaus's production, Frankfurt, 1986.

15   *Siegfried*, Act II: Günther Schneider-Siemssen's designs,
Metropolitan Opera, New York, 1989.

16   *Die Walküre*, Act III: François Rochaix's production, Seattle, 1986-91.

Epiphany and apocalypse in the 'Ring'

ROGER HOLLINRAKE

THE POETIC TEXT OF *Der Ring des Nibelungen*, as it appeared in the private edition of 1853, had occupied Wagner's attention intermittently for some four-and-a-half years: the reader readily perceives the feat of erudition it entailed. Although Wagner went to extraordinary lengths to achieve parity with his sources, in the process of conflation the material acquired a far more personal emphasis.

A Hegelian by upbringing, conditioned to ideas of historical progress and human perfectibility – ideas celebrated in his quest for a new synthetic art form and in his elevated notion of the role of the artist in the modern world – Wagner was irresistibly drawn, almost from the outset, to the progressive thought of the day. By the mid-1830s he had started to identify himself with the liberal views of the Young Germany in its quest for social, political and religious emancipation. Soon after his appointment to the Dresden Court of Friedrich August II of Saxony, encouraged by his colleague August Röckel – a socialist radical and disciple of Proudhon as he is described in *My Life* – he entered freely into the activities of a group of local republican malcontents whose struggle for reform, carried forward by the more general unrest that pervaded Europe in the last years of the decade, was to culminate in the disastrous uprising of May 1849. Inevitably the Romantic operas completed at Dresden were imbued with the new ideology; and by the time the scenario *The Nibelung Legend (Myth)* and the 'grand heroic opera' *Siegfried's Tod* (the prototype of *Götterdämmerung*) were written towards the end of 1848, the allegory and symbolism of a prehistorical pagan mythology had been pressed into service to underscore a message of uncompromising modernity.

The inspiration for *The Nibelung Legend* was unquestionably Siegfried, the perfect human being, as Wagner subsequently described him to Röckel, who recognizes that 'all consciousness always manifests itself solely in the most immediate vitality and action' (letter of 23 August 1856). Later, the idea of the learning of fear, borrowed from the Brothers Grimm and deftly worked into *Der junge Siegfried* (the preliminary drama written in Zurich in May-June 1851 as part of an unfinished bipartite redaction of the Nibelung scenario), would complete the portrait of hedonistic youth guided by instinct and uncorrupted by civilization: a modern protagonist of the messianic religion of nature with which Rousseau had inflamed the imagination of an earlier revolutionary epoch. Already in the scenario, however, the hero of the *Nibelungenlied* and the gods of Old Norse vernacular literature were brought together in a highly contrived, dependent relationship. As a result, Siegfried, the harbinger of a future egalitarian society, came to be set in the context of an authoritarian, quasi-Hegelian philosophy of political power as in the concluding scene at Valhalla, Brünnhilde, fully armed, conducted the hero in triumph before Wotan, his divine progenitor:

| Biet' ihm minnlichen Gruß, | Grant him a loving greeting, |
| dem Bürgen ewiger Macht! | the bondsman of boundless might! |

The contradiction between an ideology of social if not socialist emancipation (before long, in the last section of the essay *The Wibelungs*, the Nibelungs' hoard would be identified with Proudhon's notion of private property) and an extravagant act of homage to an entrenched monarchical establishment was perhaps never completely resolved. In the years that followed, the question of priorities would play a crucial part in the struggle to reduce the dramatic material to tractable form.

1

When, as a political refugee in Zurich three years later, Wagner returned to the scenario, his sense of identification with the republican cause had, if anything, intensified.

The circumstances of Wagner's introduction to the writings of Ludwig Feuerbach and, consequently, the extent of Feuerbach's influence on *The Nibelung Legend* are shrouded in obscurity. Since the early 1840s the works of the Young Hegelians, David Strauss, Bruno Bauer and Feuerbach, had been readily to hand. It is difficult to doubt that, long before his meeting with Metzdorf and indoctrination into the principles of utopian socialism by the ardent Feuerbachian, Mikhail Bakunin, during his last year in Dresden, he was conversant with the thought of the humanist philosopher, who in his *Principles of the Philosophy of the Future* had defined the tenets of a new secular morality, replacing a stifling ecclesiastical orthodoxy with the primacy of human relationships. 'The task today', Feuerbach announced, 'is the reification and humanization of god, the supersession and dissolution of theology in the study of man' (Feuerbach 1986: 5). Now, in Zurich, prompted by Wilhelm Baumgartner and a providential acquaintance with the exiled revolutionary poet Georg Herwegh – a friend of Bakunin and Marx and one of Feuerbach's more intimate associates – Wagner embarked on a systematic study of Feuerbach's works, recommending them in turn to Röckel (who, as a political prisoner at Waldheim, was to be the recipient of a particularly revealing series of letters on the genesis of the *Ring*). 'I gave myself up', Wagner recalled in his introduction to *The Art-Work of the Future* in his *Collected Writings*, 'to the guidance of a brilliant writer who approached most nearly to my prevailing frame of mind in that he abandoned philosophy, in which he thought he detected only a masked theology, and took refuge in a conception of human nature in which I believed I clearly recognized my own ideal of artistic manhood' (GS III,3; PW I,25).

Although it finds no place in *Siegfried's Tod*, the idea of the supersession of the divine by the human sphere of influence was not alien to *The Nibelung Legend*, where, however, it was eclipsed by the triumphant ending proclaiming Siegfried as the surety of the gods' 'boundless might'. A series of amendments of uncertain date, hastily written in the margins of one of the manuscripts of *Siegfried's Tod* (see Ill. 1), gave the first hint of a drastic alteration in the programme of the drama. The final scene is still set at Valhalla (the stage-directions are unaffected), but Wotan's triumph is no longer in prospect:

Erbleichet in Wonne vor des	Fade away in bliss before man's
[Menschen That,	[deed,
vor dem Helden, den ach ihr	before the hero whom, alas,
[gezeugt!	[you created!

Here, in the notion of the gods' deposition by man, was a theme that brought the action of the ideologically outmoded, neo-Hegelian *Nibelung Legend* into line with the most progressive thought of the day. Essentially, this conception dominated the process of evolution from which, piecemeal, in roughly the reverse order and with a growing refinement of detail, the remaining instalments of the cycle came into being. The main features of the text of the cycle completed by 15 December 1852 may be summarized as follows:

2

The chief result of the humanization of the plot was the reappraisal of the character of Wotan, who already in *Der junge Siegfried*, in a series of scenes adapted from the *Poetic Edda*, had emerged as the leader of a benighted and ineffectual *ancien régime*: a restless and invading presence replacing Hagen as Siegfried's traditional antithesis. The trilogy continued this trend by enhancing the portrait of the god caught in his own machinations, the 'least free of all things living', despite the moral concern that leads him to seek redress. In *Das Rheingold*, to be sure, Wotan enjoys a brief respite as he surveys the distant prospect of the newly completed citadel, the visible expression of his craving for power:

Mannes Ehre,	Manhood's honour,
ewige Macht,	boundless might,
ragen zu endlosem Ruhm!	redound to endless renown!

As the action unfolds, Valhalla is transformed into the dreaded symbol of a corrupt and sinister despotism; Wotan's warrant of authority, the covenant spear on which the laws of the gods are engraved – a notable addition to the story in *Der junge Siegfried* – exists only to be shattered by Siegfried's free, fearless sword as he makes his way to the sleeping valkyrie. '[Wotan] is the sum total of present-day intelligence,' Wagner told Röckel on 25/26 January 1854, 'whereas Siegfried is the man of the future whom we desire and long for but who cannot be made by us, since he must create himself on the basis of *our own annihilation*.' After this, in effect, Wotan has become obsolete and expendable: a symbolic repudiation figure throwing Siegfried's messianic destiny into relief. The rending of the Norns' rope of fate, intact in the original version of the prologue to *Siegfried's Tod*, gives the signal for the passing of the old order and is the prerequisite for the redeeming world-deed of Brünnhilde, the emancipated woman of the future, as she announces the precept that purges Valhalla and cleanses the earth of its curse.

Feuerbach's influence on the humanism of the *Ring* has been strenuously debated. William Ashton Ellis, in particular, was at pains to show that such intimations as are to be found in Wagner's early writings (notably the sketches for *Jesus of Nazareth*, which now provided a copious quarry of material) predated his study of Feuerbach's anti-theological *The Essence of Christianity*, the charter of the revolution, which had set the seal on the philosopher's meteoric ascendancy. At the time of his homage to Feuerbach in *The Art-Work of the Future* (published before his meeting with Herwegh), Ellis claimed that Wagner could have had hardly any first-hand knowledge of the mentor he celebrated. Be this as it may, it is certain that by 1852 Wagner was in no doubt at all of the connotations of the work he was in the process of creating. From Alberich's renunciation of love in the newly invented opening scene with the taunting Rhinedaughters, the eudemonistic teaching of love sanctioned by, if not derived from, Feuerbach was carefully superimposed on the outlines of *The Nibelung Legend*, replacing the Hegelian ideology of power that had been the starting-point. 'Here you have the structural motif that leads up to Siegfried's death,' Wagner told Uhlig on 12 November 1851, some three years after the 'love'-less *Legend* was written: 'Imagine the consequences!' Alberich's renunciation, the theft of the gold and legalistic quarrel over ownership among the giants are balanced with an acute feeling for dramatic symmetry by a closing scene in which a Proudhonian Brünnhilde, as she redresses the theft of the ring, dispenses with private property and, in a world without rulers, proclaims the restitution of love to a humanity from which hitherto it has been consistently withheld. The *ragnarök* of the *Völuspá*, in prospect at least since Wagner introduced a graphic description of the Norse apocalypse into the third act of *Der junge Siegfried*, comes as the fitting culmination: a moment of epiphany, according to the humanist logic of the completely rewritten closing scene, bringing with it the long-awaited death-redemption of the gods, simultaneously restoring hope to man and meaning to the earth.

This hope and meaning were expounded in the long, self-revealing letter to Röckel of 25/26 January 1854, a year after the poem was printed. Here, albeit without acknowledgement, we have the fullest account of the message of the trilogy construed in terms of the 'I-you' relationship of Feuerbach's philosophy. 'Egoism', Wagner writes, 'ceases only when the "I" is subsumed by the "you": this "I" and "you", however, no longer show themselves as such the moment I align myself with the wholeness of the world.' This is the legacy that Brünnhilde, made wise by Siegfried's love, vouchsafes on Siegfried's behalf to a future humanity, a legacy that redresses the trend of the action which otherwise, bereft of any promise for the future, veers dangerously in the direction of a nihilistic void. Only at the age of thirty-six (the year of his flight to Zurich and renewed study of Feuerbach), Wagner goes on to say, did he recognize the goal that gave meaning to his creative endeavours:

> This goal, however, has not yet been recognized as such by the majority of people: but I have indicated above what I understand it to be; it is to render love possible as the most perfect realization of reality – truth; not a conceptual, abstract, non-sensuous love [...] but the love of the 'I' and 'you'.

3

There is an irony in the fact that in around October 1854, only a few months after this letter clinching the case for a Feuerbachian interpretation of the *Ring*, again prompted by Herwegh, Wagner began to study a book that seemed to upset all his philosophical preconceptions: Schopenhauer's long-neglected masterpiece, *The World as Will and Representation*. Once more, it came down to a question of

Wotan's standing in the drama whose message lay in the peroration pointing the moral drawn from the Siegfried epic. Schopenhauer suggested an alternative:

Weißt du, was Wotan – will?   Do you know what Wotan wills?

the god demands as he rises to the tragic height of willing his passing. Might not the god's retreat in the face of a deterministic necessity be construed as a moral advance? his abandonment of his quest for power as the attainment of a higher metaphysical end? Was this not precisely what Schopenhauer had meant when, in setting out the defining characteristics of modern (as distinct from Classical) tragedy in his chapter on the aesthetics of poetry, he wrote: 'What gives tragedy its ethical force is the recognition that the world – that life – offers no real satisfaction and hence does not deserve our loyalty? This is the tragic spirit, it leads to renunciation' (Schopenhauer 1966: II,433–4)?

Up to this point, the possibility of a Wotan 'tragedy' had not entered seriously into Wagner's calculations; yet, incredibly, it required no feat of reconstruction to bring the *Ring* into line with Schopenhauer: 'I recognized to my amazement that the very things I now found so unpalatable in the theory were long familiar to me in my own poetic conception' (ML 523; Eng. trans., 510). All that was needed to make the turn from epiphany to apocalypse was a slight shift of emphasis in the reading of the existing text.

It was at this juncture, therefore, that Franz von Bizonfy, acting as spokesman for Wagner's circle, made his historic attempt to entice Schopenhauer to Zurich, an attempt that now replaced the invitation Wagner and Herwegh had extended to Feuerbach on 3 December 1851, soon after the four instalments of the *Ring* had been sketched out. 'My experience of life', Wagner wrote with heartfelt relief and no apparent sense of self-contradiction in his next letter to Röckel on 5 February 1855, almost exactly a year after his adamantly Feuerbachian letter,

has brought me to a point where only Schopenhauer's philosophy could wholly satisfy me and exert a decisive influence on my whole life. By accepting unreservedly the profound truths of his teaching I was able to follow my own inner bent, and although he has given my line of thought a new direction, yet only this direction harmonized with the profoundly sorrowful conception I had already formed of the world.

The obstacle to a Schopenhauerian *Ring* lay in the peroration which spelled out the drama's now outmoded 'revolutionary' premises. By May 1856, Wagner's latest obsession had yielded a sketch for a new peroration, 'a truly fitting keystone for my poem', as he called it in his letter to Röckel of 23 August, which with its brief reference to the (quasi-Buddhist) doctrine of metempsychosis and hint of an oriental nirvana clearly showed just how deeply Schopenhauer's influence had penetrated. From the same letter to Röckel, we see that Wagner's first impulse was to distance himself from the ubiquitous love idea, if not to try to banish it altogether from his conceptual scheme. Here, after all, was the particular object of Schopenhauer's impassioned tirades – the primary manifestation of the elemental 'Will', the source of all suffering life. The idea, he now declared, had always rankled and had intervened at a crucial moment only to set him off course. In fact, the singularity of the poem all along had consisted in the teaching of world-renunciation, the basic principle of morality: a teaching enshrined not only in the

Ring cycle but in all the works of the 1840s – *Der fliegende Holländer, Tannhäuser* and *Lohengrin* – as well.

None the less, Feuerbach's discredited love idea had been too deliberately invoked for it to be possible to dismiss it as some sort of miscalculation.

The justification for the extraordinary process of dialectical synthesis by which, in 1858, during the composition of *Tristan und Isolde*, the teaching of love was to have been assimilated to the teaching of world-abnegation was never written (it was no more than hinted at in an entry in the Venice Diary for 1 December 1858, in a note in the Annals, in *My Life* and in a handful of jottings for an unrealized 'correction' of Schopenhauer published posthumously). In fairness to Wagner, it should be noted that the equation of love with renunciation, the extinction of personal identity and even death was not at all new, but had been developed at some length in published writings and notes long before he alighted upon Schopenhauer's book. 'What could this yearning for love, the noblest impulse of my nature, be,' he asked in *A Communication to my Friends* in 1851, 'but a longing for release from the present, for absorption into an element of endless love, denied in life, and attainable only through death' (GS IV,279; PW I,323). Not that such a theory, cogently reformulated, would have provided a way out of his exegetical difficulties regarding the *Ring*. Schopenhauer may have been Wagner's great intellectual discovery, bearing on all the music dramas (*Tristan und Isolde, Die Meistersinger von Nürnberg* and *Parsifal*) of his later years. No doubt, too, paradoxically, the trilogy with its infrastructure compounded of Hegelian, Proudhonian, anarchistic, utopian, materialistic, socialistic and Feuerbachian elements had become more completely intelligible in the light of Schopenhauer's defiantly unpolitical, pessimistic precepts. 'No one', Wagner is said to have remarked to Eliza Wille, 'has penetrated more deeply into the spirit of this philosophy than I.' Schopenhauer, for all that, certainly acted as a conservative force insofar as he served to establish that the *Ring* cycle belonged to a corpus of creative work that was *sui generis* and wholly compatible with neither the humanism of the 1840s nor the fashionable pessimism of the later 1850s, which at different times acted as catalysts in the creative process. Both in scale and scope the gigantic edifice had exceeded its theoretical brief. In 1858, Wagner's study of philosophy was leading to the point at which philosophy itself would become largely irrelevant.

Consistent with the catalyst theory is the fact that when at Tribschen in 1872 Wagner reached the last scene of *Götterdämmerung* (as *Siegfried's Tod* in deference to Wotan had been re-entitled), he set aside the two perorations with their 'tendentious' or 'sententious' moralizing and centered the musical score on the single preexisting line in which Brünnhilde entrusts Wotan's ravens with a message of rest:

Ruhe, ruhe, du Gott!   Rest now, rest now, you god!

It was an inspired compromise, which reinstated Wotan as the architect of the action as in the original scenario and overcame the opposition between the two perorations by a Hegelian synthesis in which each was both transcended and preserved. This final alteration may not have been unpremeditated. 'I can conceive of only one salvation,' Wagner had written to Mathilde Wesendonck in early July 1858: 'It is rest! Rest from longing! The stilling of every desire!'

It may be said, therefore, that in his concern to understand his own imaginative processes, Wagner resorted to philosophy for clarification, successively accepting and rejecting many of the most controversial theories of the 19th century, traces of which remain inextricably embedded in the penumbra of thought surrounding the work he created. Yet the meaning of the trilogy today (and in the future) is not bounded by the horizons of the period to which it owed so much and which it did so much to illuminate; nor are the criteria relevant to its interpretation necessarily those which Wagner himself adopted in his attempts to explain it to himself and to his contemporaries. 'I believe that a true instinct led me to guard against an excessive eagerness to make things plain', he told Röckel on 25/26 January 1854 at the height of his period of allegiance to Feuerbach, 'for I have learned to feel that to make one's intention too obvious risks impairing a proper understanding.' A year later, as his infatuation for Schopenhauer began to develop into a consuming passion, he wrote with greater emphasis: 'But how can an artist hope to find his own intuitions perfectly reproduced in those of another person, since he himself stands before his own work of art – if it really *is* a work of art – as though before some puzzle, which is just as capable of misleading *him* as it is of misleading anyone else.' If, in the end, the trilogy cannot be reduced to any single level of meaning, this may well be a measure of Wagner's achievement and of the *Ring*'s significance.

'The World Belongs to Alberich!' Wagner's changing attitude towards the 'Ring'

WARREN DARCY

IT HAS BECOME COMMONPLACE, in discussing Wagner's *Ring*, to remark upon the work's numerous dramatic inconsistencies. It has become no less a cliché to explain (and rather patronizingly forgive) these inconsistencies as the inevitable result of the tetralogy's protracted genesis and to argue that, compared with the work's indisputable strengths, they really do not matter. Wagner, after all, changed his mind many times about the scope, content and meaning of the *Ring* and it is hardly surprising that the completed work bears a few traces of its rather convoluted evolution. In any case, the typical *Ring* audience, overwhelmed by the work's dramatic power, emotional impact and musical brilliance, is unlikely to be troubled by a few minor paradoxes.

So runs the usual argument, and in some cases it may be justified. For example, few people are overly concerned that, in the second act of *Siegfried*, Mime taunts Alberich with having allowed the giants to steal the ring from him, when both dwarfs (along with the audience) know perfectly well that it was Wotan who committed that fatal theft. However, some of these 'inconsistencies' are of a more serious nature. For instance, the pivotal Erda episode of *Das Rheingold* invariably provokes questions: why do the gods ultimately perish even though Wotan heeds Erda's warning and relinquishes the ring? If the gods are ineluctably doomed from the outset, what sense does her warning make at all? Queries such as these go to the very core of what the *Ring* is all about (see Bibliography, Darcy 1986 and 1988).

No less problematical is Wagner's treatment of Siegfried. *Das Rheingold* and *Die Walküre* spend an enormous amount of time preparing the way for this hero who, it is implied, will finally set to rights the current sad state of affairs. *Siegfried* concludes with the apparent establishment of the reign of love, a new social order destined to supersede the power-hungry Wotans, Mimes and Alberichs of the world. Yet when Siegfried sets forth in *Götterdämmerung* to spread the new gospel, he promptly forgets his love for Brünnhilde, and love itself surrenders to power as completely and inevitably as it had in the first two dramas. The 'runes of knowledge' imparted by Brünnhilde appear to have robbed Siegfried of his youthful perspicacity without appreciably increasing his wisdom: once he intuitively recognized Mime's evil nature, but now he allows Hagen and Gunther to lead him around by the nose. In short, the hero's actions do not seem to follow logically from premises established earlier in the cycle and there appears to be no convincing reason why Wagner's 'man of the future', his symbolic portrait of regenerate humanity, should so decisively crash to his ruin.

The inconsistencies themselves are fairly easy to explain. When Wagner in 1848 drafted *Siegfried's Tod*, he planned only a single opera based upon the Nibelung myth. Within this drama, Siegfried's behaviour made perfect sense and was totally consistent with the moral/ethical framework Wagner had imposed upon his mythological material. But as the single drama gradually expanded into a tetralogy, this framework changed considerably, so that Siegfried's actions grew increasingly dissonant with it. Although Wagner subsequently revised *Siegfried's Tod* in order to reconcile it with the newly written portions of the *Ring*, he left the character of Siegfried largely untouched; in effect, he abandoned his hero, leaving him to play out a role whose dramatic *raison d'être* had long since collapsed.

However, although the inconsistencies in Siegfried's actions may be more or less satisfactorily explained by reference to early versions of the *Ring*, one crucial question remains. Wagner's keen dramatic instinct could not have failed to sense the discordance he had created by surrounding Siegfried's actions with a new moral/ethical framework. Why, then, did he allow this discordance to persist? He must have believed that Siegfried's original actions would still possess meaning – albeit a drastically altered one – within the context of the completed *Ring*.

To say that Wagner conceived the text of the *Ring* 'backwards' is to oversimplify and distort an extremely complex process. The *Ring* poem evolved through several clearly demarcated phases, the first of which comprised the writing of *Siegfried's Tod*. Wagner's usual procedure for constructing an operatic libretto involved four distinct steps: a brief, succinct prose sketch, a more elaborate prose draft, a verse draft and a fair copy of the poem. In the case of *Siegfried's Tod*, the usual prose sketch was replaced by a lengthy 'scenario' entitled *The Nibelung Legend (Myth)*, in which Wagner outlined his entire reconstruction of the Nibelung myth. Completed on 4 October 1848, and followed four days later by a fair copy entitled *The Legend of the Nibelungs*, this draft begins with Alberich's theft of the gold (for which, significantly, no renunciation of love is required) and concludes with Siegfried's death and Brünnhilde's self-immolation. Unlike most of the later *Ring* manuscripts, this one contains an interpretative commentary which clearly sets forth its moral/ethical framework.

The fundamental notion underlying the 1848 scenario is that of Siegfried as the gods' redeemer. Taking advantage of a conflict between Alberich and the race of giants, the gods (not just Wotan) steal the dwarf's hoard and ring, using them as payment for Valhalla. The giants create a dragon to guard their treasure, while Alberich and the Nibelungs toil fruitlessly in bondage to the ring. As the years pass, the gods attempt to order the world; their goal is moral consciousness, but their rule is flawed, established as it was through force and deceit. Their guilt can be purged only if the ring is stolen from the dragon and returned to the Rhine; this would release the Nibelungs from servitude. Yet the gods themselves cannot undertake such an action without committing a further sin. Only one who is independent of the gods may perform the beneficent deed of liberation, one who does it of his own free will. This capacity the gods see in mankind, in whom they strive to implant their divinity – realizing, however, that they might ultimately be forced to relinquish their influence to the freedom of human consciousness.

Several generations finally produce the needed hero. Following only his inner dictates, Siegfried kills the dragon and gives the ring to Brünnhilde, who bestows upon him her godly wisdom. Yet Siegfried does not use this gift; he still relies solely upon himself. Disguised as Gunther, he wrests the ring from Brünnhilde, thereby recreating the gods' fatal theft and assuming their guilt. Warned by the Rhinedaughters, he refuses to relinquish the ring; he defies the Norns, the gods and death itself. He thus atones for the gods' guilt through his independence, his fearlessness and ultimately his downfall. After Hagen murders him, Brünnhilde repossesses her unused wisdom, which vouchsafes her the necessary insight to complete Siegfried's work; returning the ring to the Rhine, she finally liberates

Alberich and the Nibelungs. Armed as a valkyrie, she immolates herself in order to lead Siegfried in triumph to Valhalla. The gods' rule is firmly re-established, although the implication is that ultimately they will pass away, leaving mankind – now brought to full moral consciousness – to reign supreme.

Within the context of this 1848 scenario, Siegfried's actions are not at all problematic. His innocence and 'ignorance' are crucial: knowing nothing of any higher scheme of things, he follows only his instincts. Because he must not accept aid from the gods, he cannot even avail himself of Brünnhilde's wisdom. His deeds not only redeem the gods but ultimately benefit the human race. In fact, Siegfried comes remarkably close to fulfilling Hegel's concept of the world-historical figure, the hero who, heeding only inner necessity, unwittingly assists the dialectical process of history (see Hegel 1956: 29–31).

By 20 October 1848 Wagner had finished a prose draft entitled *Siegfried's Death (Opera in Three Acts)*, which fleshed out the events beginning with Siegfried's arrival at the Gibichung court. However, this draft naturally lacked not only the drama's extensive prehistory but also the interpretative commentary which, in the earlier scenario, had established its ethical framework. To remedy this loss, Wagner in late October or early November drafted a two-part prologue. In a scene quite different from that which opens what we now know as *Götterdämmerung*, the Norns explained the moral significance of Siegfried's mission. The leave-taking scene which followed (almost identical with the one we know) emphasized Siegfried's dependence upon Brünnhilde, a connection which had to be broken if the hero was to fulfil his destiny. This, incidentally, explains the original purpose behind the potion of forgetfulness: it enabled Siegfried to regain his independence. Although Wagner probably drafted the farewell scene with an eye towards its possibilities for heroic love music, the concept of redemptive love as yet played no part in the drama: *Lohengrin* had cooled Wagner's enthusiasm for this theme and his interest in it was not rekindled until he began reading Feuerbach.

Between 12 and 28 November, Wagner drafted the poem of *Siegfried's Tod*, which had now become 'A Grand Heroic Opera in Three Acts'. Probably in early December he prepared a fair copy, in which he altered some scenic directions but left the verses largely unchanged. Almost immediately he revised the drama, entering revisions in both manuscripts; he then made a second fair copy of the poem, reflecting the changes of the first revision. The work was now designated a 'Heroic Opera in Three Acts', and this second fair copy contains two significant marginal alterations to Brünnhilde's closing speech (see Ill. 1 and appendix 3b). In the original scenario, the prose draft and both versions of the poem, Brünnhilde had concluded the drama by proclaiming Wotan's continuing rule. However, in the first marginal entry, Brünnhilde announced 'blessed atonement' for the eternal gods and urged them to welcome Siegfried into their midst; Wagner here attempted to restore the notion of Siegfried as the gods' redeemer, a concept crucial to the 1848 scenario but somehow missing from both the prose draft and the poem of *Siegfried's Tod*. In the second entry, added later, Brünnhilde admonished the gods to 'depart without power' and 'fade away in bliss' before Siegfried's deed and she concluded by foretelling their 'blessed redemption in death' from their anxious fear. The notion of the gods' demise, already alluded to in the first scenario, was coming into ever sharper focus.

Sometime during the summer of 1850, Wagner began and abandoned some musical sketches for *Siegfried's Tod*; he then threw his energy into writing *Opera and Drama*. The next spring (presumably during early May 1851) he jotted down some prose sketches for *Der junge Siegfried* and between 24 May and 1 June he completed a lengthy prose draft of this 'comic counterpart' to *Siegfried's Tod*. The verse draft, dated 3–24 June, was soon followed by two fair copies and this second stage in the evolution of the *Ring* text terminated, like the first, in an abortive attempt at composing the music, followed by yet another long essay (*A Communication to my Friends*).

The notion of the gods' demise had now crystallized: in *Der junge Siegfried* Wagner set Wotan himself upon the stage, to be informed by Erda of his approaching end. However, the god genially yielded place to Siegfried without a struggle and the second opera would still have concluded with the temporary re-establishment of Wotan's rule.

Wagner conceived the remaining two dramas more or less simultaneously, the prose sketch and prose draft of *Das Rheingold* preceding their respective counterparts for *Die Walküre* (in these two instances, then, the text was written in 'normal' order). The expansion into a trilogy with prefatory prelude was motivated by Wagner's desire to dramatize the entire tragedy of Wotan. For it was now Wotan the god, not Siegfried the hero, who fascinated him. His reading of Feuerbach had suggested a possible foundation for the entire cycle: the eternal conflict between love and power (perhaps a manifestation of Hegelian dialectic). While versifying the two new dramas, Wagner decided to destroy the gods by fire, demonstrating how Wotan's original misdeed led ultimately to the collapse of his whole world. Yet he failed to apprise Siegfried of this radical change of plan.

Wagner next (late 1852) revised *Der junge Siegfried* but, his interest in the title character having waned, he primarily altered those scenes involving Wotan: the doomed god now embraced his own annihilation as he willed his spear to be shattered on Siegfried's sword. The new love/power conflict proved difficult to work in, for this third drama had always revolved around the concept of fear, not love. However, Wagner's identification of the fear of death as the source of all lovelessness permitted him to view fearless Siegfried as 'the man who never ceases to love' (letter to August Röckel of 25/26 January 1854). In any case, he probably realized that the closing duet could be understood as the long-awaited triumph of love over power, and his musical setting certainly underscores that interpretation.

Finally Wagner revised *Siegfried's Tod*, replacing the liberation of the Nibelungs with the destruction of the gods. Unable to inject a heavy dose of love into this drama, he appended to Brünnhilde's closing lines a rather Feuerbachian speech extolling love over worldly possessions (see appendix 3c). Released from Alberich's curse, love was again free to rule the world: 'Blessed in joy and sorrow / love alone can be!' The drama had apparently come full circle; just as Alberich had once renounced love for the sake of power, Brünnhilde, by restoring the ring to the Rhine, now renounced power for the sake of love. (The notion that the *Ring* ends with the release of love from Alberich's curse on it is undoubtedly what led Hans von Wolzogen to dub the drama's final musical theme '*Liebeserlösung*' – literally, the 'redemption, or release, of love', a meaning obscured by the traditional translation 'redemption through love'. It should be noted that Wolzogen based his interpretation upon the 1852 ending, an ending which Wagner not only discarded but actually repudiated in his letter to Röckel of 23 August 1856. In any case, Wagner himself referred to the concluding theme as 'the glorification of Brünnhilde', as Cosima reported in an unpublished letter of 6 September 1875 to the chemist Edmund von Lippmann.)

This totally ineffectual attempt to bring *Siegfried's Tod* into line with *Das*

Rheingold and *Die Walküre* was not likely to satisfy Wagner for long, especially since he had come to view its concluding catastrophe as the destruction, not only of the gods, but of the world as well (see his letter to Liszt of 11 February 1853).

Wagner concluded the fourth and final stage in the evolution of the *Ring* text by making fair copies of *Das Rheingold* and *Die Walküre* and a fourth fair copy of *Siegfried's Tod*; for some reason, he never made another fair copy of the extensively revised *Der junge Siegfried*. The entire process was completed by 15 December 1852, after which he had fifty copies of the poem privately printed at his own expense although this still did not represent the final version of the text.

In the autumn of 1854 Wagner was introduced to the works of Arthur Schopenhauer, and he claims to have read *The World as Will and Representation* four times over the course of the following year. The philosopher's writings afforded him an almost cosmic vision of the true meaning of the work. Love, he now realized, is not the final remedy; rather, the suffering it causes may vouchsafe an insight into the essential nullity of existence, the reality of human misery and the necessity for rejecting the phenomenal world as an evil illusion. The only right course is to renounce the Will, as Brünnhilde demonstrates by relinquishing both the ring of power and life itself. Consequently, Wagner decided to replace his heroine's 'Feuerbachian' lines with a 'Schopenhauerian/Buddhist' speech; he wrote out a prose sketch for this in 1856, but did not versify it until 1871 or 1872. Although ultimately not set to music, this speech expressed for him the final meaning of the *Ring*. It concludes: 'Grieving love's profoundest suffering opened my eyes for me: I saw the world end' (see appendix 3d).

Yet where did all this leave poor Siegfried? Stripped of his role as the gods' redeemer, totally uninterested in metaphysical speculation, he doggedly fights on in a world which no longer understands him. Not content with abandoning his hero, Wagner musically undercuts him. When Siegfried ostentatiously ignores the Rhinedaughters' warning in Act III of *Götterdämmerung*, metaphorically throwing life away, the orchestra accompanies this gesture with the final portion of Alberich's Curse; his life is already forfeit and he deceives only himself by claiming otherwise. In 1872 Wagner could scoff at Siegfried's pretensions to free will.

Siegfried's dramatic function had changed drastically. In *Siegfried's Tod* he had been the gods' redeemer and the benefactor of humanity. In *Götterdämmerung*, however, his actions may be understood as recreating Wotan's mistakes: he embraces power, entangles himself in false treaties and renounces true love. Wagner had come to believe that social progress was an illusion, that humanity was fated endlessly to repeat past errors and that the ideal future he had once envisaged could never be realized. The Act III Funeral March serves simultaneously as a commentary upon Wotan's plan for moral regeneration (symbolized by the Sword and Wälsung motifs) – an idea which had dominated the 1848 scenario – and as a lament for the futility of that idea.

That Wagner no longer believed the world worth saving is beyond question. In July 1872 he mentioned to Cosima that Wotan 'has recognized the guilt of existence and atones for the error of creation' (CT, 2 July 1872). But already in October 1854, in a passage that reads almost like a gloss on the new direction the *Ring* had taken, Wagner wrote to Liszt: 'Let us treat the world only with contempt; for it deserves no better; but let no hope be placed in it, that our hearts be not deluded! It is evil, evil, *fundamentally evil* [. . .]. It belongs to *Alberich*: no one else!! Away with it!'

The Ring of the Nibelung

TRANSLATED BY STEWART SPENCER

[The numbers in square brackets refer to the
Thematic Guide on pp. 17–24]

Das Rheingold

THE RHINEGOLD

Synopsis

Scene 1

THE ACTION OPENS AT THE BOTTOM of the Rhine, where the three Rhinedaughters, Woglinde, Wellgunde and Flosshilde, are disporting themselves in the waves. The dwarf Alberich climbs out of a dark chasm lower down and after watching the Rhinedaughters at play, calls out to them. They initially recoil at his loathsome appearance, but then decide to reward his lubricious advances by teaching him a lesson. Each in turn appears to lead him on but then mocks and rejects him. As he looks up, speechless with rage, a bright light shines through the waters from high above. Alberich, mesmerized by the sight, asks what it is. He is told that it is the Rhinegold, from which a ring can be made that will confer limitless power. Only he who forswears the power of love can fashion the ring, adds Woglinde – in which case they have nothing to fear from the lascivious dwarf. But Alberich climbs to the top of the central rock, declares his curse on love, and wrests the gold away with terrible force. He scrambles away with it, deaf to the lamenting cries of the Rhinedaughters.

Scene 2

Wotan, the ruler of the gods, and his consort Fricka are asleep on an open space on a mountain height. Behind them, his magnificent new fortress-home, built for him by the giants, gleams in the light of dawn. Fricka, awaking first, sees the fortress and rouses her husband. Wotan sings a paean to the completed work, but Fricka reminds him that it was her sister, Freia, the goddess of love, who was rashly offered to the giants in payment for their work. Wotan brushes aside her fears. But now Freia enters in terrified haste, followed closely by the giants Fasolt and Fafner. Wotan wonders what has detained Loge, the fire god, on whom he had been relying to disengage him from the contract. Fasolt demands their fee for the work done, but when he insists on Freia as the agreed payment, Wotan tells him that some other reward must be asked. Fasolt indignantly reminds Wotan that the runes on his spear symbolize his contractual agreements and it is they that legitimize his power. Fafner is less interested in Freia for her beauty, but realizes that if she is abducted, the gods, denied her youth-perpetuating apples, will wither and die.

As the giants prepare to take Freia away, her brothers Froh and Donner (the god of thunder) rush in to protect her. Wotan prevents Donner from exercising force and is relieved to see Loge arrive at last. Loge relates how he has circled the world attempting to find out what men hold dearer than the virtues of womankind. No one would give up love, except a Nibelung dwarf, who stole the Rhinegold after suffering the rejection of his sexual advances. Loge calls on Wotan to secure the return of the gold to the custody of the Rhinemaidens. When Loge explains that a ring forged from it would give absolute power, the giants, Wotan and Fricka all begin to lust after it. Loge suggests that it be obtained by theft, and Fafner demands that it then be handed over in payment. Meanwhile they will hold Freia hostage.

As the giants trudge away, dragging Freia behind them, a mist descends on the gods, who, denied Freia's golden apples, begin to wilt. Wotan, accompanied by Loge, descends through a sulphur cleft in pursuit of the gold.

Scene 3

In the depths of Nibelheim, Alberich is tormenting his weaker brother Mime, and demands the magic tarnhelm that he has forced Mime to make. The tarnhelm renders its wearer invisible, and Alberich proves its efficacy by disappearing and raining blows on the defenceless Mime. Alberich eventually leaves, and Wotan and Loge arrive. Loge, offering to help Mime, hears from him how the carefree race of Nibelung blacksmiths has been held in thrall by Alberich since he forged a ring from the Rhinegold.

Alberich returns, driving his slaves with whiplashes to pile up the gold. He brandishes the ring and they scatter in all directions. Alberich now turns his attention to the strangers. He boasts about the power he now wields, obtained by relinquishing love, and threatens one day to vanquish the gods and force his favours on their women. Loge tricks him into transforming himself into first a dragon, then a toad. The gods are thus able to tie him and drag him up to the surface.

Scene 4

Back on the mountain heights, Loge and Wotan deride Alberich and his pretensions to world domination. Intending to keep the ring, which he knows he can use to generate more wealth, Alberich agrees to hand over the gold. His right hand is untied and he summons the Nibelungs with the ring. The gods then demand not only the tarnhelm but also the ring. Alberich, crushed, is untied, but before he goes, he lays a curse on the ring. It will bring anxiety and death to whoever owns it; those who possess it will be racked with torment, those who do not will be consumed with envy.

Donner, Froh and Fricka welcome back Wotan and Loge, who show them Freia's ransom: the pile of gold. The air lightens as Freia returns with the giants. Fasolt is reluctant to relinquish Freia and insists that the gold be piled up so as to hide her from sight. Loge and Froh pile up the treasure, filling up all the gaps. Fafner demands even the ring on Wotan's finger. The god refuses to yield it, until Erda, the earth goddess, appears from a rocky cleft to warn him that possession of the ring condemns him to irredeemable dark perdition. Wotan tosses the ring on the pile and Fafner begins to stow it away. The giants struggle for the ring and Fafner clubs Fasolt to death. Wotan realizes with horror the power of the curse.

The gods prepare to enter the fortress. Donner swings his hammer and there is thunder and lightning. Suddenly the clouds lift and a rainbow bridge is visible, stretching across the valley to the fortress. Wotan invites his wife to follow him into the fortress, which he now calls Valhalla. As the couple walk to the bridge, followed by Froh, Donner and Freia, Loge looks on nonchalantly. The wail of the Rhinemaidens, lamenting their lost gold, rises out of the valley. Wotan ignores them and leads the gods over the bridge as the curtain falls.

Preliminary Evening to the Stage Festival 'The Ring of the Nibelung'

First performed at the Munich Court Theatre on 22 September 1869

Gods
    Wotan (bass-baritone)   August Kindermann
    Donner (bass-baritone)   Karl Samuel Heinrich
    Froh (tenor)   Franz Nachbaur
    Loge (tenor)   Heinrich Vogl

Nibelungs
    Alberich (bass-baritone)   Wilhelm Fischer
    Mime (tenor)   Max Schlosser

Giants
    Fasolt (bass-baritone)   Anton Petzer
    Fafner (bass)   Kaspar Bausewein

Goddesses
    Fricka (mezzo-soprano)   Sophie Stehle
    Freia (soprano)   Henriette Müller
    Erda (contralto)   Emma Seehofer

Rhinedaughters
    Woglinde (soprano)   Anna Kaufmann
    Wellgunde (soprano)   Therese Vogl
    Flosshilde (mezzo-soprano)   Wilhelmine Ritter

Nibelungs

Scene 1.   In the depths of the Rhine
Scenes 2 and 4.   Open space on mountain heights overlooking the Rhine
Scene 3.   The subterranean clefts of Nibelheim

First performed as part of cycle, Bayreuth Festspielhaus, 13 August 1876

Wotan (Franz Betz), Donner (Eugen Gura), Froh (Georg Unger), Loge (Heinrich Vogl), Alberich (Karl Hill), Mime (Max Schlosser), Fasolt (Albert Eilers), Fafner (Franz von Reichenberg), Fricka (Friederike Sadler-Grün), Freia (Marie Haupt), Erda (Luise Jaide), Woglinde (Lilli Lehmann), Wellgunde (Marie Lehmann), Flosshilde (Minna Lammert)

First UK performance: Her Majesty's Theatre, London, 5 May 1882

First US performance: Metropolitan Opera, New York, 4 January 1889

Das Rheingold

Scene One

On the bed of the Rhine

Greenish twilight, lighter above, darker below. The top of the stage is filled with billowing waters that flow unceasingly from left to right. Towards the bottom the waves dissolve into an increasingly fine mist-like spray, so that a space the height of a man appears to be left there completely free of the water, which flows like scudding clouds over the dusk-enshrouded river bed. Rocky ledges rise up everywhere out of the depths and mark the confines of the stage; the whole river bed is broken up into a wild confusion of crags, so that it is nowhere completely level, while deeper gullies may be imagined leading off on all sides into impenetrable darkness. The orchestra begins while the curtain is still closed.[1] [1a, 1b, 1c]

WOGLINDE
(circling the central rock with a graceful swimming motion)

Weia! Waga![2]	[2]	Weia! Waga![2]
Woge, du Welle,		Welter, you wave,
walle zur Wiege![3]		swirl round the cradle![3]
Wagalaweia!		Wagalaweia!
Wallala weiala weia!		Wallala weiala weia!

WELLGUNDE'S VOICE
(from above)

Woglinde, wach'st du allein?　　　　Woglinde, watching alone?

WOGLINDE

Mit Wellgunde wär' ich zu zwei.　　With Wellgunde there would be two
　　　　　　　　　　　　　　　　　　[of us!

WELLGUNDE
(diving down through the waves to the rocky ledge)

Lass' seh'n, wie du wach'st.　　　　Let's see how you watch!

WOGLINDE
(swimming away from her)

Sicher vor dir.　　　　[1c]　　Safe from your reach!
(They tease and playfully try to catch one another.)

FLOSSHILDE'S VOICE
(from above)

Heiala weia!	Heiala weia!
Wildes Geschwister!	High-spirited sisters!

WELLGUNDE

Floßhilde, schwimm'!	Flosshilde, swim!
Woglinde flieht:	Woglinde's fleeing:
hilf mir die fließende⁴ fangen!	help me to catch your sleek sister!⁴

FLOSSHILDE
(diving down and interrupting them in their play)

Des Goldes Schlaf	The sleeping gold
hütet ihr schlecht;	you guard badly;
besser bewacht	pay better heed
des Schlummernden Bett,	to the slumberer's bed
sonst büß't ihr beide das Spiel! [1c]	or you'll both atone for your sport.

(With shrieks of high-spirited laughter, the two of them move apart: Flosshilde tries to catch first one and then the other; they slip away from her and finally join forces in pursuit of Flosshilde. Thus they dart, like fish, from rock to rock, joking and laughing. Meanwhile Alberich has emerged from a dark gully below and climbed up on to one of the rocky ledges. He pauses, still surrounded by darkness, and with increasing delight watches the Rhinedaughters playing.)

ALBERICH

He he! Ihr Nicker!	Ha ha! You nixies!
Wie seid ihr niedlich,	How dainty you are,
neidliches Volk!	you delectable creatures!
Aus Nibelheim's⁵ Nacht	From Nibelheim's⁵ night
naht' ich mich gern,	I'd gladly draw near
neigtet ihr euch zu mir.	if only you'd look on me kindly.

(The girls stop playing as soon as they hear Alberich's voice.)

WOGLINDE

Hei! wer ist dort?	Hey! Who is there?

FLOSSHILDE

Es dämmert und ruft.	Darkness descends and a voice cries [out!

WELLGUNDE

Lugt, wer uns belauscht!	See who is spying upon us.

(They dive down deeper and see the Nibelung.)

WOGLINDE AND WELLGUNDE

Pfui! der Garstige!	Ugh! The foul creature!

FLOSSHILDE
(darting swiftly upwards)

Hütet das Gold!	Look to the gold!

Vater warnte	Father warned
vor solchem Feind.	against such a foe.

(The other two follow her, and all three quickly gather round the central ledge.)

ALBERICH

Ihr da oben!	You up there!

ALL THREE

Was willst du dort unten?	What is it, down there, that you want?

ALBERICH

Stör' ich eu'r Spiel,	Would it spoil your sport
wenn staunend ich still hier steh'?	if I stood here in silent amazement?
Tauchtet ihr nieder,	If you dived down here,
mit euch tollte	how gladly the Niblung
und neckte der Niblung sich gern!	would romp and tease you!

WOGLINDE

Mit uns will er spielen?	Would he join in our games?

WELLGUNDE

Ist ihm das Spott?	Do you think he's in jest?

ALBERICH

Wie scheint im Schimmer	How bright and comely
ihr hell und schön!	you shine in the shimmering light!
Wie gern umschlänge	How I long to embrace
der Schlanken eine mein Arm,	just one of those slender creatures,
schlüpfte hold sie herab!	if only she'd deign to slip down here!

FLOSSHILDE

Nun lach' ich der Furcht:	Now I laugh at my fear:
der Feind ist verliebt.	the fiend is in love.

WELLGUNDE

Der lüsterne Kauz!	The lecherous rogue!

WOGLINDE

Laßt ihn uns kennen!	Let's teach him a lesson!

(She lowers herself to the top of the rock the foot of which Alberich has reached.)

ALBERICH

Die neigt sich herab.	She's drawing down here.

WOGLINDE

Nun nahe dich mir!	Come close to me now!

(His progress repeatedly obstructed, Alberich clambers up to the top of the ledge with goblin-like agility.)

ALBERICH
(angrily)

Garstig glatter
glitschriger Glimmer!
Wie gleit' ich aus!
Mit Händen und Füßen
nicht fasse noch halt' ich
das schlecke Geschlüpfer!
Feuchtes Naß
füllt mir die Nase:
verfluchtes Niesen!

Slimily smooth and
slippery slate!
I can't stop sliding!
With my hands and my feet
I can't capture or hold
those delightfully slippery creatures.
Dank water
fills my nose –
accursèd sneezing!

(He is now close to Woglinde.)

WOGLINDE
(laughing)

Pruhstend naht
meines Freiers Pracht!

Spluttering comes
my suitor in splendour!

ALBERICH

Mein Friedel[6] sei,
du fräuliches Kind!

Be my lover,[6]
you winsome child!

(He tries to put his arms round her.)

WOGLINDE
(slipping away from him)

Willst du mich frei'n,
so freie mich hier!

If you want to woo me,
then woo me here!

(She darts up to another ledge. Alberich scratches his head.)

ALBERICH

O weh! du entweich'st?
Komm' doch wieder!
Schwer ward mir,
was so leicht du erschwing'st.

Alas! You evade me?
Come back again!
What you scaled with such ease
was much harder for me.

WOGLINDE
(swinging herself across to a third rock, deeper down)

Steig' nur zu Grund:
da greif'st du mich sicher!

Come down to the depths,
where you'll surely be able to catch
[me!

ALBERICH
(quickly clambering down)

Wohl besser da unten!

It's certainly better down there.

WOGLINDE
(darting swiftly upwards to a higher rock at the side)

Nun aber nach oben!

Now up once again!

WELLGUNDE AND FLOSSHILDE
(laughing)

Hahahahahaha!   Hahahahahaha!

ALBERICH

Wie fang' ich im Sprung	How can I catch
den spröden Fisch?	this cold fish in flight?
Warte, du Falsche!	Wait, you false creature!

(He tries to clamber up after her.)

WELLGUNDE
(settling on a lower ledge on the other side)

Heia! du Holder!	Hey, my sweetheart!
hör'st du mich nicht?	Can you not hear me?

ALBERICH
(turning round)

Ruf'st du nach mir?   Are you calling to me?

WELLGUNDE

Ich rathe dir wohl:	I counsel you well:
zu mir wende dich,	come over to me and
Woglinde meide!	avoid Woglinde!

ALBERICH
(clambering hastily over the river bed to be with Wellgunde)

Viel schöner bist du	You're far more fair
als jene Scheue,	than that faint-hearted child,
die minder gleißend	who glitters less
und gar zu glatt. –	and is far too glib. –
Nur tiefer tauche,	Only dive deeper
willst du mir taugen!	if you'd avail me!

WELLGUNDE
(descending a little closer towards him)

Bin nun ich dir nah?   Am I near to you now?

ALBERICH

Noch nicht genug!	Not yet near enough!
Die schlanken Arme	Entwine your slender
schlinge um mich,	arms around me
daß ich den Nacken	that, teasingly, I may
dir neckend betaste,	touch your neck and
mit schmeichelnder Brunst	with fawning fervour
an die schwellende Brust mich dir	nestle up to your heaving breast.
[schmiege.	

WELLGUNDE

Bist du verliebt	If you're in love
und lüstern nach Minne?[7]	and lusting for love's delights,[7]

Lass' seh'n, du Schöner,
wie bist du zu schau'n! –
Pfui, du haariger,
höck'riger Geck!
Schwarzes, schwieliges
Schwefelgezwerg!
Such' dir ein Friedel,
dem du gefällst!

let's see, my beauty,
just what you are like! –
Ugh! You hairy,
hunchbacked fool!
Brimstone-black
and blistered dwarf!
Look for a lover
who looks like yourself!

(Alberich tries to restrain her by force.)

ALBERICH

Gefall' ich dir nicht,
dich fass' ich doch fest!

Although you don't like me,
I still hold you tight.

WELLGUNDE
(darting up to the central ledge)

Nur fest, sonst fließ' ich dir fort!

Hold tight, or I'll slip through your
[hands!

WOGLINDE AND FLOSSHILDE
(laughing)

Hahahahahaha!

Hahahahahaha!

ALBERICH
(shouting angrily after Wellgunde)

Falsches Kind!
Kalter, grätiger[8] Fisch!
Schein' ich nicht schön dir,
niedlich und neckisch,
glatt und glau –
hei! so buhle mit Aalen,
ist dir eklig mein Balg!

False-hearted child!
Cold-blooded, bony[8] fish!
If I seem unsightly,
not pretty or playful,
sleek and sharp-sighted –
have your way, then, with eels,
if my skin is so foul!

FLOSSHILDE[9]

Was zank'st du, Alp?
Schon so verzagt?
Du frei'test um zwei:
frügst du die dritte,
süßen Trost
schüfe die Traute dir!

Why scold, you elf?
Already downhearted?
Two you have wooed:
if you asked but the third,
sweet solace
your true love would bring you!

ALBERICH

Holder Sang
singt zu mir her. –
Wie gut, daß ihr
eine nicht seid!
Von vielen gefall' ich wohl einer:
bei einer kies'te mich keine! –
Soll ich dir glauben,
so gleite herab!

What lovely singing
wafts this way. –
How good there's not
just one of you:
with many, one might like me,
with one, none would choose me! –
If I'm to believe you,
glide down here!

FLOSSHILDE
(diving down to Alberich)

Wie thörig seid ihr,	How foolish you are,
dumme Schwestern,	you dull-witted sisters,
dünkt euch dieser nicht schön!	not to find him good-looking!

ALBERICH
(hastily drawing near her)

Für dumm und häßlich	Dull-witted and ugly
darf ich sie halten,	they seem to me
seit ich dich holdeste seh'.	now I see *you*, the fairest of all.

FLOSSHILDE

O singe fort	O go on singing
so süß und fein;	so sweetly and subtly;
wie hehr verführt es mein Ohr!	how it bewitches my ear!

ALBERICH
(caressing her confidingly)

Mir zagt, zuckt	My heart quakes and quivers
und zehrt sich das Herz,	and burns with desire,
lacht mir so zierliches Lob.	when such fulsome praise smiles upon [me.

FLOSSHILDE
(gently restraining him)

Wie deine Anmuth	How your charm
mein Aug' erfreut,	cheers my eye,
deines Lächelns Milde	how your mellowing smile
den Muth mir labt!	makes my spirits rise!

(She draws him tenderly towards her.)

Seligster Mann!	Most blissful of men!

ALBERICH

Süßeste Maid!	Sweetest of maids!

FLOSSHILDE

Wär'st du mir hold!	Would you were mine!

ALBERICH

Hielt' ich dich immer!	Might I hold you forever!

FLOSSHILDE
(ardently)

Deinen stechenden Blick,	Your piercing eyes,
deinen struppigen Bart,	your bristling beard,
o säh' ich ihn, faßt' ich ihn stets!	might I always see and hold them!
Deines stachligen Haares	May your prickly hair's
strammes Gelock,	unruly locks
umflöss' es Floßhilde ewig!	flow round Flosshild' for ever!

Deine Krötengestalt,
deiner Stimme Gekrächz,
o dürft' ich staunend und stumm,
sie nur hören und seh'n!

Your toad-like build,
the croak of your voice,
could I hear and see only them
in mutely silent amazement!

(Woglinde and Wellgunde have dived down close.)

WOGLINDE AND WELLGUNDE
(laughing)

Hahahahahaha!   Hahahahahaha!

ALBERICH
(starting up in alarm)

Lacht ihr Bösen mich aus?   You're laughing at me, you wicked
                                                      [women?

FLOSSHILDE
(suddenly breaking free)

Wie billig am Ende vom Lied.   As befits the end of the song!

(She darts away upwards with her sisters.)

WOGLINDE AND WELLGUNDE
(laughing)

Hahahahahaha!   Hahahahahaha!

ALBERICH
(in a screeching tone of voice)[10]

Wehe! ach wehe!   [3]   Woe! Woe is me!
O Schmerz! O Schmerz!   O grief! O grief!
Die dritte, so traut,   Has the third one, so true,
betrog sie mich auch? –   betrayed me as well?
Ihr schmählich schlaues,   You contemptibly cunning,
liederlich schlechtes Gelichter!   lewdly iniquitous creatures!
Nährt ihr nur Trug,   So deceit is all you foment,
ihr treuloses Nickergezücht?   you faithless brood of nixies?

THE THREE RHINEDAUGHTERS

Wallala! Wallala!   [2]   Wallala! Wallala!
Lalaleia, leialalei!   Lalaleia, leialalei!
Heia! Heia! Haha!   Heia! Heia! Haha!
 Schäme dich, Albe!   Shame on you, elf!
 Schilt nicht dort unten!   Stop shouting abuse!
Höre, was wir dich heißen!   Hear what we bid you do!
 Warum, du Banger,   Why, faint-hearted dwarf,
 bandest du nicht   did you fail to bind fast
das Mädchen, das du minnst?   the maiden that you love?
 Treu sind wir   We are trusty
 und ohne Trug   and true
dem Freier, der uns fängt. –   to the wooer who traps us. –
 Greife nur zu   Grab what you can
 und grause dich nicht!   and don't be afraid:

In der Fluth entflieh'n wir nicht [leicht.	in the floodtide we'll not lightly flee.
Wallala! Lalaleia! Leialalei!	Wallala! Lalaleia! Leialalei!
Heia! Heia! Hahei!	Heia! Heia! Hahei!

(They swim apart, hither and thither, now deeper, now higher, inciting Alberich to pursue them.)

ALBERICH

Wie in den Gliedern	In every limb
brünstige Gluth	a blazing fire
mir brennt und glüht!	burns and glows!
Wuth und Minne,	Rage and desire,
wild und mächtig	wild and all-powerful,
wühlt mir den Muth auf! –	throw my thoughts into turmoil! –
Wie ihr auch lacht und lügt,	Though you may laugh and lie,
lüstern lechz' ich nach euch,	lusting, I languish after you
und eine muß mir erliegen!	and one of you must yield to me!

(With a desperate effort he sets off in pursuit of them, clambering from ledge to ledge with appalling agility, leaping from one ledge to another and attempting to catch now one, now another of the girls, who repeatedly elude him to the sounds of shrieking laughter. [2] He stumbles, plunges headlong back to the river bed, then clambers back up to the top to renew the chase. They move a little closer to him. He almost reaches them when he falls back down again and begins all over again. He finally stops, foaming with rage and out of breath, and shakes his clenched fist up at the girls.)

ALBERICH

| Fing' eine diese Faust! . . . | Might this fist catch even one! |

(He remains where he is, speechless with rage, his gaze directed upwards where it is suddenly attracted and held by the following spectacle. An increasingly bright glow penetrates the floodwaters from above, flaring up as it strikes a point high up on the central rock and gradually becoming a blinding and brightly beaming gleam of gold; a magical golden light streams through the water from this point.)

WOGLINDE

| Lugt, Schwestern! | Look, sisters! |
| Die Weckerin lacht in den Grund. | The wakening sun smiles into the deep. |

WELLGUNDE

| Durch den grünen Schwall | Through the green billows |
| den wonnigen Schläfer sie grüßt. | she greets the glad sleeper. |

FLOSSHILDE

| Jetzt küßt sie sein Auge, | Now she kisses his eyelid |
| daß er es öff'ne. | that it may open. |

WELLGUNDE

| Schaut, er lächelt | See how he smiles |
| in lichtem Schein. | in the gleaming light. |

Durch die Fluthen hin
fließt sein strahlender Stern.

Through the floodtide
flows its glittering ray.

THE THREE RHINEDAUGHTERS
(gracefully swimming round the rocky ledge together)

Heiajaheia!	[5]	Heiajaheia!
Heiajaheia!		Heiajaheia!
Wallalalalala leiajahei!		Wallalalalala leiajahei!
Rheingold!		Rhinegold!
Rheingold!		Rhinegold!
Leuchtende Lust,		Light-bringing joy,
wie lach'st du so hell und hehr!		how bright and sublime your laughter!
Glühender Glanz		A glowing gleam breaks awesomely[11] [forth
entgleißt dir weihlich[11] im Wag!		from the gold in the seething waves!
Heiajahei!		Heiajahei!
Heiajahei!		Heiajahei!
Wache, Freund,		Awaken, friend,
wache froh!		awake to joy!
Wonnige Spiele		Gladdening games
spenden wir dir:		we'll play for you now:
flimmert der Fluß,		when the river glows
flammet die Fluth,		and the flood is aflame,
umfließen wir tauchend,		your bed we encircle, diving
tanzend und singend,		and dancing and singing,
im seligen Bade dein Bett.		in blithely blissful abandon!
Rheingold!		Rhinegold!
Rheingold!		Rhinegold!
Heiajaheia!		Heiajaheia!
Heiajaheia!		Heiajaheia!
Wallalalalalaleia jahei!		Wallalalalalaleia jahei!

(The girls swim round the ledge in increasingly exuberant delight. The whole of the water glistens in the bright gleam of the gold.) [4]

ALBERICH
(his eyes powerfully attracted by the gleam, staring fixedly at the gold)

Was ist's, ihr Glatten,
das dort so glänzt und gleißt?

What is it, sleek creatures,
that glints and glitters there so?

THE THREE GIRLS

Wo bist du Rauher denn heim,
daß vom Rheingold nicht du
[gehört? –

Where is your home, you ruffian,
that you've never heard of the
[Rhinegold? –

WELLGUNDE

Nichts weiß der Alp
von des Goldes Auge,
das wechselnd wacht und schläft?

The elf knows naught
of the eye of the gold
that wakes and sleeps by turns?

WOGLINDE

Von der Wassertiefe	Of the joy-giving star
wonnigem Stern,	in the watery deep
der hehr die Wogen durchhellt? –	that illumines the waves with its noble [light?

ALL THREE

Sieh', wie selig	See how blithely
im Glanze wir gleiten!	we glide in its glow.
Willst du Banger	Faint-hearted dwarf,
in ihm dich baden,	if you'd fain bathe within it,
so schwimm' und schwelge mit [uns! [2]	then swim and make merry with us!
Wallala lalaleialalei!	Wallala lalaleialalei!
Wallala lalaleia jahei!	Wallala lalaleia jahei!

ALBERICH

Eu'rem Taucherspiele	Is the gold only good
nur taugte das Gold?	for your diving games?
Mir gält' es dann wenig!	Then it would serve me little!

WOGLINDE

Des Goldes Schmuck	The golden jewel
schmähte er nicht,	he'd not despise
wüßte er all seine Wunder!	if only he knew all its wonders.

WELLGUNDE

Der Welt Erbe [6]	The world's wealth
gewänne zu eigen,	would be won by him
wer aus dem Rheingold	who forged from the Rhinegold
schüfe den Ring,	the ring
der maaßlose Macht ihm verlieh'.	that would grant him limitless power.

FLOSSHILDE

Der Vater sagt' es,	Father told us
und uns befahl er	and bound us over
klug zu hüten	to guard
den klaren Hort,	the bright hoard wisely
daß kein Falscher der Fluth ihn [entführe:	that no false thief should filch it from the [flood:
d'rum schweigt, ihr schwatzendes [Heer!	be silent, then, you babbling brood!

WELLGUNDE

Du klügste Schwester!	Wisest of sisters,
Verklag'st du uns wohl?	why complain?
Weißt du denn nicht,	Do you not know
wem nur allein,	to whom alone
das Gold zu schmieden vergönnt?	it is given to forge the gold?

WOGLINDE

Nur wer der Minne
Macht versagt,
nur wer der Liebe
Lust verjagt,
nur der erzielt sich den Zauber
zum Reif zu zwingen das Gold.

[7] Only the man who forswears
love's sway,
only he who disdains
love's delights
can master the magic spell
[6] that rounds a ring from the gold.

WELLGUNDE

Wohl sicher sind wir
und sorgenfrei:
denn was nur lebt will lieben;
meiden will keiner die Minne.

We're safe enough
and free from care
since all that lives must love;
no one wants to abjure its delights.

WOGLINDE

Am wenigsten er,
der lüsterne Alp:
vor Liebesgier
möcht' er vergeh'n!

Least of all he,
the lecherous elf:
he's almost dying
of lustful desire!

FLOSSHILDE

Nicht fürcht' ich den,
wie ich ihn erfand:
seiner Minne Brunst
brannte fast mich.

I do not fear him
as I found him:
the flames of his lust
fairly scorched me.

WELLGUNDE

Ein Schwefelbrand
in der Wogen Schwall:
vor Zorn der Liebe
zischt er laut.

A brimstone brand
in the surging swell,
with the frenzy of love
he sizzles aloud.

ALL THREE

Wallala! Wallaleialala!
Lieblichster Albe,
lach'st du nicht auch?
In des Goldes Scheine
wie leuchtest du schön!
O komm', Lieblicher, lache mit uns!
Heiajaheia! Heiajaheia!
Wallalalalalaleia jahei!

[2] Wallala! Wallaleialala!
Loveliest elf,
why won't you laugh too?
In the gold's gleaming light
how handsome you look!
O come, my love, and laugh with us!
Heiajaheia! Heiajaheia!
[4] Wallalalalalaleia jahei!

(They swim to and fro, laughing in the glittering light.) [2]

ALBERICH

(his eyes fixed firmly on the gold, listening attentively to the sisters' chatter)

Der Welt Erbe
gewänn' ich zu eigen durch dich?
Erzwäng' ich nicht Liebe,
doch listig erzwäng' ich mir Lust?

[6] The world's wealth
might I win through you?
Though love can't be gained by force,
through cunning might I enforce its
[7] [delights?

(terribly loud)

Spottet nur zu!	Scoff if you like!
Der Niblung naht eu'rem Spiel!	The Niblung draws near your gold!

(Furiously, he leaps across to the central ledge and clambers up to the top of it. The girls scatter, screaming raucously, and resurface on different sides.)

ALL THREE

Heia! Heia! Heiajahei!	Heia! Heia! Heiajahei!
Rettet euch!	Run for your lives!
es raset der Alp!	The elf is raving!
in den Wassern sprüht's,	The water sprays
wohin er springt:	wherever he springs:
die Minne macht ihn verrückt!	love has driven him mad!

(laughing)

Hahahahahahaha!	Hahahahahahaha!

ALBERICH

(reaching the top with one last bound)

Bangt euch noch nicht?	Still not afraid?
So buhlt nun im Finstern,	Then whore in the dark,
feuchtes Gezücht!	you watery brood!

(He reaches out his hand towards the gold.)

Das Licht lösch' ich euch aus,	[4]	Your light I'll put out,
entreiße dem Riff das Gold,		wrench the gold from the rock
schmiede den rächenden Ring:		and forge the avenging ring:
denn hör' es die Fluth –		so hear me, you waters: –
so verfluch' ich die Liebe!	[7]	thus I lay a curse on love!

(He tears the gold from the rock with terrible force and plunges swiftly into the depths, where he quickly disappears. [4] Impenetrable darkness suddenly descends on all sides. The girls dive down abruptly into the depths in pursuit of the robber.)

FLOSSHILDE

Haltet den Räuber!	Stop, you thief!

WELLGUNDE

Rettet das Gold!	Look to the gold!

WOGLINDE AND WELLGUNDE

Hilfe! Hilfe!	Help! Help!

ALL THREE

Weh! Weh!	Alas! Alas!

(The waters subside, taking the Rhinedaughters with them into the depths. From the lowest level Alberich's piercingly mocking laughter is heard. The rocky ledges disappear into the densest darkness, the whole stage is filled from top to bottom with black billowing water, which for a time seems to keep on sinking. [7] Gradually the waves turn into clouds, which resolve into a fine mist as an increasingly bright light emerges behind them. [6] When the mist has completely disappeared from the top of the stage in the form of delicate little clouds, an open space on a mountain summit becomes visible in the dawning light. At one side, on a flowery bank, lies Wotan, with Fricka at his side.[12] Both are asleep.) [8]

SCENE TWO

(An open space on a mountain summit)

In the growing light of the dawning day a castle with glittering battlements can be seen standing on a rocky summit in the background; between it and the front of the stage a deep valley must be imagined, with the River Rhine flowing through it. (Wotan and Fricka asleep. The castle is now fully visible. Fricka wakes up: her eye falls on the castle.)

FRICKA
(alarmed)

Wotan! Gemahl! erwache!   Wotan, husband! Awake!

WOTAN
(still dreaming)

Der Wonne seligen Saal	[6]	The happy hall of delight
bewachen mir Thür' und Thor:		is guarded by door and gate:
Mannes Ehre,	[8b]	manhood's honour,
ewige Macht,		boundless might
ragen zu endlosem Ruhm!		redound to endless renown!

FRICKA
(shaking him)

  Auf, aus der Träume   Awake from the blissful
  wonnigem Trug!   deception of dreams!
Erwache, Mann, und erwäge!   Husband, wake up and reflect!

WOTAN
(waking and raising himself a little; his gaze is at once arrested by the sight of the castle)

Vollendet das ewige Werk:	[8]	The everlasting work is ended!
auf Berges Gipfel		On mountain peak
die Götter-Burg,		the gods' abode;
prächtig prahlt		resplendent shines
der prangende Bau!		the proud-standing hall!
Wie im Traum ich ihn trug,		As in my dream I conceived it,
wie mein Wille ihn wies,		just as my will decreed it,
stark und schön		sturdy and fair
steht er zur Schau:		it stands on show,
hehrer, herrlicher Bau!		august and glorious building!

FRICKA

Nur Wonne schafft dir,		You feel only joy
was mich erschreckt?		at what fills me with dread?
Dich freut die Burg,		The stronghold delights you,
mir bangt es um Freia.		but I fear for Freia.
Achtloser, laß dich erinnern		Heedless husband, don't you recall
des ausbedungenen Lohn's!		the payment that was agreed?
Die Burg ist fertig,	[9]	The fortress is finished,
verfallen das Pfand:		the forfeit is due:

vergaßest du, was du vergab'st?   have you forgot what you gave away?

WOTAN

Wohl dünkt mich's, was sie
  [bedangen,
die dort die Burg mir gebaut;
  durch Vertrag[13] zähmt' ich
  ihr trotzig Gezücht,
  daß sie die hehre
  Halle mir schüfen;
die steht nun – Dank den Starken: –
um den Sold sorge dich nicht.

I well remember what they demanded

who built the stronghold for me there;
  through a contract[13] I tamed
  their froward breed,
  bidding them build
  the lordly hall;
it stands there – thanks to the giants: –
as for the payment, give it no thought.

FRICKA

O lachend frevelnder Leichtsinn!
Liebelosester Frohmuth!
Wußt' ich um eu'ren Vertrag,
dem Truge hätt' ich gewehrt;
  doch muthig entferntet
  ihr Männer die Frauen,
um taub und ruhig vor uns

allein mit den Riesen zu tagen.
  So ohne Scham
  verschenktet ihr Frechen
Freia, mein holdes Geschwister,
froh des Schächergewerb's. –
  Was ist euch Harten
  doch heilig und werth,
giert ihr Männer nach Macht!

O laughingly wanton folly!
Most loveless joviality!
Had I known about your contract,
I'd have hindered such deceit;
  but you mettlesome menfolk
  kept us women out of the way,
so that, deaf to all entreaty, you could
  [calmly
deal with the giants alone.
  So without shame
  you brazenly bargained with
Freia, my gracious sister,
well pleased with your shabby deal! –
  What is still sacred and precious
  to hard hearts such as yours
when you menfolk lust after power?

[6]

WOTAN
(calmly)

    Gleiche Gier
    war Fricka wohl fremd,
als selbst um den Bau sie mich bat?

    Was such lust
    unknown to Fricka
when she begged me for the building?

FRICKA

Um des Gatten Treue besorgt
muß traurig ich wohl sinnen,
wie an mich er zu fesseln,
zieht's in die Ferne ihn fort:
  herrliche Wohnung,
  wonniger Hausrath,
  sollten dich binden
  zu säumender Rast.
Doch du bei dem Wohnbau sannst
auf Wehr und Wall allein:
  Herrschaft und Macht
  soll er dir mehren;

Heedful of my husband's fidelity,
I'm bound in my sadness to brood
on ways of binding him fast
whenever he feels drawn away:
  a glorious dwelling,
  domestic bliss
  were meant to entice you
  to tarry and rest.
But, in having it built,
you thought of bulwark and berm alone:
  it is meant to enhance
  your dominion and power;

nur rastlosern Sturm zu erregen
erstand dir die ragende Burg.

yet only to whip up greater unrest
has the towering stronghold arisen.

WOTAN
(smiling)

Wolltest du Frau
in der Feste mich fangen,
mir Gotte mußt du schon gönnen,
daß, in der Burg
gefangen, ich mir
von außen gewinne die Welt.　[8b]
Wandel und Wechsel　[8d, 8e]
liebt wer lebt:
das Spiel drum kann ich nicht sparen.

If your aim, as my wife,
was to hold me fast in the fortress,
you must grant that I, as a god,
while confined to the
stronghold, might win
for myself the world outside.
All who live
love renewal and change:
that pleasure I cannot forgo!

FRICKA

Liebeloser,
leidigster Mann!
Um der Macht und Herrschaft
müßigen Tand
verspielst du in lästerndem Spott

Liebe und Weibes Werth?　[7]

Loveless husband,
most heartless of men!
For the barren bauble
of might and dominion
you'd gamble away, with ungodly
[contempt,
love and womanhood's worth?

WOTAN

Um dich zum Weib zu gewinnen,　[9]
mein eines Auge
setzt' ich werbend daran:[14]
wie thörig tadelst du jetzt!
Ehr' ich die Frauen
doch mehr als dich freut!
Und Freia, die gute,
geb' ich nicht auf:
nie sann dieß ernstlich mein Sinn.

In order to win you as wife,
my one remaining eye
I staked that I might woo you:[14]
how foolish you are to blame me now!
I worship women
more than you like!
And Freia the good
I'll not give up:
it never seriously entered my thoughts.

FRICKA
(peering offstage, tense with anxiety) [3]

So schirme sie jetzt:
in schutzloser Angst
läuft sie nach Hilfe dort her!

Then shield her now:
in defenceless fear
she comes running hither for help!

FREIA
(entering, as if in headlong flight) [10]

Hilf mir, Schwester!
Schütze mich, Schwäher![15]
Vom Felsen drüben
drohte mir Fasolt,
mich holde käm' er zu holen.

Help me, sister!
Help me, kinsman![15]
Fasolt has threatened
from yonder fell,
saying he'll come for Freia the fair.

Lass' ihn droh'n!
Sah'st du nicht Loge?

Let him threaten!
Did you see Loge?

FRICKA

Daß am liebsten du immer
dem listigen trau'st!
Viel Schlimmes schuf er uns schon,
doch stets bestrickt er dich wieder.

So you still prefer to trust
in that cunning trickster?
Much ill he has caused us already,
yet ever again he ensnares you.

WOTAN

Wo freier Muth frommt,
allein frag' ich nach keinem;
doch des Feindes Neid[16]
zum Nutz' sich fügen
lehrt nur Schlauheit und List,

wie Loge verschlagen sie übt.
Der zum Vertrage mir rieth,
versprach mir Freia zu lösen:
auf ihn verlass' ich mich nun.

Where freedom of mind is called for,
I ask for help from no man;
but to turn to advantage
an enemy's grudge[16]
is a lesson that only cunning and
[craft can teach
of the kind that Loge slyly employs.
He who counselled me on the contract
promised to ransom Freia:
on him I now rely.

FRICKA

Und er läßt dich allein. –
Dort schreiten rasch
die Riesen heran:
wo harrt dein schlauer Gehilf?

And he leaves you in the lurch! –
There come the giants
striding swiftly along:
where's your crafty accomplice now?

FREIA

Wo harren meine Brüder,
daß Hilfe sie brächten,
da mein Schwäher die Schwache
[verschenkt?
Zu Hilfe, Donner!
Hieher! hieher!
Rette Freia, mein Froh!

[10]   Where are my brothers,
who ought to bring help
when my kinsman abandons the weak!

Help me, Donner!
This way, this way!
Rescue Freia, my Froh!

FRICKA

Die in bösem Bund dich verriethen,
sie alle bergen sich nun.

All who betrayed you in evil alliance
have fled to save their skins.

(Enter Fasolt and Fafner, both of gigantic stature and armed with stout staves.) [11]

FASOLT

Sanft schloß
Schlaf dein Aug':
wir beide bauten
Schlummers bar die Burg.
Mächt'ger Müh'
müde nie,
stauten starke

Gentle slumber
sealed your eyes:
we both, unsleeping,
built the stronghold.
Never tiring
of mighty toil,
we stowed the heavy

Stein' wir auf;	stones away;
steiler Thurm,	steep-sided tower,
Thür und Thor,	door and gate
deckt und schließt	cover and close
im schlanken Schloß den Saal.	the hall within the lofty keep.

(pointing to the castle) [8b]

Dort steht's,	There it stands,
was wir stemmten;	what we hewed;
schimmernd hell	shimmering brightly
bescheint's der Tag:	the day shines upon it:
zieh' nun ein,	move in now,
uns zahl' den Lohn!	to us pay our due!

WOTAN

Nennt, Leute, den Lohn:	Name your due, good people;
was dünkt euch zu bedingen?	what are you minded to ask?

FASOLT

Bedungen ist,	[9]	We already asked
was tauglich uns dünkt:		for what seems to us fitting;
gemahnt es dich so matt?		is your memory of it so faint?
Freia, die holde,	[10]	Freia the fair,
Holda, die freie[17] –		Holda the free[17] –
vertragen ist's –		it's already agreed:
sie tragen wir heim.		we carry her home.

WOTAN

Seid ihr bei Trost	Are you out of your minds
mit eurem Vertrag?	with this contract of yours?
Denkt auf andren Dank:	Think of some other thanks:
Freia ist mir nicht feil.	Freia isn't for sale.

FASOLT

(momentarily speechless, in utter consternation) [9]

Was sag'st du, ha!	What's that you say? Ha!
Sinn'st du Verrath?	You're plotting betrayal?
Verrath am Vertrag?	Betrayal of our agreement?
Die dein Speer birgt,[18]	The runes of well-considered contract,
sind sie dir Spiel,	safeguarded by your spear,[18]
des berath'nen Bundes Runen?	are they no more than sport to you?

FAFNER

Getreu'ster Bruder!	Most trusty brother,
Merk'st du Tropf nun Betrug?	you see their deception now, you fool?

FASOLT

Lichtsohn du,	Son of light,
leicht gefügter,	lightly swayed,
hör' und hüte dich:	listen and beware:
Verträgen halte Treu'!	keep your faith with contracts!

Was du bist,
bist du nur durch Verträge: [9]
bedungen ist,
wohl bedacht deine Macht.
  Bist weiser du
  als witzig wir sind,
  bandest uns Freie
  zum Frieden du:
all' deinem Wissen fluch' ich,
fliehe weit deinen Frieden,[19]
  weißt du nicht offen, [12]
  ehrlich und frei,
Verträgen zu wahren die Treu'! —
  Ein dummer Riese
  räth dir das:
du Weiser, wiss' es von ihm!

What you are
you are through contracts alone: [9]
  your power, mark me well,
is bound by sworn agreements.
  Though you are wiser
  than we in our wits,
  you bound us freemen
  to keep the peace:
I'll curse all your wisdom,
fly far away from your close,[19]
  if, openly, fairly and [12]
  freely, you cannot
keep faith with your contracts!
  A dull-witted giant
  enjoins you thus:
you witling, learn it of him!

WOTAN

Wie schlau für Ernst du achtest,
was wir zum Scherz nur beschlossen!
  Die liebliche Göttin,
  licht und leicht,
was taugt euch Tölpeln ihr Reiz?

How cunning to take in earnest
what was decided in jest!
  The lovely goddess,
  radiant and light,
what use are her charms to you churls?

FASOLT

  Höhn'st du uns?
  Ha! wie unrecht! —
Die ihr durch Schönheit herrscht, [10a]
schimmernd hehres Geschlecht,
  wie thörig strebt ihr
  nach Thürmen von Stein, [8b]
setzt um Burg und Saal
Weibes Wonne zum Pfand!
Wir Plumpen plagen uns [11]
schwitzend mit schwieliger Hand,
  ein Weib zu gewinnen,
  das wonnig und mild [10a]
bei uns armen wohne: —
und verkehrt nenn'st du den Kauf?

  You jeer at us?
  Ha, how unjust!
You who rule through beauty, [10a]
you augustly glittering race,
  how foolish to strive
  after towers of stone, [8b]
placing woman's delights in pawn
for the sake of castle and hall!
We blunderheads toil away, [11]
sweating with blistered hand,
  to win a wife
  who, fair and meek, [10a]
would dwell with us poor creatures: —
and you say that the deal is invalid?

FAFNER

Schweig' dein faules Schwatzen!
Gewinn werben wir nicht:
  Freia's Haft
  hilft wenig;[20]
  doch viel gilt's
den Göttern sie zu entreißen.

Stop your idle chatter!
We'll gain no good like this:
  holding Freia
  helps us little;[20]
  much, however, will be gained
if we wrest her away from the gods.

(softly)

  Gold'ne Äpfel [13]
wachsen in ihrem Garten;

  Golden apples [13]
grow in her garden;

sie allein
weiß die Äpfel zu pflegen:
  der Frucht Genuß
  frommt ihren Sippen
  zu ewig nie
  alternder Jugend;
  siech und bleich
  doch sinkt ihre Blüthe,
  alt und schwach
  schwinden sie hin,
müssen Freia sie missen:

(roughly)

ihrer Mitte drum sei sie entführt! [13, 11]

she alone
knows how to tend them;
  the taste of the fruit
  confers on her kinsfolk
  endlessly never-
  ageing youth;
  but, sick and wan,
  their bloom will wither,
  old and weak
  they'll waste away,
if Freia they have to forgo:

so let her be plucked from their midst!

WOTAN

Loge säumt zu lang!

Loge delays too long!

FASOLT

Schlicht gieb nun Bescheid!

Quick, give us your answer!

WOTAN

Fordert andern Sold![21]

Demand some other pay![21]

FASOLT

Kein and'rer: Freia allein!

No other: Freia alone!

FAFNER

Du da, folge uns!

You there! Follow us!

(Fasolt and Fafner threaten Freia. Froh and Donner come running in.)

FREIA

Helft! helft vor den Harten!

Help! Save me from these hard-hearted
[brutes!

FROH

(taking Freia in his arms)

Zu mir, Freia! –

To me, Freia! –

(to Fafner)

Meide sie, Frecher!
Froh schützt die Schöne.

Get back from her, you bully!
Froh protects fair Freia.

DONNER

(planting himself in the path of both the giants)

Fasolt und Fafner,
  fühltet ihr schon
meines Hammers harten Schlag?

Fasolt and Fafner,
  you've felt my hammer's
heavy blow before?

FAFNER

Was soll das Droh'n?

What do you hope to gain by your
[threats?

FASOLT

Was dringst du her?

Kampf kies'ten wir nicht,
verlangen nur unsern Lohn.

What do you hope to gain by such
[meddling?
Strife was not what we sought,
we only want our reward.

DONNER

Schon oft zahlt' ich
Riesen den Zoll;
kommt her! des Lohnes Last
wäg' ich mit gutem Gewicht!

Often before I've
paid giants their due;
come here, the debt's discharge
I'll weigh out in good measure.

(He swings his hammer.)

WOTAN

(stretching out his spear between the disputants)

Halt, du Wilder!   [9]   Stop, you firebrand!
Nichts durch Gewalt!   Nothing by force!
Verträge schützt   My spearshaft
meines Speeres Schaft: safeguards contracts:
spar' deines Hammers Heft!   spare your hammer's haft.

FREIA

Wehe! Wehe!   Sorrow! Sorrow!
Wotan verläßt mich!   Wotan forsakes me!

FRICKA

Begreif' ich dich noch,   Have I heard you aright,
grausamer Mann?   merciless man?

WOTAN

(turning away and seeing Loge coming)

Endlich Loge!   Loge at last!
Eiltest du so,   [14a]   Have you come in such haste
den du geschlossen,   to resolve
den schlimmen Handel zu schlichten?   the bad bargain you struck?

(Loge has climbed up through the valley at the back.) [14b]

LOGE

Wie? welchen Handel   What? Which bargain is that
hätt' ich geschlossen?   that I'm said to have struck?
Wohl was mit den Riesen   The one you discussed
dort im Rathe du dangst? –   with the giants in council? –
In Tiefen und Höhen   [8a, 8b] To hollow and height
treibt mich mein Hang;   my hankering drives me;
Haus und Herd   house and hearth
behagt mir nicht: delight me not:
Donner und Froh,   Donner and Froh,
die denken an Dach und Fach;   think only of house and home;
wollen sie frei'n,   if they'd go awooing,
ein Haus muß sie erfreu'n: a home must make them happy:

ein stolzer Saal,	a stately hall,
ein starkes Schloß,	a sturdy keep,
danach stand Wotan's Wunsch. –	such was Wotan's wish. –
Haus und Hof, [8]	House and court,
Saal und Schloß,	hall and keep,
die selige Burg,	your blissful abode
sie steht nun fest gebaut;	now stands there, solidly built;
das Prachtgemäuer	the proud-standing walls
prüft' ich selbst;	I tested myself;
ob alles fest,	I looked to see
forscht' ich genau:	if all was firm:
Fasolt und Fafner	Fasolt and Fafner
fand ich bewährt;	have done their work well;
kein Stein wankt im Gestemm'. [14b]	no stone stirs in the studwork.
Nicht müßig war ich,	I've not been idle,
wie mancher hier:	like many here:
der lügt, wer lässig mich schilt!	he lies who calls me lazy!

WOTAN

Arglistig	Slyly
weich'st du mir aus:	you seek to elude me;
mich zu betrügen	take care, in truth,
hüte in Treuen dich wohl!	that you don't deceive me.
Von allen Göttern	Of all the gods
dein einz'ger Freund,	your only friend,
nahm ich dich auf	I took you
in der übel trauenden Troß. –	into the ill-trusting tribe. –
Nun red' und rathe klug! [9]	Now speak and counsel wisely!
Da einst die Bauer der Burg	When the citadel's builders
zum Dank Freia bedangen,	demanded Freia by way of thanks,
du weißt, nicht anders	you know that
willigt' ich ein,	I only acquiesced
als weil auf Pflicht du gelobtest	because you promised on oath
zu lösen das hehre Pfand.	to redeem the noble pledge.

LOGE

Mit höchster Sorge	With utmost care
d'rauf zu sinnen,	to ponder on ways
wie es zu lösen,	by which to redeem it –
das – hab' ich gelobt:	*that* I did indeed promise:
doch daß ich fände,	but that I would find
was nie sich fügt,	what never befell and
was nie gelingt,	what's bound to fail,
wie ließ sich das wohl geloben?	how could such a promise be made?

FRICKA
(to Wotan)

Sieh', welch' trugvollem	See what a treacherous
Schelm du getraut!	rogue you trusted!

FROH
(to Loge)

Loge heißt du,	Loge's your name,
doch nenn' ich dich Lüge!	but I call you Liar!

DONNER

Verfluchte Lohe,	Accursèd flame,
dich lösch' ich aus!	I'll snuff you out!

LOGE

Ihre Schmach zu decken	To hide their shame
schmähen mich Dumme.	the fools defame me.

(Donner aims a blow at Loge.)

WOTAN
(intervening)

In Frieden laßt mir den Freund!	Leave my friend in peace!
Nicht kennt ihr Loge's Kunst:	You don't know Loge's art:
reicher wiegt	greater the value
seines Rathes Werth,	of his advice
zahlt er zögernd ihn aus.	when he pays it out delayingly.

FAFNER

Nichts gezögert:	[11] No more delay!
rasch gezahlt!	Pay up quickly!

FASOLT

Lang' währt's mit dem Lohn.	The wage is long overdue.

WOTAN
(turning sharply to Loge, insistently)

Jetzt hör', Störrischer!	Now listen, you stubborn creature!
halte Stich!	Keep your promised word!
Wo schweiftest du hin und her?	Where have you been roaming?

LOGE

Immer ist Undank	Ingratitude ever
Loge's Lohn!	is Loge's wage.
Für dich nur besorgt	For your sake alone,
sah ich mich um,	I looked all around me,
durchstöbert' im Sturm	stormily scouring
alle Winkel der Welt,	the ends of the earth,
Ersatz für Freia zu suchen,	seeking a ransom for Freia
wie er den Riesen wohl recht:	that the giants might approve:
umsonst sucht' ich	I sought in vain
und sehe nun wohl,	and see full well:
in der Welten Ring	in the whole wide world
nichts ist so reich,	there's naught so rare
als Ersatz zu muthen dem Mann	as to strike mankind as a worthy ransom
für Weibes Wonne und Werth.	for woman's delights and worth.

(All express astonishment and various forms of consternation.)

So weit Leben und Weben,	Wherever there's life and breath
in Wasser, Erd' und Luft,	in water, earth and air,
viel frug ich,	I asked a good deal,
forschte bei allen,	enquired of all,
wo Kraft nur sich rührt	where the lifeforce moves
und Keime sich regen:	and seedbuds stir:
was wohl dem Manne	what might man
mächt'ger dünk',	deem mightier
als Weibes Wonne und Werth?	than woman's delights and worth?
Doch so weit Leben und Weben,	But wherever there's life and breath,
verlacht nur ward	my inquisitive skill
meine fragende List:	was laughed to scorn:
in Wasser, Erd' und Luft	in water, earth and air
lassen will nichts	none will relinquish
von Lieb' und Weib. –	love and woman. –

(General agitation.)

Nur einen sah ich,	Only one man I saw
der sagte der Liebe ab: [4]	who forswore love's delights:
um rothes Gold	for the sake of red gold
entrieth er des Weibes Gunst.	he forwent women's favours.
Des Rheines klare Kinder [5]	The Rhine's fair children
klagten mir ihre Noth:	complained to me of their plight:
der Nibelung,	the Nibelung,
Nacht-Alberich,	Night-Alberich,
buhlte vergebens [2]	wooed in vain
um der Badenden Gunst;	for the nixies' favours;
das Rheingold da	the thief robbed
raubte sich rächend der Dieb: [4]	the Rhinegold then in revenge:
das dünkt ihm nun	it seems to him now
das theuerste Gut,	the rarest jewel,
hehrer als Weibes Huld.	greater than woman's grace.
Um den gleißenden Tand, [5]	For the glittering toy
der Tiefe entwandt,	that was torn from the deep
erklang mir der Töchter Klage:	the daughters' lament rang out:
an dich, Wotan,	to you, Wotan,
wenden sie sich,	they now appeal
daß zu Recht du zögest den Räuber,	to call the thief to account

(with increasing warmth)

das Gold dem Wasser [4]	and give back the gold
wieder gebest,	to the waters,
und ewig es bliebe ihr Eigen. –	to remain their own forever. –

(All show signs of approval.) [5]

Dir's zu melden	To tell you this
gelobt' ich den Mädchen: [14b]	I promised the maidens:
nun lös'te Loge sein Wort.	now Loge has kept his word.

WOTAN

Thörig bist du,	You're foolish,
wenn nicht gar tückisch!	not to say spiteful!

Mich selbst sieh'st du in Noth:
wie hülf' ich andern zum Heil?

You see me in need myself:
how might I offer help to others?

FASOLT
(who has been listening attentively, to Fafner)

Nicht gönn' ich das Gold dem Alben;
viel Noth schon schuf uns der
  [Niblung,
doch schlau entschlüpfte unserm
Zwange immer der Zwerg.

The gold I begrudge the elf;
the Nibelung's caused us much distress,

but the dwarf has always slyly
slipped from our clutches.

FAFNER

Neue Neidthat
  sinnt uns der Niblung,
giebt das Gold ihm Macht. –
  Du da, Loge!
  Sag' ohne Lug:
was Großes gilt denn das Gold,
daß dem Niblung es genügt?

The Niblung will think up
  new ways to harm us,
as long as the gold gives him power. –
  You there, Loge!
  Say without lying:
what is the gold's great virtue
that it satisfies the Niblung?

LOGE

[5]

Ein Tand ist's
  in des Wassers Tiefe,
lachenden Kindern zur Lust:
  doch, ward es zum runden
  Reife geschmiedet,
hilft es zur höchsten Macht,
gewinnt dem Manne die Welt.

A toy it is
  in the watery deep,
delighting laughing children:
  but once it is forged

[6]

  to a rounded hoop,
it helps to confer unending power
and wins the world for its master.

WOTAN
(reflectively)

Von des Rheines Gold
  hört' ich raunen:
  Beute-Runen
berge sein rother Glanz;
  Macht und Schätze
schüf' ohne Maaß ein Reif.

Of the gold in the Rhine
  I've heard it whispered
  that booty-runes
lie hid in its fiery glow;
  power and riches
beyond all measure may be gained
  [through a ring.

FRICKA
(softly to Loge)

Taugte wohl
  des gold'nen Tandes
  gleißend Geschmeid
auch Frauen zu schönem Schmuck?

Might the golden trinket's
  glittering gem
  be worn by women
and serve as fair adornment?

LOGE

Des Gatten Treu'
  ertrotzte die Frau,
  trüge sie hold

A wife might ensure
  that her husband was true
  if she lovingly wore

den hellen Schmuck,
den schimmernd Zwerge schmieden,
rührig im Zwange des Reif's.

the bright-shining jewel,
which, shimmering, dwarfs have forged,
bestirred by the spell on the ring.

FRICKA
(cajolingly, to Wotan)

Gewänne mein Gatte
sich wohl das Gold?   [4]

Might my husband
win the gold for himself?

WOTAN
(as though in a state of increasing enchantment)

Des Reifes zu walten,
räthlich will es mich dünken. –
Doch wie, Loge,
lernt' ich die Kunst?
Wie schüf' ich mir das Geschmeid?

To wield the ring
seems wise to me. –
But, Loge, how
might I learn the art?
How could I make the jewel?

LOGE

Ein Runenzauber   [6]
zwingt das Gold zum Reif:
keiner kennt ihn;   [7]
doch einer übt ihn leicht,
der sel'ger Lieb' entsagt.

A rune-spell
makes a ring from the gold:
no one knows what it is,
yet the spell is easily cast
by him who forswears love's delights.

(Wotan turns away in displeasure.)

Das spar'st du wohl;
zu spät auch käm'st du:
Alberich zauderte nicht;
zaglos gewann er   [6]
des Zaubers Macht:

You'd rather not;
you'd be too late in any case:
Alberich did not hesitate;
fearless, he gained
the magic power

(harshly)

gerathen ist ihm der Ring.

and managed to make the ring.

DONNER
(to Wotan)

Zwang uns allen
schüfe der Zwerg,
würd' ihm der Reif nicht entrissen.

The dwarf would
enslave us all
were the ring not wrested from him.

WOTAN

Den Ring muß ich haben!

I must have the ring!

FROH

Leicht erringt
ohne Liebesfluch er sich jetzt.

It's easily won now,
without cursing love.

LOGE
(harshly)

Spott-leicht,
ohne Kunst wie im Kinder-Spiel!

Absurdly easy, no skill
is needed, it's child's play indeed!

WOTAN

So rathe, wie? Then tell us, how?

LOGE

Durch Raub!		By theft!
Was ein Dieb stahl,		What a thief stole
das stiehl'st du dem Dieb:		you steal from the thief:
ward leichter ein Eigen erlangt? –	[14b]	could what is your own be more easily won? –
Doch mit arger Wehr		But with cunning defence
wahrt sich Alberich;	[4]	is Alberich armed;
klug und fein		shrewd and subtle
mußt du verfahren,		must be your approach
zieh'st den Räuber du zu Recht,		when you call the thief to account
um des Rheines Töchtern	[5]	and make him give back
den rothen Tand,		the red trinket,

(with warmth)

das Gold, wieder zu geben;		the gold, to the daughters of the Rhine:
denn darum flehen sie dich.	[4]	for that is what they beg of you.

WOTAN

Des Rheines Töchter?	The daughters of the Rhine?
Was taugt mir der Rath?	What use is such advice to me?

FRICKA

Von dem Wassergezücht	[2]	Of the watery brood
mag ich nichts wissen:		I'd rather not know;
schon manchen Mann		for many a man
– mir zum Leid –		– to my grief! –
verlockten sie buhlend im Bad.		they have lewdly lured to their watery [lair.

(Wotan is struggling silently with himself, while the other gods, tense and silent, stare fixedly at him. Meanwhile, to one side, Fafner has been conferring with Fasolt.)

FAFNER
(to Fasolt)

Glaub' mir, mehr als Freia		Believe you me, the glittering gold
frommt das gleißende Gold:		is worth far more than Freia:
auch ew'ge Jugend erjagt,		eternal youth may also be gained by him
wer durch Goldes Zauber sie zwingt.	[4]	who obtains it by force through the [gold's magic spell.

(Fasolt's reaction indicates that he has been persuaded against his will. Accompanied by Fasolt, Fafner approaches Wotan.) [11]

Hör', Wotan,	Hear, Wotan,
der Harrenden Wort!	the word of us who have waited!
Freia bleib' euch in Frieden;	Freia may live in peace with you;
leicht'ren Lohn	an easier payment
fand ich zur Lösung:	I've found as ransom:
uns rauhen Riesen genügt	we uncouth giants will be content
des Niblungen rothes Gold.	with the Niblung's bright red gold.

Seid ihr bei Sinn?
Was nicht ich besitze,
soll ich euch Schamlosen schenken?

Are you out of your minds?
What I myself do not own
you expect me to give to you shameless
[creatures?

FAFNER

Schwer baute
dort sich die Burg:
leicht wird dir's
mit list'ger Gewalt,
was im Neidspiel²² nie uns gelang,
den Niblungen fest zu fah'n.   [14b]

The stronghold there
was hard to build;
it's easy for you
with your cunning and power
to bind the Nibelung fast –
which we've never achieved in war.²²

WOTAN

Für euch müht' ich
mich um den Alben?
Für euch fing' ich den Feind?
Unverschämt
und überbegehrlich
macht euch Dumme mein Dank!

For you should I trouble
myself with the dwarf?
For you should I capture your foe?
Unabashed
and over-demanding
my debt has made you, you fools.

FASOLT
(suddenly seizing Freia and taking her to one side with Fafner)

Hieher, Maid!
in uns're Macht!
Als Pfand folg'st du uns jetzt,
bis wir Lösung empfah'n.

Come here, child!
You're in our power!
As hostage you'll follow us now,
until we receive a ransom.

FREIA
(calling out)

Wehe! Wehe! Weh!

Alas! Woe's me! Alas!

FAFNER

Fort von hier
sei sie entführt!
Bis Abend, achtet's wohl,
pflegen wir sie als Pfand:
wir kehren wieder;
doch kommen wir,
und bereit liegt nicht als Lösung   [6]
das Rheingold licht und roth –

Away from here
let her be led!
Till evening – mark me well –
we'll take good care of our hostage:
we'll then return;
but if we come back
and the Rhinegold, bright and red,
is not lying ready as ransom –

FASOLT

Zu End' ist die Frist dann,
Freia verfallen:
für immer folge sie uns!

your term will be up then,
Freia forfeit:
she'll follow us for ever!

FREIA
(calling out)

Schwester! Brüder!
Rettet! helft!

Sister! Brothers!
Save me! Help!

(Freia is carried off by the giants as they hurry away.)

FROH

Auf, ihnen nach!

Up, go after them!

DONNER

Breche denn alles!

May they all perish!

(They look inquiringly at Wotan.)

FREIA
(in the distance)

Rettet! Helft!

Save me! Help!

LOGE
(gazing after the giants)

Über Stock und Stein zu Thal
   stapfen sie hin;
durch des Rheines Wasserfurth
   waten die Riesen:
fröhlich nicht
hängt Freia
den Rauhen über den Rücken! —
   Heia! hei!
Wie taumeln die Tölpel dahin!
Durch das Thal talpen sie schon:

   wohl an Riesenheim's Mark
   erst halten sie Rast!

Over hedge and ditch they trudge
   down into the valley;
through the ford on the Rhine
   the giants are wading:
far from happy,
Freia is hanging
over the ruffians' backs!
   Heia! hey!
How the louts are lurching along!
Already they're lumbering down through
   [the valley;
   only at Riesenheim's border
   will they stop for rest!

(turning to the gods)

Was sinnt nun Wotan so wild?[23] —
Den sel'gen Göttern wie geht's?

Why's Wotan so strangely thoughtful?[23]
What ails the blessed immortals?

A pale mist, growing gradually denser, fills the stage, so that the gods acquire an increasingly wan and aged appearance; they all stand gazing anxiously and expectantly at Wotan, who is lost in thought, his eyes fixed firmly on the ground.

   Trügt mich ein Nebel?
   Neckt mich ein Traum?
   Wie bang und bleich
   verblüht ihr so bald!
Euch erlischt der Wangen Licht;
der Blick eures Auges verblitzt! —
   Frisch, mein Froh,
   noch ist's ja früh! —
   Deiner Hand, Donner,
   entsinkt ja der Hammer! —
   Was ist's mit Fricka?
   freut sie sich wenig

[13]

   Is the mist playing tricks?
   Does a dream delude me?
   How fearful and wan
   you wither away so soon!
The bloom in your cheeks is fading;
the light has gone from your eyes!
   Take heart, my Froh!
   It's early yet!
   From your hand, Donner,
   your hammer is sinking!
   What ails Fricka?
   Is she little pleased

ob Wotan's grämlichem Grau,
das schier zum Greisen ihn schafft?

at Wotan's sullen greyness,
that suddenly makes him old?

FRICKA

Wehe! Wehe!
Was ist gescheh'n?

Woe! Ah woe!
What has happened?

DONNER

Mir sinkt die Hand.

My hand is sinking!

FROH

Mir stockt das Herz.

My heartbeat falters!

LOGE

Jetzt fand ich's: hört was euch fehlt!
    Von Freia's Frucht
genosset ihr heute noch nicht:
    die gold'nen Äpfel   [13]
    in ihrem Garten,
sie machten euch tüchtig und jung,
aß't ihr sie jeden Tag.
    Des Gartens Pflegerin
    ist nun verpfändet;
    an den Ästen darbt
    und dorrt das Obst:
bald fällt faul es herab. –   [14b]
    Mich kümmert's minder;
    an mir ja kargte
    Freia von je
knausernd die köstliche Frucht:
    denn halb so ächt nur
bin ich wie, Selige, ihr!

I have it! Hear what you lack!
    Of Freia's fruit
you've not yet tasted today:
    the golden apples
    in her garden
kept you hale and young
when you ate them every day.
    She who tends the garden
    has now been placed in pawn;
    on the branches the fruit
    dries out and withers:
soon it will rot and fall. –
    It troubles me less:
    in her niggardly fashion
    Freia always
begrudged me the luscious fruit:
    for I'm only half as godlike
as you, you immortals!

(freely, but animatedly and harshly)

    Doch ihr setztet alles
    auf das jüngende Obst:
das wußten die Riesen wohl;
    auf euer Leben
    legten sie's an:
nun sorgt, wie ihr das wahrt!
    Ohne die Äpfel
    alt und grau,
    greis und grämlich,
welkend zum Spott aller Welt,

erstirbt der Götter Stamm.

    But you staked all
    on the youth-giving fruit,
as the giants knew full well;
    your very lives
    they've threatened:
now look to ways of saving yourselves.
    Without the apples,
    old and grey,
    grizzled and grim,
withered and scorned by the whole of
[the world,
the race of gods will perish.

FRICKA
(anxiously)

Wotan, Gemahl,
unsel'ger Mann!

Wotan, my husband,
unhappy man!

Sieh', wie dein Leichtsinn
lachend uns allen
Schimpf und Schmach erschuf!

See how your folly
has laughingly brought us
naught but shame and disgrace!

WOTAN
(starting up with sudden resolve)

Auf, Loge!
hinab mit mir!
Nach Nibelheim fahren wir nieder:
gewinnen will ich das Gold.

Get up, Loge!
Come down with me!
To Nibelheim let's descend:
the gold I mean to win.

LOGE

Die Rheintöchter
riefen dich an:
so dürfen Erhörung sie hoffen?

[5] The Rhinedaughters
cried out for your help:
so may they hope to be heard?

WOTAN
(vehemently)

Schweige, Schwätzer!
Freia, die gute,
Freia gilt es zu lösen.

Silence, you babbler!
Freia the good,
Freia must be redeemed.

LOGE

Wie du befiehlst,
führ' ich dich gern:
steil hinab
steigen wir denn durch den Rhein?

As you command,
I'll gladly guide you:
shall we descend
straight down through the Rhine?

WOTAN

Nicht durch den Rhein!

Not through the Rhine!

LOGE

So schwingen wir uns
durch die Schwefelkluft:
dort schlüpfe mit mir hinein!
(He leads the way and disappears sideways into a crevice from which sulphurous vapours immediately start to seep.)

Then let's swing ourselves down
through the sulphurous cleft:
come, slip with me through there!

WOTAN

Ihr andern harrt
bis Abend hier:
verlor'ner Jugend
erjag' ich erlösendes Gold!
(He climbs down into the crevice after Loge: the sulphurous vapours rising from it spread out over the whole stage, quickly filling it with dense clouds. The remaining gods are already invisible.)

You others wait
here till evening:
I go in search of redeeming gold
to ransom our lost youth!

DONNER

Fahre wohl, Wotan!

Fare well, Wotan!

FROH

Glück auf! Glück auf!   Good luck! Good luck!

FRICKA

O kehre bald   O come back soon
zur bangenden Frau!   to your worried wife!

*(The sulphurous mists darken in colour to form a completely black cloud, which moves from
below to above; this is then transformed into a solid, dark rocky chasm that continues moving
upwards, thus giving the impression that the stage is sinking deeper and deeper into the earth.
[14b, 3, 4, 6, 10b, 15] A dark red light begins to glow at various points in the distance: a noise
as though of people forging can be heard on all sides. The ringing of the anvils dies away. A
subterranean cavern, stretching away endlessly into the distance, can be made out, apparently
opening into narrow shafts on every side.)*

SCENE THREE

(Nibelheim)

(Alberich drags the screeching Mime by his ears from a side gallery.)

ALBERICH

Hehe! hehe!   Hihi! Hihi!
hieher! hieher!   This way! This way!
Tückischer Zwerg!   You shifty dwarf!
Tapfer gezwickt   You'll be
sollst du mir sein,   properly pinched
schaff'st du nicht fertig,   if you don't finish making
wie ich's bestellt,   the delicate jewel
zur Stund' das feine Geschmeid!   on time, as I ordered.

MIME
(howling)

Ohe! Ohe!   Oh! Oh!
Au! Au!   Ow! Ow!
Lass' mich nur los!   Just let me go!
Fertig ist's,   It's already finished,
wie du befahlst;   just as you asked;
mit Fleiß und Schweiß   with toil and sweat
ist es gefügt: it was fitted together:
                                                (piercingly)
nimm nur die Nägel vom Ohr!   only let go of my ear!

ALBERICH

Was zögerst du dann   So why are you waiting?
und zeig'st es nicht?   Why don't you show it me?

MIME

Ich Armer zagte,   Poor wretch that I am, I feared
daß noch 'was fehle.   that something was missing.

ALBERICH

Was wär' noch nicht fertig?   What's not yet ready?

MIME
(embarrassed)
Hier . . . und da . . .   Here – and there –

ALBERICH

Was hier und da?   What here and there?
Her das Geschmeid!   Give me the trinket!

(He makes as though to seize Mime's ear again: in his terror, Mime drops a piece of metalwork that he had been clutching tightly in his hands. Alberich snatches it up and examines it closely.) [16]

Schau', du Schelm!   Look, you knave!
Alles geschmiedet   Everything forged
und fertig gefügt,   and fitted together,
wie ich's befahl!   just as I asked!
So wollte der Tropf   So the simpleton slyly
schlau mich betrügen,   wanted to trick me,
für sich behalten   keep for himself
das hehre Geschmeid,   the costly jewel
das meine List   that my cunning alone
ihn zu schmieden gelehrt?   had taught him to craft?
Kenn' ich dich dummen Dieb?   Have I caught you out, you dim-witted
                                         [thief?

(He places the metalwork on his head as a 'tarnhelm'.)[24]

Dem Haupt fügt sich der Helm: The helm fits tightly over my head:
ob sich der Zauber auch zeigt?   will the magic also work?

(very quietly)

– »Nacht und Nebel,   'Night and mist,
Niemand gleich!« –   like to none!' –

(He disappears and in his place can be seen a column of mist.)

Sieh'st du mich, Bruder?   Can you see me, brother?

MIME
(looking round in bewilderment)

Wo bist du? Ich sehe dich nicht.   Where are you? I can't see you.

ALBERICH
(invisible)

So fühle mich doch,   Then feel me,
du fauler Schuft!   you idle wretch!

Nimm das für dein Dieb'sgelüst!   Take that for your thieving greed!

(Mime writhes beneath the blows of a whip, whose strokes can be heard even though the whip itself is invisible.)

MIME

Ohe! Ohe!   Oh! Oh!
Au! Au! Au!   [3]   Ow! Ow! Ow!

ALBERICH
(laughing, invisible)

Ha ha ha ha ha ha!   Ha ha ha ha ha ha!
Hab Dank, du Dummer!   My thanks, you dimwit!
Dein Werk bewährt sich gut. –   Your work has proved its worth. –
Hoho! hoho!   Hoho! Hoho!
Niblungen all',   Nibelungs all,
neigt euch nun Alberich!   bow down to Alberich!
Überall weilt er nun,   Everywhere now he lies in wait
euch zu bewachen;   in order to keep you under guard;
Ruh' und Rast   rest and repose
ist euch zerronnen;   have melted away;
ihm müßt ihr schaffen,   for him you must toil
wo nicht ihr ihn schaut;   where you cannot see him;
wo ihr nicht ihn gewahrt,   where you don't expect him,
seid seiner gewärtig: there you shall find him:
unterthan seid ihr ihm immer!   you're subject to him for ever!

(harshly)

Hoho! hoho!   Hoho! Hoho!
hört ihn: er naht,   Hear him, he nears:
der Niblungen-Herr!   the Nibelungs' lord!

(The column of mist disappears towards the back of the stage: Alberich's voice can be heard receding into the distance, venting his fury as he goes. Mime has sunk to the ground in pain. [15] Wotan and Loge descend through a crevice.) [14b]

LOGE

Nibelheim hier: Nibelheim's here:
durch bleiche Nebel   through leaden mists
was blitzen dort feurige Funken!   what fiery sparks are flashing there!

MIME
(on the ground)

Au! Au! Au!   [3]   Ow! Ow! Ow!

WOTAN

Hier stöhnt es laut: Something's groaning loudly here:
was liegt im Gestein?   what's lying among the stones?

LOGE
(bending over Mime)

Was Wunder wimmerst du hier?   Why whimper here, you wondrous
                              [thing?

90 DAS RHEINGOLD, Scene Three

MIME

Ohe! Ohe!	Oh! Oh!
Au! Au!	Ow! Ow!

LOGE

Hei, Mime! Munt'rer Zwerg!	Hey, Mime! Blithe-spirited dwarf!
Was zwingt und zwackt dich denn so?	What plagues and pinches you so?

MIME

Lass' mich in Frieden!	Leave me in peace!

LOGE

Das will ich freilich,	Of course I'll do so,
und mehr noch, hör':	and even more, listen:
helfen will ich dir, Mime!	I want to help you, Mime!

(He sets him on his feet with difficulty.)

MIME

Wer hälfe mir?	[17]	Who'd ever help me?
Gehorchen muß ich		I'm bound to obey
dem leiblichen Bruder,		my own bloodbrother,
der mich in Bande gelegt.		who's bound me in fetters fast.

LOGE

Dich, Mime, zu binden,	What gave him the power,
was gab ihm die Macht?	Mime, to bind you?

MIME

Mit arger List	[17]	With cunning artifice
schuf sich Alberich		Alberich crafted
aus Rheines Gold		a yellow ring
einen gelben Reif:		of gold from the Rhine:
seinem starken Zauber		at its powerful spell
zittern wir staunend;		we tremble in awe;
mit ihm zwingt er uns alle,		for with it he bends us all to his will,
der Niblungen nächt'ges Heer. –	[15]	the Nibelungs' army of night. –
Sorglose Schmiede,		Carefree smiths,
schufen wir sonst wohl		we used to fashion
Schmuck uns'ren Weibern,		trinkets for our womenfolk,
wonnig Geschmeid,		delightful gems and
niedlichen Niblungentand:		delicate Nibelung toys:
wir lachten lustig der Müh'.		we cheerfully laughed at our pains.
Nun zwingt uns der Schlimme	[3]	Now the criminal makes us
in Klüfte zu schlüpfen,		crawl into crevices,
für ihn allein		ever toiling
uns immer zu müh'n.		for him alone.
Durch des Ringes Gold		Through the gold of the ring
erräth seine Gier,		his greed can divine
wo neuer Schimmer		where more gleaming veins
in Schachten sich birgt:		lie buried in shafts:

da müssen wir spähen,
spüren und graben,
die Beute schmelzen
und schmieden den Guß,
ohne Ruh' und Rast,
dem Herrn zu häufen den Hort.

there we must seek
and search and dig,
smelting the spoils
and working the cast
without rest or repose,
to heap up the hoard for our lord.

LOGE

Dich Trägen so eben
traf wohl sein Zorn?

You idler roused
his wrath just now?

MIME

Mich Ärmsten, ach!
mich zwang er zum ärgsten:
ein Helmgeschmeid   [16, 15]
hieß er mich schweißen;
genau befahl er,
wie es zu fügen.
Wohl merkt' ich klug,
welch' mächt'ge Kraft
zu eigen dem Werk,
das aus Erz ich wob:
für mich drum hüten
wollt' ich den Helm,
durch seinen Zauber
Alberich's Zwang mich entzieh'n –
vielleicht, ja vielleicht
den Lästigen selbst überlisten,
in meine Gewalt ihn zu werfen,
den Ring ihm zu entreißen,   [6]
daß, wie ich Knecht jetzt dem
[Kühnen,

(harshly)

mir Freien er selber dann fröhn'!

On me, the most wretched of all,
he forced the worst of all tasks:
a metal helm
he bade me weld;
he told me exactly
how to craft it.
I cleverly noted
what magic power
lay in the work
that I forged from the ore:
so I wanted to keep
the helm for myself,
by means of its magic
free me from Alberich's sway –
perhaps – yes, perhaps
outwit my tormentor
and, placing him in my power,
wrest the ring away from his grasp,
so that, just as I'm now a slave to that
[bully,

he'd serve me, a free man, in turn!

LOGE

Warum, du Kluger,
glückte dir's nicht?

If you're so clever,
why did you fail?

MIME

Ach, der das Werk ich wirkte,
den Zauber, der ihm entzuckt,   [16]
den Zauber errieth ich nicht recht!
Der das Werk mir rieth,
und mir's entriß,
der lehrte mich nun
– doch leider zu spät! –
welche List läg' in dem Helm:
meinem Blick entschwand er,
doch Schwielen dem Blinden

Alas, I who wrought the work
failed to guess the spell aright,
the spell that stirs within it!
He who ordered the work
and snatched it away
has taught me now
– too late, alas! –
what artifice lies in the helmet:
he vanished from sight,
but his arm, unseen,

schlug unschaubar sein Arm.	[3]	dealt weals to one who was blind.

(howling and sobbing)

Das schuf ich mir Dummen		Fool that I am, that's all the thanks
schön zu Dank!	[6]	that I earned for myself.

(He rubs his back. Wotan and Loge laugh.)

LOGE
(to Wotan)

Gesteh', nicht leicht	Admit it, his capture
gelingt der Fang.	won't be easy.

WOTAN

Doch erliegt der Feind,		But our foe will fall
hilft deine List.	[14b]	with the help of your cunning.

MIME
(observing the gods more closely)

Mit eurem Gefrage	Who are you strangers,
wer seid denn ihr Fremde?	with all your questions?

LOGE

Freunde dir;		Friends of yours;
von ihrer Noth		from their plight
befrei'n wir der Niblungen Volk.	[15]	we shall free the Nibelung folk.

MIME
(starting up in terror on hearing Alberich returning)

Nehmt euch in Acht!	Be on your guard!
Alberich naht.	Alberich's coming.

(He runs to and fro in fear.)

WOTAN
(seating himself calmly on a rock)

Sein' harren wir hier.	We'll wait for him here.

(Alberich, who has removed the tarnhelm from his head and hung it from his belt, enters brandishing a whip, with which he drives a group of Nibelungs before him, urging them up from one of the deeper-lying shafts beneath them: they are laden with gold and silver trinkets which, under Alberich's constant coercion, they add to a pile which thus turns into a hoard.)

ALBERICH

Hieher! Dorthin!	[3]	This way! That way!
Hehe! Hoho!		Hihi! Hoho!
Träges Heer,		You idle herd,
dort zu Hauf		there in a heap
schichtet den Hort!		pile up the hoard!
Du da, hinauf!		You there, get up!
Willst du voran?		Move to the front!
Schmähliches Volk,		Contemptible creatures,
ab das Geschmeide!		put down the trinkets!
Soll ich euch helfen?		Do you want me to help you?

Alles hieher!	Everything here!

(He suddenly becomes aware of Wotan and Loge.)

He! wer ist dort?	Hey! Who's that there?
Wer drang hier ein? –	Who's broken in here? –
Mime! Zu mir,	Mime! To me,
schäbiger Schuft!	you scurvy wretch!
Schwatzest du gar	Have you blabbed all
mit dem schweifenden Paar?	to this pair of vagrants?
Fort, du Fauler!	Away, you idler!
Willst du gleich schmieden und [schaffen?	Back to your smelting and smithying!

(With blows of his whip he drives Mime into the crowd of Nibelungs.)

He! an die Arbeit!	Hey! Get to work!
Alle von hinnen!	Away with you all!
Hurtig hinab!	Get down there at once!
Aus den neuen Schachten	Gather the gold
schafft mir das Gold!	from the newly-sunk shafts!
Euch grüßt die Geißel,	You'll taste my whip
grabt ihr nicht rasch!	if you don't dig quickly!
Daß keiner mir müßig	That none shall be idle
bürge mir Mime,	Mime shall answer,
sonst birgt er sich schwer	or else he'll not scape
meiner Geißel Schwunge:	the swing of my scourge:
daß ich überall weile,	that I'm lying in wait
wo keiner mich wähnt,	where no one expects me –
das weiß er, dünkt mich, genau. –	he knows, I think, well enough. –
Zögert ihr noch?	You're lingering still?
Zaudert wohl gar?	You dare to delay?

(He draws the ring from his finger, kisses it and holds it out threateningly.) [6]

Zitt're und zage,	[3]	Tremble and quail,
gezähmtes Heer:		downtrodden herd:
rasch gehorcht		be quick and obey
des Ringes Herrn!		the lord of the ring!

(Amidst howling and shrieking the Nibelungs – Mime among them – scatter and slip away into the shafts all around them. Alberich gives Wotan and Loge a long, suspicious stare.) [15]

Was wollt ihr hier?	What do you want here?

WOTAN

Von Nibelheim's nächt'gem Land	Of Nibelheim's night-shrouded land
vernahmen wir neue Mähr':	new tidings we've heard tell:
mächt'ge Wunder	it's said here that Alberich
wirke hier Alberich;	works mighty wonders;
daran uns zu weiden	the urge to feast our eyes on them
trieb uns Gäste die Gier.	has driven us here as your guests.

ALBERICH

Nach Nibelheim	[14b]	Envy brings you
führt euch der Neid:		to Nibelheim:
so kühne Gäste,		such dauntless guests,
glaubt, kenn' ich gut.		believe me, I know well.

LOGE

Kenn'st du mich gut,	You know me well,
kindischer Alp?	you childish elf?
Nun sag': wer bin ich,	Then say who I am
daß du so bell'st?	that you yelp like that.
Im kalten Loch,	In a frozen hole,
da kauernd du lag'st,	where you coweringly lay,
wer gab dir Licht	who'd have given you light
und wärmende Lohe,	and warming fire
wenn Loge nie dir gelacht?	if Loge hadn't smiled upon you?
Was hülf' dir dein Schmieden,	What use would your forgework
	[have been
heizt' ich die Schmiede dir nicht?	if I hadn't heated your forge?
Dir bin ich Vetter,	I am your kinsman
und war dir Freund:	and once was your friend:
nicht fein drum dünkt mich dein Dank!	so your thanks seem far from fitting!

ALBERICH

Den Lichtalben[25]	So Loge now smiles
lacht jetzt Loge,	on the light-elves,[25]
der list'ge Schelm:	cunning rogue that he is?
bist du Falscher ihr Freund,	If, false traitor, you're now their friend,
wie mir Freund du einst war'st –	as you once were a friend to me,
haha! mich freut's! –	haha! – I'm glad –
von ihnen fürcht' ich dann nichts.	from them I've nothing to fear.

LOGE

So denk' ich, kannst du mir trau'n?	And so, I think, you can trust me.

ALBERICH

Deiner Untreu' trau' ich,	I trust your dishonesty,
nicht deiner Treu'! –	not your honesty! –

(adopting a defiant attitude)

Doch getrost trotz' ich euch allen!	I can safely defy you all!

LOGE

Hohen Muth	Your power has made you
verleiht deine Macht:	very high-minded:
grimmig groß	fearsomely great
wuchs dir die Kraft.	your strength has grown.

ALBERICH

Sieh'st du den Hort,	Do you see the hoard
den mein Heer	that my army
dort mir gehäuft?	heaped up for me there?

LOGE

So neidlichen sah ich noch nie.	Such a splendid one I never yet saw!

Das ist für heut',
ein kärglich Häufchen:
kühn und mächtig
soll er künftig sich mehren.

That's just for today,
a pitiful pile:
daunting and great
it shall grow hereafter.

WOTAN

Zu was doch frommt dir der Hort,
da freudlos Nibelheim,
und nichts für Schätze hier feil?

But what good is the hoard
since Nibelheim's joyless
and naught can be bought here with
[wealth?

ALBERICH

Schätze zu schaffen
und Schätze zu bergen,
nützt mir Nibelheim's Nacht;
doch mit dem Hort,
in der Höhle gehäuft,
denk' ich dann Wunder zu wirken:
die ganze Welt
gewinn' ich mit ihm mir zu eigen.

To create yet more wealth
and to hide away wealth
Nibelheim's night serves me well;
and yet with the hoard,
heaped up in the cave,
I shall then, I think, work wonders:
the whole of the world
I'll win with it as my own.

WOTAN

Wie beginn'st du, Gütiger, das?

And how, good friend, will you go
[about that?

ALBERICH

Die in linder Lüfte Weh'n
da oben ihr lebt,
lacht und liebt:
mit gold'ner Faust
euch Göttliche fang' ich mir alle!
Wie ich der Liebe abgesagt,   [7]
Alles was lebt
soll ihr entsagen:
mit Golde gekirrt,
nach Gold nur sollt ihr noch
[gieren.
Auf wonnigen Höh'n   [8b, 8d]
in seligem Weben
wiegt ihr euch,
den Schwarz-Alben
verachtet ihr ewigen Schwelger: –
habt Acht!
habt Acht! –
denn dient ihr Männer
erst meiner Macht,
eure schmucken Frau'n –
die mein Frei'n verschmäht –
sie zwingt zur Lust sich der Zwerg,

You who live, laugh and love
up there in the breath
of gentle breezes:
in my golden grasp
I'll capture all you gods!
As love has been forsworn by me,
so all that lives
shall also forswear it:
lured by gold,
you'll lust after gold alone.

Rocked in
blissful abandon
on radiant heights,
you eternal free-livers
scorn the black elf: –
Beware!
Beware! –
For when your menfolk
yield to my power,
your pretty women,
who spurned my wooing,
shall forcibly sate the lust of the dwarf,

lacht Liebe ihm nicht. –

though love may no longer smile upon
[him. –

(laughing wildly)

Hahahaha!
habt ihr's gehört?
Habt Acht!
Habt Acht vor dem nächtlichen Heer,
entsteigt des Niblungen Hort   [3]
aus stummer Tiefe zu Tag!   [4, 8b]

Ha ha ha ha!
Do you hear?
Beware!
Beware of my army of night,
when the Nibelung's hoard arises
from silent depths to the light of day!

WOTAN

(flying into a rage)

Vergeh', frevelnder Gauch!

Out of my sight, you impious fool!

ALBERICH

Was sagt der?

What does he say?

LOGE

(intervening)

Sei doch bei Sinnen!
Wen doch faßte nicht Wunder,
erfährt er Alberich's Werk?
Gelingt deiner herrlichen List,
was mit dem Horte du heischest,
den Mächtigsten muß ich dich
[rühmen: [8b, 14b]
  denn Mond und Stern'
  und die strahlende Sonne,
sie auch dürfen nicht anders,
dienen müssen sie dir. –
Doch wichtig acht' ich vor allem   [15]
  daß des Hortes Häufer,
  der Niblungen Heer,
neidlos dir geneigt.
Einen Reif rührtest du kühn,   [6]
dem zagte zitternd dein Volk:
  doch wenn im Schlaf
  ein Dieb dich beschlich',
den Ring schlau dir entriss',
wie wahrtest du Weiser dich dann?

Don't lose your head!
Who'd not be struck with wonder
on learning of Alberich's work?
If your marvellous guile can achieve
what you claim with the hoard,
as the mightiest of men I must hail you:

  for the moon and the stars
  and the beaming sun,
they too have no choice
but to serve you. –
Yet I think it important above all else
  that those who heap up the hoard,
  the Nibelung army,
should bow before you ungrudgingly.
A ring you boldly flourished;
trembling, your people shrank before it:
  but what if a thief
  crept upon you, asleep,
and slyly snatched it away –
how would you ward yourself then in
[your wisdom?

ALBERICH

Der listigste dünkt sich Loge;   [14b]
  and're denkt er
  immer sich dumm:
  daß sein' ich bedürfte
  zu Rath und Dienst,
  um harten Dank,
das hörte der Dieb jetzt gern! –

Loge thinks himself smartest of all;
  others he always
  deems dim-witted:
  that I might perhaps need him
  to help and advise me
  and earn his weighty thanks –
the thief would now be glad to hear! –

Den hehlenden Helm [16]
ersann ich mir selbst;
der sorglichste Schmiedt,
Mime, mußt' ihn mir schmieden:
schnell mich zu wandeln
nach meinem Wunsch,
die Gestalt mir zu tauschen,
taugt der Helm;
Niemand sieht mich,
wenn er mich sucht;
doch überall bin ich,
geborgen dem Blick.
So ohne Sorge
bin ich selbst sicher vor dir,
du fromm sorgender Freund! [8b, 14b]

The masking helmet
I thought up myself;
but Mime – most heedful of smiths –
had to forge it for me:
to transform me swiftly
and change my shape
to whatever I want
the helmet serves;
no one sees me,
though he may seek me;
yet I am everywhere,
hidden from sight.
And so, free from care,
I'm safe from you, too,
my fondly caring friend!

LOGE

Vieles sah ich,
Seltsames fand ich:
doch solches Wunder
gewahrt' ich nie.
Dem Werk ohne Gleichen
kann ich nicht glauben;
wäre dieß eine möglich,
deine Macht währte dann ewig.

Much I have seen,
strange things I have found,
but such a wonder
I've never beheld.
I can scarcely believe
in so matchless a work;
were such a thing likely,
your power would last for ever.

ALBERICH

Mein'st du, ich lüg'
und prahle wie Loge?

Do you think that I'm lying
and boasting like Loge?

LOGE

Bis ich's geprüft,
bezweifl' ich, Zwerg, dein Wort.

Till I've proved it myself,
dwarf, I doubt in your word.

ALBERICH

Vor Klugheit bläht sich [15]
zum platzen der Blöde:
nun plage dich Neid!
Bestimm', in welcher Gestalt
soll ich jach vor dir steh'n?

The fool's fit to burst,
he's so swollen with cunning:
may envy torment you!
Decide in what shape
I'm to stand here before you.

LOGE

In welcher du willst:
nur mach' vor Staunen mich stumm!

In whatever you will:
only strike me dumb with amazement!

ALBERICH
(putting on the helmet) [16]

»Riesen-Wurm[26]
winde sich ringelnd!«

'Giant dragon,[26]
wind in coils!'

(He immediately disappears and in his place an enormous giant serpent writhes on the ground; it rears up and snaps at Wotan and Loge.) [18]

LOGE
(pretending to be terror-struck)

Ohe! Ohe!	Oh! Oh!
schreckliche Schlange,	Fearsome serpent,
verschlinge mich nicht!	don't swallow me up!
Schone Logen das Leben!	Spare Loge's life for him!

WOTAN

Hahaha! Hahaha!	Hahaha! Hahaha!
Gut, Alberich!	Good, Alberich!
gut, du Arger!	Good, you rogue!
Wie wuchs so rasch	How quickly the dwarf
zum riesigen Wurme der Zwerg!	grew into a giant dragon!

(The serpent disappears and is immediately replaced by Alberich in his own shape.)

ALBERICH

Hehe! Ihr Klugen,	Hihi! You know-alls,
glaubt ihr mir nun?	do you believe me now?

LOGE
(with a quavering voice)

Mein Zittern mag dir's bezeugen.		My trembling may prove it to you.
Zur großen Schlange		You turned yourself swiftly
schuf'st du dich schnell:		into a giant serpent:
weil ich's gewahrt,		since I saw it myself,
willig glaub' ich dem Wunder.	[8b]	I'm willing to believe the wonder.
Doch, wie du wuchsest,		But, just as you grew,
kannst du auch winzig		can you also make yourself
und klein dich schaffen?		tiny and small?
Das klügste schien' mir das,		That would seem the cleverest way
Gefahren schlau zu entflieh'n:		of cunningly fleeing from danger:
das aber dünkt mich zu schwer!		but that, I think, would be too hard!

ALBERICH

Zu schwer dir,	Too hard for you,
weil du zu dumm!	since you're too dim!
Wie klein soll ich sein?	How small shall I be?

LOGE

Daß die feinste Klinze dich fasse,	So small that the finest crack can hold [you,
wo bang die Kröte sich birgt.	in which a frightened toad might hide.

ALBERICH

Pah! nichts leichter!		Pah! Nothing simpler!
Luge du her!	[16]	Look over here!

(He puts on the helmet.)

»Krumm und grau   'Crook-legged and grey,
krieche Kröte!«   creep, you toad!'

(He disappears: the gods become aware of a toad creeping towards them over the stones.)

LOGE
(to Wotan)

Dort die Kröte,   There, the toad!
greife sie rasch!   Grab it quickly!

(Wotan places his foot on the toad: Loge seizes it by the head and takes the tarnhelm in his hand.)

ALBERICH

Ohe! Verflucht!   Oh! Curse it!
Ich bin gefangen!   I'm caught!

(Alberich has suddenly become visible in his own form, writhing beneath Wotan's foot.)

LOGE

Halt' ihn fest,   Hold him fast
bis ich ihn band.   until I've bound him.

(Loge binds his hands and feet with a length of rope.)

Nun schnell hinauf!   Quickly up now!
Dort ist er unser.   There he'll be ours!

(Both of them seize their prisoner, who makes furious attempts to resist, and drag him with them towards the crevice through which they had entered. They disappear, climbing upwards. The scene changes as before, but in reverse order. [15, 3] Once again the change of scene leads past the forges. [10b, 11, 8b] Continuous upward movement. [3, 11, 14b, 5, 3] Wotan and Loge emerge from a cleft, leading the bound figure of Alberich.)

SCENE FOUR

An open space on a mountain summit

(The stage is still veiled in pale mists, as at the end of the second scene.)

LOGE

Da, Vetter,   There, kinsman,
sitze du fest!   you sit tight now!
Luge, Liebster,   Look, dearest fellow,
dort liegt die Welt,   there lies the world
die du Lung'rer gewinnen dir willst: that you long to win for yourself:
welch' Stellchen, sag',   which spot in it, say,
bestimmst du drin mir zum Stall?   have you set aside as my sty?

(He dances round him, snapping his fingers.)

ALBERICH

Schändlicher Schächer!   Infamous robber!
du Schalk! du Schelm!   You wretch! You rogue!

Löse den Bast,
binde mich los,
den Frevel sonst büßest du Frecher!

Loosen the rope,
untie my bonds,
else you'll pay for this outrage, you upstart!

WOTAN

Gefangen bist du,
fest mir gefesselt,
wie du die Welt,
was lebt und webt,
in deiner Gewalt schon wähntest.
In Banden liegst du vor mir,
du Banger kannst es nicht läugnen:
zu ledigen dich
bedarf's nun der Lösung.

You're captured
and firmly fettered,
just as you thought that the world
and all that lives and moves in it
was already in your power.
You lie before me in shackles,
you can't deny that, you craven dwarf:
to set you free
a ransom is needed.

ALBERICH

O, ich Tropf!
ich träumender Thor!
Wie dumm traut' ich
dem diebischen Trug!
Furchtbare Rache
räche den Fehl!

O dunce that I am!
A dreamy-eyed fool!
How stupid to trust
their thievish deceit!
Fearful revenge
shall atone for my failing!

LOGE

Soll Rache dir frommen,
vor allem rathe dich frei:
dem gebund'nen Manne
büßt kein Freier den Frevel.
Drum sinn'st du auf Rache,
rasch ohne Säumen
sorg' um die Lösung zunächst!

If revenge is to serve you,
think first how to set yourself free:
no freeman atones
for a bondsman's crime.
If you're plotting revenge,
be quick, don't delay,
think first of the ransom!

(Rubbing his fingers he indicates the nature of the ransom.)

ALBERICH

So heischt, was ihr begehrt!

Then say what you desire!

WOTAN

Den Hort und dein helles Gold.

The hoard and your bright-shining gold.

ALBERICH

Gieriges Gaunergezücht!

[6]   You greedy gang of swindlers!

(aside)

Doch behal' ich mir nur den Ring,
des Hortes entrath' ich dann leicht:
denn von neuem gewonnen
und wonnig genährt
ist er bald durch des Ringes Gebot.
Eine Witzigung wär's,
die weise mich macht:
zu theuer nicht zahl' ich die Zucht,

But if I can keep the ring for myself,
I can easily manage without the hoard:
for it's soon replenished
and splendidly fattened
by means of the ring's command.
It would serve as a warning
that makes me wise:
I don't count the lesson too dearly bought

lass' für die Lehre ich den Tand. –   if all I give up is the golden dross. –

WOTAN

WOTAN

Erleg'st du den Hort?   You'll hand the hoard over?

ALBERICH

Lös't mir die Hand,   Untie my hand
so ruf' ich ihn her.   and I'll call it here.

(Loge unties the rope from his right hand. Alberich raises the ring to his lips and secretly murmurs a command.) [6, 3, 15]

– Wohlan, die Niblungen   Well then, I've called
rief ich mir nah':   the Nibelungs here:
ihrem Herrn gehorchend   obeying their lord,
hör' ich den Hort   I hear them bringing the hoard
aus der Tiefe sie führen zu Tag. –   from the depths into daylight. –
Nun lös't mich vom lästigen Band!   Untie me now from my irksome bonds!

WOTAN

Nicht eh'r, bis alles gezahlt.   Not until everything's paid!

(The Nibelungs emerge from the crevice, laden with trinkets from the hoard. Throughout the following, the Nibelungs pile up the hoard.)

ALBERICH

O schändliche Schmach,   O shameful disgrace!
daß die scheuen Knechte   That my faint-hearted slaves
geknebelt[27] selbst mich erschau'n! –   should see me shackled[27] myself! –

(to the Nibelungs)

Dorthin geführt,   Put it down there,
wie ich's befehl'!   just as I tell you!
All' zu Hauf'   All in a heap
schichtet den Hort!   pile up the hoard!
Helf' ich euch Lahmen? –   Shall I help you cripples? –
Hieher nicht gelugt! –   Don't look this way! –
Rasch da! rasch!   Quick there! Be quick!
Dann rührt euch von hinnen: Then get yourselves hence!
daß ihr mir schafft,   Back to your work!
fort in die Schachten!   Away to the shafts!
Weh' euch, treff'[28] ich euch faul!   Woe betide if I find you idle!
Auf den Fersen folg' ich euch nach.   I'll be following hard on your heels.

(He kisses his ring and stretches it out commandingly. All at once, the timid, fearful Nibelungs crowd into the crevice through which they swiftly slip away.)

Gezahlt hab' ich: I've paid:
nun lass' mich zieh'n!   now let me go!
Und das Helmgeschmeid,   [16]   And the metal helm
das Loge dort hält,   that Loge's holding:
das gebt mir nun gütlich zurück!   kindly give it me back!

LOGE

(tossing the tarnhelm on to the hoard)

Zur Buße gehört auch die Beute.   The booty is part of the ransom.

ALBERICH

Verfluchter Dieb! –	[6]	Confounded thief! –
Doch nur Geduld!		But only be patient!
Der den alten mir schuf,		He who made the old one
schafft einen andern:		will make me another:
noch halt' ich die Macht,		I still wield the power
der Mime gehorcht.		that Mime obeys.
Schlimm zwar ist's,		It's hard, I confess,
dem schlauen Feind		to abandon this cunning defence
zu lassen die listige Wehr! –	[16]	to my craftily scheming foe!
Nun denn! Alberich		Well then! Alberich's
ließ euch alles:		left you everything:
jetzt lös't, ihr Bösen, das Band!		loosen my bonds now, you evil pair!

LOGE
(to Wotan)

Bist du befriedigt? Are you content?
Lass' ich ihn frei? Shall I let him go?

WOTAN

Ein gold'ner Ring A golden ring
ragt dir am Finger: stands proud on your finger:
hör'st du, Alp? do you hear me, elf?
der, acht' ich, gehört mit zum Hort. It too is part of the hoard, I think.

ALBERICH
(appalled)

Der Ring? The ring?

WOTAN

Zu deiner Lösung You must leave it here
mußt du ihn lassen. by way of a ransom.

ALBERICH
(trembling)

Das Leben – doch nicht den Ring! My life, but not the ring!

WOTAN
(more forcefully)

Den Reif verlang' ich: I demand the ring:
mit dem Leben mach' was du willst! with your life you can do what you want!

ALBERICH

Lös' ich mir Leib und Leben, If I ransom life and limb,
den Ring auch muß ich mir lösen: I must also ransom the ring:
  Hand und Haupt,   hand and head,
  Aug' und Ohr,   eye and ear
  sind nicht mehr mein Eigen,   are no more my own
als hier dieser rothe Ring? than this bright red ring?

Dein Eigen nenn'st du den Ring?   You call the ring your own?
Rasest du, schamloser Albe?   [3]   Are you raving mad, you shameless elf?
  Nüchtern sag',   Tell me calmly,
  wem entnahm'st du das Gold,   from whom did you take the gold
daraus du den schimmernden schuf'st?   from which you made the glittering
                                 [jewel?

  War's dein Eigen,   Was it your own
  was du Arger   what you stole
der Wassertiefe entwandt?   from the watery depths, you wretch?
  Bei des Rheines Töchtern   [5]   Consult with
  hole dir Rath,   the Rhine's fair daughters
  ob ihr Gold sie   and ask if they gave you
  zu eigen dir gaben,   the gold as your own
das du zum Ring dir geraubt.   which you stole to make a ring.

  Schmähliche Tücke!   Disgraceful trickery!
  Schändlicher Trug!   Shameless deceit!
  Wirf'st du Schächer   You upbraid me, you crook,
  die Schuld mir vor,   for the wrong
die dir so wonnig erwünscht?   you so fondly desired?
  Wie gern raubtest   [6]   How glad you'd have been
du selbst dem Rheine das Gold,   to have robbed the gold from the Rhine,
  war nur so leicht   were the skill
die Kunst,[29] es zu schmieden, erlangt?   to forge it so lightly gained!
  Wie glückt' es nun   How lucky for you,
  dir Gleißner zum Heil,   you smooth-tongued god,
  daß der Niblung ich   that I, the Niblung,
  aus schmählicher Noth,[30]   from shameful necessity,[30]
  in des Zornes Zwange,   slave to my anger,
den schrecklichen Zauber gewann,   mastered the fearful magic
dess' Werk nun lustig dir lacht?   whose work now smiles so gaily upon
                                 [you.

  Des Unseligen,   Shall the curse-heavy,
  Angstversehrten[31]   harrowing deed
  fluchfertige,   of the hapless,
  furchtbare That,   fearstricken[31] dwarf
  zu fürstlichem Tand   serve haply to gain you
soll sie fröhlich dir taugen?   a princely toy?
zur Freude dir frommen mein   Shall my curse redound to your joy? –
  [Fluch? –   [6]
  Hüte dich,   Be on your guard,
  herrischer Gott!   you haughty god!
  Frevelte ich,   If ever I sinned,
so frevelt' ich frei an mir: I sinned freely against myself:
doch an allem, was war,   but you, you immortal, will sin
  ist und wird,   against all that was,
frevelst, Ewiger, du,   is and shall be –
entreißest du frech mir den Ring!   if you brazenly wrest the ring from me now!

Her den Ring! [9] Give the ring here!
Kein Recht an ihm No right to it
schwör'st du schwatzend dir zu. will you claim with your chatter.
(He seizes Alberich and tears the ring from his finger with terrible force.) [4]

ALBERICH
(with a hideous scream)

Ha! Zertrümmert! Zerknickt! Ha! Ruined! Crushed!
Der Traurigen traurigster Knecht! The saddest of all sad slaves!

WOTAN
(contemplating the ring)

Nun halt' ich, was mich erhebt, Now I hold that which exalts me,
der Mächtigen mächtigsten Herrn! the mightiest lord of the mighty!
(He puts on the ring.) [6]

LOGE
(to Wotan)

Ist er gelös't? Is he ransomed?

WOTAN

Bind' ihn los! Set him free!
(Loge frees Alberich from his bonds.)

LOGE
(to Alberich)

Schlüpfe denn heim! Slip away home!
Keine Schlinge hält dich: No snare still holds you:
frei fahre dahin! you're free to go on your way!

ALBERICH
(raising himself)

Bin ich nun frei? Am I free now?
(laughing wildly)

Wirklich frei? – Really free? –
So grüß' euch denn Then let my freedom's
meiner Freiheit erster Gruß! – first greeting salute you! –
Wie durch Fluch er mir gerieth, [19] Just as it came to me through a curse,
verflucht sei dieser Ring! so shall this ring be accursed in turn!
Gab sein Gold Just as its gold once endowed me
mir – Macht ohne Maaß, with might beyond measure,
nun zeug' sein Zauber so shall its spell now deal
Tod dem – der ihn trägt! death to whoever shall wear it!
Kein Froher soll [6] No joyful man
seiner sich freu'n; shall ever have joy of it;
keinem Glücklichen lache on no happy man
sein lichter Glanz; shall its bright gleam smile;
wer ihn besitzt, may he who owns it
den sehre die Sorge, be wracked by care,

und wer ihn nicht hat,
den nage der Neid!
Jeder giere
nach seinem Gut,
doch keiner genieße
mit Nutzen sein';
ohne Wucher hüt' ihn sein Herr,
doch den Würger zieh' er ihm zu!

Dem Tode verfallen,
fess'le den Feigen die Furcht;
  so lang' er lebt,
sterb' er lechzend dahin, ·
  des Ringes Herr
  als des Ringes Knecht:
  bis in meiner Hand
den geraubten wieder ich halte! –
  So – segnet
  in höchster Noth
der Nibelung seinen Ring. –
  Behalt' ihn nun,

  (laughing)
  hüte ihn wohl:

  (grimly)
meinem Fluch fliehest du nicht!

and he who does not
be ravaged by greed!
Each man shall covet
its acquisition,
but none shall enjoy
it to lasting gain;
its lord shall guard it without any profit,
and yet it shall draw down his bane upon
[him.
Doomed to die,
may the coward be fettered by fear;
  as long as he lives,
let him pine away, languishing,
  lord of the ring
  as the slave of the ring:
  till the stolen circlet
I hold in my hand once again! –
  And so in direst need
  the Nibelung
blesses his ring. –
  Keep it now

and guard it well:

you'll not escape from my curse!

(He disappears quickly into the crevice. [3] The thick mists in the foreground slowly clear.)

LOGE

Lauschtest du
seinem Liebesgruß?

Did you hear
his fond farewell?

WOTAN
(lost in contemplation of the ring on his finger)
Gönn' ihm die geifernde Lust!   Don't begrudge him his bilious pleasure!
(It continues to grow lighter.)

LOGE
(looking offstage to the left)
Fasolt und Fafner   Fasolt and Fafner
nahen von fern;   approach from afar;
Freia führen sie her.   [13]   They're bringing Freia here.
(Donner, Froh and Fricka emerge from the mists, which continue to disperse, and hurry towards the front of the stage.)

FROH

Sie kehrten zurück.   They've come back again.

DONNER

Willkommen, Bruder!   Welcome, brother!

FRICKA
(anxiously, to Wotan)

Bring'st du gute Kunde?   Do you bring good tidings?

LOGE
(pointing to the hoard)

Mit List und Gewalt   With cunning and force
gelang das Werk: our task succeeded:
dort liegt, was Freia lös't.   there lies Freia's ransom!

DONNER

Aus der Riesen Haft   From the giants' hold
naht dort die Holde.   fair Holda approaches.

FROH

Wie liebliche Luft   What sweet-scented air
wieder uns weht,   wafts round us again
wonnig Gefühl   as blissful emotion
die Sinne erfüllt!   steals over our senses!
Traurig ging' es uns allen,   Sad it would be for us all
getrennt für immer von ihr,   to be severed for ever from her
die leidlos ewiger Jugend   who grants us the jubilant bliss
jubelnde Lust uns verleiht.   of sorrowless youth everlasting.

The front of the stage is now brightly lit again; the light restores the gods' former youthful appearance; a veil of mist still hangs over the back of the stage, however, so that the distant castle remains hidden. (Fasolt and Fafner enter, leading Freia between them.)

FRICKA
(hurrying joyfully towards her sister)

Lieblichste Schwester,   Loveliest sister,
süßeste Lust!   sweetest delight!
Bist du mir wieder gewonnen?   Are you won back again for me now?

FASOLT
(restraining her)

Halt! Nicht sie berührt!   [11]   Stop! Don't touch her!
Noch gehört sie uns. −   She is still ours. −
   Auf Riesenheim's   On Riesenheim's
   ragender Mark   towering marches
   rasteten wir;   we rested;
   mit treuem Muth   with true-hearted zeal
   des Vertrages Pfand   we tended
   pflegten wir: the pledge of our pact:
so sehr mich's reut,   much as I rue it,
zurück doch bring' ich's,   I'll yet bring her back
erlegt uns Brüdern   [12]   if you pay us brothers
die Lösung ihr.   the ransom.

WOTAN

Bereit liegt die Lösung: The ransom is lying ready:

| des Goldes Maaß | let the gold's measure |
| sei nun gütlich gemessen. | be measured out fairly. |

FASOLT

Das Weib zu missen,	To lose the woman,
wisse, gemuthet mich weh: [10]	you know, grieves me deeply:
soll aus dem Sinn sie mir schwinden,	if she's to fade from my thoughts,
des Geschmeides Hort	then heap up
häufet denn so,	the hoard of trinkets
daß meinem Blick	so that it hides
die Blühende ganz er verdeck'!	the radiant child from my sight!

WOTAN

| So stellt das Maaß | Then set the measure |
| nach Freia's Gestalt. | to Freia's form. |

(Freia is placed in the middle by the two giants. They then drive their staves into the ground on either side of her so as to measure her height and breadth.) [11, 12]

FAFNER

Gepflanzt sind die Pfähle	Our staves have been set
nach Pfandes Maaß:	to the pledge's size:
gehäuft nun füll' es der Hort.	let the hoard, when heaped high, fill the [space!

WOTAN

| Eilt mit dem Werk: | Make haste with the work: |
| widerlich ist mir's! | it irks me greatly! |

LOGE

| Hilf mir, Froh! | Help me, Froh! |

FROH

| Freia's Schmach | Freia's shame |
| eil' ich zu enden. | I hasten to end. |

(Loge and Froh hurriedly pile up the trinkets between the staves.) [12, 15]

FAFNER

| Nicht so leicht | Don't pack it |
| und locker gefügt: | so lightly and loosely: |

(He roughly presses the trinkets closer together.)

| fest und dicht | tightly and densely |
| füll' er das Maaß! | get him to fill the measure! |

(He bends down to look for chinks.)

| Hier lug' ich noch durch: | Here I can still see through: |
| verstopft mir die Lücken! | stop up those gaps! |

LOGE

| Zurück, du Grober! | Get back, you churl! |
| greif' mir nichts an! | Keep your hands to yourself! |

FAFNER

Hieher! die Klinze verklemmt!   Over here! Close up the crack!

WOTAN
(turning away in displeasure)

Tief in der Brust   Deep in my breast
brennt mir die Schmach.   [10b]   the shame of it sears me

FRICKA

Sieh', wie in Scham   See the goddess
schmählich die Edle steht: standing there, outraged in her disgrace,
um Erlösung fleht   her suffering glance
stumm der leidende Blick.   begging silently for redemption.
Böser Mann!   You wicked man!
der Minnigen botest du das!   It's you brought this down on the
                                [goddess of love!

FAFNER

Noch mehr hieher!   [11, 15]   Still more over here!

DONNER

Kaum halt' ich mich: I can scarcely control my anger:
schäumende Wuth   [10b]   the shameless creature
weckt mir der schamlose Wicht! –   rouses my seething rage! –
Hieher, du Hund!   Over here, you cur!
willst du messen,   If you want to measure,
so miß dich selber mit mir!   measure yourself against me!

FAFNER

Ruhig, Donner!   Calm down, Donner!
Rolle wo's taugt: Roar where it helps:
hier nützt dein Rasseln dir nichts!   here your bluster's no use.

DONNER
(preparing to strike)

Nicht dich Schmähl'chen zu   No use to crush you, you insolent churl?
[zerschmettern?

WOTAN

Friede doch!   [12]   Peace now!
Schon dünkt mich Freia verdeckt.   I think that Freia's already hidden.

LOGE

Der Hort ging auf.   [15]   The hoard is spent.

FAFNER
(casting a careful eye over the hoard, looking for chinks) [13]

Noch schimmert mir Holda's Haar: Holda's hair still glints through the gold:
dort das Gewirk   that trinket yonder
wirf auf den Hort!   add to the hoard!

LOGE

Wie? auch den Helm?   What? The helmet as well?

FAFNER

Hurtig her mit ihm!   [16]   Be quick, give it here!

WOTAN

Lass' ihn denn fahren!   All right, let it go!

LOGE
(throwing the tarnhelm on to the hoard)

So sind wir denn fertig! –   So we seem to be finished! –
Seid ihr zufrieden?   Are you content?

FASOLT

Freia, die schöne,   Freia the fair
schau' ich nicht mehr: I see no longer:
so ist sie gelös't?   and so she's been ransomed?
muß ich sie lassen?   Have I to lose her?
        (He moves closer and peers through the hoard.) [10]
Weh! noch blitzt   Alas! Her glance
ihr Blick zu mir her;   still gleams on me here;
des Auges Stern   her starry eye
strahlt mich noch an: still shines upon me:
durch eine Spalte   [10]   I cannot but see it
muß ich's erspäh'n! –   through the crack! –
                    (beside himself)
Seh' ich dieß wonnige Auge,   While I still see this lovely eye,
von dem Weibe lass' ich nicht ab.   I'll not give up the woman.

FAFNER

He! euch rath' ich,   Hey! I advise you,
verstopft mir die Ritze!   stop up the cranny!

LOGE

Nimmer-Satte!   You're never satisfied!
seht ihr denn nicht,   Can't you see
ganz schwand uns der Hort?   that the hoard's all gone?

FAFNER

Mit nichten, Freund!   By no means, friend!
An Wotan's Finger   On Wotan's finger
glänzt von Gold noch ein Ring: a ring of gold still glints:
den gebt, die Ritze zu füllen!   give that to fill the cranny!

WOTAN

Wie! diesen Ring?   What? This ring?

LOGE

Laßt euch rathen!   [5]   Let me advise you!

Den Rheintöchtern
gehört dieß Gold:
ihnen giebt Wotan es wieder.

This gold belongs
to the Rhine's fair daughters:
Wotan is giving it back to them.

WOTAN

Was schwatzest du da?
Was schwer ich mir erbeutet,
ohne Bangen wahr' ich's für mich.

What nonsense is that?
What was hard for me to capture
I'll fearlessly keep for myself.

LOGE

Schlimm dann steht's
um mein Versprechen,
das ich den Klagenden gab.

[4] Then things look black
for the promise
I gave to the grieving sisters.

WOTAN

Dein Versprechen bindet mich nicht:
als Beute bleibt mir der Reif.

Your promise isn't binding on me:
the ring remains mine as booty.

FAFNER

Doch hier zur Lösung
mußt du ihn legen.

[6] But as ransom
you have to leave it here.

WOTAN

Fordert frech was ihr wollt:
alles gewähr' ich;
um alle Welt doch
nicht fahren lass' ich den Ring!

Brazenly ask for whatever you want,
everything will I grant you;
but not for the world
shall I give up the ring!

FASOLT
(angrily pulling Freia out from behind the hoard)

Aus denn ist's,
beim Alten bleibt's:
nun folgt uns Freia für immer!

Then it's all off!
We're back where we started:
Freia will follow us now for ever.

FREIA

Hilfe! Hilfe!

[3] Help me! Help me!

FRICKA

Harter Gott,
gieb ihnen nach!

Hard-hearted god,
give in to them!

FROH

Spare das Gold nicht!

Don't stint the gold!

DONNER

Spende den Ring doch!

Let them have the ring!

WOTAN

Lass't mich in Ruh'!
Den Reif geb' ich nicht.

Leave me in peace:
The ring I'll not give up.

(Fafner prevents Fasolt from hurrying away. All stand dismayed. Wotan turns away in anger. The stage has grown dark again. A bluish light breaks forth from a rocky fissure at one side and in it Erda suddenly appears, rising up to half her height.) [20]

ERDA
(stretching out her hand to Wotan in a gesture of remonstration)

Weiche, Wotan, weiche!	Yield, Wotan! Yield!
Flieh' des Ringes Fluch!	Flee the curse on the ring!
Rettungslos	To irredeemably
dunklem Verderben	dark destruction
weiht dich sein Gewinn.[32]	its gain will ever ordain you.[32]

WOTAN

Wer bist du, mahnendes Weib?	What woman are you that warns me [thus?

ERDA

Wie alles war, weiß ich;		How all things were – I know;
wie alles wird,		how all things are,
wie alles sein wird,		how all things will be,
seh' ich auch:		I see as well:
der ew'gen Welt		the endless earth's
Ur-Wala,		primeval vala,
Erda mahnt deinen Muth.		Erda, bids you beware.
Drei der Töchter,		Ere the world was,
ur-erschaff'ne,		my womb brought forth
gebar mein Schooß:		three daughters:
was ich sehe,		what I see
sagen dir nächtlich die Nornen.		the Norns unfold each night.
Doch höchste Gefahr		But gravest danger
führt mich heut'		brings me myself
selbst zu dir her:		to you today:
höre! höre! höre!	[3]	hearken! Hearken! Hearken!
Alles was ist, endet.	[20]	All things that are – end.
Ein düst'rer Tag	[21]	A day of darkness
dämmert den Göttern:		dawns for the gods:
dir rath' ich, meide den Ring!	[6]	I counsel you: shun the ring!

WOTAN

Geheimnis-hehr	[20]	Sublimely awesome
hallt mir dein Wort:		your words resound:
weile, daß mehr ich wisse!		tarry, till I know more!

(Erda sinks down to chest height, as the bluish light begins to fade.)

ERDA
(sinking)

Ich warnte dich –	I've warned you –
du weißt genug:	you know enough:
sinn' in Sorg' und Furcht!	brood in care and fear!

(She disappears completely.)

(Wotan tries to follow her into the fissure in order to stop her; Froh and Fricka throw themselves in his way and hold him back.)

WOTAN

Soll ich sorgen und fürchten –	If care and fear must consume me,
dich muß ich fassen,	then I must seize you
alles erfahren!	and find out everything!

FRICKA

Was willst du, Wüthender?	What would you do, you madman?

FROH

Halt' ein, Wotan!	Stay your hand, Wotan!
Scheue die Edle,	Fear the goddess
achte ihr Wort!	and heed her words!

(Wotan stares ahead, deep in thought.)

DONNER
(turning decisively to the giants)

Hört, ihr Riesen!	Listen, you giants!
Zurück und harret:	Come back and wait:
das Gold wird euch gegeben.	to you the gold will be given.

FREIA

Darf ich es hoffen?	Dare I yet hope so?
Dünkt euch Holda	Does Holda really seem to you
wirklich der Lösung werth?	worthy of ransom?

(All stare expectantly at Wotan; [20] the latter rouses himself from his thoughts, seizes his spear and brandishes it, as though to indicate a courageous decision.) [9]

WOTAN

Zu mir, Freia!	To me, Freia!
Du bist befreit:	You are freed:
wieder gekauft	now it's bought back,
kehr' uns die Jugend zurück! –	may our youth return! –
Ihr Riesen, nehmt euren Ring!	You giants, take your ring!

(He throws the ring on to the hoard. The giants release Freia: joyfully she hurries over to the gods, each of whom embraces her at length in an access of joy. Fafner has wasted no time in spreading out an enormous sack, into which he prepares to pack the hoard.)

FASOLT
(to Fafner)

Halt, du Gieriger!	[11, 15]	Don't be so greedy!
gönne mir auch 'was!		Grant me some, too!
Redliche Theilung		Equal shares
taugt uns beiden.		befit us both.

FAFNER

Mehr an der Maid als am Gold	You set greater store by the maid
lag dir verliebtem Geck:	than you did by the gold, you lovesick loon!

mit Müh' zum Tausch
vermocht' ich dich Thoren.
Ohne zu theilen
hättest du Freia gefreit:
  theil' ich den Hort,
  billig behalt' ich
die größte Hälfte für mich.

It was hard to make you
exchange her, you fool.
You wouldn't have shared her
if you'd wooed Freia;
  if I now share the hoard,
  it's fair that I keep
the biggest half for myself.

FASOLT

Schändlicher du!
Mir diesen Schimpf? –

You infamous rogue!
You'd insult me so? –

(to the gods)

Euch ruf' ich zu Richtern:
  theilet nach Recht
  uns redlich den Hort!

I call on you as judges:
  justly and fairly
  divide the hoard!

(Wotan turns contemptuously away.)

LOGE
(to Fasolt)

Den Hort lass' ihn raffen:
halte du nur auf den Ring!

Let him snatch up the hoard:
[6] look to the ring alone!

FASOLT
(hurling himself at Fafner, who has been busily packing away the gold)

Zurück, du Frecher!
Mein ist der Ring:
mir blieb er für Freia's Blick.

Get back! You upstart!
The ring is mine:
I got it for Freia's glance.

(He tries to grab the ring: they struggle.)

FAFNER

Fort mit der Faust!
Der Ring ist mein.

Take your hands off!
The ring is mine.

(Fasolt tears the ring from Fafner's hand.)

FASOLT

Ich halt' ihn, mir gehört er!

I hold it, it's mine!

FAFNER
(preparing to strike him with his stave)

Halt' ihn fest, daß er nicht fall'!

Hold it fast or else it may fall!

(He fells Fasolt with a single blow, then wrenches the ring from his dying brother.)

Nun blinz'le nach Freia's Blick:
an den Reif rühr'st du nicht mehr!

Now gaze your fill on Freia's glance:
never again will you touch the ring!

(He puts the ring in the sack, then calmly finishes packing away the rest of the hoard. All the gods look on in horror: solemn silence.) [19]

WOTAN
(shaken)

Furchtbar nun
erfind' ich des Fluches Kraft!

Fearful now
I find the curse's power!

LOGE

Was gleicht, Wotan,
wohl deinem Glücke?
Viel erwarb dir
des Ringes Gewinn;
daß er nun dir genommen,

nützt dir noch mehr:
deine Feinde, sieh',   [11]
fällen sich selbst
um das Gold, das du vergabst.

Wotan, what can compare
with your luck?
Winning the ring
gained you much;
that it's now been taken away from
[you
serves you even more:
behold, your enemies
fell one another
for the sake of the gold that you gave
[away.

WOTAN

Wie doch Bangen mich bindet!   [6]

Sorg' und Furcht   [20]
fesseln den Sinn;
wie sie zu enden
lehre mich Erda:
zu ihr muß ich hinab!

And yet how a sense of unease binds me
[fast!
Care and fear
fetter my thoughts –
how I may end them
Erda shall teach me:
to her I must descend!

FRICKA
(nestling up to him, cajolingly)

Wo weil'st du, Wotan?
Winkt dir nicht hold
die hehre Burg,   [8b]
die des Gebieters
gastlich bergend nun harrt?

Your thoughts are elsewhere.
Does the noble stronghold
not beckon you gladly,
awaiting its lord
with its welcoming shelter?

WOTAN
(sombrely)

Mit bösem Zoll   [6]
zahlt' ich den Bau!

With evil wage
I paid for the building!

DONNER
(pointing to the back of the stage, which is still hidden in mist)

Schwüles Gedünst
schwebt in der Luft;
lästig ist mir
der trübe Druck:
das bleiche Gewölk
samml' ich zu blitzendem Wetter;
das fegt den Himmel mir hell.

A sultry haze
hangs in the air;
its lowering weight
lies heavy upon me:
the leaden clouds
I'll gather into a raging storm;
it will sweep the heavens clear.

(Donner climbs on to a rocky promontory overlooking the valley and swings his hammer; during the following, mists gather around him.)

He da! He da! Hedo!   [22]
  Zu mir, du Gedüft!
  ihr Dünste, zu mir!
  Donner, der Herr,

Heda! Heda! Hedo!
  To me, you haze!
  You mists, to me!
  Donner, your lord,

ruft euch zu Heer.

musters his hordes.

(He swings his hammer.)

Auf des Hammers Schwung	At the swing of his hammer
schwebet herbei:	sweep to me here!
dunstig Gedämpf!	Misty steam-clouds!
Schwebend Gedüft!	Hovering haze!
Donner, der Herr,	Donner, your lord,
ruft euch zu Heer!	musters his hordes.
He da! He da! Hedo!	Heda! Heda! Hedo!

(Donner disappears completely in a thundercloud which grows increasingly dense and black. The blow of his hammer is heard striking the rock. A brilliant flash of lightning issues from the cloud, followed by a violent clap of thunder. Froh has vanished with him in the cloud.)

DONNER
(invisible)

Bruder, hieher!	Brother, this way!
weise der Brücke den Weg!	Mark out the way for the bridge!

(The cloud suddenly lifts, revealing Donner and Froh. From their feet a rainbow bridge of blinding radiance stretches out across the valley to the castle, which now glints in the glow of the evening sun.)

FROH
(to the gods, indicating with outstretched hand the path which the bridge has taken over the valley)

Zur Burg führt die Brücke,		The bridge leads to the stronghold,
leicht, doch fest eurem Fuß:		light yet firm to the foot:
beschreitet kühn		tread undaunted
ihren schrecklosen Pfad!	[8]	its terrorless path!

(Wotan and the other gods are lost in speechless astonishment at the glorious sight.)

WOTAN

Abendlich strahlt		In the evening light
der Sonne Auge;[33]		the sun's eye[33] gleams;
in prächtiger Gluth		in its glittering glow
prangt glänzend die Burg:		the stronghold shines resplendent:
in des Morgens Scheine		glinting bravely
muthig erschimmernd,		in the morning light,
lag sie herrenlos		it still lay lordless and
hehr verlockend vor mir.		nobly alluring before me.
Von Morgen bis Abend	[6]	From morn until evening
in Müh' und Angst		in toil and anguish
nicht wonnig ward sie gewonnen!		it wasn't happily won!
Es naht die Nacht:		Night draws on:
vor ihrem Neid		from its envious sway
biete sie Bergung nun.		may it offer shelter now.

(very resolutely, as though seized by a grandiose idea) [23]

So – grüß' ich die Burg,	Thus I salute the stronghold,
sicher vor Bang und Grau'n. –	safe from dread and dismay. –

(He turns solemnly to Fricka.) [8e]

Folge mir, Frau:	Follow me, wife:

in Walhall wohne mit mir! [8] in Valhalla dwell with me!

FRICKA

Was deutet der Name? What meaning lies in the name?
Nie, dünkt mich, hört' ich ihn nennen. Never, I think, have I heard it before.

WOTAN

Was, mächtig der Furcht What, mastering fear,
mein Muth mir erfand, my mind conceived
wenn siegend es lebt – shall reveal its sense
leg' es den Sinn dir dar! [14b] if it lives victorious.
(He takes Fricka by the hand and moves slowly with her towards the bridge; Froh, Freia and Donner follow.)

LOGE
(remaining at the front of the stage and looking back at the gods)
Ihrem Ende eilen sie zu, [8a, 14b] They're hurrying on towards their end,
die so stark im Bestehen sich wähnen. though they think they will last for ever.
Fast schäm' ich mich I'm almost ashamed
mit ihnen zu schaffen; to share in their dealings;
zur leckenden Lohe to turn myself
mich wieder zu wandeln into guttering flame
spür' ich lockende Lust. I feel a seductive desire.
Sie aufzuzehren, To burn them up
die einst mich gezähmt, who formerly tamed me,
statt mit den blinden instead of feebly[34]
blöd[34] zu vergeh'n – fading away with the blind –
und wären es göttlichste Götter – and were they the godliest gods –
nicht dumm dünkte mich das! that seems to me not so foolish!
Bedenken will ich's: I'll think it over:
wer weiß was ich thu'! who knows what I'll do!
(He goes nonchalantly to join the gods.) [8c, 8d]

THE THREE RHINEDAUGHTERS
(from the depths of the valley, invisible)
Rheingold! Rheingold! [5] Rhinegold! Rhinegold!
Reines Gold, Guileless gold!
wie lauter und hell How clear and bright
leuchtetest hold du uns! you shone on us so sweetly!
Um dich, du klares, For you, bright toy,
wir nun klagen! we now lament!
Gebt uns das Gold, Give us the gold,
o gebt uns das reine zurück! O give us the guileless gold back again!

WOTAN
(on the point of setting foot on the bridge, stops and turns round)
Welch' Klagen dringt zu mir her? [4] What sounds of wailing waft this way?

LOGE
(peering down into the valley)

Des Rheines Kinder	The River Rhine's children
beklagen des Goldes Raub.	bewail the rape of the gold.

WOTAN

Verwünschte Nicker! –	Confounded nixies! –
(to Loge)	
Wehre ihrem Geneck'!	Put an end to their teasing!

LOGE
(calling down into the valley)

Ihr da im Wasser!	[8b]	You there in the water!
was weint ihr herauf?		Why weep at us up here?
Hört, was Wotan euch wünscht.		Hear what Wotan wishes of you:
Glänzt nicht mehr		if the gold no longer
euch Mädchen das Gold,		gleams on you maidens,
in der Götter neuem Glanze		blissfully bask henceforth
sonnt euch selig fortan!		in the gods' new-found splendour!

(The gods laugh and, during the following, stride across the bridge.)

THE RHINEDAUGHTERS

Rheingold! Rheingold!		Rhinegold! Rhinegold!
Reines Gold!		Guileless gold!
O leuchtete noch		Would that your glittering toy
in der Tiefe dein laut'rer Tand!	[4]	still shone in the depths!
Traulich und treu		Trusty and true
ist's nur in der Tiefe:		it is here in the depths alone:
falsch und feig[35]		false and fated[35]
ist was dort oben sich freut!	[8b, 23]	is all that rejoices above!

(As the gods pass over the bridge on their way to the castle, the curtain falls.)

Die Walküre

The Valkyrie

Act I

THE ORCHESTRAL PRELUDE DEPICTS a violent thunderstorm. The curtain rises on the interior of Hunding's hut. Siegmund enters, exhausted, and is tended by Hunding's wife Sieglinde. A bond is immediately forged between them. Hunding arrives and roughly extends his own hospitality. Urged to tell his story, Siegmund describes how one day he returned from hunting with his father, Wolfe, to find their home burnt down, his mother murdered and his twin-sister brutally abducted. Siegmund goes on to tell how he lost track of his father and how he always found himself at odds with society. He went to the aid of a young woman forced into a loveless marriage; he killed her savage kinsmen, but with spear and shield hacked from his arms, he was unable to protect the woman. Hunding now realizes that the men attacked by Siegmund were his kinsmen and that he is harbouring the enemy in his house. The laws of hospitality compel him to give Siegmund shelter for the night, but in the morning he will have to fight for his life.

Sieglinde drugs Hunding's night drink and leaves the room with a lingering gaze at Siegmund, indicating a spot on the trunk of the ash-tree around which the room is constructed. She now enters and narrates how at the wedding of Hunding and herself, a stranger interrupted the festivities, thrusting a sword into the tree trunk. Not even the strongest men could move it an inch. Embracing Sieglinde passionately, Siegmund exclaims that both sword and wife will be his: she is everything he has yearned for. Suddenly the main door flies open, revealing a glorious spring night with full moon. Siegmund speaks of Spring and Love as brother and sister, to which Sieglinde replies that he is the spring for whom she has so longed. To her delight, he pulls the sword out of the tree. They embrace rapturously and the curtain – at least in traditional productions – falls with decorous swiftness.

Act II

On a wild, rocky mountain ridge Wotan instructs his daughter Brünnhilde, the valkyrie of the title, to ensure that Siegmund wins the ensuing battle with Hunding. As Brünnhilde leaves, Wotan's wife Fricka arrives angrily in a ram-drawn chariot. As the guardian of wedlock, she demands that the incestuous adulterers be punished. After a long confrontation, in which he is forced to accept that Siegmund is not a free hero but the god's own tool, Wotan yields to Fricka's demand. Left alone with his daughter, Wotan gives vent to his anger and shame, but then confides his ambitions and fears to Brünnhilde in a long narration. He now instructs Brünnhilde to protect not Siegmund in the coming battle, but Hunding. She tries to change his mind, but he is implacable.

Siegmund and Sieglinde enter breathlessly. She, tormented by guilt, feverishly imagines Hunding's dogs tearing at Siegmund's flesh, and falls into a faint. In the following Annunciation of Death Scene, Brünnhilde appears, announcing to Siegmund that he must follow her to Valhalla. Told that he cannot take his sister-bride, Siegmund determines not to go. Brünnhilde eventually relents and promises to protect him, in defiance of Wotan's command. In the ensuing fight, Brünnhilde attempts to shield Siegmund, only for Wotan to appear and shatter Siegmund's sword with his spear. Hunding kills Siegmund, but is himself despatched by Wotan in a gesture of bitter anger. Wotan sets off in pursuit of Brünnhilde.

Act III

In the prelude, known as The Ride of the Valkyries, the warmaidens gather, on the summit of a rocky mountain, collecting their heroes for Valhalla. Brünnhilde enters in fearful haste, carrying Sieglinde, whom she rescued from the battlefield. None of her sisters will risk helping her. Sieglinde escapes to the forest in the east and is given the fragments of Siegmund's sword from which one day his son will forge a new weapon.

Wotan storms in and the valkyries attempt to shield Brünnhilde. They protest, but in vain, at the severity of her sentence: she is to be confined in sleep on the mountain top, a prey to the first man to find her. Left alone with Wotan, Brünnhilde begs him to be merciful to his favourite child. She recounts how the Wälsung touched her heart and how she decided to protect him, knowing that that was Wotan's innermost wish. She pleads that at least she be spared the disgrace of an ignoble union: let her be surrounded by a circle of fire that will deter all but the bravest of heroes. Deeply moved, Wotan lays Brünnhilde down on a rock and kisses her shining eyes closed. He summons Loge and points with his spear to where he should blaze round the rock. Wotan sorrowfully departs.

Die Walküre

First Day of the Stage Festival 'The Ring of the Nibelung'

First performed at the Munich Court Theatre on 26 June 1870

Siegmund (tenor)	Heinrich Vogl
Hunding (bass)	Kaspar Bausewein
Wotan (bass–baritone)	August Kindermann
Sieglinde (soprano)	Therese Vogl
Brünnhilde (soprano)	Sophie Stehle
Fricka (mezzo-soprano)	Anna Kaufmann

Valkyries
Gerhilde (soprano)	Karoline Leonoff
Ortlinde (soprano)	Henriette Müller
Waltraute (contralto)	Frl. Hemauer
Schwertleite (contralto)	Emma Seehofer
Helmwige (soprano)	Anna Possart
Siegrune (mezzo-soprano)	Walburga Eichheim
Grimgerde (contralto)	Wilhelmine Ritter
Rossweisse (mezzo-soprano)	Frl. Tyroler

Act I.   The interior of Hunding's dwelling
Act II.   A wild craggy mountain landscape
Act III.   On the summit of a rocky mountain ('Brünnhilde's rock')

First performed as part of cycle, Bayreuth Festspielhaus, 14 August 1876

Siegmund (Albert Niemann), Hunding (Joseph Niering), Wotan (Franz Betz), Sieglinde (Josephine Schefsky), Brünnhilde (Amalie Materna), Fricka (Friederike Sadler-Grün), Gerhilde (Marie Haupt), Ortlinde (Marie Lehmann), Waltraute (Luise Jaide), Schwertleite (Johanna Jachmann–Wagner), Helmwige (Lilli Lehmann), Siegrune (Antonie Amann), Grimgerde (Hedwig Reicher-Kindermann), Rossweisse (Minna Lammert)

First UK performance: Her Majesty's Theatre, London, 6 May 1882

First US performance: Academy of Music, New York, 2 April 1877

Die Walküre

Act One

PRELUDE AND SCENE ONE

The curtain rises.[36] *The interior of a dwelling. The room is built round the trunk of a mighty ash-tree,*[37] *which forms its central point. Downstage left is the hearth, behind it the storeroom; at the back of the stage is the main entrance to the room; upstage right, steps lead up to an inner chamber; on the same side, at the front of the stage, is a table, behind it a broad bench, let into the wall, and wooden stools in front of it. (The stage remains empty for a while; outside, a storm is on the point of abating. [22] Siegmund opens the main door from outside and enters. [24] He keeps his hand on the latch and looks round the room: he seems exhausted by extreme exertion; it is evident from his clothing and appearance that he is on the run. Seeing no one, he closes the door behind him and, with the extreme effort of someone half-dead with exhaustion, moves towards the hearth, where he throws himself down on a bear-skin rug.) [3]*

SIEGMUND

Wess' Herd dieß auch sei,　　　　Whosoever's hearth this may be,
hier muß ich rasten.　　　　here shall I have to rest.

(He sinks back and remains stretched out, motionless. [24] Thinking that her husband has returned, Sieglinde enters from the inner room; her grave look changes to one of surprise when she sees a stranger stretched out by the hearth.)

SIEGLINDE
(still in the background)

Ein fremder Mann!　　　　An unknown man!
Ihn muß ich fragen.　　　　I must ask who he is.

(She comes closer.)

Wer kam in's Haus　　　　Who came to this house
und liegt dort am Herd?　　　　and lies over there by the hearth?

(Since Siegmund does not move, she comes closer still and observes him.) [24]

Müde liegt er　　　　Weary he lies
von Weges Müh'n: –　　　　from the toils of his way here: –
schwanden die Sinne ihm?　　　　has he lost consciousness?
wäre er siech? –　　　　Could he be ill? –

(She bends over him and listens.) [24, 25]

Noch schwillt ihm der Athem;　　　　His breath is still stirring;
das Auge nur schloß er: –　　　　his eyes he but shut: –
muthig dünkt mich der Mann,　　　　stout-hearted the man seems to me,
sank er müd' auch hin.　　　　though he sank wearily down.

SIEGMUND

(abruptly raising his head) [24]

Ein Quell! ein Quell!   A drink! A drink!

SIEGLINDE

Erquickung schaff' ich.   I'll fetch some refreshment.

(She hurries to fetch a drinking-horn, goes out of the house with it and, returning with it full, offers it to Siegmund.) [24, 25]

Labung biet' ich   Comfort I offer
dem lechzenden Gaumen: to lips that are parched:
Wasser, wie du gewollt!   water, just as you wanted!

(Siegmund drinks and hands back the drinking-horn. As he signals his thanks with a movement of his head, his gaze fixes on her features with growing interest.) [26]

SIEGMUND

Kühlende Labung   Cooling comfort
gab mir der Quell,   [25]   came from the spring,
des Müden Last   the weary man's burden
machte er leicht;   it helped to make light;
erfrischt ist der Muth,   my courage revives,
das Aug' erfreut   my eye is rejoiced
des Sehens selige Lust: –   by the blissful delight of seeing: –
wer ist's, der so mir es labt?   [25]   who is it who comforts me so?

SIEGLINDE

Dieß Haus und dieß Weib   This house and this wife
sind Hunding's Eigen;   are Hunding's own;
gastlich gönn' er dir Rast: as host may he grant you rest:
harre bis heim er kehrt!   [24]   tarry until he comes home.

SIEGMUND

Waffenlos bin ich: Weaponless am I:
dem wunden Gast   a wounded guest
wird dein Gatte nicht wehren.   won't be turned away by your husband.

SIEGLINDE

(with anxious haste)

Die Wunden weise mir schnell!   Quickly, show me your wounds!

SIEGMUND

(shaking himself and raising himself quickly into a sitting position)

Gering sind sie,   But slight they are,
der Rede nicht werth;   not worthy of mention;
noch fügen des Leibes   my body's limbs
Glieder sich fest.   are still sound.
Hätten halb so stark wie mein Arm   Had shield and spear held out
Schild und Speer mir gehalten,   but half as well as my arm,
nimmer floh' ich dem Feind; –   I'd never have fled from my foe; –
doch zerschellten mir Speer und Schild.   but spear and shield were shattered.
   Der Feinde Meute   The enemy horde

hetzte mich müd',	hounded me till I was weary;
Gewitter-Brunst	a raging tempest
brach meinen Leib;	battered my body;
doch schneller als ich der Meute,	but, fast as I fled the hounds,
schwand die Müdigkeit mir: [24]	my faintness has fled yet faster:
sank auf die Lider mir Nacht,	though night had closed on my eyelids,
die Sonne lacht mir nun neu.	the sun smiles upon me anew.

(Sieglinde goes to the storeroom, fills a horn with mead and offers it to Siegmund with friendly concern.) [25]

SIEGLINDE

Des seimigen Methes	A sweetened draught
süßen Trank	of honeyed mead
mög'st du mir nicht verschmäh'n.	you'll not, I hope, disdain.

SIEGMUND

Schmecktest du mir ihn zu?	Will you not taste it first?

(Sieglinde sips from the horn and hands it back to him. [26b] Siegmund takes a long draught, while fixing his eyes on her with growing warmth. [26a] He takes the horn from his lips and slowly lets it sink, while the expression on his face turns to one of powerful emotion. He sighs deeply, and gloomily casts his eyes to the ground.) [24]

(with a trembling voice)

Einen Unseligen labtest du: −	You've tended an ill-fated man: −
Unheil wende	may Wotan[38] avert
der Wunsch[38] von dir!	ill-fortune from you!

(He starts up to go.)

Gerastet hab' ich	I'm rested now
und süß geruh't:	and sweet was my ease:
weiter wend' ich den Schritt.	now shall I wend my way further.

(He moves towards the back of the stage.)

SIEGLINDE

(turning round quickly)

Wer verfolgt dich, daß du schon	Who's hunting you down, that you flee
[flieh'st?	[so soon?

SIEGMUND

(stopping)

Miswende folgt mir	Ill-fortune follows
wohin ich fliehe;	wherever I flee;
Miswende naht mir	ill-fortune draws near me
wo ich mich neige:	wherever I turn:
dir Frau doch bleibe sie fern! [26b]	from you, woman, may it stay far away!
Fort wend' ich Fuß und Blick.	I'll turn my steps and eyes from here.

(He moves quickly towards the door and raises the latch.)

SIEGLINDE

(impulsively forgetting herself and calling after him)

So bleibe hier!	Then tarry here!

(guardedly)

Nicht bringst du Unheil dahin,   Ill-luck you cannot bring

(slower)

wo Unheil im Hause wohnt!   to a house where ill-luck lives!

(Deeply shaken, Siegmund remains where he is; he gazes searchingly at Sieglinde, who lowers her eyes, ashamed and sad.) [27]

SIEGMUND
(returning)

Wehwalt hieß ich mich selbst: –   Wehwalt I have called myself: –

Hunding will ich erwarten.   Hunding I'll await.

(He leans against the hearth; his gaze is fixed on Sieglinde in calm and resolute sympathy: the latter slowly raises her eyes again to his. A deep silence ensues, during which they both gaze into each other's eyes with an expression of great emotion.) [27, 25, 26b]

SCENE TWO

(Sieglinde suddenly starts up, listens and hears Hunding leading his horse to the stable outside. She hurries over to the door and opens it. Hunding, armed with shield and spear, enters and stops in the doorway on noticing Siegmund. Hunding turns to Sieglinde with an expression of stern enquiry.) [28]

SIEGLINDE
(in reply to Hunding's enquiring expression)

Müd' am Herd   Faint by the hearth

fand ich den Mann: I found the man:

Noth führt' ihn in's Haus.   [24]   need has brought him to our house.

HUNDING

Du labtest ihn?   You tended him?

SIEGLINDE
(calmly)

Den Gaumen letzt' ich ihm,   His lips I moistened,

gastlich sorgt' ich sein'.   I cared for him as any host would.

SIEGMUND
(observing Hunding calmly and resolutely)

Dach und Trank   For shelter and drink

dank' ich ihr: I have to thank her:

willst du dein Weib drum schelten?   would you chide your wife for that?

HUNDING

Heilig ist mein Herd: –   Sacred is my hearth: –

heilig sei dir mein Haus!   may my house be sacred to you!

(He removes his weapons and hands them to Sieglinde.) (to Sieglinde) [28]

Rüst' uns Männern das Mahl!   Prepare a meal for us men!

(Sieglinde hangs the weapons from the branches of the ash-tree, then fetches food and drink from

the storeroom and sets the table for the evening meal. Involuntarily she stares at Siegmund again. Hunding examines Siegmund's features closely and with surprise, comparing them with those of his wife.) [25, 26a]

HUNDING
(aside)

Wie gleicht er dem Weibe!	How like the woman he looks!
Der gleißende Wurm	The selfsame glittering serpent
glänzt auch ihm aus dem Auge.[39]	is glinting in his eye, too.[39]

(He conceals his dismay and turns to Siegmund as though quite naturally.) [24, 28]

Weit her, traun,	Far, indeed,
kam'st du des Weg's;	have you fared on your way;
ein Roß nicht ritt,	no horse rode he
der Rast hier fand:	who found rest here:
welch' schlimme Pfade	what impassable pathways
schufen dir Pein?	caused you pain?

SIEGMUND

Durch Wald und Wiese,	Through forest and field,
Haide und Hain,	heathland and hurst,
jagte mich Sturm	storm and great need
und starke Noth:	have driven me here:
nicht kenn' ich den Weg, den ich kam.	I know not the way that I came.
Wohin ich irrte	Whither I've wandered
weiß ich noch minder:	I know still less:
Kunde gewänn' ich dess' gern.	I should be glad to learn.

HUNDING
(at the table, offering Siegmund a seat)

Dess' Dach dich deckt,		He whose roof is your shelter,
dess' Haus dich hegt,		whose house is your haven,
Hunding heißt der Wirth;	[28]	Hunding's the name of your host;
wendest von hier du		if you turn your steps
nach West den Schritt,		to the west of here,
in Höfen reich		in wealthy homesteads
hausen dort Sippen,		kinsmen dwell
die Hunding's Ehre behüten.		who safeguard Hunding's honour.
Gönnt mir Ehre mein Gast,		My guest would do me honour
wird sein Name nun mir genannt.		by telling me his name.

(Siegmund stares thoughtfully ahead of him. Sieglinde, who has sat down beside Hunding and opposite Siegmund, fixes her gaze on the latter with evident interest and attention.)
(observing both of them) [26b, 27, 25]

Träg'st du Sorge,	If you're wary
mir zu vertrau'n,	of placing your trust in me,
der Frau hier gieb doch Kunde:	then tell your tale to my wife here:
sieh', wie gierig sie dich frägt!	see how eagerly she asks you!

SIEGLINDE
(unembarrassed and interested)

Gast, wer du bist	Guest, who you are

wüßt' ich gern.   I'd gladly know.

SIEGMUND
(looks up, gazes into her eyes and begins gravely) [27]

Friedmund darf ich nicht heißen;
Frohwalt möcht' ich wohl sein:
doch Wehwalt muß ich mich nennen.
Wolfe,[40] der war mein Vater;
zu zwei kam ich zur Welt,
eine Zwillingsschwester und ich.
   Früh schwanden mir
   Mutter und Maid;
   die mich gebar,
   und die mit mir sie barg,
kaum hab' ich je sie gekannt. –
Wehrlich und stark war Wolfe;
der Feinde wuchsen ihm viel.
   Zum Jagen zog
   mit dem Jungen der Alte;
   von Hetze und Harst[41]
   einst kehrten sie heim:
da lag das Wolfsnest leer;
   zu Schutt gebrannt
   der prangende Saal,
   zum Stumpf der Eiche
   blühender Stamm;
   erschlagen der Mutter
   muthiger Leib,[42]
   verschwunden in Gluthen
   der Schwester Spur: –
uns schuf die herbe Noth
der Neidinge harte Schaar.   [28]
   Geächtet floh
   der Alte mit mir;
   lange Jahre
   lebte der Junge
mit Wolfe im wilden Wald:
   manche Jagd
   ward auf sie gemacht;
   doch muthig wehrte
   das Wolfspaar sich.

(turning to Hunding)

Ein Wölfing kündet dir das,
den als Wölfing mancher wohl
[kennt.   [28]

Friedmund I may not call myself;
Frohwalt fain would I be:
but Wehwalt I must name myself.
Wolfe[40] was my father;
as one of twain I came into the world,
a twin-born sister and I.
   Mother and maid
   soon disappeared;
   she who bore me
   and she whom she carried with me –
I scarcely ever knew them. –
Stout-hearted and strong was Wolfe;
many foes he made.
   With the boy
   the old man used to go hunting;
   from chase and encounter[41]
   they came home one day:
the wolf's lair lay deserted;
   burned to ashes
   the splendent hall,
   the oak-tree's sturdy
   trunk a stump;
   murdered lay
   my valiant mother,
   all trace of my sister
   lost in the embers: –
the Neidings' hard-hearted host
had wrought us this bitter distress.
   Outlawed, the old man
   fled with me;
   deep in the wildwood
   the youngster lived
with Wolfe for many a year:
   many's the time
   they were hunted down;
   but wolf and whelp
   would put up a stout defence.

A Wölfing tells you this,
whom as Wölfing many know well.

HUNDING

Wunder und wilde Märe
kündest du, kühner Gast,
Wehwalt – der Wölfing!

Marvels and wondrous tales
you tell us, stout-hearted guest:
Wehwalt – the Wölfing!

Mich dünkt, von dem wehrlichen Paar	Dark tales of that dauntless pair
vernahm ich dunkle Sage,	I think that I've heard tell,
kannt' ich auch Wolfe	though I knew neither Wolfe
und Wölfing nicht.	nor Wölfing.

SIEGLINDE

Doch weiter künde, Fremder:	But, stranger, tell us more:
wo weilt dein Vater jetzt?	where is your father now?

SIEGMUND

Ein starkes Jagen auf uns	The Neidings launched
stellten die Neidinge an:	a fierce onslaught against us:
der Jäger viele	full many a huntsman
fielen den Wölfen,	fell to the wolves,
in Flucht durch den Wald	in flight through the forest
trieb sie das Wild:	their quarry drove them:
wie Spreu zerstob uns der Feind.	like chaff our foe was scattered.
Doch ward ich vom Vater versprengt;	But I from my father was parted;
seine Spur verlor ich,	the longer I searched,
je länger ich forschte;	the more I lost his trail;
eines Wolfes Fell	a wolfskin was all
nur traf ich im Forst:	that I found in the forest:
leer lag das vor mir,	empty it lay there before me,
den Vater fand ich nicht. – [8]	my father I could not find. –
Aus dem Wald trieb es mich fort;	I longed to leave the wildwood
mich drängt' es zu Männern und	and felt drawn to men and women: –
[Frauen: – [26b]	
wie viel ich traf,	however many I met,
wo ich sie fand,	wherever I might find them,
ob ich um Freund,	though I sued for a friend
um Frauen warb, –	or for women, –
immer doch war ich geächtet,	ever was I treated as an outcast.
Unheil lag auf mir.	Ill-fortune lay upon me.
Was rechtes je ich rieth,	Whatever I held to be right
Andern dünkte es arg;	others thought was wrong;
was schlimm immer mir schien,	to whatever seemed to me bad
And're gaben ihm Gunst.	others gave their approval.

(animatedly)

In Fehde fiel ich	I was caught up in feuds
wo ich mich fand;	wherever I went
Zorn traf mich	and met by anger
wohin ich zog;	wherever I fared;

(hesitatingly)

gehrt' ich nach Wonne,	though I craved for bliss,
weckt' ich nur Weh': – [3]	I caused only woe: –
drum mußt' ich mich Wehwalt nennen;	and so I must call myself Wehwalt;
des Wehes waltet' ich nur.	for woe is all I have known.

(He looks up at Sieglinde and notices her sympathetic glance.) [28, 26b, 3]

Die so leidig Loos dir beschied,

nicht liebte dich die Norn:
froh nicht grüßt dich der Mann,

dem fremd als Gast du nah'st.

The Norn who decreed so wretched a
[fate
felt little love for you:
the man you draw near as stranger and
[guest
will not be glad to greet you.

SIEGLINDE

Feige nur fürchten den,
der waffenlos einsam fährt! –   [25]
    Künde noch, Gast,
    wie du im Kampf
zuletzt die Waffe verlor'st!   [27]

Only cowards fear a man
who, weaponless, fares alone! –
    Tell us, guest,
    how at last you lost
your weapon in the fray.

SIEGMUND

Ein trauriges Kind
rief mich zum Trutz:
vermählen wollte
der Magen Sippe
dem Mann ohne Minne die Maid.
    Wider den Zwang
    zog ich zum Schutz;
    der Dränger Troß
    traf ich im Kampf:
dem Sieger sank der Feind.
Erschlagen lagen die Brüder:
die Leichen umschlang da die Maid;
den Grimm verjagt' ihr der Gram.
Mit wilder Thränen Fluth   [3]
betroff sie weinend die Wal:
um des Mordes der eig'nen Brüder
klagte die unsel'ge Maid. –
    Der Erschlag'nen Sippen
    stürmten daher;
    übermächtig
    ächzten nach Rache sie:
    rings um die Stätte
    ragten mir Feinde.
    Doch von der Wal
    wich nicht die Maid;
    mit Schild und Speer
    schirmt' ich sie lang',
    bis Schild und Speer
    im Harst mir zerhau'n.   [24]
Wund und waffenlos stand ich –
sterben sah ich die Maid:
mich hetzte das wüthende Heer[43] –
auf den Leichen lag sie todt.   [27]

A sorrowing child
had called me to arms:
her kinsmen's clan
was wanting to marry
the maid, unloved, to a man.
    To meet that force
    I flew to her aid;
    the horde of oppressors
    I faced in battle:
the enemy fell to the victor.
Her brothers lay there slain:
the maid enclasped their corpses;
grief drove out her anger.
In floods of unstaunchable tears
she bathed the slain with her weeping:
the murder of her brothers
the hapless maid bewailed. –
    The dead men's kin
    came storming along;
    vast in number,
    they groaned for vengeance:
    all round the battlefield
    foemen rose to meet me.
    But the maid would not stir
    from the slain;
    with shield and spear
    I long gave her shelter
    till shield and spear
    were hewn from my hand in the fray.
Wounded and weaponless, there I stood –
and saw the maiden die:
I was harried by the Wild Hunt[43] –
on the lifeless bodies she lay dead.

(turning to Sieglinde with a look of sorrowful fervour)

Nun weißt du, fragende Frau,   Now you know, you questioning woman,
warum ich – Friedmund nicht heiße!   why Friedmund is not my name!

(He stands up and walks over to the hearth. [29] Sieglinde turns pale and stares, deeply shaken, at the ground.)

HUNDING
(rising to his feet)

Ich weiß ein wildes Geschlecht,   I know an unruly race:
  nicht heilig ist ihm   what others hold dear
  was And'ren hehr: they deem unholy:

(more forcefully)

verhaßt ist es Allen und mir.   [28]   they're hated by all – and by me.
Zur Rache ward ich gerufen,   I was called to vengeance,
  Sühne zu nehmen   to seek requital
  für Sippen-Blut: for kinsmen's blood:
  zu spät kam ich,   I came too late
  und kehre nun heim   and now come home
des flücht'gen Frevlers Spur   to find the fleeing traitor's trace
im eig'nen Haus zu erspäh'n. –   here inside my own house. –

(advancing downstage)

  Mein Haus hütet,   My house, Wölfing,
  Wölfing, dich heut';   protects you today;
für die Nacht nahm ich dich auf: for the night I have taken you in:

(more animatedly)

  mit starker Waffe   [28]   but with sturdy weapon
  doch wehre dich morgen;   defend yourself in the morning;
zum Kampfe kies' ich den Tag: I choose the day for the fight;
für Todte zahl'st du mir Zoll.   you'll pay me tribute for all who died.

(With an anxious gesture, Sieglinde steps between the two men.) [25]

Fort aus dem Saal!   Get out of the hall!
Säume hier nicht!   Stop lingering here!
Den Nachttrunk rüste mir drin,   Prepare my drink for the night,
und harre mein' zur Ruh'.   and wait for me in bed.

(For a moment, Sieglinde remains where she is, undecided and pensive. [25] Then she turns, slowly and with hesitant steps, to the stillroom. There she pauses once again and remains standing, lost in thought, with her face half turned away. With quiet resolve she opens the cupboard, fills a drinking-horn and shakes some spices into it from a container. She then turns to Siegmund in order to meet his gaze, which he keeps permanently fixed on her. She notices that Hunding is watching them and turns at once to the bedchamber. On the steps she turns round once again, gazes yearningly at Siegmund and indicates with her eyes, continuously and with eloquent explicitness, a particular spot in the ash-tree's trunk. [26a, 23] Hunding flares up and drives her on her way with a violent gesture. With a final glance at Siegmund, she goes into the bedchamber and closes the door behind her. Hunding takes down his weapons from the tree-trunk.) [28]

Mit Waffen wahrt sich der Mann. – With weapons a man defends himself. –

(turning to Siegmund as he leaves)

Dich Wölfing treffe ich morgen: Tomorrow, Wölfing, we shall meet;
  mein Wort hörtest du –   you heard what I said –
  hüte dich wohl!   guard yourself well!

(He goes into the bedchamber and can be heard closing the bolt from within.)

SCENE THREE

(Siegmund alone. It is completely dark outside; the room is lit only by the faint glimmer of a fire in the hearth. Siegmund settles down on the couch near the fire and broods silently for a while in a state of great inner turmoil.)

SIEGMUND

Ein Schwert verhieß mir der Vater,[23b]
ich fänd' es in höchster Noth. –   [28]
    Waffenlos fiel ich
    in Feindes Haus;
    seiner Rache Pfand
    raste ich hier: –
    ein Weib sah' ich,
    wonnig und hehr;   [26b]
    entzückend Bangen
    zehrt mein Herz: –   [28]
zu der mich nun Sehnsucht zieht,
die mit süßem Zauber mich sehrt –

im Zwange hält sie der Mann,
der mich – wehrlosen höhnt. –
    Wälse! Wälse!   [23b]
    Wo ist dein Schwert?
    Das starke Schwert,
    das im Sturm ich schwänge,
bricht mir hervor aus der Brust
was wüthend das Herz noch hegt?

My father promised me a sword:
I'd find it in direst need. –
    Unarmed I chanced
    on my enemy's house;
    in pawn to his vengeance
    I rest here now: –
    I saw a woman,
    winsome and fair;
    exquisite terror
    consumes my heart: –
she to whom yearning draws me now
and who wounds me with sweet
    [enchantment
is held in thrall by the man
who mocks me, weaponless as I am. –
    Wälse! Wälse!
    Where is your sword?
    The mighty sword
    that I'd wield in the fray,
when forth from my breast breaks
the furious rage yet harboured within my
    [heart?

(The fire collapses, causing a fierce glow to flare up and strike the spot on the ash-tree's trunk indicated by Sieglinde's eyes, where the hilt of a buried sword can be clearly seen.) [23]

    Was gleißt dort hell
    im Glimmerschein?
    Welch' ein Strahl bricht   [23]
    aus der Esche Stamm? –
    Des Blinden Auge
    leuchtet ein Blitz:
lustig lacht da der Blick. –   [23]
    Wie der Schein so hehr
    das Herz mir sengt!
    Ist es der Blick
    der blühenden Frau,
    den dort haftend
    sie hinter sich ließ,
als aus dem Saal sie schied?

    What glints there so bright
    in the glimmering light?
    What blaze breaks forth
    from the ash-tree's bole?
    A blind man's eyes
    are lit by its flash:
gaily his gaze lights in laughter. –
    How the heavenly glow
    sears this heart of mine!
    Is it the glorious
    woman's glance,
    which she left behind her,
    clinging there,
when she passed out of the hall?

(From this point on, the fire in the hearth gradually dies out.)

    Nächtiges Dunkel
    deckte mein Aug';
    ihres Blickes Strahl

    Nighttime's shadows
    shielded my eyes;
    the flash of her gaze

streifte mich da:
Wärme gewann ich und Tag.
  Selig schien mir
  der Sonne Licht;
  den Scheitel umgliß mir
  ihr wonniger Glanz –
bis hinter Bergen sie sank.

then glanced upon me,
bringing me warmth and light.
  Blessed to me seemed
  the light of the sun;
  its bliss-bringing glow
  girt the crown of my head,
ere it sank behind the mountains.

(The fire flares up feebly again.)

Noch einmal, da sie schied,
traf mich Abends ihr Schein:
selbst der alten Esche Stamm
erglänzte in gold'ner Gluth:
  da bleicht die Blüthe –
  das Licht verlischt –
  nächtiges Dunkel
  deckt mir das Auge:
tief in des Busens Berge
glimmt nur noch lichtlose Gluth!

Yet once again, as it set,
I was caught in its evening light;
even the ancient ash-tree's bole
[23] gleamed in the golden glow:
  now the blossom fades,
  the light dies out;
  nighttime's shadows
  shield my eyes:
deep in my sheltering breast
a flameless fire still smoulders.

*(The fire has gone out completely: total darkness. [28] The door to the sideroom opens gently.
Sieglinde enters in a white nightdress and moves softly but quickly over to the hearth.)*

SIEGLINDE

Schläf'st du, Gast?

Are you sleeping, guest?

SIEGMUND
(in joyful surprise)

Wer schleicht daher?

Who steals this way?

SIEGLINDE
(in mysterious haste)

Ich bin's: höre mich an! –
In tiefem Schlaf liegt Hunding;
ich würzt' ihm betäubenden Trank.
Nütze die Nacht dir zum Heil!

'Tis I: lend an ear! –
Hunding is lying deep asleep;
I spiced his drink with a drug.
Use night's cover to save your life!

SIEGMUND
(interrupting her passionately)

Heil macht mich dein Nah'n![44]

Your coming brings me life![44]

SIEGLINDE

Eine Waffe lass' mich dir weisen –:
O wenn du sie gewänn'st!
  Den hehr'sten Helden
  dürft' ich dich heißen:
  dem Stärk'sten allein
  ward sie bestimmt. –
O merke wohl, was ich dir melde! –
  Der Männer Sippe
  saß hier im Saal,
von Hunding zur Hochzeit geladen:

Let me show you a weapon:
if only you could win it!
  As the noblest of heroes
  might I hail you:
  the strongest alone
[23] was destined to gain it. –
Heed well what I have to tell you. –
  The men from his clan
  sat here in the hall,
as guests at Hunding's wedding:

er frei'te ein Weib,
das ungefragt
Schächer ihm schenkten zur Frau.
  Traurig saß ich
  während sie tranken:
ein Fremder trat da herein –   [8]
ein Greis in grauem[45] Gewand;
tief hing ihm der Hut,
der deckt' ihm der Augen eines;
  doch des and'ren Strahl,
  Angst schuf er allen,
  traf die Männer
  sein mächtiges Dräu'n:
  mir allein
  weckte das Auge
süß sehnenden Harm,
Thränen und Trost zugleich.   [23]
  Auf mich blickt' er,
  und blitzte auf Jene,
als ein Schwert in Händen er
  [schwang;
  das stieß er nun
  in der Esche Stamm,
bis zum Heft haftet' es drin: –
dem sollte der Stahl geziemen,
der aus dem Stamm' es zög'.
  Der Männer Alle,
  so kühn sie sich müh'ten,
die Wehr sich keiner gewann;
  Gäste kamen
  und Gäste gingen,
die stärk'sten zogen am Stahl –
keinen Zoll entwich er dem Stamm':[23]
dort haftet schweigend das Schwert. –
Da wußt' ich, wer der war,   [8]
der mich gramvolle gegrüßt:
  ich weiß auch,
  wem allein
im Stamm' das Schwert er bestimmt. [23]
  O fänd' ich ihn hier
  und heut', den Freund;
käm' er aus Fremden
zur ärmsten Frau:
  was je ich gelitten
  in grimmigem Leid,
  was je mich geschmerzt
  in Schande und Schmach, –
  süßeste Rache
  sühnte dann Alles!
  Erjagt hätt' ich

he was wooing a woman
whom villains, unasked,
had given him as his wife.
  Sadly I sat there
  while they were drinking:
a stranger then came in –
an old man dressed in grey;[45]
his hat hung so low
that one of his eyes was hidden,
  but the flash of its fellow
  struck fear all around,
  as its lowering stare
  transfixed the men:
  in me alone
  his eye awakened
sweetly yearning sorrow,
mingled with tears and solace.
  He gazed at me
  and glared at them
as he brandished a sword in his hands;

  he then drove it deep
  in the ash-tree's trunk;
it was buried up to the hilt: –
the steel would rightly belong to him
who could draw it forth from the trunk.
  Of all the menfolk,
  much as they struggled,
none could win the weapon;
  guests would come
  and guests would go,
the strongest tugged at the steel –
not an inch did it stir in the trunk:
in silence the sword still cleaves there. –
I knew then who he was
who greeted me in my grief:
  I also knew
  for whom alone
he destined the sword in the tree.
  Might I find him here
  today, that friend;
  might he come from afar
  to a woman most wretched;
  whatever I suffered
  in terrible sorrow,
  however I smarted
  from shame and disgrace, –
  sweetest revenge
  would atone for it all!
  I'd then have recaptured

was je ich verlor,	whatever I'd lost,
was je ich beweint	whatever I'd wept for
wär' mir gewonnen –	would then be won back,
fänd' ich den heiligen Freund,	were I only to find that hallowed friend,
umfing' den Helden mein Arm!	were my arms to enfold the hero.

SIEGMUND
(ardently embracing Sieglinde) [29]

Dich selige Frau	That friend now holds you,
hält nun der Freund,	thrice-blessed woman,
dem Waffe und Weib bestimmt!	to whom both weapon and wife were [destined!
Heiß in der Brust	Deep in my breast
brennt mir der Eid,	there burns the vow
der mich dir Edlen vermählt.	that binds me, noble woman, to you.
Was je ich ersehnt	Whatever I longed for
ersah' ich in dir;	I saw in you;
in dir fand ich	in you I found
was je mir gefehlt!	whatever I lacked!
Littest du Schmach,	Though you suffered shame
und schmerzte mich Leid;	and though sorrow pained me;
war ich geächtet,	though I was an outlaw
und war'st du entehrt:	and you were dishonoured,
freudige Rache	joyful revenge
ruft nun den Frohen!	now bids us rejoice.
Auf lach' ich	I laugh aloud
in heiliger Lust,	in hallowed delight
halt' ich die Hehre umfangen,	as I hold the proud woman within my [embrace
fühl' ich dein schlagendes Herz!	and feel your beating heart!

(The main door flies open.)

SIEGLINDE
(starting up in alarm and tearing herself away)

Ha, wer ging? wer kam herein?	Ha, who went out? Who came inside?

(The door remains open: a glorious spring night outside; the full moon shines in and throws its bright light on the pair, so that they can suddenly see each other in total clarity.)

SIEGMUND
(in gentle ecstasy)

Keiner ging – –	No one went – –
doch Einer kam:	but someone came:
siehe, der Lenz	see how Spring
lacht in den Saal!	smiles into the hall!

(He draws Sieglinde to him on the couch with gentle force, so that she sits beside him. The moonlight grows increasingly bright.)

Winterstürme wichen	Winter's storms have waned
dem Wonnemond,	at May's awakening;
in mildem Lichte	Spring is aglow
leuchtet der Lenz;	with gentle light;

auf linden Lüften
leicht und lieblich,
Wunder webend
er sich wiegt;
durch Wald und Auen
weht sein Athem,
weit geöffnet
lacht sein Aug'.
Aus sel'ger Vöglein Sange
süß er tönt,
holde Düfte
haucht er aus;
seinem warmen Blut entblühen
wonnige Blumen,
Keim und Sproß
entsprießt seiner Kraft.
Mit zarter Waffen Zier
bezwingt er die Welt;
Winter und Sturm wichen
der starken Wehr: –
wohl mußte den tapf'ren Streichen
die strenge Thüre auch weichen,
die trotzig und starr
uns – trennte von ihm. –

on balmy breezes,
light and lovely,
working wonders
he wafts this way;
through woods and meadows
blows his breath;
wide open
his eyes are laughing.
In blissful birdsong
sweetly he sounds
and fragrant perfumes
scent his breath;
from his warming blood bloom
wondrous flowers,
buds and shoots
sprout forth from his strength.
Arrayed with delicate weapons,
he conquers the world;
winter and storm gave way
to his stout defence: –
at his doughty blows the sturdy door
had no choice but to yield
which, stubborn and stern,
divided us from him. –

[26b]

Zu seiner Schwester[46]
schwang er sich her;

[26a]

To find his sister[46]
he flew this way;

(tenderly)

die Liebe lockte den Lenz;
in uns'rem Busen
barg sie sich tief;
nun lacht sie selig dem Licht.
Die bräutliche Schwester
befreite der Bruder;
zertrümmert liegt
was je sie getrennt;
jauchzend grüßt sich
das junge Paar:
vereint sind Liebe und Lenz!

Love has lured Spring here.
Deep in our breasts
Love lay hidden;
in bliss she now laughs in the light.
The sister-bride
was freed by her brother;
in ruins lies
what held them asunder;
exulting, the couple
greet one another:
united are Love and Spring!

SIEGLINDE

Du bist der Lenz,
nach dem ich verlangte
in frostigen Winters Frist;
dich grüßte mein Herz
mit heiligem Grau'n,
als dein Blick zuerst mir erblühte. –
Fremdes nur sah ich von je,
freundlos war mir das Nahe;
als hätt' ich nie es gekannt

[26a]

You are the Spring
for which I longed
in frosty wintertime;
you my heart greeted
in holy dread
when my eyes first lighted upon you. –
All I'd ever seen seemed strange,
friendless was all that was near me;
as though I'd never known it

war was immer mir kam.
  Doch dich kannt' ich   [26b]
deutlich und klar:
als mein Auge dich sah,
war'st du mein Eigen:
was im Busen ich barg,
was ich bin,
hell wie der Tag
taucht' es mir auf,
wie tönender Schall
schlug's an mein Ohr,
als in frostig öder Fremde
zuerst ich den Freund ersah.

was everything that befell me.
  But you I recognized
plainly and clearly:
when my eye beheld you,
you were my own:
what I hid in my breast
and what I am,
it came to me
as bright as day;
like an echoing sound
it struck my ear,
when in frostily foreign wasteland
I first beheld my friend.

(She throws her arms round his neck in her ecstasy and looks closely into his face.)

SIEGMUND
(enraptured)

O süßeste Wonne!
Seligstes Weib!

O sweetest delight!
Most blessed of women!

SIEGLINDE
(staring keenly into his eyes)

O lass' in Nähe   [10a]
zu dir mich neigen,
daß hell ich schaue
den hehren Schein,
der dir aus Aug'
und Antlitz bricht,   [26b]
und so süß die Sinne mir zwingt!

O let me bend
more closely towards you,
that I see more clearly
the noble light
that breaks forth
from your eye and face
and so sweetly suborns my senses!

SIEGMUND

Im Lenzesmond
leuchtest du hell;
hehr umwebt dich
das Wellenhaar:
was mich berückt
errath' ich nun leicht –
denn wonnig weidet mein Blick.

Brightly you shine
in the springtime moon;
your waving hair
forms a wondrous halo:
what charms me now
I can easily guess –
for my gaze feasts upon you in rapture.

SIEGLINDE
(pushing his hair away from his forehead and gazing at him in astonishment)

Wie dir die Stirn
so offen steht,
der Adern Geäst
in den Schläfen sich schlingt!
Mir zagt es vor der Wonne,   [8]
die mich entzückt –
ein Wunder[47] will mich gemahnen: –
den heut' zuerst ich erschaut,
mein Auge sah dich schon!

How broad
is your brow,
the scrollwork of veins
entwines in your temples!
I tremble to tell
of the bliss that transports me –
a wonder[47] seeks to forewarn me:
you whom I first beheld today
my eyes have seen before!

SIEGMUND

Ein Minnetraum	A dream of love
gemahnt auch mich:	forewarns me, too:
in heißem Sehnen	in fervent longing
sah ich dich schon!	I've seen you before!

SIEGLINDE

Im Bach erblickt' ich	My own likeness
mein eigen Bild –	I glimpsed in the brook –
und jetzt gewahr' ich es wieder:	and now I see it again:
wie einst dem Teich es enttaucht,	as once it rose from the pool,
bietest mein Bild mir nun du!	to me now you show that likeness!

SIEGMUND

Du bist das Bild,	[26b]	You are the likeness
das ich in mir barg.		I hid within me.

SIEGLINDE
(quickly averting her eyes)

O still! lass' mich	O hush! Let me
der Stimme lauschen: –	hark to your voice:
mich dünkt, ihren Klang	I think that I heard
hört' ich als Kind – –	its sound as a child – –
doch nein! ich hörte sie neulich,	but no! I heard it of late
als meiner Stimme Schall	when the ring of my voice
mir wiederhallte der Wald.	reechoed throughout the wood.

SIEGMUND

O lieblichste Laute,	O sweetest of sounds
denen ich lausche!	to which I hearken!

SIEGLINDE
(gazing into his eyes again) [29, 23]

Deines Auges Gluth		Your eye's smouldering glance
erglänzte mir schon: –	[8]	glinted upon me ere now: –
so blickte der Greis		so the greybeard looked
grüßend auf mich,		as he greeted me once
als der Traurigen Trost er gab.		and brought comfort to me in my sadness.
An dem Blick		By his glance
erkannt' ihn sein Kind –		his child knew who he was –
schon wollt' ich bei'm Namen ihn		I wanted to call out his name – –
[nennen – –		
Wehwalt heiß'st du fürwahr?		Is Wehwalt really what you are called?

SIEGMUND

Nicht heiß' mich so	Do not call me so
seit du mich lieb'st:	now that you love me:
nun walt' ich der hehrsten Wonnen!	I'm lord of sublimest delights!

SIEGLINDE

Und Friedmund darfst du froh dich nicht nennen?	And, happy, you cannot call yourself Friedmund?

SIEGMUND

Nenne mich du wie du lieb'st daß ich heiße: den Namen nehm' ich von dir!	Name me yourself as you'd like me called: I'll take my name from you.

SIEGLINDE

Doch nanntest du Wolfe den Vater?	But Wolfe, you said, was your father?

SIEGMUND

Ein Wolf war er feigen Füchsen!
  Doch dem so stolz
  strahlte das Auge,
wie, Herrliche, hehr dir es strahlt,
der war – Wälse genannt.
	A wolf to fearful foxes!
	  But he whose eye
	  once flashed as proudly
	as yours, fair woman, flashes now –
	Wälse was his name.

SIEGLINDE
(beside herself)

War Wälse dein Vater, und bist du ein Wälsung, stieß er für dich sein Schwert in den Stamm – so lass' mich dich heißen wie ich dich liebe: Siegmund – so nenn' ich dich!	If Wälse's your father and if you're a Wälsung; if he thrust the sword in the tree for you – then let me name you as I love you: Siegmund – thus do I call you!

SIEGMUND
(leaping up) [29]

Siegmund heiß' ich, und Siegmund bin ich:	[23]	Siegmund I'm called and Siegmund I am:
bezeug' es dieß Schwert, das zaglos ich halte!		be witness this sword that I hold without flinching!
Wälse verhieß mir, in höchster Noth fänd' ich es einst: ich fass' es nun!	[9]	Wälse promised I'd find it one day in my time of greatest need: I seize it now!
Heiligster Minne höchste Noth, sehnender Liebe sehrende Noth,	[7]	Highest need of holiest love, consuming need of yearning desire
brennt mir hell in der Brust, drängt zu That und Tod! – Nothung! Nothung!	[23b]	burns brightly within my breast, urging me on to deed and death! – Nothung! Nothung!
so nenn' ich dich Schwert – Nothung! Nothung! neidlicher[48] Stahl!		So I name you, sword! Nothung! Nothung! Fearsome[48] steel!

Zeig' deiner Schärfe
schneidenden Zahn:
heraus aus der Scheide zu mir!
(With a violent effort he draws the sword from the tree and shows it to Sieglinde, who is seized by astonishment and ecstasy.) [23]

Siegmund den Wälsung	Siegmund the Wälsung
sieh'st du, Weib! [29]	you see here, wife!
Als Brautgabe	As bridal gift
bringt er dieß Schwert:	he brings this sword:
so freit er sich	for so he woos
die seligste Frau;	the most blessed of women;
dem Feindeshaus	from his enemy's house
entführt er dich so.	he thus carries you off.
Fern von hier	Far from here
folge mir nun,	follow me now,
fort in des Lenzes [23]	away to springtime's
lachendes Haus:	smiling home:

dort schützt dich Nothung das Schwert,   there Nothung the sword shall shield you,
wenn Siegmund dir liebend erlag! [26b]   when Siegmund succumbs to your love.
(He has thrown his arm round her in order to draw her away with him.)

SIEGLINDE
(tearing herself free in the utmost intoxication and standing before him)

Bist du Siegmund,	If you are Siegmund
den ich hier sehe –	whom I see here –
Sieglinde bin ich,	Sieglinde am I,
die dich ersehnt:	who has longed for you:
die eig'ne Schwester	your own true sister
gewann'st du zueins mit dem [Schwert!	you've won for yourself with the sword!

(She throws herself at his breast.)

SIEGMUND

Braut und Schwester [26b]	Bride and sister
bist du dem Bruder –	you are to your brother –
so blühe denn Wälsungen-Blut!	so let the blood of the Wälsungs blossom!

(He draws her towards him with furious passion. [23] *The curtain falls quickly.)* [26a]

Act Two

PRELUDE AND SCENE ONE

The curtain rises.[49] *A wild and rocky mountain landscape. At the back of the stage a gorge runs from below to a high ridge of rocks, from which the ground slopes down again towards the front of the stage. (Wotan, armed for battle, with his spear; before him Brünnhilde, as a valkyrie, likewise fully armed.)* [23, 26a, 30]

WOTAN

Nun zäume dein Roß,	Now harness your horse,
reisige Maid!	warrior maid!
Bald entbrennt	A furious fight
brünstiger Streit: [9]	will soon flare up:
Brünnhilde stürme zum Kampf,	let Brünnhilde fly to the fray;
dem Wälsung kiese[50] sie Sieg!	for the Wälsung let her choose[50] victory!
Hunding wähle sich	Hunding may choose
wem er gehört:	to whom he belongs:
nach Walhall taugt er mir nicht.	he's no use to me in Valhalla.
Drum rüstig und rasch	Soundly and swiftly, then,
reite zur Wal!	ride to the slaughter!

BRÜNNHILDE

(shouting exultantly as she leaps from rock to rock up to the heights on the left)

Hojotoho! Hojotoho! [30, 31]	Hojotoho! Hojotoho!
Heiaha! Heiaha!	Heiaha! Heiaha!
Hahei! Hahei! Heiaho!	Hahei! Hahei! Heiaho!

(She pauses on a high peak, looks down into the gorge at the rear of the stage and calls back to Wotan.)

Dir rath' ich, Vater,	I warn you, father,
rüste dich selbst;	forearm yourself;
harten Sturm	a violent storm
sollst du besteh'n:	you'll have to weather:
Fricka naht, deine Frau,	Fricka, your wife, draws near
im Wagen mit dem Widdergespann.	in a chariot drawn by a team of rams.
Hei! wie die gold'ne	Ha! How she whirls
Geißel sie schwingt; [3]	the golden whip;
die armen Thiere	the pitiful beasts
ächzen vor Angst;	are bleating with fear;
wild rasseln die Räder:	the wheels are rattling wildly:
zornig fährt sie zum Zank.	wrathful, she fares to the fray.
In solchem Strauße	In strife of this kind
streit' ich nicht gern,	I care not to fight,
lieb' ich auch muthiger	fond though I am of
Männer Schlacht: [30]	brave men's battles:
drum sieh', wie den Sturm du	then see how you weather the storm!
[besteh'st;	

ich Lustige lass' dich im Stich! –
  Hojotoho! Hojotoho!   [31]
  Heiaha! Heiaha!
Hahei! Hahei! Hojohei!

I'll happily leave you to it! –
  Hojotoho! Hojotoho!
  Heiaha! Heiaha!
Hahei! Hahei! Hojohei!

(Brünnhilde disappears behind the high rock at the side. Fricka arrives on the mountain ridge from the gorge in a chariot drawn by two rams: here she stops abruptly and climbs out. She strides impetuously towards Wotan, who is standing at the front of the stage.)

WOTAN

Der alte Sturm,
  die alte Müh'!
Doch Stand muß ich hier halten.

The same old storm,
  the same old strife!
But here I must make a stand.

FRICKA

(the closer she comes, the more she moderates her pace and at last places herself with dignity before Wotan)

Wo in Bergen du dich birgst
der Gattin Blick zu entgeh'n,
  einsam hier
  such' ich dich auf,
daß Hilfe du mir verhießest.

Wherever you hide in the hills
to escape the eyes of your wife,
  I seek you out
  here, all alone,
that you promise me your help.

WOTAN

Was Fricka kümmert
künde sie frei.   [28]

Let Fricka freely
confide her cares.

FRICKA

Ich vernahm Hunding's Noth,
um Rache rief er mich an:
  der Ehe Hüterin
  hörte ihn,
  verhieß streng
  zu strafen die That
des frech frevelnden Paar's,
das kühn den Gatten gekränkt.[51] –

Hunding's distress I heard;
he called on me for vengeance:
  wedlock's guardian
  gave him ear
  and promised to punish
  severely the deed
of that brazenly impious pair
that dared to wrong a husband.[51] –

WOTAN

Was so schlimmes
  schuf das Paar,
das liebend einte der Lenz?   [26b]
  Der Minne Zauber
  entzückte sie:
wer büßt mir der Minne Macht?

What was so wrong
  that was done by the couple
that Spring united in love?
  Love's enchantment
  had cast upon them its magic spell:
who'll make me amends for the power of
  [love?

FRICKA

Wie thörig und taub du dich stell'st,
als wüßtest fürwahr du nicht,
  daß um der Ehe
  heiligen Eid,

How foolish and dull you pretend to be,
as though, in truth, you did not know
  that I grieve for wedlock's
  holy vow,

den hart gekränkten, ich klage!

a vow most harshly broken!

Unheilig
acht' ich den Eid,
der Unliebende eint;
und mir wahrlich
muthe nicht zu,
daß mit Zwang ich halte
was dir nicht haftet:
denn wo kühn Kräfte sich regen,
da rath' ich offen zum Krieg.

Unholy
I deem the vow
that binds unloving hearts;
and, in truth, you cannot
expect me now
to bind by force
[9]   what won't be bound by you:
wherever forces are boldly stirring,
I openly counsel war.

FRICKA

Achtest du rühmlich
der Ehe Bruch,
so prahle nun weiter
und preis' es heilig,
daß Blutschande entblüht
dem Bund eines Zwillingspaar's!
Mir schaudert das Herz,
es schwindelt mein Hirn:
bräutlich umfing
die Schwester den Bruder![52]
Wann — ward es erlebt,
daß leiblich Geschwister sich liebten?

If you think breach
of wedlock worthy of praise,
then go on boasting
and deem it holy
that incest springs
from the bond of a twin-born pair!
My heart is quaking,
my brain is reeling:
as bride a sister
embraced her brother![52]
When was it witnessed
that natural siblings loved one another?

WOTAN

Heut' — hast du's erlebt:
erfahre so,
was von selbst sich fügt,
sei zuvor auch noch nie es
[gescheh'n.
Daß jene sich lieben,
leuchtet dir hell:
drum höre redlichen Rath!
Soll süße Lust
deinen Segen dir lohnen,
so seg'ne, lachend der Liebe,

Siegmund's und Sieglinde's Bund!

Today you have witnessed it happen:
learn thus that a thing
might befall of itself
though it never happened before.
[26b]

That those two are in love
is as plain as the day:
so hear my honest advice!
If sweet delight
shall reward your blessing,
then, smiling on love, bestow that
[blessing
on Siegmund's and Sieglinde's bond.

FRICKA
(breaking out in the most violent indignation)

So ist es denn aus
mit den ewigen Göttern,
seit du die wilden
Wälsungen zeugtest? —
Heraus sagt' ich's —
traf ich den Sinn? —

So is this the end
of the blessed immortals,
since you begot
those dissolute Wälsungs? —
I've said it now —
have I caught your meaning?

Nichts gilt dir der Hehren
heilige Sippe;
hin wirfst du alles
was einst du geachtet;
zerreißest die Bande,
die selbst du gebunden;
lösest lachend
des Himmels Haft –   [23]
daß nach Lust und Laune nur walte
dieß frevelnde Zwillingspaar,
deiner Untreue zuchtlose Frucht! –

   O, was klag' ich   [15]
   um Ehe und Eid,   [26a]
da zuerst du selbst sie versehrt!
   Die treue Gattin
   trogest du stets:
   wo eine Tiefe,
   wo eine Höhe,
   dahin lugte
   lüstern dein Blick,
wie des Wechsels Lust du gewännest,
und höhnend kränktest mein Herz!
   Trauernden Sinnes
   mußt' ich's ertragen,
   zog'st du zur Schlacht
   mit den schlimmen Mädchen,
   die wilder Minne
   Bund dir gebar;
denn dein Weib noch scheutest du so,

   daß der Walküren Schaar,
   und Brünnhilden selbst,
   deines Wunsches[53] Braut,
in Gehorsam der Herrin du gab'st.
   Doch jetzt, da dir neue
   Namen gefielen,
   als »Wälse« wölfisch
   im Walde du schweifest;
   jetzt, da zu niedrigster
   Schmach du dich neigtest,
   gemeiner Menschen
   ein Paar zu erzeugen:
jetzt dem Wurfe der Wölfin
wirfst du zu Füßen dein Weib? –
   So führ' es denn aus,
   fülle das Maaß:
die Betrog'ne lass' auch zertreten!

The gods' hallowed kin
means nothing to you;
you cast away everything
that you once cared for,
severing ties
that you yourself forged,
laughingly loosening
heaven's hold
that this impious twin-born pair,
your falsehood's wanton fruit,
might obey the dictates of pleasure and
   [whim! –
   O why do I wail over
   wedlock and vow,
when you were the first to infringe them!
   You've always played false
   with your true-hearted wife:
   where was the hollow,
   where the height
   where your lustful look
   didn't pry in seeking out ways
of indulging your fondness for change
and of tauntingly wounding my heart!
   In sadness of spirit
   I had to stand by,
   while you fared to the fray
   with those ill-mannered girls,
   who were born of the bond
   of a dissolute love;
for you still held your wife in sufficient
   [awe
   that the valkyrie band,
   and Brünnhild' herself,
   the bride of your wishes,[53]
you gave to me to obey as their mistress.
   But now new names
   have taken your fancy,
   wolf-like you roam
   through the forest as 'Wälse';
   now that you've fallen
   to fathomless shame
   and fathered a couple
   of common mortals,
would you then fling your wife
at the feet of the she-wolf's litter? –
   Then finish your work
   and fill the measure:
now you've betrayed me, trample me
   [underfoot as well!

WOTAN
(calmly)

Nichts lerntest du,
　wollt' ich dich lehren,
was nie du erkennen kannst,
eh' dir ertagte die That.
　Stets Gewohntes
　nur magst du versteh'n:
doch was noch nie sich traf,
danach trachtet mein Sinn! –　　　[23]
　Eines höre!
　Noth thut ein Held,
der, ledig göttlichen Schutzes,
sich löse vom Göttergesetz:　　　[9]
　so nur taugt er
　zu wirken die That,
die, wie noth sie den Göttern,　　[6]
dem Gott doch zu wirken verwehrt.[12]

You learned nothing at all
　when I tried to teach you
things you can never recognize
until the deed has dawned on you.
　Age-old custom
　is all you can grasp:
but *my* thoughts seek to encompass
what's never yet come to pass. –
　Hear one thing alone!
　A hero is needed
who, lacking godly protection,
breaks loose from the law of the gods:
　thus alone is he fit
　to perform that feat
which, needful though it is to the gods,
the god is forbidden to do.

FRICKA

Mit tiefem Sinne
willst du mich täuschen!
Was hehres sollten
Helden je wirken,
das ihren Göttern wäre verwehrt,

deren Gunst in ihnen nur wirkt?

You seek to deceive me
with deep-set meaning!
What lofty feat
could heroes perform
that their gods were prevented from
　　　　　　　　　　　[doing,
whose grace informs their actions alone?

WOTAN

Ihres eig'nen Muthes⁵⁴
achtest du nicht.

Have you no heed
of their own independence?[54]

FRICKA

Wer hauchte Menschen ihn ein?
Wer hellte den Blöden den Blick?
　In deinem Schutz
　scheinen sie stark,
　durch deinen Stachel
　streben sie auf:
du – reizest sie einzig,
die so mir Ew'gen du rühm'st.

Who breathed it into humankind?
Who lighted the cowards' eyes?
　Sheltered by you,
　they seem to be strong;
　spurred on by you,
　they strive for the light:
you alone urge them on
whom you thus praise to me, the
　　　　　　　　　[immortal goddess.

　Mit neuer List
　willst du mich belügen,
　durch neue Ränke
　jetzt mir entrinnen;
　doch diesen Wälsung
　gewinn'st du dir nicht:
in ihm treff' ich nur dich,
denn durch dich trotzt er allein.

　With what new guile
　you seek to gull me,
　with new devices
　evade me now:
　and yet you'll not
　win this Wälsung yourself:
in him I find only you,
for through you alone he defies us.

In wilden Leiden
     In grievous distress
(with emotion)
erwuchs er sich selbst:
    [9]   he grew up by himself:
mein Schutz schirmte ihn nie.
    my shelter never shielded him.

FRICKA

So schütz' auch heut' ihn nicht;
    Don't shelter him today then;
  nimm ihm das Schwert,
    take away the sword
  das du ihm geschenkt!
    you bestowed upon him.

WOTAN

Das Schwert?
    [23]   The sword?

FRICKA

Ja – das Schwert,
    Yes – the sword,
  das zauberstark
    the magically mighty,
  zuckende Schwert,
    flashing sword
das du Gott dem Sohne gab'st.
    which you, a god, gave your son.

WOTAN
(vehemently)

Siegmund gewann es sich
    Siegmund won it himself
(with suppressed trembling)
selbst in der Noth.
    in his need.
(From this point onwards, Wotan's whole demeanour expresses increasing gloom and deep dejection.) [32a]

FRICKA
(continuing vehemently)

Du schuf'st ihm die Noth,
    You fostered that need
  wie das neidliche Schwert:
    no less than you fashioned the
    [fearsome sword:

  willst du mich täuschen,
    would you deceive me
  die Tag und Nacht
    who, day and night,
  auf den Fersen dir folgt?
    follows you hard on your heels?
  Für ihn stießest du
    For him you thrust
  das Schwert in den Stamm;
    the sword in the tree trunk;
  du verhießest ihm
    you promised him
  die hehre Wehr:
    the noble weapon:
  willst du es leugnen,
    will you deny
  daß nur deine List
    that your cunning alone
ihn lockte wo er es fänd'?
    lured him to where he might find it?
(Wotan starts up with a gesture of anger. Fricka becomes ever more confident as she observes the impression she has made on Wotan.)
  Mit Unfreien
    No nobleman battles
  streitet kein Edler,
    with bondsmen;
den Frevler straft nur der Freie:
    the freeman alone chastises the felon:
  wider deine Kraft
    against your might
  führt' ich wohl Krieg:
    I might well wage war:

doch Siegmund verfiel mir als Knecht.	but Siegmund was destined to be my slave.

(Another violent gesture on Wotan's part, after which he sinks into a feeling of powerlessness.)

Der dir als Herren	Should he who, as bondsman
hörig und eigen,	and vassal, obeys you, his lord,
gehorchen soll ihm	bend your own eternal
dein ewig Gemahl?	wife to his will?
Soll mich in Schmach	Is the basest of men
der Niedrigste schmähen,	to heap shame on my head,
dem Frechen zum Sporn,	a goad to the brazen
dem Freien zum Spott?	and butt of the free?
Das kann mein Gatte nicht wollen,	My husband cannot want such a thing,
die Göttin entweiht er nicht so! [32]	he'd not profane the goddess so.

WOTAN
(sombrely)

Was verlang'st du?	What do you demand of me?

FRICKA

Lass' von dem Wälsung! [32]	Abandon the Wälsung!

WOTAN
(with muffled voice)

Er geh' seines Weg's.	He'll go his own way.

FRICKA

Doch du – schütze ihn nicht,	But you – don't protect him
wenn zur Schlacht ihn der Rächer	when the avenger calls him to battle.
[ruft.	

WOTAN

Ich – schütze ihn nicht.	I'll not protect him.

FRICKA
(more animatedly)

Sieh' mir in's Auge,	Look me straight in the eye
sinne nicht Trug!	and don't think to deceive me.
Die Walküre wend' auch von ihm!	Turn the valkyrie from him, too.

WOTAN

Die Walküre walte frei.	Let the valkyrie choose for herself.

FRICKA

Nicht doch! Deinen Willen	No, no! For it's *your* will
vollbringt sie allein:	alone she carries out:
verbiete ihr Siegmund's Sieg!	forbid her Siegmund's victory!

WOTAN
(breaking out in a violent inner struggle)

Ich kann ihn nicht fällen:	I cannot kill him:
er fand mein Schwert! [23]	he found my sword!

FRICKA

Entzieh' dem den Zauber,
zerknick' es dem Knecht:
schutzlos find' ihn der Feind!

Withdraw its magic,
let it break in his servile hands:
let his enemy find him defenceless!

(Brünnhilde's call can be heard from the heights.) [30]

BRÜNNHILDE

Heiaha! Heiaha! Hojotoho!

Heiaha! Heiaha! Hojotoho!

FRICKA

Dort kommt deine kühne Maid:
jauchzend jagt sie daher.

Here comes your valiant maid:
exulting, she storms this way!

BRÜNNHILDE

Heiaha! Heiaha!
Heiohotojo! Hotojoha!

Heiaha! Heiaha!
Heiohotojo! Hotojoha!

WOTAN

Ich rief sie für Siegmund zu Roß!   I called her to horse for Siegmund!

(Brünnhilde appears with her horse on the mountain path on the left. On noticing Fricka, she stops abruptly and, throughout the following, leads her horse silently and slowly down the rocky path: there she stables it in a cave.)

FRICKA

Deiner ew'gen Gattin
  heilige Ehre
beschirme heut' ihr Schild!
  Von Menschen verlacht,
  verlustig der Macht,
gingen wir Götter zu Grund,
  würde heut' nicht hehr
  und herrlich mein Recht
gerächt von der muthigen Maid. –
Der Wälsung fällt meiner Ehre: –   [9]

empfah' ich von Wotan den Eid?

Your eternal spouse's
  sacred honour
her shield must defend today.
  Derided of men,
  deprived of our might,
we gods would go to our ruin
  were my rights
  not avenged, nobly and grandly,
by your mettlesome maid today. –
The Wälsung falls for my honour's
  [sake: –
will Wotan give me his oath?

WOTAN

(throwing himself on a rocky seat in terrible dejection) [32]

Nimm den Eid!   Take my oath!

(Fricka strides towards the back of the stage: there she meets Brünnhilde and pauses for a moment before her.)

Heervater
  harret dein:
  lass' ihn dir künden
wie das Loos er gekies't!

The Lord of Battles
  awaits you:
  let him explain
the fate he has chosen!

(She drives quickly away. [19, 32] Surprised and with an expression of concern, Brünnhilde moves towards Wotan, who, leaning on the rocky seat, is sunk in gloomy brooding.)

SCENE TWO

BRÜNNHILDE

Schlimm, fürcht' ich,	The quarrel, I fear,
schloß der Streit,	must have ended badly
lachte Fricka dem Loose! – [32]	if Fricka laughed at the outcome. –
Vater, was soll	What is it, father,
dein Kind erfahren?	your child must learn?
Trübe scheinst du und traurig!	Sad you seem and downhearted.

WOTAN
(dropping his arm in a gesture of helplessness and allowing his head to sink on his breast)

In eig'ner Fessel	In my own fetters
fing ich mich: –	I find myself caught: –
ich unfreiester Aller!	I, least free of all things living!

BRÜNNHILDE

So sah ich dich nie!	Never have I seen you so!
Was nagt dir das Herz?	What is it that gnaws at your heart?

(From this point onwards, Wotan's expression and gestures grow in intensity, until they culminate in the most terrible outburst.) [19]

WOTAN

O heilige Schmach!	O righteous disgrace!
O schmählicher Harm!	O shameful sorrow!
Götternoth!	Gods' direst need!
Götternoth!	Gods' direst distress!
Endloser Grimm!	Infinite fury!
Ewiger Gram!	Grief neverending!
Der Traurigste bin ich von Allen!	The saddest am I of all living things!

BRÜNNHILDE
(startled, throwing down shield, spear and helmet and sinking down at Wotan's feet in anxious solicitude)

Vater! Vater!	Father! Father!
Sage, was ist dir?	Tell me, what ails you?
Wie erschreck'st du mit Sorge dein [Kind!	How you startle your child and fill her [with fear!
Vertraue mir:	Confide in me:
ich bin dir treu;	I'm true to you;
sieh', Brünnhilde bittet!	see, Brünnhilde begs you.

(Lovingly and anxiously she rests her head and hands on his knees and lap.) [26a, 26b]

WOTAN
(gazing at length into her eyes, after which he strokes her hair in a gesture of spontaneous tenderness. As if emerging from deep thought, he finally begins in whispered tones)

Lass' ich's verlauten,	If I let it be spoken aloud,
lös' ich dann nicht	shall I not loosen
meines Willens haltenden Haft?	my will's restraining hold?

BRÜNNHILDE
(very quietly)

Zu Wotan's Willen sprichst du,[55]	To Wotan's will you speak[55]
sag'st du mir was du willst:	when you tell me what you will:
wer – bin ich,	who am I
wär' ich dein Wille nicht?	if not your will?

WOTAN[56]
(very quietly)

Was Keinem in Worten ich künde,		What in words I reveal to no one,
unausgesprochen		let it stay
bleib' es denn ewig:		unspoken for ever:
mit mir nur rath' ich,		with myself I commune
red' ich zu dir. – – –	[32]	when I speak with you. – – –
Als junger Liebe		When youthful love's
Lust mir verblich,		delights had faded,
verlangte nach Macht mein Muth:		I longed in my heart for power:
von jäher Wünsche		impelled by the rage
Wüthen gejagt,		of impulsive desires,
gewann ich mir die Welt.		I won for myself the world.
Unwissend trugvoll		Unwittingly false
Untreue übt' ich,		I acted unfairly,
band durch Verträge		binding by treaties
was Unheil barg:		what boded ill:
listig verlockte mich Loge,		cunningly Loge lured me on
der schweifend nun verschwand. –		but vanished while roaming the world. –
Von der Liebe doch	[32]	Yet I did not like
mocht' ich nicht lassen;		to give up love;
in der Macht verlangt' ich nach		in the midst of power I longed for love's
[Minne:		[pleasures:
den Nacht gebar,		born of the night,
der bange Nibelung,		the fearful Nibelung,
Alberich brach ihren Bund;	[3]	Alberich, severed its bonds;
er fluchte der Liebe,		he laid a curse upon love
und gewann durch den Fluch		and, by that curse, won
des Rheines glänzendes Gold,	[5]	the glittering gold of the Rhine
und mit ihm maaßlose Macht.		and, with it, measureless might.
Den Ring, den er schuf,	[6]	The ring that he forged
entriß ich ihm listig:		I cunningly wrenched away from him:
doch nicht dem Rhein		not to the Rhine though
gab ich ihn zurück;		did I return it;
mit ihm bezahlt' ich		with it I paid for
Walhall's Zinnen,	[8]	Valhalla's battlements,
der Burg, die Riesen mir bauten,		the bulwark that giants had built for me,
aus der ich der Welt nun gebot. –		from which I now ruled the world. –
Die Alles weiß	[20]	She who knows all
was einstens war,		that ever was,
Erda, die weihlich		Erda, the awesomely
weiseste Wala,		all-wise vala,
rieth mir ab von dem Ring,		told me to give up the ring

warnte vor ewigem Ende.
     and warned of an end everlasting.

(somewhat more forcefully)

Von dem Ende wollt' ich
mehr noch wissen;
     Of that end I wanted
     to know yet more;

(guardedly)

doch schweigend entschwand mir
[das Weib.
     but the woman vanished in silence.

(more animated)

Da verlor ich den leichten Muth; [32]
zu wissen begehrt' es den Gott:
  in den Schooß der Welt
  schwang ich mich hinab,
  mit Liebes-Zauber
  zwang ich die Wala,
stört' ihres Wissens Stolz,
daß sie Rede nun mir stand.
Kunde empfing ich von ihr;
von mir doch empfing[57] sie ein
[Pfand:
der Welt weisestes Weib
gebar mir, Brünnhilde, dich. [26a]
  Mit acht Schwestern [30]
  zog ich dich auf:
  durch euch Walküren
  wollt' ich wenden,
  was mir die Wala
  zu fürchten schuf –
ein schmähliches Ende der Ew'gen.
  Daß stark zum Streit [30]
  uns fände der Feind,
hieß ich euch Helden mir schaffen:
  die herrisch wir sonst
  in Gesetzen hielten,
  die Männer, denen
  den Muth wir gewehrt,
  die durch trüber Verträge
  trügende Bande
  zu blindem Gehorsam
  wir uns gebunden –
  die solltet zu Sturm [30]

     Then I lost all lightness of heart;
     the god desired knowledge:
       into the womb of the world
       I descended,
       mastered the vala
       with love's magic spell
     and broke her wisdom's pride,
     that she gave account of herself.
     Knowledge I gained from her;
     from me though she gained[57] a pledge:

     the world's wisest woman
     bore to me, Brünnhilde, you.
       With eight sisters
       I brought you up:
       through you valkyries
       I hoped to avert
       the fate that the vala
       had made me fear –
     a shameful end of the gods everlasting.
       That our foe might find us
       stalwart in strife
     I bade you bring me heroes:
       those men whom, high-handed,
       we tamed by our laws,
       those men whose mettle
       we held in check
       by binding them to us
       in blind allegiance
       through troubled treaties'
       treacherous bonds –
     you'd to spur them on

(increasingly animated, but with muted force)

und Streite ihr stacheln,
ihre Kraft reizen
zu rauhem Krieg,
daß kühner Kämpfer Schaaren
ich samm'le in Walhall's Saal. [8]

     to onslaught and strife,
     honing their strength
     for hot-blooded battle,
     so that hosts of valiant warriors
     I'd gather in Valhalla's hall.

BRÜNNHILDE

Deinen Saal füllten wir weidlich:
viele schon führt' ich dir zu.

     Bravely we filled your hall:
     many I brought you myself.

Was macht dir nun Sorge,		What is it you fear
da nie wir gesäumt?		since we've never yet failed?

WOTAN
(more muted again)

Ein Andres ist's:	[20]	There's something else
achte es wohl,		– mark me well –
wess' mich die Wala gewarnt! –	[6]	of which the vala warned me. –
Durch Alberich's Heer		Through Alberich's host
droht uns das Ende:		our end now threatens:
mit neidischem Grimm		burning with envious rage,
grollt mir der Niblung;		the Nibelung bears me ill-will;

(more animated)

doch scheu' ich nun nicht		but I'm not now afraid
seine nächtigen Schaaren –		of his forces of night –
meine Helden schüfen mir Sieg.		my heroes would defeat him.

(more muted)

Nur wenn je den Ring	[6]	Only were he
zurück er gewänne –		to win back the ring

(even more muted)

dann wäre Walhall verloren:		would Valhalla then be lost:
der der Liebe fluchte,		he who laid a curse on love,
er allein		he alone
nützte neidisch		in his envy would use
des Ringes Runen		the runes of the ring
zu aller Edlen		to the noble gods'
endloser Schmach;		unending shame;
der Helden Muth		my heroes' hearts

(more animated)

entwendet' er mir;		he'd turn against me,
die kühnen selber		forcing the brave
zwäng' er zum Kampf;		to battle with me
mit ihrer Kraft		and, with their strength,
bekriegte er mich.		wage war against me.

(muted)

Sorgend sann ich nun selbst	[6]	Troubled, I brooded in turn
den Ring dem Feind zu entreißen:		how to wrest the ring from my foe:

(muted)

der Riesen einer,	[11]	one of the giants,
denen ich einst		whose work
mit verfluchtem Gold		I rewarded
den Fleiß vergalt,		with gold that was cursed,
Fafner hütet den Hort,		Fafner broods on the hoard
um den er den Bruder gefällt.		for which he killed his brother.
Ihm müßt' ich den Reif entringen,		From him I must wrest the ring,
den selbst als Zoll ich ihm zahlte:		which I paid him once as tribute:
doch mit dem ich vertrug,	[12]	having treated with him,
ihn darf ich nicht treffen;		I cannot meet him;
machtlos vor ihm		fatally weakened, my courage
erläge mein Muth.		would fail me.

(bitterly)

Das sind die Bande,
die mich binden:
der durch Verträge ich Herr,   [9]
den Verträgen bin ich nun
[Knecht.   [32b, 23]
Nur Einer könnte
was ich nicht darf:
ein Held, dem helfend
nie ich mich neigte;
der fremd dem Gotte,
frei seiner Gunst,
unbewußt,
ohne Geheiß,
aus eig'ner Noth
mit der eig'nen Wehr
schüfe die That,
die ich scheuen muß,
die nie mein Rath ihm rieth,
wünscht sie auch einzig mein
[Wunsch. –   [32b]
Der entgegen dem Gott
für mich föchte,
den freundlichen Feind,
wie fände ich ihn?
Wie schüf' ich den Freien,
den nie ich schirmte,
der im eig'nen Trotze
der trauteste mir?
Wie macht' ich den And'ren,
der nicht mehr ich,
und aus sich wirkte
was ich nur will? –
O göttliche Noth!   [3, 20]
Gräßliche Schmach!
Zum Ekel find' ich
ewig nur mich
in Allem was ich erwirke!
Das And're, das ich ersehne,
das And're erseh' ich nie;
denn selbst muß der Freie sich
[schaffen –
Knechte erknet' ich mir nur!   [32a, 32b]

These are the bonds
that hold me in thrall:
I, lord of treaties,
am now a slave to those treaties.

One man alone could do
what I myself may not:
a hero I never
stooped to help;
who, unknown to the god
and free of his favours,
all unwitting,
without his bidding,
by his own need alone
and with his own weapon
might do the deed
which *I* must shun
and which my urging urged not on him,
though it were wished by my wish
[alone. –
He who, against the god,
would fight for me,
o how might I find
that friendly foe?
How fashion a free man
whom I never sheltered
and who, in his own defiance,
is yet the dearest of men to me?
How can I make that other man
who's no longer me
and who, of himself, achieves
what I alone desire? –
O godly distress!
O hideous shame!
To my loathing I find
only ever myself
in all that I encompass!
That other self for which I yearn,
that other self I never see;
for the free man has to fashion
himself –
serfs are all I can shape!

BRÜNNHILDE

Doch der Wälsung, Siegmund?
wirkt er nicht selbst?   [24]

But the Wälsung, Siegmund?
Does he not act of himself?

WOTAN

Wild durchschweift' ich

I roamed the wildwood

mit ihm die Wälder;
gegen der Götter Rath
reizte kühn ich ihn auf –
gegen der Götter Rache
schützt ihn nun einzig das Schwert, [23a]

with him;
against the gods' advice,
I boldly urged him on –
against the gods' revenge,
he's shielded now by that sword

(slowly and bitterly)

das eines[58] Gottes
Gunst ihm beschied. –   [32]
Wie wollt' ich listig
selbst mich belügen?
So leicht ja entfrug
mir Fricka den Trug!
Zu tiefster Scham
durchschaute sie mich: –

which the grace
of a[58] god bestowed upon him. –
How slyly I sought
to deceive myself!
How easily Fricka
uncovered the fraud!
To my deepest shame
she saw straight through me: –

(quickly)

ihrem Willen muß ich gewähren!   now I must yield to her will!

BRÜNNHILDE

So nimmst du von Siegmund den Sieg?   And so you'll not let Siegmund win?

WOTAN

Ich berührte Alberich's Ring –   [6]
gierig hielt ich das Gold!
   Der Fluch, den ich floh,   [26a]
   nicht flieht er nun mich: –
was ich liebe, muß ich verlassen,
morden, wen je ich minne,
   trügend verrathen
   wer mir traut! –   [19]

I once held Alberich's ring,
greedily grasped the gold!
   The curse that I fled
   won't flee from me now: –
what I love I must relinquish,
murder him whom I cherish
   and foully betray
   him who trusts me! –

(Wotan's demeanour passes from an expression of the most terrible anguish to one of desperation.) [23]

Fahre denn hin,
herrische Pracht,
göttlichen Prunkes
prahlende Schmach!
Zusammen breche
was ich gebaut!
Auf geb' ich mein Werk;
nur Eines will ich noch:
   das Ende – –   [23b]
   das Ende! –

Farewell, then,
imperious pomp!
Godly show's
resplendent shame!
Let all I raised
now fall in ruins!
My work I abandon;
one thing alone do I want:
   the end – –
   the end! –

(He pauses in thought.)

Und für das Ende
sorgt Alberich! –
Jetzt versteh' ich
den stummen Sinn
des wilden Wortes der Wala: –
»Wenn der Liebe finst'rer Feind
zürnend zeugt einen Sohn,
   der Sel'gen Ende

And Alberich will see
to that end! –
Only now do I fathom
the silent sense
of the vala's mysterious words: –
'When love's dark foe
begets a son in his fury,
   the end of the gods

säumt dann nicht!« –   [23a, 28, 8, 4]
Vom Niblung jüngst
vernahm ich die Mär',
daß ein Weib der Zwerg bewältigt,

dess' Gunst Gold ihm erzwang.
Des Hasses Frucht
hegt eine Frau;
des Neides Kraft
kreiß't ihr im Schooß:
das Wunder gelang
dem Liebelosen;
doch der in Lieb' ich frei'te,
den Freien erlang' ich mir nicht! –

(rising in bitter anger)

So nimm meinen Segen,   [28, 8, 4]
Niblungen-Sohn!
Was tief mich ekelt,
dir geb' ich's zum Erbe,
der Gottheit nichtigen Glanz:
zernage ihn gierig dein[59] Neid!

won't long be delayed!' –
Of the Niblung I lately
heard it told
that the dwarf had had his way with a
[woman,
whose favours gold had gained him.
A woman harbours
the seed of hate;
the force of envy
stirs in her womb:
this wonder befell
the loveless dwarf;
yet I who wooed in love
cannot father one who is free! –

So take my blessing,
Nibelung son!
What I loathe most deeply
I leave as your legacy:
godhood's empty glitter.
May your envy greedily gnaw it away!

BRÜNNHILDE
(alarmed)

O sag', künde!
Was soll nun dein Kind?

Speak, o tell me,
what must your child do now?

WOTAN
(embittered)

Fromm streite für Fricka,
hüte ihr Eh' und Eid'!

(dryly)

Was sie erkor,
das kiese auch ich:
was frommte mir eig'ner Wille?
Einen Freien kann ich nicht wollen –
für Fricka's Knechte
kämpfe nun du!

Fight bravely for Fricka,
for her, guard both wedlock and vows!

What she has chosen
I choose, too:
what use would my own will be to me?
I cannot will a free man –
for Fricka's slaves
now fight!

BRÜNNHILDE

Weh! nimm reuig
zurück das Wort!
Du lieb'st Siegmund:
dir zu Lieb' –
ich weiß es – schütz' ich den Wälsung.

In pity's name
take back your word!
You love Siegmund:
out of love for you –
I know – I'll shield the Wälsung.

WOTAN

Fällen sollst du Siegmund,
für Hunding erfechten den Sieg!
Hüte dich wohl

Siegmund you must kill
and master the field for Hunding!
Guard yourself well

und halte dich stark;
all' deiner Kühnheit
entbiete im Kampf:
ein Sieg-Schwert [23]
schwingt Siegmund –
schwerlich fällt er dir feig.

and save your strength;
summon up all your boldness
for battle:
Siegmund wields
a victorious sword –
even to you he'll not easily fall.

BRÜNNHILDE

Den du zu lieben
stets mich gelehrt,
der in hehrer Tugend
dem Herzen dir theuer –
gegen ihn zwingt mich nimmer
dein zwiespältig Wort.

Him whom you always
taught me to love,
whose lofty valour
is dear to your heart –
never will your two-faced words
force me to turn against him.

WOTAN

Ha, Freche du!
Frevelst du mir?
Wer bist du, als meines Willens
blind wählende Kür? – [9]
Da mit dir ich tagte,
sank ich so tief,
daß zum Schimpf der eig'nen
Geschöpfe ich ward?
Kenn'st du Kind meinen Zorn?
Verzage dein Muth,
wenn je zermalmend
auf dich stürzte sein Strahl!
In meinem Busen
berg' ich den Grimm,
der in Grau'n und Wust
wirft eine Welt,
die einst zur Lust mir gelacht: –
wehe dem, den er trifft!
Trauer schüf' ihm sein Trotz! – [32b]
Drum rath' ich dir,
reize mich nicht;
besorge was ich befahl: –
Siegmund falle! – [23a]
Dieß sei der Walküre Werk.

Ha, insolent child!
How dare you insult me!
What *are* you if not the blindly
elective tool of my will? –
In conferring with you,
have I sunk so low
that I'm scorned
by creatures of my own making?
Do you know my anger, child?
May your courage fail
if its lightning flash
were to strike you with crushing force!
Within my breast
I harbour the rage
that can plunge into dread
and confusion a world
which once smiled upon me in joy: –
woe unto him whom it strikes!
His defiance would bring him grief! –
And so I warn you:
don't provoke me;
see that you do as I said: –
Siegmund shall fall! –
Let this be the valkyrie's task.

(He storms away and is soon lost from sight among the mountains on the left.) [32b, 8, 31, 32]

BRÜNNHILDE
(remaining where she is, shocked and stunned)

So – sah ich
Siegvater nie,
erzürnt' ihn sonst wohl auch ein
[Zank!

Thus have I never seen
Father of Victories,
oft though wrangle roused him to wrath!

(She bends down sadly and picks up her weapons, with which she again arms herself.)
[32a, 30]

Schwer wiegt mir	The weight of my weapons
der Waffen Wucht: –	weighs heavy upon me: –
wenn nach Lust ich focht,	when I fought to my liking
wie waren sie leicht! –	how light they were then! –
Zu böser Schlacht	To an evil fight
schleich' ich heut' so bang! –	I creep today in fear! –

(She broods to herself and then sighs.)

Weh', mein Wälsung!	[32]	Alas, my Wälsung!
Im höchsten Leid		In deepest grief
muß dich treulos die Treue		a faithful woman must faithlessly forsake
[verlassen! –		[you! –

(She turns slowly towards the back of the stage.) [32b]

SCENE THREE

(On reaching the mountain ridge, Brünnhilde gazes down into the gorge and sees Siegmund and Sieglinde; she watches them approaching for a moment, then goes into the cave where her horse is stabled, thus disappearing completely from the audience. Siegmund and Sieglinde appear on the mountain ridge. Sieglinde is hurrying on ahead; Siegmund tries to restrain her.) [26a]

SIEGMUND

Raste nun hier:	Rest here now:
gönne dir Ruh'!	grant yourself respite!

SIEGLINDE

Weiter! Weiter!	Further! Further!

SIEGMUND
(embracing her with gentle force)

Nicht weiter nun!	No further now!

(He clasps her firmly to him.)

Verweile, süßestes Weib! –	Tarry here, sweetest of wives!
Aus Wonne-Entzücken	From the transports of bliss
zucktest du auf,	you started up
mit jäher Hast	and rushed away
jagtest du fort;	in headlong haste;
kaum folgt' ich der wilden Flucht:	I could scarcely follow your breakneck
	[flight:
durch Wald und Flur,	through forest and field,
über Fels und Stein,	over crag and rock,
sprachlos schweigend	speechless, silent,
sprang'st du dahin;	onward you sprang;
kein Ruf hielt dich zur Rast.	no call would bring you to rest.

(She stares wildly ahead of her.)

Ruhe nun aus:		Rest here awhile:
rede zu mir!		speak but a word!
Ende des Schweigens Angst!	[26]	End this speechless fear!

Sieh', dein Bruder
hält seine Braut:
Siegmund ist dir Gesell!

See, your brother
holds his bride:
Siegmund is your helpmeet!

SIEGLINDE

*(gazing into Siegmund's eyes with growing ecstasy; she then throws her arms passionately
about his neck and so remains for a moment; then she starts up in sudden terror.)*

Hinweg! hinweg!
flieh' die Entweihte!
Unheilig
umfängt dich ihr Arm;
entehrt, geschändet
schwand dieser Leib:
flieh' die Leiche,
lasse sie los!
Der Wind mag sie verweh'n,
die ehrlos dem Edlen sich gab! − − [26a]

Away! Away!
Flee one who's defiled!
Unhallowed
her arm enfolds you;
dishonoured, disgraced,
this body is dead:
flee from the corpse
and let it go!
May the wind waft her away
who, honourless, gave herself up to the
[hero! − −

Da er sie liebend umfing,
da seligste Lust sie fand,
da ganz sie minnte der Mann,
der ganz ihr Minne geweckt −
vor der süßesten Wonne
heiligster[60] Weihe,
die ganz ihr Sinn
und Seele durchdrang,
Grauen und Schauder
ob gräßlichster Schande
mußte mit Schreck
die Schmähliche fassen
die je dem Manne gehorcht,
der ohne Minne sie hielt! −

When he held her in loving embrace
and she herself found joy supreme
and was wholly loved by the man
who wholly awakened her love,
in the face of sweet rapture's
most hallowed[60] solemnity,
wholly imbuing
her senses and soul,
what horror and dread
at most horrible shame
were bound to inspire
with terror the whore
who had ever obeyed a man
who held her without any feelings of
[love! −

Lass' die Verfluchte,
lass' sie dich flieh'n!
Verworfen bin ich,
der Würde bar!
Dir reinstem Manne
muß ich entrinnen;
dir herrlichem darf ich
nimmer gehören:
Schande bring' ich dem Bruder,
Schmach dem freienden Freund! [29]

Forsake the accursèd creature,
let her flee far away!
Depraved am I
and devoid of all worth!
You purest of men,
from you I must run;
to so lordly a man
I may never belong:
shame I bring to my brother,
offence to the friend who has wooed me!

SIEGMUND

Was je Schande dir schuf,
das büßt nun des Frevlers Blut!
Drum fliehe nicht weiter;
harre des Feindes;
hier − soll er mir fallen:

Whatever shame has done to you
the villain's blood shall now blot out!
So fly no further;
wait for our foe;
it's here he'll fall before me:

wenn Nothung ihm		when Nothung now
das Herz zernagt,	[23]	but gnaws his heart,
Rache dann hast du erreicht!		vengeance then you'll have won!

SIEGLINDE
(starting up and listening) [28]

Horch! die Hörner –	Hark! The horns –
hör'st du den Ruf? –	do you hear their call? –
Ringsher tönt	The furious bray rings
wüthend Getös';	forth all around;
aus Wald und Gau	yonder it yells
gellt es herauf.	from forest and shire.
Hunding erwachte	Hunding has woken
aus hartem Schlaf;	from heavy sleep;
Sippen und Hunde	kinsmen and hounds
ruft er zusammen;	he calls together;
muthig gehetzt	soundly harried,
heult die Meute,	the pack is howling
wild bellt sie zum Himmel	and baying wildly heavenwards
um der Ehe gebrochenen Eid!	at wedlock's broken vow!

(staring ahead of her, as if demented)

Wo bist du, Siegmund?	Where are you, Siegmund?
seh' ich dich noch?	Can I still see you?
Brünstig geliebter	Ardently cherished,
leuchtender Bruder?	light-bringing brother!
Deines Auges Stern	Let your star-bright eye
lass' noch einmal mir strahlen:	shine upon me again
wehre dem Kuß	and shun not the kiss
des verworf'nen Weibes nicht! –	of a fallen woman! –

(She has thrown herself, sobbing, on his breast; she then starts up again in fear.)

Horch! o horch!		Hark! O hark!
das ist Hunding's Horn!		That is Hunding's horn!
Seine Meute naht	[32]	His pack is approaching,
mit mächt'ger Wehr.		mightily armed!
Kein Schwert frommt		No sword can resist
vor der Hunde Schwall: –		the hounds' seething horde: –
wirf es fort, Siegmund! –		cast it off, Siegmund! –
Siegmund – wo bist du? –	[20]	Siegmund – where are you? –
Ha dort – ich sehe dich –		Ha! There! I can see you –
schrecklich Gesicht! –		terrible sight! –
Rüden fletschen		Scenting flesh,
die Zähne nach Fleisch;		the dogs bare their fangs;
sie achten nicht		they pay no heed
deines edlen Blick's;		to your noble mien;
bei den Füßen packt dich		their firm-gripping teeth
das feste Gebiß –		tear at your feet –
du fällst –		you fall –
in Stücken zerstaucht das Schwert: –		the sword is shivered in shards: –
die Esche stürzt –	[23]	the ash-tree topples –
es bricht der Stamm! –		the trunk is riven! –

Bruder! mein Bruder!		Brother! My brother!
Siegmund – ha! –		Siegmund – ha! –

(She sinks senseless into Siegmund's arms.)

SIEGMUND

Schwester! Geliebte!		Sister! Beloved!

(He listens to her breathing and convinces himself that she is still alive. [26a] He lets her sink down with him so that, as he himself sinks into a sitting position, her head rests on his lap. They both remain in this position until the end of the following scene. Long silence, during which Siegmund bends over Sieglinde with tender care and presses a long kiss upon her brow.)

SCENE FOUR

(Leading her horse by the bridle, Brünnhilde emerges from the cave and advances slowly and solemnly to the front of the stage. She pauses and observes Siegmund from a distance. Again she advances slowly. She stops, somewhat closer to him. She carries her shield and spear in one hand, resting the other on her horse's neck, and thus observes Siegmund with a grave expression.)

BRÜNNHILDE

Siegmund! –		Siegmund! –
Sieh' auf mich!	[34]	Look on me!
Ich – bin's,		I am she
der bald du folg'st.		whom you'll follow soon.

SIEGMUND
(raising his eyes to her)

Wer bist du, sag',	[33]	Who are you, say,
die so schön und ernst mir erscheint?		who appears before me so fair and [solemn?

BRÜNNHILDE

Nur Todgeweihten		The death-doomed alone
taugt mein Anblick:		are destined to look on me:
wer mich erschaut,		he who beholds me
der scheidet vom Lebens-Licht.		goes hence from life's light.
Auf der Walstatt allein	[8]	In battle alone
erschein' ich Edlen:		I appear before heroes:
wer mich gewahrt,		him who perceives me
zur Wal kor ich ihn mir.		I've chosen as one of the slain.

SIEGMUND
(gazing at length into her eyes, steadfastly and searchingly, then lowering his head in thought and finally turning to her resolutely again) [34]

Der dir nun folgt,	[33]	The hero who follows you –
wohin führ'st du den Helden?		where will you lead him?

BRÜNNHILDE

Zu Walvater,	[8] The Lord of the Slain
der dich gewählt,	has chosen you –
führ' ich dich:	to him do I lead you now:
nach Walhall folg'st du mir.	you'll follow me to Valhalla.

SIEGMUND

In Walhall's Saal
Walvater find' ich allein?

In Valhalla's hall
shall I find the Lord of the Slain alone?

BRÜNNHILDE

Gefall'ner Helden
hehre Schaar
umfängt dich hold
mit hoch-heiligem Gruß.

The noble host
of fallen heroes
welcomes you fondly
[30]   with greeting most holy.

SIEGMUND

Fänd' ich in Walhall
Wälse, den eig'nen Vater?

Might I find my own father,
Wälse, in Valhalla?

BRÜNNHILDE

Den Vater findet
der Wälsung dort.

[8]   The Wälsung will find
his father there.

SIEGMUND

Grüßt mich in Walhall
froh eine Frau?

Will a woman greet me
gladly in Valhalla?

BRÜNNHILDE

Wunschmädchen
walten dort hehr:
Wotan's Tochter
reicht dir traulich den Trank.

[10a]   There Wish-Maidens
hold sublime sway:
Wotan's daughter
will lovingly hand you your drink.

SIEGMUND

Hehr bist du,
und heilig gewahr' ich
das Wotanskind:
doch Eines sag' mir, du Ew'ge!
Begleitet den Bruder
die bräutliche Schwester?
Umfängt Siegmund
Sieglinde dort?

Awesome are you,
and Wotan's child
I behold with holy wonder:
but tell me one thing, immortal!
[33]   Will the sister-bride
go with her brother?
Will Siegmund embrace
Sieglinde there?

BRÜNNHILDE

Erdenluft
muß sie noch athmen:
Sieglinde
sieht Siegmund dort nicht!

Earthly air
she must breathe awhile:
Siegmund
will not see Sieglinde there!

SIEGMUND

(bending gently over Sieglinde, kissing her softly on the brow and turning calmly to Brünnhilde once more) [26b]

So grüße mir Walhall,   [8]   Then greet for me Valhalla,
grüße mir Wotan,   greet for me Wotan,
grüße mir Wälse   greet for me Wälse
und alle Helden −   and all the heroes −
grüß' auch die holden   greet, too, Wotan's
Wunsches-Mädchen: −   [10a] gracious daughters: −

(very emphatically)

zu ihnen folg' ich dir nicht.   [34] to them I follow you not.

BRÜNNHILDE

Du sah'st der Walküre   [33]   You saw the valkyrie's
sehrenden Blick: searing glance:
mit ihr mußt du nun zieh'n!   with her you must now go!

SIEGMUND

Wo Sieglinde lebt   [26]   Where Sieglinde lives
in Lust und Leid,   in delight and sorrow,
da will Siegmund auch säumen: there, too, shall Siegmund tarry:
noch machte dein Blick   [34]   your gaze has yet
nicht mich erbleichen: to make me blench:
vom Bleiben zwingt er mich nie![61]   it will never[61] force me from staying!

BRÜNNHILDE

So lange du leb'st   As long as you live,
zwäng' dich wohl nichts;   nothing, no doubt, would force you;
doch zwingt dich Thoren der Tod: [33] but death, you fool, will force you: −
ihn dir zu künden   hither I came
kam ich her.   to tell you this.

SIEGMUND

Wo wäre der Held,[62]   Where might the hero[62] be found
dem heut' ich fiel'?   to whom I'd fall today?

BRÜNNHILDE

Hunding fällt dich im Streit. [34] Hunding will slay you in single combat.

SIEGMUND

Mit stärk'rem drohe   Threaten things stronger
als Hunding's Streichen!   than Hunding's blows!
Lauerst du hier   If you're lurking here,
lüstern auf Wal,   lusting for slaughter,
jenen kiese zum Fang: choose Hunding as your booty:
ich denk' ihn zu fällen im Kampf.   I mean to slay him in battle.

BRÜNNHILDE

(shaking her head)

Dir, Wälsung −   For you, Wälsung,

höre mich wohl! –
dir ward das Loos gekies't.

                      – mark me well –
                      for you the lot was cast.

SIEGMUND

Kenn'st du dieß Schwert?   [23]   Do you know this sword?
Der mir es schuf,   He who sent it
beschied mir Sieg: decreed I should win:
deinem Drohen trotz' ich mit ihm!   with it I'll defy your threats!

BRÜNNHILDE
(with great emphasis)

Der dir es schuf,   He who sent it
beschied dir jetzt Tod: has now decreed your death:
seine Tugend nimmt er dem Schwert!   its virtue he takes from the sword!

SIEGMUND
(violently)

Schweig', und schrecke   Hush, or you'll frighten
die Schlummernde nicht!   my slumbering sister!
   (He bends tenderly over Sieglinde in an access of grief.) [26a]
Weh! Weh!   Woe! Ah woe!
Süßestes Weib!   O sweetest of wives!
Du traurigste aller Getreuen!   You saddest of all who are true!
 Gegen dich wüthet   Against you the world
 in Waffen die Welt: has taken up arms:
und ich, dem du einzig vertraut,   and I, whom you trusted alone
für den du ihr einzig getrotzt –   and for whom you defied the world alone,
 mit meinem Schutz   may I not[63] shield you
 nicht soll[63] ich dich schirmen,   with my shelter
die Kühne verrathen im Kampf? –   but must I betray my brave sister
                               [in battle?

Ha, Schande ihm,   Ha, shame upon him
 der das Schwert mir schuf,   who sent me the sword
beschied er mir Schimpf für Sieg!   if he now decrees not conquest but
                               [shame!

Muß ich denn fallen,   If I must fall,
 nicht fahr' ich nach Walhall –   I'll not go to Valhalla –
Hella halte mich fest!   Hella shall hold me fast!
   (He bends low over Sieglinde.) [26a]

BRÜNNHILDE
(shaken) [34]

So wenig achtest du   You're so little heedful
ewige Wonne?   of bliss everlasting?
   (hesitantly and cautiously)
Alles wär' dir   Is she all to you,
das arme Weib,   this pitiful woman
das müd' und harmvoll   who, tired and sorrowful,
matt auf dem Schooße dir hängt?   lies there, faint, in your lap?
Nichts sonst hieltest du hehr?   Is there nothing else you hold dear?

(gazing up at her, bitterly) [10]

So jung und schön	[33]	Young and fair
erschimmerst du mir:		though you shimmer before me:
doch wie kalt und hart		cold and hard
erkennt dich mein Herz! −		my heart now knows you to be! −
Kannst du nur höhnen,		Can you only scoff,
so hebe dich fort,		then be on your way,
du arge, fühllose Maid!		you false, unfeeling maid!
Doch mußt du dich weiden		But if you must gloat
an meinem Weh',		at this grief of mine,
mein Leiden letze dich denn;		then let my anguish gladden you;
meine Noth labe		may my plight regale
dein neidvolles Herz: −		your spiteful heart: −
nur[64] von Walhall's spröden Wonnen		but[64] of Valhalla's cold delights
sprich du wahrlich mir nicht!		speak not, in truth, to me!

BRÜNNHILDE

Ich sehe die Noth,	[26a]	I can see the need
die das Herz dir zernagt;		that gnaws at your heart;
ich fühle des Helden		I can feel the hero's
heiligen Harm − −		holy sorrow.
Siegmund, befiehl mir dein Weib:		Siegmund, commend your wife to me:
mein Schutz umfange sie fest!		let my shelter shield her securely!

SIEGMUND

Kein and'rer als ich	No one but I shall touch
soll die Reine lebend berühren:	the pure woman as long as she lives:
verfiel ich dem Tod,	if I'm fated to die,
die betäubte tödt' ich zuvor!	I shall kill her first as she lies here, dulled
	[by sleep.

BRÜNNHILDE
(with growing emotion)

Wälsung! Rasender!		Wälsung! Madman!
Hör' meinen Rath:	[26b]	Hear my plan:
befiehl mir dein Weib		commend me your wife
um des Pfandes willen,	[21]	for the sake of the pledge
das wonnig von dir es empfing!		she received from you in her bliss.

SIEGMUND
(drawing his sword)

Dieß Schwert −	[23]	This sword −
das dem Treuen ein Trugvoller schuf;		which a traitor gave to one who is true;
dieß Schwert −		this sword −
das feig vor dem Feind mich		which betrays me, fey, to my foe:
[verräth: −		
frommt es nicht gegen den Feind,		if it cannot avail against that foe,
so fromm' es denn wider den		then let it avail against a friend!
[Freund! −	[23]	

(He aims the sword at Sieglinde.)

Zwei Leben	Two lives
lachen dir hier: –	smile upon you here: –
nimm sie, Nothung,	take them, Nothung,
neidischer Stahl!	envious steel!
Nimm sie mit einem Streich!	Take them at a stroke!

BRÜNNHILDE
(in the most passionate and tempestuous show of sympathy)

Halt' ein, Wälsung,	[34]	Stay your hand, Wälsung!
höre mein Wort!		Hark to my word!
Sieglinde lebe –		Sieglind' shall live –
und Siegmund lebe mit ihr!		and Siegmund with her!
Beschlossen ist's;		My mind is made up;
das Schlachtloos wend' ich:		I'll change the course of the battle:
dir, Siegmund,		Siegmund, on you
schaff' ich Segen und Sieg!		both blessing and victory I bestow!
Hör'st du den Ruf?		Do you hear the call?
Nun rüste dich, Held!		Now arm yourself, hero!
Traue dem Schwert		Trust in the sword
und schwing' es getrost:		and wield it securely:
treu hält dir die Wehr,		the weapon will ever be steadfast,
wie die Walküre treu dich schützt! –		just as the valkyrie steadfastly shields [you! –
Leb' wohl, Siegmund,		Fare you well, Siegmund,
seligster Held!		most blessed of heroes!
Auf der Walstatt seh' ich dich wieder!		I'll see you again on the battlefield.

(She storms away and, together with her horse, disappears in a side gully on the left. Siegmund gazes after her in joy and elation. The stage has slowly become darker; heavy stormclouds descend over the back of the stage, gradually concealing the mountain walls, gorge and elevated ridge.) [26, 34]

SCENE FIVE

SIEGMUND
(bending over Sieglinde again and listening to her breathing)

Zauberfest		Proof against magic,
bezähmt ein Schlaf		slumber soothes
der Holden Schmerz und Harm: –		my sweetheart's pain and sorrow: –
da die Walküre zu mir trat,	[26b]	when the valkyrie came to my side,
schuf sie ihr den wonnigen Trost?		did she bring her this blissful solace?
Sollte die grimmige Wahl[65]	[34]	Should so fell a choice[65]
nicht schrecken ein gramvolles [Weib? –		not affright a sorrowing woman?
Leblos scheint sie,		Lifeless she seems
die dennoch lebt:		who is yet alive:
der Traurigen kos't		a smiling dream
ein lächelnder Traum. –		now speaks to her in her sadness. –

So schlumm're nun fort,	Sleep on
bis die Schlacht gekämpft,	till the battle be fought
und Frieden dich erfreu'!	and peace bring you joy once again.

(He lays her gently on the stone seat and kisses her brow in farewell. [10] He hears Hunding's horn-call and starts up resolutely.) [28]

Der dort mich ruft,	Let him who calls me
rüste sich nun;	arm himself now;
was ihm gebührt,	what he deserves
biet' ich ihm:	I offer unto him:

(He draws his sword.) [23]

| Nothung zahl' ihm den Zoll! | Nothung shall pay him his due! |

(He hurries to the back of the stage and, having reached the ridge, disappears at once in the dark stormclouds, from which flashes of lightning immediately break forth.)

SIEGLINDE
(beginning to stir more restlessly in her dreams)

Kehrte der Vater nun heim!	Would that our father were home!
Mit dem Knaben noch weilt er im	With the lad he yet lingers away in the
[Wald.⁶⁶ [28]	[wildwood.⁶⁶
Mutter! Mutter!	Mother! Mother!
mir bangt der Muth: –	my spirit fails me: –
nicht freund und friedlich [26b]	the strangers seem
scheinen die Fremden! –	neither friendly nor peaceful! –
Schwarze Dämpfe –	Dense black smoke –
schwüles Gedünst –	sultry mists –
feurige Lohe	tongues of flame
leckt schon nach uns –	are licking around us already –
es brennt das Haus –	the house is on fire –
zu Hilfe, Bruder!	help me, brother!
Siegmund! Siegmund!	Siegmund! Siegmund!

(She leaps up. Violent thunder and lightning.)

| Siegmund! – Ha! | Siegmund! – Ha! |

(She stares around her in mounting fear: almost the entire stage is shrouded in black stormclouds. Hunding's horn-call can be heard close at hand.)

HUNDING'S VOICE
(in the background from the direction of the mountain ridge)

Wehwalt! Wehwalt! [3]	Wehwalt! Wehwalt!
Steh' mir zum Streit,	Stand firm and fight,
sollen dich Hunde nicht halten!	or else the hounds will stop you!

SIEGMUND'S VOICE
(from further off in the ravine)

Wo birg'st du dich,	Where are you hiding
daß ich vorbei dir schoß?	that I shot straight past you?
Steh', daß ich dich stelle!	Stand still, that I may face you!

SIEGLINDE
(listening in a state of terrible anxiety)

| Hunding – Siegmund – | Hunding – Siegmund – |

könnt' ich sie sehen!   could I but see them!

Hieher, du frevelnder Freier: This way, you wicked wooer:
Fricka fälle dich hier!   let Fricka fell you here!

SIEGMUND
(now also from the ridge)
Noch wähn'st du mich waffenlos,   You still think me weaponless,
feiger Wicht!   cowardly wretch!
Droh'st du mit Frauen,   Though you threaten women,
so ficht nun selber,   fight now yourself,
sonst läßt dich Fricka im Stich!   lest Fricka should leave you in the lurch!
Denn sieh': deines Hauses   For lo! From your house's
heimischem Stamm   [23]   home-built trunk
entzog ich zaglos das Schwert;   I fearlessly drew forth the sword;
seine Schneide schmecke jetzt du!   its edge you now shall taste!

SIEGLINDE
(with the utmost force)
Haltet ein, ihr Männer!   Stop, you menfolk!
Mordet erst mich!   Kill me first!

(She rushes towards the mountain ridge but a light, which breaks out on the left over the combatants, suddenly dazzles her, so that she staggers away to the side, as though blinded. Brünnhilde appears in the blaze of light, hovering over Siegmund and protecting him with her shield.)

BRÜNNHILDE
Triff ihn, Siegmund!   Strike him, Siegmund!
Traue dem Schwert!   Trust in your sword!

(Siegmund is on the point of dealing Hunding a fatal blow when a bright red glow breaks through the clouds on the right; in it can be seen Wotan, standing over Hunding and holding his spear diagonally at Siegmund.) [30, 23]

WOTAN
Zurück vor dem Speer!   Get back from the spear!
In Stücken das Schwert!   In splinters the sword!

(Still holding her shield, Brünnhilde recoils in terror before Wotan: Siegmund's sword shatters on the outstretched spear. Hunding plunges his spear into the defenceless Siegmund's breast. Siegmund falls to the ground dead. Hearing his death-sigh, Sieglinde sinks to the ground with a scream, apparently lifeless. As Siegmund falls, the glowing lights at either side disappear; dense, dark clouds extend to the front of the stage: Brünnhilde is dimly discernible in them, turning to Sieglinde in precipitate haste.) [9, 23, 3, 29, 34]

BRÜNNHILDE
Zu Roß, daß ich dich rette!   To horse, that I may save you!

(She lifts Sieglinde quickly on to her horse, which is standing near the side gully, and immediately disappears with her. [30] The clouds then part in the middle, revealing Hunding in the act of drawing his spear from the fallen Siegmund's breast. [34] Surrounded by clouds, Wotan can be seen standing on a rock behind him, leaning on his spear and gazing in anguish at Siegmund's body.)

WOTAN
(to Hunding)

Geh' hin, Knecht!		Be gone, slave!
Kniee vor Fricka:		Kneel before Fricka:
meld' ihr, daß Wotan's Speer		tell her that Wotan's spear
gerächt, was Spott ihr schuf. –	[9]	has avenged what brought her disgrace. –
Geh'! – Geh'! –		Go! – Go! –

(At a contemptuous wave of his hand, Hunding falls to the ground, dead.)
(suddenly erupting in terrible anger) [32a]

Doch Brünnhilde –	[32b]	But Brünnhilde –
weh' der Verbrecherin!		woe betide the betrayer!
Furchtbar sei		The shameless child
die Freche gestraft,		shall be fearfully punished
erreicht mein Roß ihre Flucht!		once my horse overtakes her flight!

(He disappears amidst thunder and lightning. [32b] The curtain falls quickly.)

Act Three

SCENE ONE

(The curtain rises.[67] On the summit of a rocky mountain. A pinewood borders the stage on the left. On the right is the entrance to a rocky cave which forms a natural chamber: above it the cliff rises to its highest point. At the back, the view is completely open; rocks of varying height form the parapet of the precipice. Isolated cloudbanks scud past the edge of the cliff, as though driven by a storm. Gerhilde, Ortlinde, Waltraute and Schwertleite have taken up their positions on the peak, outside and above the cave; they are fully armed.) [30]

GERHILDE
(from her position at the top, calling towards the back of the stage, from where a dense cloud can be seen approaching)

Hojotoho! Hojotoho!	[31, 30]	Hojotoho! Hojotoho!
Heiaha! Heiaha!		Heiaha! Heiaha!
Helmwige, hier!		Helmwige, here!
Hieher mit dem Roß!		This way with your horse!

HELMWIGE'S VOICE
(from the back of the stage, through a speaking-trumpet)

Hojotoho! Hojotoho!	Hojotoho! Hojotoho!
Heiaha!	Heiaha!

(A flash of lightning breaks forth from the cloud, revealing a valkyrie on horseback: over her saddle hangs a slain warrior. The apparition draws closer, moving from right to left past the edge of the rock.)

GERHILDE, WALTRAUTE, SCHWERTLEITE

Heiaha! Heiaha!   Heiaha! Heiaha!
(The cloud with the apparition disappears behind the pinewood on the left.)

ORTLINDE
(calling into the pinewood)

Zu Ortlinde's Stute   Put your stallion
stell' deinen Hengst: with Ortlinde's mare:
mit meiner Grauen   your bay likes to graze
gras't gern dein Brauner!   with my grey!

WALTRAUTE
(calling into the wood)

Wer hängt dir im Sattel?   Who's that on your saddle?

HELMWIGE
(emerging from the pinewood)

Sintolt der Hegeling!   Sintolt the Hegeling!

SCHWERTLEITE

Führ' deinen Braunen   Take your bay
fort von der Grauen: well away from my grey:
Ortlinde's Mähre   Ortlinde's mare
trägt Wittig den Irming!⁶⁸   bears Wittig the Irming!⁶⁸

GERHILDE
(coming somewhat lower)

Als Feinde nur sah ich   Only as foes saw I
Sintolt und Wittig.   Sintolt and Wittig.

ORTLINDE
(leaping up)

Heiaha! Die Stute   [30]   Heiaha! Your stallion's
stößt mir der Hengst!   jostling my mare!
(She runs into the pinewood. Gerhilde, Helmwige and Schwertleite burst into laughter.) [31]

GERHILDE

Der Recken Zwist   The warriors' hate
entzweit noch die Rosse!   still embroils the horses!

HELMWIGE
(calling back into the pinewood)

Ruhig, Brauner!   Calm down, bay!
Brich nicht den Frieden!   Stop making trouble!

WALTRAUTE
(calling out from the highest peak, where she has replaced Gerhilde on watch)

Hojoho! Hojoho!   Hojoho! Hojoho!
(calling out upstage left)

Siegrune, hier!   Siegrune, here!

Wo säum'st du so lang? [30] What kept you so long?

(She listens to the left.)

SIEGRUNE'S VOICE
(through a speaking-trumpet, from upstage left)

Arbeit gab's! There was work to be done!
Sind die And'ren schon da? Are the others all ready?

SCHWERTLEITE, WALTRAUTE
(calling out upstage left)

Hojotoho! Hojotoho! [31] Hojotoho! Hojotoho!
Heiaha! Heiaha!

GERHILDE
(calling out upstage left)

Heiaha! Heiaha!

(Their gestures, together with the bright glow behind the wood, show that Siegrune has just arrived there.)

GRIMGERDE, ROSSWEISSE
(from upstage right, through a speaking-trumpet)

Hojotoho! Hojotoho! [31, 30] Hojotoho! Hojotoho!
Heiaha! Heiaha!

WALTRAUTE
(to the right)

Grimgerd' und Roßweiße! Grimgerd' and Rossweisse!

GERHILDE
(as before)

Sie reiten zu zwei. They ride as a pair.

(In a cloudbank which, lit by lightning, moves past from the right, Rossweisse and Grimgerde appear, also on horseback, each with a dead warrior on her saddle. Helmwige, Ortlinde and Siegrune have emerged from the pinewood and beckon to the new arrivals from the edge of the cliff.)

HELMWIGE, ORTLINDE, SIEGRUNE

Gegrüßt, ihr Reißige! Greetings, you riders!
Roßweiß' und Grimgerde! Rossweiss' and Grimgerde!

ROSSWEISSE'S AND GRIMGERDE'S VOICES
(through a speaking-trumpet)

Hojotoho! Hojotoho! Hojotoho! Hojotoho!
Heiaha! Heiaha!

(The apparition disappears behind the wood.)

THE SIX OTHER VALKYRIES

Hojotoho! Hojotoho! Hojotoho! Hojotoho!
Heiaha! Heiaha! Heiaha! Heiaha!

GERHILDE
(calling into the wood)

In Wald mit den Rossen   Into the woods with the horses
zu Rast und Weid'!   where they may rest and graze!

ORTLINDE
(similarly calling into the wood)

Führet die Mähren   Set the fillies
fern von einander,   far apart,
bis uns'rer Helden   until our heroes'
Haß sich gelegt!   hate has abated.
(The valkyries laugh.)

HELMWIGE

Der Helden Grimm[69]   The grey has atoned
büßte schon die Graue!   for the heroes' anger.[69]
(The valkyries laugh.)

ROSSWEISSE, GRIMGERDE
(coming out of the wood)

Hojotoho! Hojotoho!   Hojotoho! Hojotoho!

THE OTHER SIX VALKYRIES

Willkommen! Willkommen!   Welcome! Welcome!

SCHWERTLEITE

War't ihr Kühnen zu zwei?   Did you ride as a pair, brave sisters?

GRIMGERDE

Getrennt ritten wir   We rode apart
und trafen uns heut'.   and met today.

ROSSWEISSE

Sind wir alle versammelt,   If we're all assembled,
so säumt nicht lange: delay no longer:
nach Walhall brechen wir auf,   [8]   to Valhalla let's set out
Wotan zu bringen die Wal.   and bring the slain to Wotan.

HELMWIGE

Acht sind wir erst: We're only eight:
eine noch fehlt.   one is still missing.

GERHILDE

Bei dem braunen[70] Wälsung   With the tawny[70] Wälsung
weilt wohl noch Brünnhild'.   Brünnhilde must be delayed.

WALTRAUTE

Auf sie noch harren   We must wait
müssen wir hier: for her here:
Walvater gäb' uns   the Lord of the Slain would give us

grimmigen Gruß,		a grim-hearted greeting,
säh' ohne sie er uns nah'n!		were he to see us approach him without [her!

SIEGRUNE
(from her rocky vantage-point, from where she has been keeping watch)

Hojotoho! Hojotoho!		Hojotoho! Hojotoho!

(calling towards the back of the stage)

Hieher! Hieher!		This way! This way!

(to the others)

In brünstigem Ritt	[30]	At a furious pace
jagt Brünnhilde her.		Brünnhilde flies this way.

THE EIGHT VALKYRIES
(hurrying up to the look-out point)

Hojotoho! Hojotoho!	[31]	Hojotoho! Hojotoho!
Brünnhilde! hei!		Brünnhilde! Hey!

(They watch with growing astonishment.) [32b]

WALTRAUTE

Nach dem Tann lenkt sie		To the pinewood she steers
das taumelnde Roß.		the stumbling horse.

GRIMGERDE

Wie schnaubt Grane		How Grane groans
vom schnellen Ritt!		at the reckless ride!

ROSSWEISSE

So jach sah ich nie		I never saw valkyries
Walküren jagen!		flee so fast!

ORTLINDE

Was hält sie im Sattel?		What hangs from her saddle?

HELMWIGE

Das ist kein Held!		No hero it is.

SIEGRUNE

Eine Frau führt sie.	[26a]	She's bringing a woman.

GERHILDE

Wie fand sie die Frau?		Where did she find her?

SCHWERTLEITE

Mit keinem Gruß		No greeting
grüßt sie die Schwestern?		does she have for her sisters?

WALTRAUTE
(calling down, very loudly)

Heiaha! Brünnhilde!		Heiaha! Brünnhilde!

| hör'st du uns nicht? | Don't you hear us? |

ORTLINDE

| Helft der Schwester | Help your sister |
| vom Roß sich schwingen! | dismount from her horse! |

HELMWIGE, GERHILDE
(both running into the pinewood)

| Hojotoho! Hojotoho! | [31] | Hojototo! Hojotoho! |

SIEGRUNE, ROSSWEISSE
(running after them)

| Hojotoho! Hojotoho! | Hojotojo! Hojotoho! |

WALTRAUTE, GRIMGERDE, SCHWERTLEITE

| Haiaho! Heiaha! | Haiaho! Heiaha! |

WALTRAUTE
(looking into the wood)

| Zu Grunde stürzt | Grane the strong |
| Grane der starke! | drops to the ground! |

GRIMGERDE

| Aus dem Sattel hebt sie | From the saddle |
| hastig das Weib. | she hastily lifts the woman. |

ORTLINDE, WALTRAUTE, GRIMGERDE, SCHWERTLEITE
(all running into the wood)

| Schwester! Schwester! | Sister! Sister! |
| Was ist gescheh'n? | What has happened? |

(All eight valkyries return to the stage; with them comes Brünnhilde, supporting and leading Sieglinde.)

BRÜNNHILDE
(breathlessly)

| Schützt mich, und helft | Shield me, and help me |
| in höchster Noth! | in direst need! |

THE EIGHT VALKYRIES

Wo rittest du her	Whence have you ridden
in rasender Hast?	in furious haste?
So fliegt nur wer auf der Flucht!	Only one who is fleeing flies so fast!

BRÜNNHILDE

Zum ersten Mal flieh' ich	For the first time I flee
und bin verfolgt!	and am being pursued!
Heervater hetzt mir nach!	Father of Battles is hunting me down!

THE EIGHT VALKYRIES
(deeply alarmed)

Bist du von Sinnen?	Have you lost your senses?
Ha! Sprich! Sage uns! Wie?	Ha! Speak! Tell us! What?
Verfolgt dich Heervater?	Father of Battles pursues you?
Flieh'st du vor ihm?	Is it from him that you're fleeing?

BRÜNNHILDE
(turning anxiously to see what is happening, then coming back)

O Schwestern, späht	O sisters, watch
von des Felsens Spitze!	from the top of the crag.
Schaut nach Norden,	Look northwards to see
ob Walvater naht!	if the Lord of the Slain's drawing near!

(Ortlinde and Waltraute leap up to the vantage-point on the mountain summit.)

Schnell! Seht ihr ihn schon?	[32b]	Quick! Can you see him yet?

ORTLINDE

Gewittersturm	A thunder-storm's
weht von Norden.	blowing down from the north.

WALTRAUTE

Starkes Gewölk	Heavy clouds
staut sich dort auf!	are gathering there!

THE OTHER SIX VALKYRIES

Heervater reitet	The Father of Battles is riding
sein heiliges Roß![71]	his sacred steed.[71]

BRÜNNHILDE

Der wilde Jäger,[72]	The Wild Huntsman,[72]
der wüthend mich jagt,	who hunts me down in his fury,
er naht, er naht von Norden!	draws near, draws near from the north.
Schützt mich, Schwestern!	Shield me, sisters!
Wahret dieß Weib!	Save this woman!

SIX VALKYRIES
(without Ortlinde and Waltraute)

Was ist mit dem Weibe!	What ails the woman?

BRÜNNHILDE

Hört mich in Eile!	Hear me in haste!
Sieglinde ist es,	She's Sieglinde,
Siegmund's Schwester und Braut:	Siegmund's sister and bride:
gegen die Wälsungen	against the Wälsungs
wüthet Wotan in Grimm: —	Wotan angrily rages: —
dem Bruder sollte	Brünnhilde should have
Brünnhilde heut'	deprived her brother
entziehen den Sieg;	of victory today;
doch Siegmund schützt' ich	but I sheltered Siegmund
mit meinem Schild,	with my shield,

trotzend dem Gott: –
der traf ihn da selbst mit dem Speer.
　Siegmund fiel;
　doch ich floh
　fern mit der Frau:
　sie zu retten,
　eilt' ich zu euch,
　ob mich bange auch

defying the god,
who struck him himself with his spear.
　Siegmund fell;
　but I fled away
　with the woman:
　to save her
　I hurried to you,
　that, afraid as I am,

(faint-heartedly)

ihr berget vor dem strafenden
　[Streich.

you might hide me away from the
　[punishing blow.

SIX VALKYRIES
(without Ortlinde and Waltraute)

Bethörte Schwester!
Was thatest du?
Wehe! Wehe!
Brünnhilde, wehe!
Brach ungehorsam
Brünnhilde
Heervaters heilig Gebot?

O foolish sister!
What have you done?
Alas! Alas!
Brünnhild', alas!
Has Brünnhilde
wilfully broken
the Battle-Lord's holy behest?

WALTRAUTE
(on look-out)

Nächtig zieht es
von Norden heran.

[32b]　Night-like the storm
　　blows down from the north.

ORTLINDE
(on look-out)

Wüthend steuert
hieher der Sturm.

Hither in fury
the tempest is driven.

ROSSWEISSE, GRIMGERDE, SCHWERTLEITE

Wild wiehert
Walvaters Roß!

[3]　The Battle-Lord's steed
　　is whinnying wildly!

HELMWIGE, GERHILDE, SIEGRUNE

Schrecklich schnaubt es daher!

Fearfully snorting, it storms this way!

BRÜNNHILDE

Wehe der Armen,
wenn Wotan sie trifft:
den Wälsungen allen
droht er Verderben! –
Wer leih't mir von euch
das leichteste Roß,
das flink die Frau ihm entführ'?

Woe betide the wretched woman
if Wotan finds her here:
he threatens the ruin
of all the Wälsungs! –
Which of you'll lend me
the fleetest of steeds
that will swiftly spirit the woman away?

SIEGRUNE

Auch uns räth'st du

Us, too, you urge

rasenden Trotz?

to frenzied defiance?

BRÜNNHILDE

Roßweiße, Schwester!
Leih' mir deinen Renner!

Rossweisse, sister!
Lend me your racer!

ROSSWEISSE

Vor Walvater floh
der fliegende nie.

From the Father of Battles
my flying steed's never fled.

BRÜNNHILDE

Helmwige, höre!

Helmwige, hear me!

HELMWIGE

Dem Vater gehorch' ich.

I obey our father!

BRÜNNHILDE

Grimgerde! Gerhilde!
Gönnt mir eu'r Roß!
Schwertleite! Siegrune!
Seht meine Angst!
O seid mir treu,
wie traut ich euch war:
rettet dieß traurige Weib!

Grimgerde! Gerhilde!
Grant me your horses!
Schwertleite! Siegrune!
See, I'm afraid!
Dear to you as I was,
be true to me now
and save this sorrowing woman!

SIEGLINDE

(has been staring ahead, sombrely and coldly, but now starts up with a gesture of rejection as Brünnhilde embraces her warmly as if to protect her.)

Nicht sehre dich Sorge um mich:
einzig taugt mir der Tod!
  Wer hieß dich Maid
  dem Harst mich entführen?
  Im Sturm dort hätt' ich
  den Streich empfah'n
  von derselben Waffe,
  der Siegmund fiel:
  das Ende fand ich
  vereint mit ihm!
  Fern von Siegmund –
  Siegmund, von dir! –
  O deckte mich Tod,
  daß ich's denke!
  Soll um die Flucht
  dir Maid ich nicht fluchen,
so höre heilig mein Flehen –
stoße dein Schwert mir in's Herz!

Let care not afflict you for my sake:
death alone avails me!
Who bade you, maid,
bear me hence from the fray?
In the onslaught there
I'd have been struck down
by the selfsame spear
to which Siegmund fell:
I'd have met my end
united with him!
Far from Siegmund –
Siegmund, from you! –
Let death enfold me
lest I think of it!
Ere I curse you, maid,
for fleeing with me,
hear my holy entreaty and
drive your sword into my heart!

BRÜNNHILDE

Lebe, o Weib,
um der Liebe willen!

O woman, live
for the sake of love!

Rette das Pfand,
das von ihm du empfing'st:
(forcefully and insistently)
ein Wälsung wächst dir im Schooß!

Save the pledge
you received from him:

a Wälsung stirs in your womb!

(Sieglinde initially starts up violently, but her face immediately lights up with sublime joy.)

SIEGLINDE

Rette mich, Kühne!
Rette mein Kind!
Schirmt mich, ihr Mädchen,
mit mächtigstem Schutz!

Save me, brave woman!
Rescue my child!
Shield me, you maidens,
with mightiest shelter!

(An ever-darkening tempest rises in the background.) [32b]

WALTRAUTE
(on look-out)

Der Sturm kommt heran.

The storm's drawing nearer.

ORTLINDE
(also on look-out)

Flieh' wer ihn fürchtet!

Flee, all who fear it!

THE OTHER SIX VALKYRIES

Fort mit dem Weibe,
droht ihm Gefahr:
der Walküren keine
wag' ihren Schutz!

Away with the woman,
if danger besets her:
let none of the valkyries
dare to protect her!

SIEGLINDE
(kneeling before Brünnhilde)

Rette mich, Maid!
Rette die Mutter!

Save me, o maiden!
Rescue a mother!

BRÜNNHILDE
(raising Sieglinde to her feet with lively resolve)

So fliehe denn eilig –
und fliehe allein!
Ich – bleibe zurück,
biete mich Wotan's Rache:
an mir zögr' ich
den Zürnenden hier,
während du seinem Rasen
[entrinn'st. [32b]

Flee then in haste –
and flee alone!
I'll stay here
and face Wotan's vengeance:
here I'll forestall
the furious god,
while you escape from his frenzy.

SIEGLINDE

Wohin soll ich mich wenden?

Whither then should I turn?

BRÜNNHILDE

Wer von euch Schwestern
schweifte nach Osten?

Which of you sisters
has roamed to the east?

SIEGRUNE

Nach Osten weithin
dehnt sich ein Wald:
der Niblungen Hort
entführte Fafner dorthin.

Away to the east
a forest stretches:
there Fafner has taken
the Nibelung hoard.

SCHWERTLEITE

Wurmes-Gestalt
schuf sich der Wilde:
in einer Höhle
hütet er Alberich's Reif!

[6] The savage assumed
the shape of a dragon
and in a cave
he guards Alberich's ring.

GRIMGERDE

Nicht geheu'r ist's dort
für ein hilflos Weib.

[18] No place it is
for a helpless woman.

BRÜNNHILDE

Und doch vor Wotan's Wuth
schützt sie sicher der Wald:
ihn scheut der Mächt'ge
und meidet den Ort.[73]

And yet the forest
will surely shield her from Wotan's wrath:
the mighty god shuns it
and shies from the spot.[73]

WALTRAUTE
(on look-out)

Furchtbar fährt
dort Wotan zum Fels.

[32b] How fearfully Wotan
approaches the fell.

SIX VALKYRIES

Brünnhilde, hör'
seines Nahens Gebraus'!

Brünnhilde, hear
the roar as he nears!

BRÜNNHILDE

Fort denn eile
nach Osten gewandt!
Muthigen Trotzes
ertrag' alle Müh'n –
Hunger und Durst,
Dorn und Gestein;
lache, ob Noth,
ob Leiden dich nagt!
Denn eines wiss'
und wahr' es immer:
den hehrsten Helden der Welt
heg'st du, o Weib,
im schirmenden Schooß! –

Then hurry away
and head for the east!
In brave defiance
bear all burdens –
hunger and thirst,
thorns and stones;
[26a] laugh if need
or suffering plague you!
Know this alone
and ward it always:
[35] the world's noblest hero,
o woman, you harbour
within your sheltering womb! –

(She takes the fragments of Siegmund's sword from beneath her coat of mail and hands them to Sieglinde.)

Verwahr' ihm die starken
Schwertes-Stücken;
seines Vaters Walstatt

For him keep safe
the sword's stout fragments;
from his father's field

entführt' ich sie glücklich:		I haply took them:
der neu gefügt [35]		let him who'll wield
das Schwert einst schwingt,		the newly forged sword
den Namen nehm' er von mir –		receive his name from me –
»Siegfried« erfreu' sich des Sieg's! [23]		may 'Siegfried' joy in victory!

SIEGLINDE
(deeply stirred)

O hehrstes Wunder! [36]		Sublimest wonder!
Herrliche Maid!		Glorious maid!
Dir treuen dank' ich		You true-hearted woman, I thank you
heiligen Trost!		for sacred solace!
Für ihn, den wir liebten, [35]		For him whom we loved
rett' ich das liebste:		I'll save what's most dear:
meines Dankes Lohn		may my gratitude's guerdon
lache dir einst!		smile upon you one day!
Lebe wohl!		Fare you well!
Dich segnet Sieglinde's Weh'!		Let Sieglinde's woe be your blessing!

(She hurries away downstage left. The rocky height is surrounded by black thunderclouds; a terrible storm blows up from the back of the stage, while a fiery glow to the left of it grows ever brighter.) [3]

WOTAN'S VOICE
(through a speaking-trumpet)

Steh', Brünnhild'!	Stay, Brünnhild'!

(Having watched Sieglinde go, Brünnhilde turns upstage, looks into the pinewood, then returns downstage in her fear.)

ORTLINDE, WALTRAUTE
(descending from their vantage-point)

Den Fels erreichten	Horse and rider
Roß und Reiter!	have reached the rock!

ALL EIGHT VALKYRIES

Weh', Brünnhild'!	Alas, Brünnhild'!
Rache entbrennt!	Vengeance blazes.

BRÜNNHILDE

Ach, Schwestern, helft!	Ah, sisters, help!
Mir schwankt das Herz!	How my heart is pounding!
Sein Zorn zerschellt mich, [32b]	His wrath will crush me,
wenn euer Schutz ihn nicht zähmt.	unless your shelter can curb it.

THE EIGHT VALKYRIES
(retreating in fear up the rocky cliff and drawing Brünnhilde with them)

Hieher, Verlor'ne!	Hither, lost sister!
Lass' dich nicht seh'n!	Let him not see you!
Schmiege dich an uns,	Huddle closer
und schweige dem Ruf!	and heed not his call!

(They hide Brünnhilde in their midst and look anxiously in the direction of the pinewood,

which is now lit up by a brilliant fiery glow, while the front of the stage has become completely dark.)

Weh'!	Alas!
Wüthend schwingt sich	In his fury Wotan dismounts
Wotan vom Roß –	from his horse –
hieher ras't	hither he storms
sein rächender Schritt!	with vengeful step!

SCENE TWO

(Wotan emerges from the pinewood in an access of fury and strides impetuously towards the group of valkyries on the cliff, looking for Brünnhilde.) [8]

WOTAN

Wo ist Brünnhild',	Where is Brünnhild',
wo die Verbrecherin?	where the delinquent?
Wagt ihr, die böse	How dare you hide
vor mir zu bergen?	the traitress from me?

THE EIGHT VALKYRIES

Schrecklich ertos't dein Toben: –	How fearful your fury resounds: –
was thaten, Vater, die Töchter,	father, what've your daughters done
daß sie dich reizten	to rouse you
zu rasender Wuth?	to raging anger?

WOTAN

Wollt ihr mich höhnen?	How dare you mock me?
Hütet euch, Freche!	Beware, brazen creatures!
Ich weiß: Brünnhilde	I know that you're hiding
bergt ihr vor mir.	Brünnhilde from me.
Weichet von ihr,	From her, the eternal
der ewig Verworf'nen,	outcast, turn aside,
wie ihren Werth	as she herself
von sich sie warf! [32a]	has cast aside her worth!

ROSSWEISSE

Zu uns floh die Verfolgte.	To us the fugitive fled.

ALL EIGHT VALKYRIES

Uns'ren Schutz flehte sie an:	She entreated our protection:
mit Furcht und Zagen	with fear and trembling
faßt sie dein Zorn.	your anger fills her.
Für die bange Schwester	For our faint-hearted sister
bitten wir nun,	we beg in turn
daß den ersten Zorn du bezähm'st.	that you curb your initial anger.

Lass' dich erweichen für sie,	Unbend towards her
zähme deinen Zorn!	and curb your anger!

WOTAN

Weichherziges	You weak-hearted
Weibergezücht!	herd of women!
So matten Muth	Such feeble wits
gewannt ihr von mir?	did you win from me?
Erzog ich euch kühn,	Did I bring you up boldly
zum Kampfe zu zieh'n,	to fare to the fight,
schuf ich die Herzen	did I render your hearts
euch hart und scharf,	both hard and keen
daß ihr wilden nun weint und greint,	that you hoydens now wail and whine
wenn mein Grimm eine Treulose	when my wrath chastises a traitor?
[straft? [32a]	
So wiss't denn, winselnde,	Know then, you whimperers,
was die verbrach,	what she did wrong,
um die euch zagen	for whom you fainthearts
die Zähre entbrennt!	shed a hot tear.
Keine wie sie	No one, as she did,
kannte mein innerstes Sinnen;	knew my innermost thinking;
keine wie sie	no one, as she did,
wußte den Quell meines Willens;	watched at the well-spring of my will;
sie selbst war	she herself was
meines Wunsches schaffender	my wish's life-giving womb: –
[Schooß: –	
und so nun brach sie	and now she has broken
den seligen Bund,	the holy bond
daß treulos sie	by faithlessly
meinem Willen getrotzt,	flouting my will
mein herrschend Gebot	and openly spurning
offen verhöhnt,	my sovereign command,
gegen mich die Waffe gewandt,	turning against me the very weapon
die mein Wunsch allein ihr schuf! –	my will alone had created for her! –
Hör'st du's, Brünnhilde?	Do you hear me, Brünnhilde?
du, der ich Brünne,	You, on whom brinie,
Helm und Wehr,	helmet and weapon,
Wonne und Huld,	bliss and favour,
Namen und Leben verlieh?	name and life I bestowed?
Hör'st du mich Klage erheben,	Do you hear me make complaint
und birg'st dich bang dem Kläger,	and hide in fear from the plaintiff
daß feig du der Straf' entflöh'st?	in the faint-hearted hope of avoiding
	[chastisement?

BRÜNNHILDE

(emerges from the group of valkyries and, humbly but with firm steps, descends from the top of the cliff, coming to a rest a short distance from Wotan.) [32a]

Hier bin ich, Vater:	Here I am, father,
gebiete die Strafe!	dictate my punishment!

WOTAN

Nicht – straf' ich dich erst:
deine Strafe schuf'st du dir selbst.
  Durch meinen Willen
  war'st du allein:
gegen mich doch hast du gewollt;
  meine Befehle nur
  führtest du aus:
gegen mich doch hast du befohlen;
  Wunsch-Maid
  war'st du mir: [9]
gegen mich doch hast du gewünscht;
  Schild-Maid
  war'st du mir:
gegen mich doch hob'st du den
  [Schild;
  Loos-Kieserin
  war'st du mir:
gegen mich doch kies'test du Loose;
  Helden-Reizerin
  war'st du mir:
gegen mich doch reiztest du Helden.
  Was sonst du war'st,
  sagte dir Wotan:
  was jetzt du bist,
  das sage dir selbst!
Wunschmaid bist du nicht mehr;
Walküre bist du gewesen: –
  nun sei fortan,

(sharply)

was so du noch bist!

It is not for me to punish you:
your punishment you yourself ordained.
  Through my will
  alone you existed:
but against me you have willed;
  my orders alone
  you carried out:
but against me you have given orders;
  Wish-Maid
  you were to me:
but against me you have wished;
  Shield-Maid
  you were to me;
but against me you have raised your
  [shield;
  Chooser of Lots
  you were to me:
but against me you have chosen lots;
  Inciter of Heroes
  you were to me:
but against me you have incited heroes.
  What once you were
  Wotan has said to you:
  what you are now
  say to yourself!
Wish-Maid you are no more;
valkyrie you have been: –
  now henceforth be

what you are even now!

BRÜNNHILDE
(deeply shocked)

Du verstößest mich?
Versteh' ich den Sinn?

You're casting me out?
Do I grasp your meaning?

WOTAN

Nicht send' ich dich mehr aus
  [Walhall,
  nicht weis' ich dir mehr   [33]
  Helden zur Wal;
  nicht führ'st du mehr Sieger
  in meinen Saal:
bei der Götter trautem Mahle
  das Trinkhorn nicht reich'st
  du traulich mir mehr;
  nicht kos' ich dir mehr
  den kindischen Mund.
Von göttlicher Schaar

No more shall I send you forth from
  [Valhalla,
  no more show you
  heroes to add to the slain;
  no victors you'll guide
  again to my hall:
nevermore at the gods' friendly feast
  will you lovingly hand me
  the drinking-horn;
  nevermore shall I fawn on
  your childlike mouth.
From the gods' own host

bist du geschieden,
ausgestoßen
aus der Ewigen Stamm;
gebrochen ist unser Bund: [9]
aus meinem Angesicht bist du
[verbannt!

you're now cut off,
cast out
from the kin of immortals;
our bond is broken:
you're banished from my sight!

THE EIGHT VALKYRIES

(abandoning their former position in their consternation and moving somewhat further down the cliff)

Wehe! Weh'!
Schwester! Ach Schwester!

Alas! Alas!
Sister, ah sister!

BRÜNNHILDE

Nimmst du mir alles,
was einst du gab'st?

Will you take away all
that you ever gave me?

WOTAN

Der dich zwingt, wird dir's entzieh'n![3]
  Hieher auf den Berg
  banne ich dich;
  in wehrlosen Schlaf
  schließ' ich dich fest;   [9]
der Mann dann fange die Maid,
der am Wege sie findet und weckt.

He who subdues you will take it away!
  Here on the mountain
  I'll lay you under a spell;
  in shelterless sleep
  I'll shut you fast;
the maiden shall fall to the man
who stumbles upon her and wakes her.

THE EIGHT VALKYRIES

(coming right down from the cliff and, in anxious groups, surrounding Brünnhilde, who lies half-kneeling in front of Wotan)

Halt' ein, o Vater,
halt' ein den Fluch!
Soll die Maid verblüh'n   [33]
und verbleichen dem Mann?
Hör' unser Fleh'n!
Du schrecklicher Gott, wende
die schreiende Schmach: [3]
wie die Schwester träfe uns selber
[der Schimpf!   [32b]

Stop, o father,
stay the curse!
Is the maiden to fade
and grow wan with a man?
Hear our entreaty!
You terrible god, avert
this flagrant disgrace:
such shame we should surely share with
[our sister!

WOTAN

Hörtet ihr nicht,
was ich verhängt?   [9]
Aus eurer Schaar
ist die treulose Schwester geschieden;
  mit euch zu Roß
durch die Lüfte nicht reitet sie
[länger;
  die magdliche Blume
  verblüht der Maid;
  ein Gatte gewinnt

Did you not hear
what I decreed?
From your host
shall your faithless sister be sundered;
with you she shall
nevermore ride through the air on her
[steed;
the maid's maidenly
flower will fade;
a husband will win

ihre weibliche Gunst:
dem herrischen[74] Manne
gehorcht sie fortan,
am Herde sitzt sie und spinnt,   [9]
aller Spottenden Ziel und Spiel.

her woman's favours;
henceforth she'll obey
the high-handed[74] man;
she'll sit by the hearth and spin,
the butt and plaything of all who despise
[her.

(Brünnhilde sinks to the ground with a cry; appalled, the valkyries shrink from her side with a violent clatter of arms.)

Schreckt euch ihr Loos?
So flieht die verlor'ne!
Weichet von ihr
und haltet euch fern!
Wer von euch wagte
bei ihr zu weilen,
wer mir zum Trotz
zu der traurigen hielt' –
die Thörin theilte ihr Loos:
das künd' ich der kühnen an! –
Fort jetzt von hier!
Meidet den Felsen!
Hurtig jagt mir von hinnen,
sonst erharrt Jammer euch hier!

Does her fate affright you?
Then flee your lost sister!
Be gone from her side
and keep well away!
If any one dares
to tarry here with her,
if any defies me
and helps the sad child –
that fool shall surely share her fate:
this do I say to you valiant maids! –
Now get you all gone!
Keep clear of the crag!
Swiftly speed on your way,
else sorrow await you here!

THE EIGHT VALKYRIES

Weh'! Weh'!

Alas! Alas!

(They scatter to the sound of wild cries and, in their headlong flight, plunge into the pinewood. Black clouds gather close to the edge of the cliff: a wild tumult is heard in the wood. A blinding flash of lightning breaks through the cloudbank; in it can be seen the valkyries, pressed closely together, their reins hanging loose as they storm wildly away. [30] The tempest soon abates; the stormclouds gradually disperse. During the following scene, once the weather is calm, twilight descends and finally night.)

SCENE THREE

(Wotan and Brünnhilde, who still lies at his feet, are left alone. A long, solemn silence: their positions remain unchanged.) [37, 34]

BRÜNNHILDE
(slowly beginning to raise her head a little; starting timidly, then with increasing intensity)

War es so schmählich,
was ich verbrach,
daß mein Verbrechen so schmählich
[du bestraf'st?
War es so niedrig,
was ich dir that,
daß du so tief mir Erniedrigung
[schaff'st?

Was it so shameful
what I did wrong
that you punish that wrong in so
[shameful a way?
Was it so base
what I did unto you
that you seek to debase me to fathomless
[depths?

War es so ehrlos,
was ich beging,
daß mein Vergeh'n nun die Ehre mir
[raubt?

Was what I did
so lacking in honour
my lapse must deprive me of honour?

(raising herself gradually into a kneeling position)

O sag', Vater!
Sieh' mir in's Auge:
schweige den Zorn,
zähme die Wuth
und deute mir klar
die dunkle Schuld,
die mit starkem Trotze dich zwingt,
zu verstoßen dein trautestes Kind! [32a]

O tell me, father!
Look in my eyes
and silence your anger;
curb your wrath
and explain to me clearly
what hidden guilt
forces you now, in stubborn defiance,
your dearest child to disown!

WOTAN
(his position unchanged, gravely and sombrely)

Frag' deine That –
sie deutet dir deine Schuld!   [30]

Question your deed,
it explains to you your guilt!

BRÜNNHILDE

Deinen Befehl
führte ich aus.

I carried out
your orders.

WOTAN

Befahl ich dir,
für den Wälsung zu fechten?   [34]

Did I order you
to fight for the Wälsung?

BRÜNNHILDE

So hießest du mich
als Herrscher der Wal.

So you bade me act
as Lord of the Slain.

WOTAN

Doch meine Weisung
nahm ich wieder zurück.

But I took
my instruction back again.

BRÜNNHILDE
(more animatedly)

Als Fricka den eig'nen
Sinn dir entfremdet:
da ihrem Sinn du dich fügtest,
war'st du selber dir Feind.   [32a]

When Fricka had turned
your own mind against you:
in conforming with her thinking,
you became an enemy unto yourself.

WOTAN
(quietly and bitterly)

Daß du mich verstanden, wähnt' ich,
und strafte den wissenden Trotz;
doch feig und dumm
dachtest du mich:
so hätt' ich Verrath nicht zu rächen,
zu gering wär'st du meinem Grimm? [37]

I believed you had understood me
and punished your knowing defiance;
but craven and foolish
you thought me:
had I not to avenge betrayal,
you'd be unworthy of my wrath!

Nicht weise bin ich;
doch wußt' ich das Eine –

(very slowly)

daß den Wälsung du liebtest:

(more animatedly)

ich wußte den Zwiespalt,   [33]
der dich zwang,
dieß Eine ganz zu vergessen.
Das And're mußtest   [27, 32a]
einzig du seh'n,
was zu schau'n so herb
schmerzte dein Herz –
daß Siegmund Schutz du versagtest.

Not wise am I,
but one thing I knew –

that you loved the Wälsung:

I knew the discord
that made you
forget this one thing altogether.
Yet something else
you had to see,
the sight of which
so sorely pained your heart
you withheld your protection from
[Siegmund.

WOTAN

Du wußtest es so,
und wagtest dennoch den Schutz?

You knew it was so
and yet you dared to protect him?

BRÜNNHILDE
(beginning quietly)

Weil für dich im Auge
das Eine ich hielt,
dem, im Zwange des And'ren
schmerzlich entzweit,
rathlos den Rücken du wandtest!
Die im Kampfe Wotan
den Rücken bewacht,
die sah nun Das nur,
was du nicht sah'st: –
Siegmund mußt' ich seh'n.   [33]
Tod kündend
trat ich vor ihn,
gewahrte sein Auge,
hörte sein Wort;
ich vernahm des Helden
heilige Noth;
tönend erklang mir
des Tapfersten Klage –
freiester Liebe
furchtbares Leid,
traurigsten Muthes   [26]
mächtigster Trotz:
meinem Ohr erscholl,
mein Aug' erschaute,
was tief im Busen das Herz
zu heil'gem Beben mir traf. –
Scheu und staunend
stand ich in[75] Scham:

Since, for you, I kept sight of
that one thing alone
on which, painfully torn
by the other's constraint,
you helplessly turned your back!
She who, in battle,
guards Wotan's back,
she saw only
what you did not see: –
Siegmund had I to see.
Heralding death,
I stepped before him,
beheld his eye
and heard his word;
I noted the hero's
hallowed need;
the bravest of men's
lament rang forth –
the fearful pain
of freest love,
the mightiest scorn
of the saddest of hearts:
it rang in my ear
and my eye beheld
what, deep in my breast, caused
my heart to tremble in holy awe. –
Shy and startled
I stood there in[75] shame:

ihm nur zu dienen
konnt' ich noch denken:

all I could think of
was how to serve him:

(more animatedly)

Sieg oder Tod
mit Siegmund zu theilen –
dieß nur erkannt' ich
zu kiesen als Loos!

victory or death
to share with Siegmund –
this I now knew
[32a]   was the fate I must choose!

(slowly)

Der diese Liebe
mir in's Herz gehaucht,[76]
dem Willen, der
dem Wälsung mich gesellt,
ihm innig vertraut –

[37]   Inwardly true
to the will
which inspired[76]
this love in my heart
and which bound me to the Wälsung –

(more broadly)

trotzt' ich deinem Gebot.

I flouted your command.

WOTAN

So thatest du,
was so gern zu thun ich begehrt –
doch was nicht zu thun
die Noth zwiefach mich zwang?
So leicht wähntest du
Wonne des Herzens erworben,
wo brennend Weh'
in das Herz mir brach,
wo gräßliche Noth
den Grimm mir schuf,
einer Welt zu Liebe
der Liebe Quell

And so you did
what I longed so dearly to do –
but which I was doubly
forced not to do by need.
So lightly you thought
that heartfelt delight might be won,
when burning pain
broke into my heart
and hideous need
aroused my wrath,
so that, out of my love for the world,
I was forced to staunch the
[well-spring of love

im gequälten Herzen zu hemmen?
Wo gegen mich selber
ich sehrend mich wandte,
aus Ohnmacht-Schmerzen
schäumend ich aufschoß,
wüthender Sehnsucht
sengender Wunsch
den schrecklichen Willen mir schuf,
in den Trümmern der eig'nen Welt
meine ew'ge Trauer zu enden: –

in this harrowed heart of mine?
When I turned on myself
in consuming torment,
starting up, chafing,
in impotent pain,
furious longing's
fervent desire
inspired the terrible wish
to end my eternal grief
[19]   in the ruins of my own world: –

(somewhat freely)

da labte süß
dich selige Lust;
wonniger Rührung
üppigen Rausch
enttrank'st du lachend
der Liebe Trank –
als mir göttlicher Noth
nagende Galle gemischt? –

then blissful abandon
solaced you sweetly;
rapt emotion's
heady delights
you drank from love's cup
with lips parted in laughter –
while *my* drink was mixed
with the griping gall of godly distress? –

(dryly and curtly)

Deinen leichten Sinn
lass' dich denn leiten:
von mir sagtest du dich los.
    Dich muß ich meiden,
    gemeinsam mit dir
nicht darf ich Rath mehr raunen;
    getrennt nicht dürfen
    traut wir mehr schaffen:
so weit Leben und Luft,
darf der Gott dir nicht mehr
    [begegnen!

Be guided now
    by your own light thoughts:
[37]   from me you have cast yourself free.
    Now I must shun you
    and nevermore share
any whispered counsels with you;
    divided, we may not
    act in close concert;
wherever there's life and breath,
the god may no longer meet you!

BRÜNNHILDE
(simply)

Wohl taugte dir nicht
die thör'ge Maid,
die staunend im Rathe
nicht dich verstand,
wie mein eig'ner Rath
nur das Eine mir rieth –
zu lieben, was du geliebt. –
    Muß ich denn scheiden
    und scheu dich meiden,
    mußt du spalten
    was einst sich umspannt,
    die eig'ne Hälfte
fern von dir halten –
daß sonst sie ganz dir gehörte,
du Gott, vergiß das nicht!
    Dein ewig Theil
    nicht wirst du entehren,
    Schande nicht wollen,
    die dich beschimpft:
dich selbst ließest du sinken,
säh'st du dem Spott mich zum
    [Spiel!

Little use, I fear,
    was the foolish maid,
    who, stunned by your counsel,
    understood nothing,
    for my private counsel
    counselled but one thing –
to love whatever you loved. –
    If I must leave you
    and shyly shun you,
    if you must sunder
    what once was whole,
    and hold far off
    one half of yourself –
o god, don't forget
that it once belonged to you wholly!
    You cannot want to dishonour
    that part of you which is ageless
    nor suffer a shame
    that brings you disgrace:
you'd only abase yourself
if you saw me as mockery's plaything!

[26b]

WOTAN
(calmly)

Du folgtest selig
der Liebe Macht:
folge nun dem,
den du lieben mußt!

You blissfully followed
the force of love:
now follow him
whom you're forced to love!

BRÜNNHILDE

Soll ich aus Walhall scheiden,
nicht mehr mit dir schaffen und
    [walten,
    dem herrischen Manne
    gehorchen fortan –
    dem feigen Prahler

If I must leave Valhalla,
no more to work beside you,

    henceforth obeying
    a high-handed husband –
    don't give me as prey

gieb mich nicht preis:
nicht werthlos sei er,
der mich gewinnt.

to some craven braggart:
let him who wins me
not be worthless.

WOTAN

Von Walvater schiedest du –

nicht wählen darf ich für dich.

You've severed all links with the Lord of
[the Slain –
for you I cannot choose.

BRÜNNHILDE
(quietly, with intimate secrecy)

Du zeugtest ein edles Geschlecht;   [29]
kein Zager kann je ihm entschlagen:
der weihlichste Held – ich weiß es – [35]
entblüht dem Wälsungenstamm!

You fathered a noble race;
no coward can spring from its stock:
the holiest hero – I know –
will arise from the race of the Wälsungs!

WOTAN

Schweig' von dem Wälsungenstamm!
   Von dir geschieden,
   schied ich von ihm:
vernichten mußt' ihn der Neid.

Speak not of the race of the Wälsungs!
   Parted from you,
   I have parted from them:
spite was bound to destroy them.

BRÜNNHILDE

Die von dir sich riß –
rettete ihn:

She who tore herself from you
has saved them:

(confidingly)

Sieglinde hegt
die heiligste Frucht;
in Schmerz und Leid,
wie kein Weib sie gelitten,
wird sie gebären
was bang sie birgt.

[35]   Sieglinde nurtures
the holiest seed;
in pain and grief
such as no woman suffered
she'll one day bring forth
what she hides in her fear.

WOTAN

Nie suche bei mir
Schutz für die Frau,
noch für ihres Schooßes Frucht!

Seek not my shelter
[35]   for that woman
nor for the fruit of her womb!

BRÜNNHILDE
(confidingly)

Sie wahret das Schwert,
das du Siegmund schufest –

[23]   She safeguards the sword
you made for Siegmund –

WOTAN
(violently)

Und das ich ihm in Stücken
   [schlug. –
   Nicht streb', o Maid,
   den Muth mir zu stören!
Erwarte dein Loos,

and which I struck in splinters! –
[34]
   Don't strive, o maiden,
   to alter my mind!
Await your fate,

wie sich's dir wirft:
nicht kiesen kann ich es dir! –
Doch fort muß ich jetzt,
fern mich verzieh'n:
zu viel schon zögert' ich hier.
Von der Abwendigen
wend' ich mich ab;
nicht wissen darf ich
was sie sich wünscht:
die Strafe nur
muß vollstreckt ich seh'n.

as the lot has been cast:
I cannot choose it for you! –
But now I must leave you
and fare far from here:
too long I've already delayed.
From the turncoat
I turn aside in turn;
I may not know
what she wants:
the sentence alone
I must see carried out.

BRÜNNHILDE

Was hast du erdacht,
daß ich erdulde?

What have you planned
that I should suffer?

WOTAN

In festen Schlaf [38]
verschließ' ich dich:
wer so die Wehrlose weckt,
dem ward, erwacht, sie zum Weib.

I'll seal you
in soundest sleep: –
he who wakes the defenceless woman
shall take her, awakened, as wife.

BRÜNNHILDE

Soll fesselnder Schlaf
fest mich binden,
dem feigsten Manne
zur leichten Beute:
dieß Eine mußt du erhören, [39]
was heil'ge Angst zu dir fleht!
Die Schlafende schütze
mit scheuchenden Schrecken:
(resolutely)
daß nur ein furchtlos [35]
freiester Held
hier auf dem Felsen
einst mich fänd'!

If fettering sleep
is to bind me fast,
as easy prey
to the basest of cowards,
this one thing alone you must grant me
that holy fear entreats of you.
Shield the sleeper
with hideous terrors

that only a fearlessly
free-born hero
shall find me
here on the fell!

WOTAN

Zu viel begehr'st du –
zu viel der Gunst!

Too much you beg for –
too great a boon!

BRÜNNHILDE
(throwing herself at Wotan's feet)

Dieß Eine
mußt du erhören![77]
Zerknicke dein Kind,
das dein Knie umfaßt;
zertritt die Traute,
zertrümm're die Maid;
ihres Leibes Spur
zerstöre dein Speer: [9]

This one thing
you must allow me![77]
Crush your child
who clasps your knee,
trample your favourite underfoot
and dash the maid to pieces;
let your spear destroy
all trace of her body:

doch gieb, Grausamer, nicht		but, pitiless god, don't give her up
der gräßlichsten Schmach sie preis!		to the shamefullest of fates!

(with wild inspiration)

Auf dein Gebot	[30]	At your behest
entbrenne ein Feuer;	[14a]	let a fire flare up;
den Felsen umglühe		let its searing flames
lodernde Gluth;		encircle the fell;
es leck' ihre Zung',		its tongue shall lick,
es fresse ihr Zahn		its tooth consume
den Zagen, der frech sich wagte,		the coward who dares to draw near
dem freislichen[78] Felsen zu nah'n!		to the fearsome[78] rock in his rashness.

WOTAN

(overcome and deeply stirred, turning impetuously towards Brünnhilde, raising her from her knees and gazing with emotion into her eyes) [30, 39]

Leb' wohl, du kühnes	Fare well, you valiant,
herrliches Kind!	glorious child!
Du meines Herzens	You, my heart's
heiligster Stolz,	most hallowed pride,
leb' wohl! leb' wohl! leb' wohl!	fare well! Fare well! Fare well!

(very passionately)

Muß ich dich meiden,		If I must shun you,
und darf nicht minnig		if no loving greeting
mein Gruß dich mehr grüßen;		may evermore greet you;
sollst du nun nicht mehr		if you may nevermore
neben mir reiten,		ride beside me
noch Meth beim Mahl mir reichen;		nor serve me mead at table;
muß ich verlieren		if I must lose
dich, die ich liebte[79],		you whom I loved[79],
du lachende Lust meines Auges: –		you laughing delight of my eye:
ein bräutliches Feuer	[38]	a bridal fire
soll dir nun brennen,		shall burn for you
wie nie einer Braut es gebrannt!		such as never blazed for a bride!
Flammende Gluth	[14a]	Fiery flames shall
umglühe den Fels;		encircle the fell;
mit zehrenden Schrecken		with withering fears
scheuch' es den Zagen;		let them fright the faint-hearted;
der Feige fliehe		the coward shall flee
Brünnhilde's Fels: –		from Brünnhilde's fell: –
denn Einer nur freie die Braut,	[35]	for one man alone shall woo the bride,
der freier als ich, der Gott!		one freer than I, the god!

(Moved and inspired, Brünnhilde sinks down on Wotan's breast; he holds her in a long embrace. She throws back her head once more and, still embracing him, gazes with solemn emotion into Wotan's eyes.) [37, 39]

Der Augen leuchtendes Paar,	That radiant pair of eyes
das oft ich lächelnd gekos't,	which I often caressed with a smile
wenn Kampfes-Lust	when a kiss requited
ein Kuß dir lohnte,	your battle lust
wenn kindisch lallend	and, childishly lilting,
der Helden Lob	the praise of heroes

von holden Lippen dir floß: –
dieser Augen strahlendes Paar,
das oft im Sturm mir geglänzt,
    wenn Hoffnungs-Sehnen
    das Herz mir sengte,
    nach Welten-Wonne
    mein Wunsch verlangte
aus wild webendem Bangen: –
    zum letzten Mal
    letz' es mich heut'
    mit des Lebewohles
    letztem Kuß!
    Dem glücklicher'n Manne
    glänze sein Stern:
dem unseligen Ew'gen
muß es scheidend sich schließen!

flowed from your lovely lips: –
this glittering pair of eyes
which often glistened on me in the storm
    when the yearning for hope
    would sear my heart
    and I wished for
    worldly delights
amidst wildly weaving fears: –
    for one last time
    let them joy me today
    with this valediction's
    final kiss!
    On a happier man
    their stars shall shine:
on the hapless immortal
they must close in parting!

(He takes her head in both hands.)

Denn so – kehrt   [7]   And so – the god
    der Gott sich dir ab: turns away from you:
so küßt er die Gottheit von dir.   so he kisses your godhead away.

(He lingeringly kisses both her eyes. She sinks back, with eyes closed, into his arms, as consciousness gently slips away. He leads her tenderly to a low mossy bank, beneath a broad-branched fir-tree. He gazes at her, then closes her helmet: his eye then rests on the form of the sleeping woman, which he now covers completely with her valkyrie's great steel shield. Slowly he turns away, before turning round again with a sorrowful expression. [38, 39, 34] With solemn resolve he then strides to the centre of the stage and directs the point of his spear towards a large rock.) [9]

Loge, hör'!   Loge, listen!
lausche hieher!   Lend an ear!
    Wie zuerst ich dich fand,   As I found you at first,
    als feurige Gluth,   a fiery glow,
    wie dann einst du mir schwandest   as you then disappeared,
    als schweifende Lohe: as a will-o'-the-wisp,
    wie ich dich band,   just as I bound you
    bann' ich dich heut'!   I tame you today!
Herauf, wabernde Lohe,   [14a, 14b]   Arise, you flickering flame,
umlod're mir feurig den Fels!   enfold the fell with fire!

(During the following, he strikes the stone three times with his spear.)

Loge! Loge! Hieher!   Loge! Loge! Come hither!

(A stream of fire springs from the rock, gradually increasing in intensity until it becomes a brilliant fiery glow. Bright flickering flames break out. Flickering wildly, tongues of lambent flame surround Wotan. With his spear, he directs the sea of fire to encircle the edge of the rock; it immediately moves towards the back of the stage, where it now continues to burn, enclosing the mountain in flames.) [39]

    Wer meines Speeres   [35]   He who fears
    Spitze fürchtet,   my spear-point
durchschreite das Feuer nie!   shall never pass through the fire!

(He stretches out his spear as though casting a spell. He then gazes sorrowfully back at Brünnhilde, turns slowly to leave and looks back once again before disappearing through the flames. The curtain falls.) [35, 39]

Siegfried

Synopsis

Act I

ACT I IS SET IN A CAVE in the rocks in the forest. The curtain rises on the dwarf Mime hammering away at an anvil. He has brought up Siegfried so that he might kill Fafner, who has transformed himself into a dragon to guard the hoard. Mime curses his wearisome labour and his hopeless attempts to forge a sword that the boy Siegfried cannot break in two. Siegfried comes in from the forest leading a huge bear on a rope. He sets it on Mime and laughs as the bear chases the dwarf round the cave. He demands to see what Mime has forged, but scorns his latest effort and smashes it on the anvil. Siegfried, wishing to know the truth of his parentage, is told that Mime once took pity on a woman whimpering out in the wood and brought her into the cave. She died in giving birth to Siegfried and he, Mime, carried out her wishes in bringing him up.

Siegfried asks, and is told, his mother's name: Sieglinde. But Mime withholds the name of the boy's father. Siegfried demands proof of this story and Mime fetches the fragments of Siegmund's sword Nothung, which were left in his custody. Siegfried excitedly instructs Mime to recreate Nothung by forging the pieces together and, happy at the prospect of the freedom it will bring, he rushes off into the forest. Mime sits dejectedly at the anvil, despairing of fashioning the fragments into an invincible sword.

The Wanderer (Wotan in disguise) enters and stakes his head on answering any questions Mime may ask. The dwarf asks who lives in the earth, on the face of the earth and on the cloudy heights. The Nibelungs, the giants and the gods respectively, come the correct answers. Demanding the same bargain in turn, the Wanderer asks first the name of the tribe treated harshly by Wotan, though dearest to him. Siegmund's tribe, the Wälsungs, replies Mime confidently. The second question concerns the name of the sword to be wielded by the hero Siegfried. Nothung, replies Mime. But when the Wanderer asks who will forge the sword, Mime jumps up in alarm: he has no idea. The Wanderer rebukes Mime for failing to ask the question he should have; the answer, he says, is 'one who has never known fear'. He leaves Mime's head forfeit to the fearless one and departs.

Siegfried returns and the dwarf determines to teach the boy fear. Siegfried demands the sword fragments and begins to do the forging himself, starting by filing the pieces into splinters. Mime plots how he will offer Siegfried a drugged drink after his tussle with the dragon, and then kill him with his own sword. At last the forging is done, and Siegfried crashes the sword down on the anvil, splitting it in two.

Act II

Alberich, keeping watch over Fafner's cave deep in the forest, is surprised by the appearance of the Wanderer and bitterly taunts him with his ambitions for world supremacy. The latter remains quietly philosophical and even warns Alberich of the approach of Siegfried and Mime. He surprises Alberich further by arousing Fafner on his behalf and asking him to yield up the ring. The dragon is unmoved. After offering further friendly advice, the Wanderer disappears into the forest.

Mime warns Siegfried of the dragon's poisonous venom and deadly tail, but Siegfried is concerned only to know where is the dragon's heart, so that he can plunge in his sword. To the music of the Forest Murmurs, the boy, left alone, expresses his relief that the ugly dwarf is not his father after all. Hearing the song of the Woodbird, he tries to imitate it, in the hope that he will understand the song. He makes a pipe from a reed, but after cutting it in vain this way and that, he gives up. He blows his horn instead and a somnolent Fafner drags himself out of the cave. After an exchange of banter, Siegfried stabs Fafner in the heart with Nothung. In withdrawing his sword from the dragon's heart, Siegfried smears his hand with blood; it burns and he involuntarily puts his hand to his mouth. As he tastes the blood, he understands at last the song of the Woodbird: it tells him to take the ring and tarnhelm from the cave.

As Siegfried disappears into the cave, Mime and Alberich argue angrily about the rightful ownership of the treasure. Siegfried reappears with ring and tarnhelm, and the Woodbird tells him to beware Mime, who now cajoles Siegfried in words, though his thoughts are revealed to Siegfried through the dragon's blood, thus betraying his real intention. Siegfried, in an access of revulsion, kills him with a blow of the sword.

He tosses Mime's body into the cave and drags Fafner's over its mouth. Lying down under the lime-tree, he listens again to the song of the Woodbird and asks its advice. The bird tells him of the bride that awaits him on a mountain top surrounded by fire. Siegfried jumps up and follows the bird as it leads the way.

Act III

The Wanderer appears at the foot of a rocky mountain and summons Erda, the earth goddess, from her slumber. She expresses surprise that the god who taught defiance should punish Brünnhilde for disobedience. He tells her that he no longer fears the end of the gods: indeed, it is what he desires. His inheritance is bequeathed to the Wälsung hero, who will defeat Alberich's evil ambitions by the goodness of his nature. Erda sinks back into the earth.

As the Wanderer waits by the cave, Siegfried comes into view, led by the Woodbird. Their exchange becomes increasingly heated until finally the Wanderer tries to block Siegfried's path by stretching out his spear; it is shattered by a stroke of Siegfried's sword. The Wanderer vanishes and Siegfried confronts the wall of fire.

The scene changes to the rocky summit of the end of *Die Walküre*. Siegfried climbs to the top and notices the form of the sleeping Brünnhilde under the trees. Her face is covered and he takes her for a man, even after removing her helmet. As he loosens the breastplate with his sword, he realizes that it is a woman. He feels weak and dizzy and invokes his mother. Now for the first time he has been taught fear, yet he longs to waken her. In desperation he kisses her on the lips, at which she opens her eyes.

She greets the daylight and tells him that she has always loved him, even before he was conceived. When Siegfried embraces her passionately, she pushes him away in terror, conscious of her vulnerability. Though frightened, she looks fondly at him; yet she begs him not to destroy the purity of their love. Gradually she is won over by the intensity of Siegfried's passion and is able to accept her new mortal status. They embrace in ecstasy and Brünnhilde bids farewell to the world of the gods. Transformed by each other's love, they invoke 'laughing death'.

Siegfried

Second Day of the Stage Festival 'The Ring of the Nibelung'

First performed at the Bayreuth Festspielhaus, 16 August 1876

Siegfried (tenor)	Georg Unger
Mime (tenor)	Max Schlosser
The Wanderer (bass)	Franz Betz
Alberich (bass)	Karl Hill
Fafner (bass)	Franz von Reichenberg
Erda (contralto)	Luise Jaide
Brünnhilde (soprano)	Amalie Materna
Woodbird (soprano)	Lilli Lehmann

Act I.   A rocky cave in the forest
Act II.   In the depths of the forest
Act III.   A wild place at the foot of a rocky mountain
        The summit of Brünnhilde's rock

First UK performance: Her Majesty's Theatre, London, 8 May 1882

First US performance: Metropolitan Opera, New York, 9 November 1887

Siegfried

Act One

Prelude and Scene One

(The curtain rises.[80] *A cave in the forest; inside it is a natural forge, with a large set of bellows. At the anvil in front of it sits Mime, busily hammering at a sword.)* [17, 15, 3, 6, 23]

MIME
(pausing)

Zwangvolle Plage!	Punishing torment!
Müh' ohne Zweck!	Toil without purpose!
Das beste Schwert,	The finest sword
das je ich geschweißt,	that ever I forged
in der Riesen Fäusten	would have held quite firm
hielte es fest:	in giants' hands:
doch dem ich's geschmiedet,	but the rascally lad
der schmähliche Knabe,	for whom I wrought it
er knickt und schmeißt es entzwei,	bends and snaps it in two
als schüf' ich Kindergeschmeid'! – –	as though I'd made some childish [trinket! – –

(Mime ill-humouredly throws the sword down on the anvil, sets his arms akimbo and stares at the ground in thought.) [15, 17, 23a]

Es giebt ein Schwert,	One sword there is
das er nicht zerschwänge:	which he'd never shatter:
Nothung's Trümmer	Nothung's fragments
zertrotzt' er mir nicht,	he'd not defy,
könnt' ich die starken	could I but weld
Stücken schweißen,	the mighty shards
die meine Kunst[81]	which no art of mine[81]
nicht zu kitten weiß.	can piece together.
Könnt' ich's dem Kühnen schmieden,	If I could only forge it for that hothead,
meiner Schmach erlangt' ich da [Lohn![82] –	I'd find a due reward for all my [shame![82] –

(He sinks further back, lowering his head in thought.) [17, 18]

Fafner, der wilde Wurm,	Fafner, the grim-hearted dragon,
lagert im finstern Wald;	dwells in the gloomy wood;
mit des furchtbaren Leibes Wucht	with the weight of his fearsome bulk
der Niblungen Hort	he watches over
hütet er dort.	the Nibelung hoard there.

Siegfried's kindischer Kraft   [23a]
erläge wohl Fafner's Leib:[83]
  des Nibelungen Ring   [6]
  erränge er mir.
Nur ein Schwert[84] taugt zu der
  [That;   [23]
nur Nothung nützt meinem Neid,
wenn Siegfried sehrend ihn
  [schwingt: –   [8b]
  und ich kann's nicht schweißen,
  Nothung das Schwert! –

To Siegfried's childlike strength
Fafner[83] would no doubt fall:
  the Nibelung's ring
  he'd win for me.
One sword alone befits the deed

and only Nothung serves my grudge,
if Siegfried wields it with fell intent: –

  yet I cannot forge it,
  Nothung the sword! –

(He has readjusted the sword and continues hammering it in a mood of profound ill-humour.)
[15]

  Zwangvolle Plage!
  Müh' ohne Zweck!
  Das beste Schwert,   [3]
  das je ich geschweißt,
  nie taugt es je
  zu der einzigen That!
  Ich tapp're und hämm're nur,
  weil der Knabe es heischt:
er knickt und schmeißt es entzwei,
und schmählt doch, schmied' ich ihm
  [nicht!

  Punishing torment!
  Toil without purpose!
  The finest sword
  that ever I forged
  will never serve
  for that single deed!
  I fumble and hammer away
  because the boy demands it:
he bends and snaps it in two
yet chides if I don't forge it for him!

(He drops the hammer.)

SIEGFRIED

(in wild forest clothing, with a silver horn on a chain, bursts in from the forest with sudden impetuousness, driving a large bear which he has tethered with a length of rope and which he now sets on Mime in boisterous high spirits.) [40]

        (still outside)
Hoiho!   Hoiho!
        (entering)
  Hoiho!   Hoiho!
Hau' ein! Hau' ein!   Tuck in! Tuck in!
Friß ihn! Friß ihn,   Gobble him up, gobble him up,
den Fratzenschmied!   the so-called smith!
        (laughing)

(Mime drops the sword in terror and takes refuge behind the forge: wherever he runs, Siegfried continues to drive the bear after him.)

MIME

Fort mit dem Thier!   Away with the beast!
Was taugt mir der Bär?   What use is the bear to me?

SIEGFRIED

Zu zwei komm' ich,   I came as a pair
dich besser zu zwicken: the better to plague you:
Brauner, frag' nach dem Schwert!   ask him, Bruin, about the sword!

He! lass' das Wild!   Hey, leave the brute!
Dort liegt die Waffe: There lies the weapon:
fertig fegt' ich sie heut'.   I finished furbishing it today.

SIEGFRIED

So fährst du heute noch heil!   Then I'll let you off for today.
(He unties the bear's bridle and strikes the animal's back with it.)
Lauf', Brauner: Be off with you, Bruin:
dich brauch' ich nicht mehr!   I need you no longer!
(The bear runs back into the forest; Mime comes out trembling from behind the hearth.)

MIME

Wohl leid' ich's gern,   I'm happy for you
erleg'st du Bären: to hunt down bears:
was bring'st du lebend   but why bring
die braunen heim?   brown bears home alive?

SIEGFRIED
(sitting down in order to recover from his laughter)

Nach bess'rem Gesellen sucht' ich, I was seeking a better companion
als daheim mir einer sitzt;   than the one sitting here at home;
im tiefen Walde mein Horn   deep in the forest I wound my horn
ließ ich hallend da ertönen: till it echoed far and wide:
   ob sich froh mir gesellte   would some good-hearted friend
   ein guter Freund?   be glad to join me,
das frug ich mit dem Getön'. [40] I asked by means of that sound.

Aus dem Busche kam ein Bär,   From the bushes came a bear,
der hörte mir brummend zu;   which, growling, gave me ear;
er gefiel mir besser als du,   I liked him better than you,
doch bess're fänd' ich wohl noch: but might find better ones yet:
   mit dem zähen Baste   I bridled him then
   zäumt' ich ihn da,   with a length of tough bast
dich, Schelm, nach dem Schwerte zu to ask you, you scoundrel, about the
   [fragen.   [sword.
(He jumps up and goes over to the anvil. Mime picks up the sword in order to hand it to Siegfried.)

MIME

Ich schuf die Waffe scharf,   I've made the weapon sharp,
ihrer Schneide wirst du dich freu'n. you'll be pleased with its keen-edged
                               [blade.
(He anxiously holds on to the sword, which Siegfried wrenches away from him with some violence.)

SIEGFRIED

Was frommt seine helle Schneide,   What use is a shining blade
ist der Stahl nicht hart und fest!   if the steel's not tough and tempered?
             (testing the sword) [35]

Hei! was ist das
für müß'ger Tand!
Den schwachen Stift
nenn'st du ein Schwert?

Hey! what worthless
toy is this?
This puny pin
you call a sword?

(He smashes it on the anvil, so that the splinters fly off in all directions; Mime cowers away in terror.)

Da hast du die Stücken,　　　　　[41]
schändlicher Stümper:
hätt' ich am Schädel
dir sie zerschlagen! –
Soll mich der Prahler
länger noch prellen?
Schwatzt mir von Riesen
und rüstigen Kämpfen,
von kühnen Thaten
und tüchtiger Wehr;
will Waffen mir schmieden,
Schwerte schaffen;
rühmt seine Kunst,
als könnt' er 'was rechts:
nehm' ich zur Hand nun
was er gehämmert,
mit einem Griff
zergreif' ich den Quark! –
Wär' mir nicht schier
zu schäbig der Wicht,
ich zerschmiedet' ihn selbst
mit seinem Geschmeid',
den alten albernen Alp!
Des Ärgers dann hätt' ich ein End'!

There, take the pieces,
you shameful bungler:
if only I'd smashed them
against your skull! –
How much more must
the braggart dupe me?
He prates about giants
and well-fought battles,
of doughty deeds
and well-made arms;
he'd make me weapons
and fashion swords;
he vaunts his art
as though he could do aught aright:
when I take in my hand
whatever he's hammered,
I can crush the trash
in a single grip! –
Were the knave not
simply too scurvy,
I'd smash him to pieces
with all his smith-work,
the old and addle-headed elf!
My anger were then at an end!

(In his anger Siegfried throws himself down on a stone bench. Mime continues to keep out of his way.)

MIME

Nun tob'st du wieder wie toll:
dein Undank, traun! ist arg.
Mach' ich dem bösen Buben
nicht alles gleich zu best,
was ich ihm Gutes schuf,
vergißt er gar zu schnell!
Willst du denn nie gedenken
was ich dich lehrt' vom Danke?
Dem sollst du willig gehorchen,
der je sich wohl dir erwies.

Now you're raving again like a madman:
your ingratitude's gross indeed.
If I don't do everything right
for the wicked boy straightaway,
he all too soon forgets
whatever good I've done him!
Will you never recall
what I said about being grateful?
You should willingly obey him
who's always proved kind towards you.

(Siegfried turns away ill-humouredly, with his face to the wall, so that his back is turned to Mime.)

Das willst du wieder nicht hören! –

But again you refuse to listen! –

(He stands there, perplexed; then he goes to the kitchen by the hearth.)

Doch speisen magst du wohl?
Vom Spieße bring' ich den Braten:

No doubt you'd like some food.
I'll fetch the roast from the spit:

versuchtest du gern den Sud?
Für dich sott ich ihn gar.

(He offers Siegfried some food; without turning round, the latter knocks the pot and roast meat out of Mime's hands.)

or would you like to try the broth?
I boiled it thoroughly for you.

SIEGFRIED

Braten briet ich mir selbst:
deinen Sudel sauf' allein!

Meat I've roasted for myself:
slurp your slops alone!

MIME
(in a pitifully screeching voice)

Das ist nun der Liebe
schlimmer Lohn!
Das der Sorgen
schmählicher Sold! –
Als zullendes Kind
zog ich dich auf,
wärmte mit Kleiden
den kleinen Wurm:
Speise und Trank
trug ich dir zu,
hütete dich
wie die eig'ne Haut.
Und wie du erwuchsest,
wartet' ich dein;
dein Lager schuf ich,
daß leicht du schlief'st.
Dir schmiedet' ich Tand
und ein tönend Horn;
dich zu erfreu'n
müht' ich mich froh:
mit klugem Rathe
rieth ich dir klug,
mit lichtem Wissen
lehrt' ich dich Witz.
Sitz' ich daheim
in Fleiß und Schweiß,
nach Herzenslust
schweif'st du umher:
für dich nur in Plage,
in Pein nur für dich
verzehr' ich mich alter
armer Zwerg!

That's the sorry
wages of love!
That's the shameful
reward for my cares!
From a suckling babe
I brought you up,
warmed the little
mite with clothes:
food and drink
I brought to you
and tended you
like a second self.
And when you grew bigger
I waited upon you;
I made you a bed
so you'd sleep more softly.
I forged for you toys
and a winding horn;
to give you pleasure
I gladly toiled:
with clever counsel
I counselled you cleverly,
with lucid lore
I taught you wit.
While, toiling and sweating,
I sit at home,
you roam around
to your heart's content:
suffering torment for you alone,
for you alone I suffer affliction
and wear myself out, a poor
old dwarf!

(sobbing)

Und aller Lasten
ist das nun mein Lohn,
daß der hastige Knabe
mich quält

And that's my reward
for the burdens I've borne,
that the quick-tempered boy
torments

(sobbing)

und haßt!

and abhors me!

(Siegfried has turned round and looks calmly and questioningly into Mime's eyes. Mime encounters Siegfried's gaze and timidly tries to avert his eyes.)

Vieles lehrtest du, Mime,
und Manches lernt' ich von dir;
doch was du am liebsten mich
[lehrtest,
zu lernen gelang mir nie: –
wie ich dich leiden könnt'. –
    Träg'st du mir Trank   [41]
    und Speise herbei –
der Ekel speis't mich allein;
    schaff'st du ein leichtes
    Lager zum Schlaf –
der Schlummer wird mir da schwer;
    willst du mich weisen
    witzig zu sein –
gern bleib' ich taub und dumm.
    Seh' ich dir erst
    mit den Augen zu,
    zu übel erkenn' ich
    was alles du thu'st:
    seh' ich dich steh'n,
    gangeln und geh'n,
    knicken und nicken,
    mit den Augen zwicken:
    beim Genick' möcht' ich
    den Nicker packen,
    den Garaus geben
    dem garst'gen Zwicker! –
So lernt' ich, Mime, dich leiden.

    Bist du nun weise,
    so hilf mir wissen,
worüber umsonst ich sann: –
    in den Wald lauf' ich,
    dich zu verlassen, –
wie kommt das, kehr' ich zurück?

(animatedly)

    Alle Thiere sind
    mir theurer als du:
    Baum und Vogel,
    die Fische im Bach,
    lieber mag ich sie
    leiden als dich: –
wie kommt das nun, kehr' ich
[zurück?
Bist du klug, so thu' mir's kund.

Much, Mime, have you taught me
and much from you have I learned;
but what you most wanted to teach me,

I never managed to learn: –
how I could ever abide you. –
    Although you may bring me
    food and drink,
I'm fed by my loathing alone;
    although you may make me
    an easy bed,
I still find it hard to sleep;
    although you would teach me
    to use my wits,
I'd rather stay dull and stupid.
    I only need
    set eyes upon you,
    to recognize evil
    in all that you do:
    when I see you standing,
    shuffling and shambling,
    week-kneed and nodding,
    blinking your eyes:
    I long to seize
    the dodderer's neck
    and finish off
    the filthy twitching creature! –
That's how I've learned to abide you,
[Mime.

    If you're so wise,
    then help me to know
what I thought about in vain: –
    though I run off into the forest
    to leave you,
how is it that I come back?

    All the beasts of the forest are
    dearer to me than you:
    every tree and bird,
    the fish in the brook
    I can far more
    abide than you: –
how is it, then, that I always come back?

If you're so clever, then tell me why.

(Mime tries to approach him, confidingly.) [42]

MIME

Mein Kind, das lehrt dich kennen,	My child, that makes you understand
wie lieb ich am Herzen dir lieg'.	how dear to your heart I must be.

SIEGFRIED

Ich kann dich ja nicht leiden, –	And yet I can't abide you –
vergiß das nicht so leicht!	do not forget that quite so quickly!

MIME
(recoiling and sitting down again at the side, facing Siegfried)

Dess' ist deine Wildheit schuld,	For that you must blame your wildness,
die du böser bänd'gen sollst. –	which you ought to curb, you wicked [boy. –
Jammernd verlangen Junge	Whimpering, young things long
nach ihrer Alten Nest:	for their parents' nest:
Liebe ist das Verlangen;	love is the name of that longing;
so lechzest du auch nach mir,	so you, too, pined for me,
so lieb'st du auch deinen Mime –	so you, too, love your Mime –
so mußt du ihn lieben!	so you *have* to love him!
Was dem Vögelein ist der Vogel,	What the baby bird is to the bird,
wenn er im Nest es nährt,	when he feeds it in the nest,
eh' das flügge mag fliegen:	before the fledgling can fly,
das ist dir kind'schem Sproß	such to you, my childish offspring,
der kundig sorgende Mime –	is wisely caring Mime –
das muß er dir sein.	such, to you, he must be.

SIEGFRIED

Ei, Mime, bist du so witzig,	Hey, Mime, if you're so clever,
so lass' mich eines noch wissen!	tell me one thing more!

(simply)

Es sangen die Vöglein	[42] In spring the birds
so selig im Lenz,	would sing so blithely,

(tenderly)

das eine lockte das and're:	the one would entice the other:
du sagtest selbst –	you said so yourself –
da ich's wissen wollt' –	since I wanted to know –
das wären Männchen	that these were fathers

(tenderly)

und Weibchen.	and mothers.
Sie kos'ten so lieblich,	They dallied so fondly,
und ließen sich nicht;	not leaving each other
sie bauten ein Nest	but building a nest
und brüteten drin:	and brooding inside it:
da flatterte junges	young fledglings then
Geflügel auf,	would flutter out
und beide pflegten der Brut. –	and both of them tended their brood. –
So ruhten im Busch	Deer, too, would rest
auch Rehe gepaart,	in pairs in the bushes

selbst wilde Füchse und Wölfe:
  Nahrung brachte
  zum Neste das Männchen,
das Weibchen säugte die Welpen.
  Da lernt' ich wohl
  was Liebe sei:
  der Mutter entwandt' ich
  die Welpen nie. –
  Wo hast du nun, Mime,
  dein minniges Weibchen,
daß ich es Mutter nenne?

with even wild foxes and wolves:
  the father brought
  food to the lair,
the mother suckled the whelps.
  There I learned
  the meaning of love:
  from their mother I never
  took the whelps. –
  Where, Mime, is
  your loving wife,
that I may call her mother?

MIME
(angrily)

Was ist dir, Thor?
Ach, bist du dumm!
Bist doch weder Vogel noch Fuchs?

What's wrong with you, fool?
How stupid you are!
You're neither a bird nor a fox.

SIEGFRIED

Das zullende Kind
zogest du auf,
wärmtest mit Kleiden
den kleinen Wurm: –
wie kam dir aber
der kindische Wurm?
Du machtest wohl gar
ohne Mutter mich?

From a suckling babe
you brought me up,
warming the little
mite with clothes: –
but how did you come
by the childish mite?
You made me, no doubt,
without a mother . . .

MIME
(in great embarrassment)

Glauben sollst du,
was ich dir sage:
ich bin dir Vater
und Mutter zugleich.

You have to believe
what I tell you:
I'm your father
and mother in one.

SIEGFRIED

Das lüg'st du, garstiger Gauch! –
Wie die Jungen den Alten gleichen,
das hab' ich mir glücklich erseh'n.
Nun kam ich zum klaren Bach:
  da erspäht' ich die Bäum'
  und Thier' im Spiegel;
  Sonn' und Wolken,
  wie sie nur sind,
im Glitzer erschienen sie gleich.
  Da sah' ich denn auch   [35]
  mein eigen Bild;
  ganz anders als du
  dünkt' ich mir da:
  so glich wohl der Kröte   [15]

You're lying, you loathsome fool! –
That the young look like their parents
I've luckily seen for myself.
When I came to the limpid brook,
  I glimpsed trees and beasts
  in its glassy surface;
  sun and clouds,
  just as they are,
appeared in the glittering stream.
  And then I saw
  my own likeness, too,
  quite different from you
  I thought myself then:
  as like to a toad

ein glänzender Fisch;
doch kroch nie ein Fisch aus der
 [Kröte.

were a glittering fish,
though no fish ever crept from a toad.

MIME
(deeply annoyed)

Gräulichen Unsinn
kram'st du da aus!

What frightful nonsense
you're spouting there!

SIEGFRIED
(with increasing animation)

Sieh'st du, nun fällt
auch selbst mir ein,
was zuvor umsonst ich besann:
 wenn zum Wald ich laufe,
 dich zu verlassen,
wie das kommt, kehr' ich doch heim?

You see, what I used
to ponder in vain –
it now occurs to me, too:
 when I run off into the forest
 to leave you,
how is it I still come home?

(He leaps up.)

Von dir erst muß ich erfahren,
wer Vater und Mutter mir sei!

First I must learn from you
who are my father and mother!

MIME

Was Vater! was Mutter!
Müßige Frage!

What father! What mother!
Idle question!

(He leaps at Mime and seizes him by the throat.)

SIEGFRIED

So muß ich dich fassen
um 'was zu wissen:
gutwillig
erfahr' ich doch nichts!
So mußt' ich Alles
ab dir trotzen:
kaum das Reden
hätt' ich errathen,
entwand ich's mit Gewalt
nicht dem Schuft!
Heraus damit,
räudiger Kerl!

[41] So I must seize you
to find out anything:
willingly
I shall learn nothing!
Thus have I had to force
all things out of you:
even speech
I'd scarcely have mastered,
had I not wrung it
out of the rogue!
Out with it,
scurvy wretch!

Wer ist mir Vater und Mutter?

Who are my father and mother?

(Having nodded his head and made signs with his hands, Mime is released by Siegfried.)

MIME

An's Leben geh'st du mir schier! –
Nun lass'! Was zu wissen dich geizt,
erfahr' es, ganz wie ich's weiß. – –
 O undankbares,
 arges Kind!
Jetzt hör', wofür du mich hassest!
 Nicht bin ich Vater

You'll be the death of me yet! –
Let go! What you're eager to know
you shall learn just as I know it. – –
 O thankless,
 wicked child!
Now hear the reason you hate me!
 I'm neither your father

noch Vetter dir, –
und dennoch verdank'st du mir dich!
  Ganz fremd bist du mir,
  dem einzigen Freund;
  aus Erbarmen allein
  barg ich dich hier:
nun hab' ich lieblichen Lohn!
Was verhofft' ich Thor mir auch
  [Dank?   [27]

  nor any kinsman –
and yet you owe me everything!
  You're a stranger to me,
  your only friend;
  out of pity alone
  I sheltered you here:
what a rich reward have I now!
What a fool I was to hope for thanks!

Einst lag wimmernd ein Weib   [25]
da draußen im wilden Wald:
zur Höhle half ich ihr her,
am warmen Herd sie zu hüten.
Ein Kind trug sie im Schooße;   [26b]
traurig gebar sie's hier;
sie wand sich hin und her,
ich half, so gut ich konnt':
groß war die Noth, sie starb – [26a, 27]
doch Siegfried, der genas.   [35]

Out there in the wildwood
a woman once lay whimpering:
I helped her into the cave
to ward her by the warming hearth.
She bore a child within her womb:
in sadness she gave it birth here;
back and forth she writhed,
I helped as best I could:
great was her travail; she died –
but Siegfried, he survived.

SIEGFRIED
(slowly)

So starb meine Mutter an mir?

So my mother died through me?

MIME

Meinem Schutz übergab sie dich:

She handed you over into my care:

(Siegfried stands deep in thought.) [27]

ich schenkt' ihn gern dem Kind.
Was hat sich Mime gemüht!
Was gab sich der gute für Noth!
  »Als zullendes Kind
  zog ich dich auf« . . .

I gave it gladly to the child.
What trouble Mime took!
What pains the good man went to!
  'From a suckling babe
  I brought you up . . .'

SIEGFRIED

Mich dünkt, dess' gedachtest du
  [schon!   [27]
Jetzt sag': woher heiß ich Siegfried?

I think you've recalled that already!

Now say why my name is Siegfried!

MIME

So hieß mich die Mutter
möcht' ich dich heißen:
als Siegfried würdest
du stark und schön. –
  »Ich wärmte mit Kleiden
  den kleinen Wurm« . . .

Your mother said
I might name you so:
as Siegfried you'd grow
to be strong and good-looking. –
  'I warmed the little
  mite with clothes . . .'

SIEGFRIED

Nun melde, wie hieß meine
  [Mutter?   [27]

Now tell me, what was my mother
  [called?

Das weiß ich wahrlich kaum! –
 »Speise und Trank
 trug ich dir zu« . . .

Truly, I scarcely know! –
 'Food and drink
 I brought to you . . .'

SIEGFRIED
(animatedly)

Den Namen sollst du mir nennen!

You have to tell me her name!

MIME

Entfiel er mir wohl? Doch halt'!
Sieglinde mochte sie heißen,
die dich in Sorge[85] mir gab. –
 »Ich hütete dich
 wie die eig'ne Haut« . . .

It's slipped my mind . . . no, wait!
She who gave you to me in her grief[85]
may well have been called Sieglinde. –
 'I tended you
 as my second self . . .'

SIEGFRIED
(with increasing insistence)

Dann frag' ich, wie hieß mein Vater? [27]

Now I ask what my father was called.

MIME
(roughly)

Den hab' ich nie geseh'n.[86]

Him have I never seen.[86]

SIEGFRIED

Doch die Mutter nannte den Namen?

But didn't my mother speak his name?

MIME

Erschlagen sei er,
das sagte sie nur;
dich Vaterlosen
befahl sie mir da: –
 »und wie du erwuchsest,
 wartet' ich dein';
 dein Lager schuf ich,
 daß leicht du schlief'st« . . .

That he'd been slain
was all she said;
to me she commended
the fatherless child: –
 'and when you grew bigger,
 I waited upon you;
 I made you a bed
 so you'd sleep more softly . . .'.

SIEGFRIED

Still mit dem alten
Staarenlied![87] –
Soll ich der Kunde glauben,
hast du mir nichts gelogen,
so lass' mich Zeichen seh'n!

Stop that eternal
squawking![87] –
If I'm to believe your story
and if you haven't lied to me,
then let me see some proof!

MIME

Was soll dir's noch bezeugen?

What else would prove it to you?

SIEGFRIED

Dir glaub' ich nicht mit dem Ohr',
dir glaub' ich nur mit dem Aug':

I won't believe you with my ears
but only with my eyes:

welch' Zeichen zeugt für dich?   what evidence bears you witness?

MIME

(reflecting for a moment, then fetching the two pieces of a broken sword) [17, 23, 15]

Das gab mir deine Mutter: Your mother gave me this:
für Mühe, Kost und Pflege   for trouble, board and care
ließ sie's als schwachen Lohn.   she left it as paltry payment.
Sieh' her, ein zerbroch'nes Schwert!   See here, a shattered sword!
Dein Vater, sagte sie, führt' es,   Your father, she said, had borne it
als im letzten Kampf er erlag.   when he fell in his final fight.

SIEGFRIED
(enthusiastically)

Und diese Stücken   And these fragments
  sollst du mir schmieden: you shall forge for me:
dann schwing' ich mein rechtes   then I'll wield my rightful sword!
[Schwert!
Auf! Eile dich, Mime,   [41]   Come on now, Mime, bestir yourself
  mühe dich rasch;   and be quick about it;
  kannst du 'was recht's,   if there's aught you're good at,
  nun zeig' deine Kunst!   then show me your art!
  Täusche mich nicht   Don't try to trick me
  mit schlechtem Tand: with worthless trinkets:
  den Trümmern allein   [23]   in those shards alone
  trau' ich 'was zu.   do I place any trust.
  Find' ich dich faul,   If I find you idle
  füg'st du sie schlecht,   or you fit them badly,
  flick'st du mit Flausen   if you spoil the firm steel
  den festen Stahl, –   with flimsy excuses,
dir Feigem fahr' ich zu Leib',   I'll have your craven hide;
das Fegen[88] lern'st du von mir!   you'll learn from me then what a
     [tanning[88] means!

Denn heute noch, schwör' ich,   For I swear that I'll have
  will ich das Schwert;   the sword today;
die Waffe gewinn' ich noch heut'.   the weapon I'll win for myself today.

MIME
(anxiously)

Was willst du noch heut' mit dem   What would you do with the sword
[Schwert?   [today?

SIEGFRIED

Aus dem Wald fort   Go forth from the forest
  in die Welt zieh'n: into the world:
nimmer kehr' ich zurück.   I'll nevermore return.
  Wie ich froh bin,   How glad I am
  daß ich frei ward,   to have gained my freedom,
nichts mich bindet und zwingt!   nothing binds or constrains me!
Mein Vater bist du nicht,   You're not my father,
in der Ferne bin ich heim;   my home's far away;

dein Herd ist nicht mein Haus,	your hearth's not my house,
meine Decke nicht dein Dach.	nor your roof my shelter.
Wie der Fisch froh	Fleet as the fish
in der Fluth schwimmt,	as it swims in the floodtide,
wie der Fink frei	free as the finch
sich davon schwingt:	as it soars aloft,
flieg' ich von hier,	I fly from here
fluthe davon,	and float away,
wie der Wind über'n Wald	wafting along like the wind
weh' ich dahin –	over woodland –
dich, Mime, nie wieder zu seh'n!	nevermore, Mime, to see you again!

(He runs into the forest.)

MIME
(in the utmost fear)

Halte! halte! wohin?	Stop! Stop! Where are you going?
He! Siegfried!	Hey! Siegfried!
Siegfried! He![89] –	Siegfried! Hey![89] –

(He gazes in astonishment as Siegfried rushes away. He returns to the forge and sits down behind the anvil.)

Da stürmt er hin! –	[6]	Away he storms! –
Nun sitz' ich da: –		And here I sit: –
zur alten Noth		to my age-old plight
hab' ich die neue;		I can now add a new one;
vernagelt bin ich nun ganz! –		I'm well and truly trapped! –
Wie helf' ich mir jetzt?	[15]	How can I help myself now?
Wie halt' ich ihn fest?	[17]	How shall I hold him fast?
Wie führ' ich den Huien		How lead the hothead
zu Fafner's Nest? –		to Fafner's lair?
Wie füg' ich die Stücken	[3]	How join the shards
des tückischen Stahl's?		of insidious steel?
Keines Ofens Gluth		No furnace's fire
glüht mir die ächten;		can fuse these sterling splinters,
keines Zwergen Hammer		nor any dwarf's hammer
zwingt mir die harten:		subdue their stubborn strength:

(harshly)

des Niblungen Neid,	the Nibelung's envy,
Noth und Schweiß	need and sweat
nietet mir Nothung nicht,	cannot join Nothung together

(sobbing)

schweißt mir das Schwert nicht zu	nor weld the sword and make it whole! –
[ganz! –	

(He sinks down in his despair on the stool behind the anvil.)

SCENE TWO

(The Wanderer (Wotan) enters from the forest through the door at the back of the cave. He is wearing a long, dark-blue cloak; he carries a spear as a staff. On his head he wears a hat with a broad, round brim, which hangs down over his face.) [43]

Heil dir, weiser Schmied!
Dem wegmüden Gast
  gönne hold
  des Hauses Herd!

[44] Hail to you, wise smith!
To a way-weary guest
  you'll not begrudge
  your house's hearth!

MIME
(starting up in terror)

Wer ist's, der im wilden
Walde mich sucht?
Wer verfolgt mich im öden Forst?

Who is it who seeks me out
in the wildwood?
Who tracks me through the desolate
[forest?

WANDERER
(approaching very slowly, one step at a time)

Wand'rer heißt mich die Welt:
weit wandert' ich schon,
  auf der Erde Rücken
  rührt' ich mich viel.

As Wanderer am I known to the world:
already I've wandered widely
  and over the earth's broad back
  have ofttimes wended my way.

MIME

So rühre dich fort
und raste nicht hier,
nennt dich Wand'rer die Welt.

Then wend your way further
and don't rest here
if you're known to the world as the
[Wanderer.

WANDERER

Gastlich ruht' ich bei Guten,
Gaben gönnten viele mir:
  denn Unheil fürchtet,
  wer unhold ist.[90]

[44] With good men I've rested as their guest,
many have granted me gifts:
  for he who's ungracious
  fears misfortune.[90]

MIME

Unheil wohnte
  immer bei mir:
willst du dem armen es mehren?

Misfortune ever
  dwelt with me:
will you make it worse for the wretch?

WANDERER
(still advancing slowly)

Viel erforscht' ich,
  erkannte viel:
wicht'ges konnt' ich
  manchem künden,
  manchem wehren,
  was ihn mühte,
nagende Herzens-Noth.

[44] Much I've fathomed,
  much made out:
matters of moment
  I've made known to many
  and many I've saved
  from whatever irked them,
cares that gnawed at their hearts.

MIME

Spürtest du klug
und erspähtest du viel,

Though you've skilfully scouted
and spied out much,

hier brauch' ich nicht Spürer noch
   [Späher.
Einsam will ich
und einzeln sein,
Lungerern lass' ich den Lauf.

I need no scouts or spies around here.

Alone and apart
I wish to be
and let loiterers go on their way.

WANDERER
(again advancing a little)

Mancher wähnte
weise zu sein,
nur was ihm noth that,
wußte er nicht;
was ihm frommte,
ließ ich erfragen:
lohnend lehrt' ihn mein Wort.

Many's the man
who thought himself wise
but what he needed
he did not know;
I let him ask me
what might avail him:
my words he found worth while.

MIME
(increasingly anxious, as he watches the Wanderer approach)

Müß'ges Wissen
wahren manche:
ich weiß mir g'rade genug;

Many men garner
idle knowledge:
I know just as much as I need;

(The Wanderer has advanced as far as the hearth.)

mir genügt mein Witz,   [15]
ich will nicht mehr:
dir Weisem weis' ich den Weg!

my wits suffice,
I want no more:
I'll show you on your way, you sage!

WANDERER
(sitting down at the hearth) [9]

Hier sitz' ich am Herd,
und setze mein Haupt
der Wissens-Wette⁹¹ zum Pfand:
mein Kopf ist dein,
du hast ihn erkies't,
erfräg'st du mir nicht
was dir frommt,
lös' ich's mit Lehren nicht ein.

I sit by the hearth here
and stake my head
as pledge in a wager of wits:⁹¹
my head is yours
to treat as you choose,
if you fail to ask
what you need to know
and I don't redeem it with my lore.

(Mime, who has been staring open-mouthed at the Wanderer, now starts violently.)

MIME
(pusillanimously to himself)

Wie werd' ich den lauernden los?   [17]
Verfänglich muß ich ihn fragen. –

How can I rid myself of this intruder?
My questions I must couch with care. –

(He pulls himself together, as though determined to show strictness.)
(aloud)

Dein Haupt pfänd' ich   [9]
für den Herd:
nun sorg', es sinnig zu lösen!

As pledge for my hearth
I accept your head:
take care you redeem it with thoughtful
   [reply!

Drei der Fragen
stell' ich mir frei.

Three are the questions
I freely ask.

WANDERER

Dreimal muß ich's treffen.   [15]   Thrice must I hit the mark.

MIME
(collecting his thoughts) [17]

Du rührtest dich viel	[44]	You've travelled much
auf der Erde Rücken,		on the earth's broad back
die Welt durchwandertest weit: –		and wandered far through the world: –
nun sage mir schlau,		now tell me cunningly
welches Geschlecht		what is the race
tagt[92] in der Erde Tiefe?		that trades[92] in the depths of the earth?

WANDERER

In der Erde Tiefe		The Nibelungs
tagen die Nibelungen:		trade in the depths of the earth:
Nibelheim ist ihr Land.		Nibelheim is their land.
Schwarzalben[93] sind sie;		Black elves[93] they are;
Schwarz-Alberich		Black Alberich
hütet' als Herrscher sie einst:		once watched over them as their lord:
eines Zauberringes	[6]	a magic ring's
zwingende Kraft		compelling power
zähmt' ihm das fleißige Volk.		tamed his toiling people.
Reicher Schätze	[5]	A glittering hoard
schimmernden Hort		of rich-gemmed jewels
häuften sie ihm:		for him they heaped on high:
der sollte die Welt ihm		it was meant to win him the world. –
[gewinnen. –	[8b, 15, 9]	

Zum zweiten was frägst du Zwerg?   What is your second question, dwarf?

MIME
(sinking into even deeper thought) [15, 17]

Viel, Wanderer,	[44]	Much, Wanderer,
weißt du mir		I see you know
aus der Erde Nabelnest:[94] –		of the earth's umbilical nest:[94] –
nun sage mir schlicht,		now tell me straight
welches Geschlecht		what's the race that rests
ruht auf der Erde Rücken?		on the earth's broad-shouldered back?

WANDERER

Auf der Erde Rücken		On the earth's broad back
wuchtet der Riesen Geschlecht:	[11]	weighs the race of giants:
Riesenheim ist ihr Land.		Riesenheim is their land.
Fasolt und Fafner,		Fasolt and Fafner,
der Rauhen Fürsten,		the roughnecks' princes,
neideten Nibelung's Macht;		envied the Nibelung's power;
den gewaltigen Hort		the mighty hoard
gewannen sie sich,		they won for themselves
errangen mit ihm den Ring:		and with it gained the ring:
um den entbrannte		strife flared up

den Brüdern Streit; [6] between the brothers;
der Fasolt fällte, [18] he who murdered Fasolt,
als wilder Wurm Fafner now guards the hoard
hütet nun Fafner den Hort. – in the form of a fearsome dragon. –

Die dritte Frage nun droht. [9] Now the third question threatens.

MIME

(completely lost to the world and deep in thought) [15, 17]
Viel, Wanderer, [44] Much, Wanderer,
weißt du mir I see you know
von der Erde rauhem Rücken: – of the broad earth's rugged back: –
nun sage mir wahr, now tell me truly
welches Geschlecht which is the race
wohnt auf wolkigen Höh'n? that dwells on cloud-covered heights?

WANDERER

Auf wolkigen Höh'n On cloud-covered heights
wohnen die Götter: [8] there dwell the gods:
Walhall heißt ihr Saal. Valhalla is their hall.
Lichtalben sind sie; Light elves they are;
Licht-Alberich, Light Alberich,
Wotan waltet der Schaar. Wotan, rules their host.
Aus der Welt-Esche [20] From the world-ash's
weihlichstem Aste holiest bough
schuf er sich einen Schaft: he made himself a shaft:
dorrt der Stamm, though the trunk may wither,
nie verdirbt doch der Speer; [9] the spear shall never fail;
mit seiner Spitze with the point of that weapon
sperrt Wotan die Welt. Wotan governs the world.
Heil'ger Verträge Hallowed treaties'
Treue-Runen binding runes
schnitt in den Schaft er ein: he whittled into its shaft:
den Haft der Welt he who wields the spear
hält in der Hand that Wotan's fist still spans
wer den Speer führt, holds within his hand
den Wotan's Faust umspannt. control over all the world.
Ihm neigte sich [3] Before him bowed
der Niblungen Heer;[95] [6] the Nibelungs' host;[95]
der Riesen Gezücht the brood of giants
zähmte sein Rath: was tamed by his counsel:
ewig gehorchen sie alle [43] forever they all obey
des Speeres starkem Herrn. [9] the mighty lord of the spear.
(In an apparently spontaneous gesture he strikes the ground with his spear; a distant roll of thunder can be heard, causing Mime to jump violently.)
Nun rede, weiser Zwerg: Now tell me, wily dwarf:
wußt' ich der Fragen Rath? am I quit of your questions?
behalte mein Haupt ich frei? Am I free to keep my head?

MIME

(after carefully observing the Wanderer with his spear, he now falls into a state of great anxiety, looking for his tools in his confusion and timidly averting his eyes) [15]

Fragen und Haupt	Questions and head
hast du gelös't:	you've resolved and redeemed:
nun, Wand'rer, geh' deines Weg's!	now, Wanderer, go on your way!

WANDERER

Was zu wissen dir frommt	[44]	You ought to have asked
solltest du fragen;		what you needed to know;
Kunde verbürgte mein Kopf: –	[43, 9]	my head stood bail for knowledge: –
daß du nun nicht weißt		since you still do not know
was dir frommt,		what you need to know,
dess' fass' ich jetzt deines als Pfand.		I'll now take yours in pledge.
Gastlich nicht		Your greeting, I thought,
galt mir dein Gruß:		was unfit for a guest;
mein Haupt gab ich		into your hands
in deine Hand,		I gave my head
um mich des Herdes zu freu'n.		to enjoy the warmth of your hearth.
Nach Wettens Pflicht		By the rules of the wager
pfänd' ich nun dich,		I'll take you as pawn
lösest du drei		if you cannot easily
der Fragen nicht leicht:		answer three questions:
drum frische dir, Mime, den Muth!		so, Mime, pluck up your courage!

MIME

(very timidly and hesitantly, but finally pulling himself together in frightened submission) [15]

Lang' schon mied ich		It's long since I quit
mein Heimathland,		my native land,
lang' schon schied ich		long since I left
aus der Mutter Schooß;		my mother's womb;
mir leuchtete Wotan's Auge,	[8]	Wotan's eye has lighted upon me,

(looking briefly and surreptitiously at the Wanderer)

zur Höhle lugt' er herein:	into my cave he peered:
vor ihm magert	my mother's wit
mein Mutterwitz.[96]	grows weak before it.[96]
Doch frommt mir's nun weise zu sein,	But since I now need to be wise,
Wand'rer, frage denn zu!	Wanderer, ask away!
Vielleicht glückt mir's gezwungen	Perhaps, when forced, I may yet succeed
zu lösen des Zwergen Haupt.	in redeeming the head of the dwarf.

WANDERER

(again seating himself more comfortably)

Nun, ehrlicher Zwerg,		Now, worthy dwarf,
sag' mir zum ersten:		tell me first:
welches ist das Geschlecht,	[29]	what is the race
dem Wotan schlimm sich zeigte,		which Wotan acted badly towards

(very softly but audibly)

und das doch das liebste ihm lebt?	and yet which is dearest of all to him?

(gaining courage) [15]

Wenig hört' ich	Little I've heard
von Heldensippen:	of heroes' kin
der Frage doch mach' ich mich frei.	and yet I can wriggle out of this question.
Die Wälsungen sind [29]	The Wälsungs
das Wunschgeschlecht,[97]	are the favoured race[97]
das Wotan zeugte	which Wotan fathered
und zärtlich liebte,	and fondly cherished,
zeigt' er auch Ungunst ihm.	while showing them disfavour.
Siegmund und Sieglind'	Siegmund and Sieglind'
stammten von Wälse,	were sired by Wälse,
ein wild-verzweifeltes	a wildly desperate
Zwillingspaar:	pair of twins:
Siegfried zeugten sie selbst, [35]	Siegfried they begat themselves,
den stärksten Wälsungensproß.	the strongest scion of the Wälsungs.
Behalt' ich, Wand'rer, [15]	Wanderer, have I kept my head
zum ersten mein Haupt?	in answer to your opening question?

WANDERER

(good-humouredly)

Wie doch genau	How well
das Geschlecht du mir nenn'st:	you name that race to me:
schlau eracht' ich dich argen!	you're a sly one, I see, you scoundrel!
Der ersten Frage	You've acquitted yourself
wardst du frei;	of my opening question;
zum zweiten nun sag' mir, Zwerg! [17]	secondly, tell me, you dwarf! –
Ein weiser Niblung	A wily Niblung
wahret Siegfried:	cares for Siegfried:
Fafner'n soll er ihm fällen, [18]	Fafner he's to kill for him,
daß den Ring er erränge,	so that he may gain the ring
des Hortes Herrscher zu sein.	and so be master of the hoard.
Welches Schwert	Which is the sword
muß Siegfried nun schwingen,	that Siegfried must wield
taug' es zu Fafner's Tod?	if Fafner's death is to follow?

MIME

(increasingly forgetful of his present situation and rubbing his hands with pleasure) [15]

Nothung heißt	Nothung's the name
ein neidliches Schwert; [23]	of a fearsome sword;
in einer Esche Stamm	Wotan drove it
stieß es Wotan:	into an ash-tree's trunk:
dem sollt' es geziemen,	it was meant for the man
der aus dem Stamm es zög'.	who could draw it forth from the trunk.
Der stärksten Helden	Of the strongest heroes
keiner bestand's:	none succeeded:
Siegmund, der Kühne,	Siegmund the valiant
konnt's allein;	alone could do so;
fechtend führt' er's im Streit,	fighting, he bore it in battle

bis an Wotan's Speer es zersprang.
    Nun verwahrt die Stücken
ein weiser Schmied;
denn er weiß, daß allein
mit dem Wotansschwert
ein kühnes dummes Kind, [35]
Siegfried, den Wurm versehrt. [23]

until it was splintered by Wotan's spear.
    A wily dwarf
now keeps the fragments;
he knows that only
with Wotan's sword
can that foolish and foolhardy child,
Siegfried, harm the dragon.

(well pleased with himself)

    Behalt' ich Zwerg
auch zweitens mein Haupt?

    Do I, the dwarf, keep
my head a second time, too?

WANDERER
(laughing)

    Der witzigste bist du
unter den Weisen:
wer käm' dir an Klugheit gleich?
    Doch bist du so klug,
den kindischen Helden
für Zwergen-Zwecke zu nützen: [15]
    mit der dritten Frage
droh' ich nun! –
Sag' mir, du weiser
Waffenschmied,
wer wird aus den starken Stücken
Nothung, das Schwert, wohl
[schweißen? [35]

    You're the wittiest
of the wise:
who could match you in cunning?
    But if you're so sly
as to use the childish hero
to further your dwarfish ends,
    I threaten you now
with the third of my questions! –
Tell me, you wily
weapon-smith,
who do you think will forge Nothung,
the sword, out of these mighty
[fragments?

(Mime starts up in utter terror.)

MIME
(in a screeching tone of voice)

Die Stücken! das Schwert! [41]
O weh! mir schwindelt! –
Was fang' ich an?
Was fällt mir ein?
Verfluchter Stahl,
daß ich dich gestohlen!
Er hat mich vernagelt
in Pein und Noth;
mir bleibt er hart,
ich kann ihn nicht hämmern:
Niet' und Löthe
läßt mich im Stich!

The fragments! The sword!
Alas! My head's swimming! –
Whatever have I started!
Whatever am I thinking of?
Accursèd steel,
alas that I ever stole you!
It has trapped me
in torment and need;
it remains unyielding,
I cannot hammer it:
rivets and solder
fail me completely!

(Like a man no longer in possession of his wits, he throws his tools around and breaks out in sheer despair.)

Der weiseste Schmied
weiß sich nicht Rath:
wer schweißt nun das Schwert,
schaff' ich es nicht?
Das Wunder, wie soll ich's wissen?

The wisest of smiths
is now at a loss:
who'll forge the sword
if I cannot do so?
How should I know of this wonder?

WANDERER
(having risen calmly from the hearth)

Dreimal solltest du fragen,	[43]	Thrice you were meant to question me,
dreimal stand ich dir frei:		thrice I was at your disposal:
nach eitlen Fernen		you asked after
forschtest du;		futile, far-off things;
doch was zunächst dir sich fand,		but what concerned you most closely
was dir nützt, fiel dir nicht ein.		and what you most needed to know, you
		[omitted to ask.

Nun ich's errathe,	[23]	Now that I've guessed it,
wirst du verrückt:	[9]	you lose your wits:
gewonnen hab' ich		I've won
das witzige Haupt. –		your wily head. –
Jetzt, Fafner's kühner Bezwinger,	[18]	Now, Fafner's valiant conqueror,
hör', verfall'ner Zwerg:		listen, you ill-fated dwarf:
nur wer das Fürchten		only he who never
nie erfuhr,	[23]	knew fear
schmiedet Nothung neu.		will forge the sword anew.

(Mime stares at him, wide-eyed: he turns to go.)

Dein weises Haupt		Henceforth ward
wahre von heut':		your wise head well:
verfallen – lass' ich es dem,	[35]	forfeit I leave it to him
der das Fürchten nicht gelernt.		who knows not the meaning of fear.

(He turns away, smiling, and disappears quickly into the forest. Mime has sunk down on the stool as though crushed.)

SCENE THREE

(Mime stares ahead into the sunlit forest and gradually begins to tremble violently.)

MIME

Verfluchtes Licht!	[14a, 14b]	Accursèd light!
Was flammt dort die Luft?		Is the air there on fire?
Was flackert und lackert,		What's flashing and gleaming,
was flimmert und schwirrt,		what's glinting and whirling,
was schwebt dort und webt		what's floating there, weaving
und wabert umher?		and wavering round?
Dort glimmert's und glitzt's		It glisters and glows
in der Sonne Gluth:		in the gleam of the sun:
was säuselt und summt		what's rustling and buzzing
und saus't nun gar?		and now even roaring?
Es brummt und braus't		It booms and crashes
und prasselt hieher!		and crackles this way!
Dort bricht's durch den Wald,		See, it bursts through the wood,
will auf mich zu!		is making towards me!

(He rears up in terror.)

Ein gräßlicher Rachen	Grisly jaws

reißt sich mir auf! –
Der Wurm will mich fangen!
Fafner! Fafner!

are gaping towards me! –
The dragon is trying to catch me!
Fafner! Fafner!

(Siegfried bursts through the undergrowth. Mime sinks down behind the anvil with a scream.)
[23]

SIEGFRIED

(still off-stage, his movements evident from the sound of twigs snapping in the bushes)

Heda! du Fauler!
bist du nun fertig?

Hey there, you idler!
Say, have you finished?

(Siegfried enters the cave.)

Schnell! wie steht's mit dem Schwert? [41]

Quick! How's the sword coming on?

(He stops in surprise.)

Wo steckt der Schmied?
Stahl er sich fort?
Hehe! Mime! du Memme!
Wo bist du? wo birg'st du dich?

Where's the smith got to?
Has he slipped away?
Hey there, Mime, you coward!
Where are you? Where are you hiding?

MIME

(in a feeble voice, from behind the anvil)

Bist du es, Kind?
Kommst du allein?

My child, is it you?
Have you come alone?

SIEGFRIED

(laughing)

Hinter dem Ambos? –
Sag', was schufest du dort?
Schärftest du mir das Schwert?

Behind the anvil? –
Tell me, what were you doing there?
Were you honing my sword for me?

MIME

(emerging, deeply disturbed and confused)

Das Schwert? das Schwert?
wie möcht' ich's schweißen? –

The sword? The sword?
How might I forge it? –

(half to himself)

»Nur wer das Fürchten
nie erfuhr,
schmiedet Nothung neu.« –
Zu weise ward ich
für solches Werk!

'Only he who never
knew fear
can forge the sword anew.' –
I've grown too wise
for work like that!

[23]

SIEGFRIED

(forcefully)

Wirst du mir reden?
Soll ich dir rathen?

[41]

Will you answer?
Or must I help you?

MIME

(as before)

Wo nähm' ich redlichen Rath? –
Mein weises Haupt
hab' ich verwettet:

[43]

Where might I take honest counsel? –
I've wagered away
my wily head:

verfallen, verlor ich's an den,	[35]	forfeit, I've lost it to him
»der das Fürchten nicht gelernt«. −		'who never learned the meaning of [fear.' −

SIEGFRIED
(impatiently)

Sind mir das Flausen?	Are these evasions?
Willst du mir flieh'n?	You want to escape me?

MIME
(gradually regaining control of himself)

Wohl flöh' ich dem,	Well might I flee
der's Fürchten kennt: −	from the man who knows fear: −
doch das ließ ich dem Kinde zu [lehren!	but that have I failed to teach the child!
Ich Dummer vergaß	Like a fool, I forgot
was einzig gut:	what's uniquely good:
Liebe zu mir	he was meant to learn
sollt' er lernen; −	to love me; −
das gelang nun leider faul!	alas, that went amiss!
Wie bring' ich das Fürchten ihm bei?	How shall I teach him what fear is?

SIEGFRIED
(seizing him)

He! Muß ich helfen?	Hey! Must I help you?
Was fegtest du heut'?	What have you furbished today?

MIME

Um dich nur besorgt,	Concerned but for you,
versank ich in Sinnen,	I was sunk in thought
wie ich dich wichtiges wiese.	of how to teach you something weighty.

SIEGFRIED
(laughing)

Bis unter den Sitz	Right under the seat
war'st du versunken:	I see you had sunk:
was wichtiges fandest du da?	what matters of weight did you find [there?

MIME
(steadily regaining his self-control)

Das Fürchten lernt' ich für dich,		For you, I have learned the meaning of [fear,
daß ich's dich Dummen lehre.	[41]	so I might teach it to you, you fool.

SIEGFRIED
(with calm astonishment)

Was ist's mit dem Fürchten?	What's this about fear?

MIME

Erfuhr'st du's noch nie,	You've never felt it
und willst aus dem Wald	and yet you want to leave the woods
doch fort in die Welt?	and go out into the world?
Was frommte das festeste Schwert, [23]	What use is the stoutest of swords
blieb dir das Fürchten fern?	if fear is still a stranger to you?

SIEGFRIED
(impatiently)

Faulen Rath	No doubt you're inventing
erfindest du wohl?	worthless advice.

MIME
(approaching Siegfried, with growing trust)

Deiner Mutter Rath [27]	Your mother's counsel
redet aus mir:	speaks through me:
was ich gelobte	what I promised her
muß ich nun lösen,	I must now discharge
in die listige Welt	and not let you leave
dich nicht zu entlassen,	for the cunning world
eh' du nicht das Fürchten gelernt.	until you've learned the meaning of fear.

SIEGFRIED
(forcefully)

Ist's eine Kunst,	If it's an art,
was kenn ich sie nicht? –	then why don't I know it? –
Heraus! Was ist's mit dem Fürchten?	Out with it? What is this fear?

MIME

Fühltest du nie	Have you never felt
im finst'ren Wald,	in the gloomy forest
bei Dämmerschein	as darkness spreads
am dunklen Ort,	to some twilit spot
wenn fern es säuselt,	and, from afar, a rustling,
summt und saus't,	humming, roaring sound draws near,
wildes Brummen	a furious booming
näher braus't,	crashes closer,
wirres Flackern	a whirling flicker
um dich flimmert, [14a, 14b]	flits around you
schwellend Schwirren	and, swelling and whirring,
zu Leib' dir schwebt, –	floats towards you, –

(trembling)

fühltest du dann nicht grieselnd	have you not felt the terror then
Grausen die Glieder dir fahen?	that, creepingly, seizes hold of your [limbs?

(quivering)

Glühender Schauer [39]	Searing shuddering
schüttelt die Glieder,	shakes your frame,

(with quavering voice)

in der Brust bebend und bang	quaking and quivering in your breast,

berstet hämmernd das Herz? –
Fühltest du das noch nicht,
das Fürchten blieb dir noch fremd.

your hammering heart is bursting? –
If you've never felt all this,
then fear remains unknown to you.

SIEGFRIED
(thoughtfully)

Sonderlich seltsam
muß das sein!
Hart und fest,   [35]
fühl' ich, steht mir das Herz.
Das Grieseln und Grausen,   [14a]
das Glühen und Schauern,
Hitzen und Schwindeln,
Hämmern und Beben –
gern begehr' ich das Bangen,
sehnend verlangt mich

Passing strange
all this must be!
I feel that my heart
beats firmly and strongly.
The shuddering and shivering,
searing and trembling,
burning and fainting,
hammering and quaking,
how dearly I long to feel this dread
and yearningly crave

(tenderly)

der Lust. –
Doch wie bring'st du,
Mime, mir's bei?
Wie wär'st du Memme mir Meister?

such delights. –
But, Mime, how
can you teach me it?
How could a coward be my master?

MIME

Folge mir nur,
ich führe dich wohl;
sinnend fand ich es aus.
Ich weiß einen schlimmen Wurm,   [18]
der würgt' und schlang schon viel:
Fafner lehrt dich das Fürchten,
folg'st du mir zu seinem Nest.   [39]

Just follow me
and I'll lead you there;
I've thought up a way of teaching you.
I know of an evil dragon
who's killed and devoured many:
Fafner will teach you fear
if you'll follow me to his lair.

SIEGFRIED

Wo liegt er im Nest?

Where does he lie in his lair?

MIME

Neid-Höhle[98]
wird es genannt:
im Ost, am Ende des Wald's.

Neidhöhle[98]
it is called:
to the east, at the edge of the wood.

SIEGFRIED

Dann wär's nicht weit von der Welt?

And so it's not far from the world?

MIME

Bei Neidhöhle liegt sie ganz nah'!

It lies very close to the cave!

SIEGFRIED

Dahin denn sollst du mich führen:
lernt' ich das Fürchten,
dann fort in die Welt!
Drum[99] schnell! Schaffe das Schwert,

Thither you shall lead me:
when I've learned the meaning of fear,
I'll away then into the world!
Be quick then! Make me the sword,

in der Welt will ich es schwingen.　　　　　in the world I mean to wield it.

MIME

Das Schwert? O Noth!　　　　[41]　　The sword? O woe!

SIEGFRIED

Rasch in die Schmiede!　　　　　　　Into the smithy with you!
Weis' was du schuf'st.　　　　　　　Show me what you've made.

MIME

Verfluchter Stahl!　　　　　　　Accursèd steel!
Zu flicken versteh' ich ihn nicht!　　　I don't understand how to patch it up!
Den zähen Zauber　　　　　　　No dwarf's resources
bezwingt keines Zwergen Kraft.　　　can master the stubborn spell.
Wer das Fürchten nicht kennt,　　　　He who's never known fear
der fänd' wohl eher die Kunst.　　　　would sooner find the art.

SIEGFRIED

Feine Finten　　　　　　　　The idler is skilled
weiß mir der Faule;　　　　　　in subtle wiles;
daß er ein Stümper　　　　　　he ought to admit
sollt' er gesteh'n:　　　　　　to being a bungler:
nun lügt er sich listig heraus. —　　by cunning he lies his way out. —
Her mit den Stücken!　　　　　Here with the fragments!
Fort mit dem Stümper!　　　[23]　Away with the bungler!
(striding over to the hearth)
Des Vaters Stahl　　　　　　For me my father's blade
fügt sich wohl mir:　　　　　will doubtless fit together:
ich selbst schweiße das Schwert!　[40]　I'll forge the sword myself!
(Scattering Mime's tools, he sets to work impetuously.)

MIME

Hättest du fleißig　　　　[15]　　Had you attentively
die Kunst gepflegt,　　　　　　studied the art,
jetzt käm' dir's wahrlich zu gut;　　it would surely have stood you in good
　　　　　　　　　　　　　　　　[stead;
doch lässig war'st du　　　　　　but you were always
stets in der Lehr':　　　　　　lax in your lessons:
was willst du rechtes nun rüsten?　　how do you plan to prepare it now?

SIEGFRIED

Was der Meister nicht kann,　　　　Could the lad achieve
vermöcht' es der Knabe,　　　　　what the master can't do,
hätt' er ihm immer gehorcht? —　　even though he had always obeyed
　　　　　　　　　　　　　　　　him? —
(He cocks a snook at him.)
Jetzt mach' dich fort,　　　　　Be off with you now,
misch' dich nicht d'rein:　　　　stop meddling here:
sonst fäll'st du mir mit in's Feuer!　[40]　or you'll fall in the fire, too.

(He has heaped up a large pile of charcoal on the hearth and keeps the fire going while fixing the fragments of the sword in the vice and filing it down.)

MIME

(sitting down to one side and watching Siegfried at work)

Was mach'st du denn da?	What are you doing?
Nimm doch die Löthe:	Here, take the solder:
den Brei braut' ich schon längst.	I made the paste some time ago.

SIEGFRIED

Fort mit dem Brei!	Away with the paste!
Ich brauch' ihn nicht:	It's not what I need:
mit Bappe[100] back' ich kein Schwert!	I'll smelt no sword with pap![100]

MIME

Du zerfeil'st die Feile,	You're filing the file away
zerreib'st die Raspel:	and rubbing the rasp to shreds:
wie willst du den Stahl zerstampfen?	why pound the steel to pieces?

SIEGFRIED

Zersponnen muß ich	Spun out into splinters
in Spähne ihn seh'n:	I have to see it:
was entzwei ist, zwing' ich mir so.	what lies in two, I thus force together.

(He continues filing with great enthusiasm.)

MIME

(aside)

Hier hilft kein Kluger,	No sage can help here,
das seh' ich klar:	I see that clearly:
hier hilft dem Dummen	here only folly
die Dummheit allein!	can help the fool!
Wie er sich rührt	How he stirs
und mächtig regt:	and mightily strives:
ihm schwindet der Stahl,	the steel's disappearing
doch wird ihm nicht schwül! –	and yet he doesn't grow hot! –

(Siegfried has fanned the forge fire until it glows brighter than ever.)

Nun ward ich so alt	I've grown as old
wie Höhl' und Wald,	as cave and wood,
und hab' nicht so 'was geseh'n!	but never saw the like!

(While Siegfried continues filing down the fragments of the sword with impetuous enthusiasm, Mime goes and sits somewhat further away.)

Mit dem Schwert gelingt's,	He'll succeed with the sword,
das lern' ich wohl:	I can see that clearly:
furchtlos fegt er's zu ganz, –	fearless, he'll furbish it whole, –
der Wand'rer wußt' es gut! –	the Wanderer knew he would! –
Wie berg' ich nun	How can I save
mein banges Haupt?	my timid head?
Dem kühnen Knaben verfiel's, [35]	It will fall to the valiant lad
lehrt' ihn nicht Fafner die Furcht. –	if Fafner doesn't teach him fear! –

(leaping up with mounting disquiet and then stooping down)

Doch weh' mir Armen!	[18]	But, alas, poor me!
Wie würgt' er den Wurm,		For how could he slay the dragon
erführ' er das Fürchten von ihm?		if he'd first learnt fear from the beast?
Wie erräng' ich mir den Ring?	[6]	How could I win the ring for myself?
Verfluchte Klemme!		Accursèd quandary!
Da klebt' ich fest,		I'd be firmly stuck
fänd' ich nicht klugen Rath,		if I couldn't find some clever means
wie den Furchtlosen selbst ich		by which to defeat the fearless lad. –
[bezwäng'. –		

(Siegfried has filed down the fragments and collected them in a crucible, which he now places on the forge fire.)

SIEGFRIED

He, Mime, geschwind:		Hey, Mime, quick:
wie heißt das Schwert,		what's the name of the sword
das ich in Spähne zersponnen?	[23]	that I've spun out into splinters?

MIME
(starting in surprise and turning to Siegfried)

Nothung nennt sich		Nothung's the name
das neidliche Schwert:		of the fearsome sword:
deine Mutter gab mir die Mär'.		your mother told me the tale.

(While singing the following, Siegfried fans the flames with the bellows.)

SIEGFRIED

Nothung! Nothung!	[23b]	Nothung! Nothung!
Neidliches Schwert!		Fearsome sword!
was mußtest du zerspringen?		Why did you have to shatter?
Zu Spreu nun schuf ich	[45]	I've turned your sharp-edged
die scharfe Pracht,		pride to chaff,
im Tigel brat' ich die Spähne!		in the melting-pot I smelt the splinters.
Hoho! hoho!		Hoho! Hoho!
Hohei! hohei! hoho!		Hohei! Hohei! Hoho!
Blase, Balg,		Blow, you bellows,
blase die Gluth! –		fan the flames!
Wild im Walde		Wild in the woodland
wuchs ein Baum,		grew a tree:
den hab' ich im Forst gefällt:		I felled it in the forest:
die braune Esche		the fallow ash
brannt' ich zur Kohl',		I burned to charcoal,
auf dem Herd nun liegt sie gehäuft!		it now lies heaped on the hearth!
Hoho! hoho!		Hoho! Hoho!
Hohei! hohei! hoho!		Hohei! Hohei! Hoho!
Blase, Balg,		Blow, you bellows,
blase die Gluth! –		fan the flames! –
Des Baumes Kohle,		How bravely
wie brennt sie kühn,		the wood-coal is burning,
wie glüht sie hell und hehr!		how bright and glorious it glows!
In springenden Funken		It spurts out

sprühet sie auf:
hohei! hoho! hohei!
zerschmilzt mir des Stahles Spreu.

Hoho! hoho!
Hohei! hohei! hoho!
  Blase, Balg,
  blase die Gluth! −

spouting sparks:
hohei! Hoho! Hohei!
It melts down the chaff-like steel.

Hoho! Hoho!
Hohei! Hohei! Hoho!
  Blow, you bellows,
  fan the flames! −

MIME
(still to himself, sitting some distance away)

Er schmiedet das Schwert,
  und Fafner fällt er:
das seh' ich nun deutlich voraus;
  Hort und Ring
  erringt er im Harst: −
wie erwerb' ich mir den Gewinn?   [6]
  Mit Witz und List   [15]
  gewinn' ich Beides,
und berge heil mein Haupt.

He'll forge the sword
  and bring down Fafner:
I see it clearly now;
  hoard and ring
  he'll wrest from the fray: −
how can I gain what he's won?
  With wit and cunning
  I'll win them both
and keep my head unharmed.

SIEGFRIED
(still at the bellows)

  Hoho! hoho!
Hoho! hohei! hohei!

  Hoho! Hoho!
Hoho! Hohei! Hohei!

MIME
(downstage, aside)

Rang er sich müd' mit dem Wurm,

von der Müh' erlab' ihn ein Trunk;
  aus würz'gen Säften,
  die ich gesammelt,
brau' ich den Trank für ihn;
  wenig Tropfen nur
  braucht er zu trinken,
sinnlos sinkt er in Schlaf:
  mit der eig'nen Waffe,   [23]
  die er sich gewonnen,

When he's fought himself weary with the
  [dragon,
a drink may refresh him from his efforts:
  from herbal juices,
  which I've gathered,
I'll brew a drink for him;
  he'll need to drink
  only very few drops
before sinking, senseless, into sleep:
  with the selfsame weapon
  he won for himself

(more and more animatedly)

räum' ich ihn leicht aus dem Weg,
erlange mir Ring und Hort.

I'll easily clear him out of the way
and attain to both ring and hoard.

(He rubs his hands with glee.)

Hei! Weiser Wand'rer,
  dünkt' ich dich dumm,
  wie gefällt dir nun
  mein feiner Witz?   [15]
Fand ich mir wohl
Rath und Ruh'?

Hey, wily Wanderer,
  though you thought me a fool,
  how does my subtle wit
  now suit you?
Have I not won me
respite and peace?

Nothung! Nothung!   [23b]   Nothung! Nothung!
neidliches Schwert!   Fearsome steel!
Nun schmolz deines Stahles Spreu: [45]   Now your chaff-like steel's been melted [down:

im eig'nen Schweiße   you're swimming
schwimm'st du nun −   in your own sweat −

(He pours the red-hot contents of the crucible into a mould, which he holds aloft.)

bald schwing' ich dich als mein   soon I'll wield you as my sword!
[Schwert!   [23]

(He plunges the mould into a bucket of water: steam and loud hissing follow as it cools.)

In das Wasser floß   A river of fire
ein Feuerfluß: flowed into the water:
grimmiger Zorn   in furious anger
zischt' ihm da auf.   it fiercely hissed.
Wie sehrend er floß,   Searingly as it flowed,
in des Wassers Fluth   it flows no more
fließt er nicht mehr;   in the water's flood;
starr ward er und steif,   rigid and stiff it's become,
herrisch der harte Stahl: lordly the tempered steel:
heißes Blut doch   soon it will flow
fließt ihm bald! −   with hot blood! −

(He thrusts the blade into the forge fire and works the bellows vigorously. [45] Mime has leapt up gleefully, he fetches various containers and from them pours spices and herbs into a cooking-pot, which he tries to place on the hearth.)

Nun schwitze noch einmal,   Now sweat once again,
daß ich dich schweiße,   so I can weld you,
Nothung, neidliches Schwert! [40, 23b]   Nothung, you fearsome sword!

(While working, he observes Mime, who carefully places his pot over the flames at the other side of the hearth.)

Was schafft der Tölpel   What's that blockhead
dort mit dem Topf?   doing there with his pot?
Brenn' ich hier Stahl,   While I'm smelting steel,
brau'st du dort Sudel?   are you brewing slops?

Zu Schanden kam ein Schmied,   A smith has been put to shame:
den Lehrer sein Knabe lehrt;   his boy is teaching his teacher;
mit der Kunst nun ist's beim Alten aus,   the old man's lost his art,
als Koch dient er dem Kind: he serves the child as cook:
brennt er das Eisen zu Brei,   while he smelts the iron to pulp,
aus Eiern brau't   the old man cooks him
der Alte ihm Sud.   broth from eggs.

(He continues cooking.)

Mime, der Künstler,   Mime the artist
lernt jetzt kochen;   [15]   is learning to cook;
das Schmieden schmeckt ihm nicht   he's lost his taste for forging:
[mehr:

seine Schwerter alle
hab' ich zerschmissen;
was er kocht, ich kost' es ihm nicht.

I've shattered
every one of his swords;
what he's cooking, I'll not savour.

(During the following Siegfried removes the mould from the fire, breaks it and places the red-hot blade on the anvil.)

Das Fürchten zu lernen
will er mich führen;
ein Ferner soll es mich lehren:
was am besten er kann,
mir bringt er's nicht bei;
als Stümper besteht er in allem!

He wants to lead me
to where I'll learn fear;
a stranger will have to teach me:
what *he* can do best
he can't impart;
he remains a bungler in all that he does!

(while forging)

Hoho! hoho! hohei!
Schmiede, mein Hammer,
ein hartes Schwert!
Hoho! hahei!
hoho! hahei!

Hoho! Hoho! Hohei!
Forge, my hammer,
a hard-edged sword!
Hoho! Hahei!
Hoho! Hahei!

Einst färbte Blut
dein falbes Blau;
sein rothes Rieseln
röthete dich:
kalt lachtest du da,
das warme lecktest du kühl!
Heiaho! haha!
haheiaha!
Nun hat die Gluth
dich roth geglüht;
deine weiche Härte
dem Hammer weicht:
zornig sprüh'st du mir Funken,
daß ich dich spröden gezähmt!
Heiaho! heiaho!
heiaho! ho! ho!
hahei!

Blood once died
your faded blue;
its bright red trickling
made you blush:
coldly then you laughed
and licked the warm blood cool!
Heiaho! Haha!
Haheiaha!
Now the glowing coals
have made you glow red;
your yielding hardness
yields to my hammer:
in anger you spit out sparks at me
for having tamed your brittleness!
Heiaho! Heiaho!
Heiaho! Ho! Ho!
Hahei!

MIME
(aside)

Er schafft sich ein scharfes Schwert, [23]
Fafner zu fällen,
der Zwerge Feind:[101]
ich braut' ein Trug-Getränk,
Siegfried zu fangen,
dem Fafner fiel.
Gelingen muß mir die List;
lachen muß mir der Lohn!

He's making a sharp-edged sword for
[himself
to bring down Fafner,
the foe of all dwarfs:[101]
I've brewed a false drink
to trap Siegfried
once Fafner has fallen before him.
My cunning is bound to succeed;
my reward must smile upon me!

(During the following, Mime busies himself pouring the contents of the pot into a flask.)

Hoho! hoho! hahei!
  Schmiede, mein Hammer,
  ein hartes Schwert!
Hoho! hahei!
hoho! hahei!

Der frohen Funken,
  wie freu' ich mich!
Es ziert den Kühnen
  des Zornes Kraft:
lustig lach'st du mich an,
stell'st du auch grimm dich und
  [gram!
  Heiaho! haha!
  haheiaha!
Durch Gluth und Hammer
  glückt' es mir;
  mit starken Schlägen
  streckt' ich dich:
nun schwinde die rothe Scham;
werde kalt und hart wie du kannst!

(He brandishes the blade and plunges it into the bucket of water.)

  Heiaho! heiaho!
  heiaho! ho! ho!
  heiah!

Hoho! Hoho! Hahei!
  Forge, my hammer,
  a sharp-edged sword!
Hoho! Hahei!
Hoho! Hahei!

How I rejoice
  in the joyous sparks!
The force of their fury
  adorns the brave:
delighting, you laugh upon me now,
though you look grim and grudging!

  Heiaho! Haha!
  Haheiaha!
Through heat and hammer
  have I succeeded;
  with mighty blows
  I hammered you flat:
now may your blushing shame disappear;
be as cold and hard as you can!

  Heiaho! Heiaho!
  Heiaho! Ho! Ho!
  Heiah!

(He laughs aloud at the hissing noise. While Siegfried attaches the newly forged blade to the hilt, Mime fusses about with his flask downstage.) [15]

MIME

Den der Bruder schuf,
  den schimmernden Reif,
in den er gezaubert
  zwingende Kraft,
das helle Gold,
  das zum Herrscher macht –
ihn hab' ich gewonnen,
  ich walte sein'! –

The glittering ring
  which my brother made
and on which he cast
  an all-powerful spell –
the shining gold
  that will make me master –
that ring have I won,
  it's mine to command! –

(Siegfried works with a small hammer, polishing and filing. Mime skips around in a lively manner, with increasing glee.)

Alberich selbst,
  der einst mich band,
zur Zwergenfrohne
  zwing' ich ihn nun:
als Niblungenfürst
  fahr' ich danieder;
gehorchen soll mir
  alles Heer! –
Der verachtete Zwerg,
  wie wird er geehrt!

Alberich, too,
  who once enslaved me,
I'll now reduce
  to dwarfish thrall:
as Nibelung lord
  I'll light below;
the whole of his host
  shall now obey me! –
The slighted dwarf,
  how he'll be honoured!

Zu dem Horte hin drängt sich
Gott und Held:

God and hero
shall haste to the hoard:

(with increasingly animated gestures)

vor meinem Nicken
neigt sich die Welt,
vor meinem Zorne
zittert sie hin! –

the world will bow
before my nod,
it will tremble
at my anger! –

(Siegfried flattens the rivets on the hilt with the final blows of his hammer and seizes the sword with both hands.)

SIEGFRIED

Nothung! Nothung!
Neidliches Schwert!
Jetzt haftest du wieder im Heft.

[23b]　　Nothung! Nothung!
Fearsome sword!
Now you are hafted once more in your
[hilt.

MIME

Dann wahrlich müht sich
Mime nicht mehr.

Then truly Mime
shall toil no more.

SIEGFRIED

War'st du entzwei,
ich zwang dich zu ganz,
kein Schlag soll nun dich mehr
[zerschlagen.

Though once in twain
I forced you together,
no blow shall ever break you again.

MIME

Ihm schaffen And're
den ew'gen Schatz.

For him shall others mine
the eternal treasure.

SIEGFRIED

Dem sterbenden Vater
zersprang der Stahl,
der lebende Sohn
schuf ihn neu:
nun lacht ihm sein heller Schein,
seine Schärfe schneidet ihm hart.

The steel sprang apart
in the hands of my dying father;
his living son
has made it anew:
on him its brilliant sheen now shines,
for him its keen-edged blade cuts cleanly.

MIME

Mime, der kühne,
Mime ist König,
Fürst der Alben,
Walter des All's!

Mime the valiant,
Mime is king,
prince of the elves,
lord of the universe!

SIEGFRIED
(brandishing the sword in front of him)

Nothung! Nothung!
Neidliches Schwert!
Zum Leben weckt' ich dich wieder.
Todt lag'st du

Nothung! Nothung!
[23]　　Fearsome sword!
I've wakened you to life again.
You lay there, dead,

| in Trümmern dort, | in ruins; |
| jetzt leuchtest du trotzig und hehr. | now you glisten, defiant and glorious. |

MIME

| Hei, Mime! wie glückte dir das! | Hey, Mime, how did you manage! |
| Wer hätte wohl das gedacht? | Whoever would have thought it? |

SIEGFRIED

Zeige den Schächern	To felons
nun deinen Schein!	show your shining blade!
Schlage den Falschen,	Slay him who is false
fälle den Schelm! –	and fell the offender! –
Schau, Mime, du Schmied: [40]	See, Mime, you smith:

(He raises the sword to strike a blow.)

| so schneidet Siegfried's Schwert! [23] | thus severs Siegfried's sword! |

(He strikes the anvil, which splits from top to bottom and falls apart with a loud crash.[102] Mime, who has climbed on to a stool in his delight, falls to the ground in terror, landing in a sitting position. Jubilantly, Siegfried holds the sword aloft. The curtain falls.)

Act Two

PRELUDE AND SCENE ONE

(The curtain rises.[103] In the depths of the forest. At the very back of the stage is the mouth of a cave. The ground rises towards the centre of the stage, where it forms a small knoll; from here it falls away again towards the cave, so that only the upper part of the entrance is visible to the audience. To the right, a rugged cliff-face can be seen through the forest trees. It is a dark night, darkest at the back of the stage, where it is initially impossible for the audience to distinguish anything at all. Alberich is stationed by the cliff-face, brooding darkly.) [46, 6, 19]

ALBERICH

In Wald und Nacht	In the forest at night
vor Neidhöhl' halt' ich Wacht:	I stand guard before Neidhöhl':
es lauscht mein Ohr,	my ear is cocked,
mühvoll lugt mein Aug'. –	my eye keeps effortful watch. –
Banger Tag,	Dreaded day,
beb'st du schon auf?	are you fitfully dawning already?
Dämmerst du dort	Are you breaking
durch das Dunkel auf?	through the darkness there?

(A stormwind blows up in the wood on the left; a bluish light also begins to glow there.)

Welcher Glanz glitzert dort	What gleam is glittering yonder?
[auf? [32b, 40, 30]	
Näher schimmert	A shining light
ein heller Schein;	comes shimmering closer;
es rennt wie ein leuchtendes Roß,	racing along like a luminous steed,

bricht durch den Wald	it breaks through the wood
brausend daher.	with a roar.
Naht schon des Wurmes Würger?	Is the dragon's killer already coming?
Ist's schon, der Fafner fällt?	Is it he who'll lay Fafner low?

(The stormwind dies down again. The light goes out.) [19]

Das Licht erlischt –	The light dies out –
der Glanz barg sich dem Blick: [46]	the glow's disappeared from sight:
Nacht ist's wieder. –	it's night once again. –

(The Wanderer emerges from the wood and stops opposite Alberich.) [19]

Wer naht dort schimmernd im	Who's coming closer, shimmering in the
[Schatten?	[shadows?

WANDERER

Zur Neidhöhle	To Neidhöhle
fuhr ich bei Nacht:	have I come by night:
wen gewahr' ich im Dunkel dort?	whom do I see in the darkness there?

(Moonlight streams in, as if through a sudden gap in the clouds, lighting up the Wanderer's form. Alberich recognizes the Wanderer and initially starts up in surprise, before breaking out in utter fury at him.)

ALBERICH

Du selbst läss'st dich hier seh'n? –	You let yourself be seen here? –
Was willst du hier?	What is it that you want here?
Fort, aus dem Weg!	Be off, on your way!
Von dannen, schamloser Dieb!	Get you hence, shameless thief!

WANDERER
(calmly)

Schwarz-Alberich,	Black Alberich,
schweif'st du hier?	are you roving here?
Hütest du Fafner's Haus?	Are you guarding Fafner's lair?

ALBERICH

Jag'st du auf neue	Are you out pursuing
Neidthat umher?	new deeds of spite?
Weile nicht hier!	Don't linger here!
Weiche von hinnen!	Betake yourself hence!
Genug des Truges	Enough deceit
tränkte die Stätte mit Noth;	has steeped this spot in suffering;
d'rum, du Frecher,	and so, brazen god,
lass' sie jetzt frei!	let the place alone!

WANDERER

Zu schauen kam ich,	[43]	I came to watch
nicht zu schaffen:	[44]	and not to act:
wer wehrte mir Wand'rers Fahrt?		who'd bar the Wanderer's way?

ALBERICH

Du Rath wüthender Ränke!	You mine of malicious tricks!
Wär' ich dir zu lieb	Were I, as you wish,

doch noch dumm wie damals,
als du mich Blöden bandest!
  Wie leicht gerieth es

(furiously)

den Ring mir nochmals zu rauben!
  Hab' Acht: deine Kunst
  kenne ich wohl;

(mockingly)

  doch wo du schwach bist,
blieb mir auch nicht verschwiegen.
  Mit meinen Schätzen
  zahltest du Schulden;
  mein Ring lohnte[104]
  der Riesen Müh',
die deine Burg dir gebaut;   [8, 9]
  was mit den trotzigen
  einst du vertragen,
dess' Runen wahrt noch heut'
deines Speeres herrischer Schaft.
  Nicht du darfst   [12]
  was als Zoll du gezahlt
den Riesen wieder entreißen:
  du selbst zerspelltest
  deines Speeres Schaft;
  in deiner Hand
  der herrische Stab,
der starke zerstiebte wie Spreu.

still as stupid as then,
when you bound the foolish dwarf,
  how easy, indeed, it would prove

to deprive me once more of the ring!
  Beware: I know
  your ways well enough;

  but where you are weak
has not escaped me either.
  With my treasures
  you paid your debts;
  my ring rewarded[104]
  the toil of those giants
who built your stronghold for you;
  what you once agreed
  with those insolent creatures
is still preserved today in runes
on your spear's all-powerful shaft.
  What you paid the giants
  by way of tribute
you cannot wrest from them again:
  you yourself would shatter
  the shaft of your spear;
  in your hand
  the all-powerful staff,
so sturdy, would scatter like chaff.

WANDERER

Durch Vertrages Treue-Runen   [43]
  band er dich
  Bösen mir nicht:
dich beugt er mir durch seine Kraft; [9]

zum Krieg d'rum wahr' ich ihn wohl.

By the faithful runes of contract
  it bound you not
  to me, you knave:
it bends you to my will by virtue of its
    [might;
and so I ward it well in case of war.

ALBERICH

  Wie stolz[105] du dräu'st
  in trotziger Stärke,
und wie dir's im Busen doch bangt! –
  Verfallen dem Tod   [19]
  durch meinen Fluch
ist des Hortes Hüter: –
wer – wird ihn beerben?
  Wird der neidliche Hort
dem Niblungen wieder gehören?
Das sehrt dich mit ew'ger Sorge.
  Denn fass' ich ihn wieder
  einst in der Faust,
anders als dumme Riesen

How proudly[105] you threaten
  with insolent strength,
yet how fearful you are at heart! –
  Doomed to die
  through my curse
is he who holds the hoard: –
who will fall heir to it?
  Will the coveted hoard
once again belong to the Nibelung?
That fills you with endless care.
  For once I grasp it
  again in my fist,
then, unlike foolish giants,

üb' ich des Ringes Kraft:　　　　　　　　　I'll use the power of the ring:
　dann zitt're der Helden　　　　　　　　　then tremble, eternal
　ewiger Hüter!　　　　　　　　　　　　　guardian of heroes!
　Walhall's Höhen　　　　　　[3]　　　　Valhalla's heights
stürm' ich mit Hella's Heer:　　　　　　　I'll storm with Hella's host:
der Welt walte dann ich!　　　　　　　　　then shall I rule the world!

WANDERER
(calmly)

Deinen Sinn kenn' ich wohl;　　　　　　　I know your mind full well;
　doch sorgt er mich nicht:　　　　　　　it gives me no cause for worry:
des Ringes waltet　　　　　　　　　　　　he shall command the ring
wer ihn gewinnt.　　　　　　　　　　　　who wins it.

ALBERICH
(more animatedly)

Wie dunkel sprichst du,　　　　　　　　　How darkly you speak
was ich deutlich doch weiß!　　　　　　　of what I know clearly!
　An Heldensöhne　　　　　　[23]　　　Defiant, you cling
　hält sich dein Trotz,　　　　　　　　　to heroes' sons

(mockingly)

die traut deinem Blute entblüht.　[26a]　who are dearly descended from your own
　　　　　　　　　　　　　　　　　　　　[blood.

Pflegtest du wohl eines Knaben,　　　　　Haven't you nurtured a boy
der klug die Frucht dir pflücke,　　　　　who would cleverly pluck the fruit

(with increasing vehemence)

die du – nicht brechen darf'st?　[32a]　which you yourself aren't allowed to pick?

WANDERER

Mit mir – nicht,　　　　　　　　　　　　Haggle with Mime,
　had're mit Mime:　　　　　　　　　　　not with me:

(lightly)

dein Bruder bringt dir Gefahr;　　　　　　your brother's bringing you danger;
einen Knaben führt er daher,　　　　　　　he's leading a youngster here
der Fafner ihm fällen soll.　　　　　　　　who's meant to kill Fafner for him.
Nichts weiß der von mir;　　　　　　　　Of me he knows nothing;
der Niblung nützt ihn für sich.　　　　　　the Niblung is using him for his own
　　　　　　　　　　　　　　　　　　　　[ends.

D'rum sag' ich dir, Gesell:　　　　　　　And so I say to you, comrade:
thue frei wie dir's frommt!　　　　　　　act in whatever way may suit you!

(Alberich's gesture shows his violent curiosity.)

Höre mich wohl,　　　　　　　　　　　　Mark me well
　sei auf der Hut:　　　　　　　　　　　and be on your guard:
nicht kennt der Knabe den Ring,　　　　　the boy doesn't know of the ring
doch Mime kundet' ihn aus.　　　　　　　but Mime's found out about it.

ALBERICH
(forcefully)

Deine Hand hieltest du vom Hort?　[9]　And would you withhold your hand
　　　　　　　　　　　　　　　　　　　　[from the hoard?

Wen ich liebe
lass' ich für sich gewähren;
  er steh' oder fall',
   sein Herr ist er:
Helden nur können mir frommen.

Him whom I love
I leave to his own devices;
  let him stand or fall,
  his own master is he:
heroes alone can help me.

ALBERICH

Mit Mime räng' ich
allein um den Ring?

With Mime alone
would I vie for the ring?

WANDERER

Außer dir begehrt er
einzig das Gold.

Save you alone, only he
desires the gold.

ALBERICH

Und dennoch gewänn' ich ihn nicht?

And yet I might not win it?

WANDERER
(calmly coming closer)

Ein Helde naht
den Hort zu befrei'n;
zwei Niblungen geizen das Gold:
  Fafner fällt,   [18]
  der den Ring bewacht: –
wer ihn rafft, hat ihn gewonnen. –
  Willst du noch mehr?
  Dort liegt der Wurm:

A hero draws near
to rescue the hoard;
two Nibelungs covet the gold:
  Fafner will fall
  as he guards the ring: –
he who snatches it up will have won it. –
  What more do you want?
  There lies the dragon:

(He turns to the cave.)

warn'st du ihn vor dem Tod,   [46]
willig wohl ließ' er den Tand. –

if you warn him that death is at hand,
then perhaps he'll be willing to give up
[his toy. –

Ich selber weck' ihn dir auf. –

I'll wake him up myself. –

(He takes up a position on the knoll in front of the cave and calls into it.)

Fafner! Fafner!
Erwache, Wurm!

Fafner! Fafner!
Wake up, you dragon!

ALBERICH
(with intense astonishment, aside)

Was beginnt der Wilde?
Gönnt er mir's wirklich?

What's the madman doing?
Will he really not begrudge it me?

FAFNER'S VOICE
(through a powerful speaking-trumpet)

Wer stört mir den Schlaf?

Who's that who disturbs my sleep?

WANDERER
(facing the cave)

Gekommen ist einer,
Noth dir zu künden:

Someone has come
to tell you of danger:

er lohnt dir's mit dem Leben,
lohn'st du das Leben ihm
mit dem Horte, den du hütest.

he'll reward you for it with your life
if, in return, you repay that life
with the treasure that you're guarding.

(He inclines his ear towards the cave to listen.)

FAFNER'S VOICE

Was will er?

What does he want?

ALBERICH

(joining the Wanderer and calling into the cave)

Wache, Fafner!
Wache, du Wurm!
Ein starker Helde naht,
dich heil'gen will er besteh'n.

Wake up, Fafner!
Wake up, you dragon!
A doughty hero is drawing near
who means to assail you, invulnerable
[beast.

FAFNER'S VOICE

Mich hungert sein'.

I'm ready to eat him.

WANDERER

Kühn ist des Kindes Kraft,
scharf schneidet sein Schwert.

[23] Bold is the youngster's strength
and keen-cutting is his sword.

ALBERICH

Den gold'nen Reif
geizt er allein:
lass' mir den Ring zum Lohn,
so wend' ich den Streit;

du wahrest den Hort,
und ruhig leb'st du lang'!

[6] The golden band
alone he covets:
give me the ring as reward
and I'll change the course of the
[conflict;
you'll keep the hoard for yourself
and live a long life of peace!

FAFNER'S VOICE

Ich lieg' und besitz':[106] –

laßt mich schlafen!

[46] What I lie on I own:[106] –
(yawning)
leave me to sleep!

WANDERER

(laughing loudly and turning back to Alberich)

Nun, Alberich, das schlug fehl!
Doch schilt mich nicht mehr Schelm!
Dieß Eine, rath' ich,
achte noch wohl:

[6] Well, Alberich, that miscarried!
But call me a knave no longer!
This one thing – I advise you –
heed it well:

(approaching him, confidingly)

Alles ist nach seiner Art;
an ihr wirst du nichts ändern. –
Ich lass' dir die Stätte:
stelle dich fest!
Versuch's mit Mime, dem Bruder:
der Art ja versieh'st du dich besser.

[20] all things go their different ways;
you can alter nothing. –
I leave the field to you:
stand firm!
Try your luck with your brother, Mime:
his kind you understand better.

(turning to go)

Was anders ist,
das lerne nun auch!

As for the rest,
learn that, too!

(He quickly disappears into the forest. The stormwind rises, a bright glow breaks out: then both pass away again. Alberich watches the Wanderer riding away.) [23, 32b, 30, 43]

ALBERICH

Da reitet er hin
auf lichtem[107] Roß:
mich läßt er in Sorg' und Spott!
Doch lacht nur zu,
ihr leichtsinniges,
lustgieriges
Göttergelichter:
euch seh' ich   [19]
noch alle vergeh'n!
So lang' das Gold
am Lichte glänzt,
hält ein Wissender Wacht: –
trügen wird euch sein Trotz.   [46]

Away he rides
on his shining[107] steed
and leaves me to care and scorn!
But laugh away,
you light-hearted,
high-living
gang of gods:
I'll see you all
perish yet!
As long as the gold
still glints in the light,
then one who knows keeps watch: –
his defiance will yet defeat you.

(He slips into the cleft at the side. The stage remains empty. Dawn.)

SCENE TWO

(As day breaks, Siegfried and Mime enter. Siegfried is wearing the sword in a belt made of rope. Mime reconnoitres the place; finally he investigates the backstage area, which remains in deep shadow while the knoll in the middle foreground is later lit by the sun with increasing brightness; he then beckons to Siegfried.) [41, 15, 39]

MIME

Wir sind zur Stelle:
bleib' hier steh'n!

We've reached the place:
wait here!

SIEGFRIED
(sitting down beneath the lime-tree and looking round)

Hier soll ich das Fürchten lernen? –
Fern hast du mich geleitet;
eine volle Nacht im Walde
selbander wanderten wir:
nun sollst du, Mime, mich meiden!
  Lern' ich hier nicht
  was ich lernen soll,
allein zieh' ich dann weiter:
dich endlich werd' ich da los!

So this is where I'll learn what fear is? –
Far indeed have you led me;
a whole night in the forest
the two of us have wandered:
now, Mime, you must leave me!
  If I don't learn here
  what I'm meant to learn,
I'll go on my way alone
and be rid of you then at last!

MIME

Glaube, Liebster,
lern'st du heut'

Believe you me, dear boy,
if you don't learn

und hier das Fürchten nicht:
  an and'rem Ort
  zu and'rer Zeit
schwerlich erfähr'st du's je. –
  Sieh'st du dort
den dunklen Höhlenschlund?
  Darin wohnt
ein gräulich wilder Wurm: [46]
  unmaßen grimmig
  ist er und groß;
  ein schrecklicher Rachen
  reißt sich ihm auf;
  mit Haut und Haar
  auf einen Happ
verschlingt der Schlimme dich wohl.

the meaning of fear here today,
  you're unlikely to find out
  what it is
at any other place and any other time. –
  Do you see over there
the mouth of that gloomy cave?
  Within it dwells
a fearsomely savage dragon:
  grim beyond compare
  he is, and huge;
  awesome jaws
  gape open;
  hide and hair,
  at a single gulp,
the brute may bolt you down.

SIEGFRIED

(still sitting beneath the lime-tree)

Gut ist's, den Schlund ihm zu
  [schließen;
d'rum biet' ich mich nicht dem
  [Gebiß.

A good thing, then, to stop up his gullet;

and so I'll avoid his teeth.

MIME

Giftig gießt sich
ein Geifer ihm aus:
wen mit des Speichels
Schweiß er bespei't,
dem schwinden wohl Fleisch und
  [Gebein.

Poisonous spittle
spews from his lips:
if you're spattered
by gobbets of spit,
your flesh and bones will waste away.

SIEGFRIED

Daß des Geifers Gift mich nicht
  [sehre,
weich' ich zur Seite dem Wurm.

That the spittle's bane won't harm me,

I'll step to one side of the beast.

MIME

Ein Schlangenschweif
schlägt sich ihm auf:
wen er damit umschlingt
und fest umschließt,
dem brechen die Glieder wie Glas.

A serpent's tail
he uncoils:
if he twines it about you
and grips you tight,
your limbs will break like glass.

SIEGFRIED

Vor des Schweifes Schwang mich zu
  [wahren,
halt' ich den argen im Aug'. –
  Doch heiße mich das: [29]
  hat der Wurm ein Herz?

To save me from the lash of his tail

I'll keep the wicked beast in view. –
  But tell me this:
  has the dragon a heart?

Ein grimmiges, hartes Herz!   [46]   A fierce and inhuman heart!

SIEGFRIED

Das sitzt ihm doch
   wo es jedem schlägt,
trag' es Mann oder Thier?

But does it lie
   where it beats in everyone,
be he man or beast?

MIME

Gewiß, Knabe,
   da führt's auch der Wurm;
jetzt kommt dir das Fürchten wohl
[an?

Of course, my lad,
   the dragon's lies there, too;
are you starting to feel afraid now?

SIEGFRIED

(who until now has been stretched out nonchalantly on the ground, raises himself quickly into a sitting position)

Nothung stoß' ich
   dem Stolzen in's Herz:
soll das etwa Fürchten heißen?
   He, du Alter,
   ist das alles,
   was deine List
   mich lehren kann?
Fahr' deines Weg's dann weiter;
das Fürchten lern' ich hier nicht.

[23b]

[41]

Nothung I'll thrust
   in the proud beast's heart:
is that what people call fear?
   Hey, old man,
   if that's all
   that your cunning
   can teach me,
then be on your way;
I'll not learn what fear is here.

MIME

Wart' es nur ab!
   Was ich dir sage,
dünke dich tauber Schall:
   ihn selber mußt du
   hören und seh'n,
die Sinne vergeh'n dir dann schon!
   Wann dein Blick verschwimmt,
   der Boden dir schwankt,
   im Busen bang
   dein Herz erbebt: –

[39]

[46]

Just wait awhile!
   For all that I say
may seem to you empty sound:
   you have to see
   and hear him himself,
then your senses will surely fail you!
   When your gaze grows blurred
   and the ground starts to shake
   and your heart is quaking
   with fear in your breast: –

(in a very friendly tone of voice)

dann dank'st du mir, der dich führte,
gedenk'st, wie Mime dich liebt.

you'll thank me that I brought you here
and recall how much Mime loves you.

SIEGFRIED

Du sollst mich nicht lieben, –
   sagt' ich's dir nicht?
Fort aus den Augen mir;
   lass' mich allein:
sonst halt' ich's hier länger nicht aus,
fängst du von Liebe gar an!
   Das eklige Nicken

You're not to love me, –
   haven't I told you?
Out of my sight
   and leave me alone
or I'll not stand it here any longer
if you start on the subject of love!
   That loathsome nodding

und Augenzwicken,
wann endlich soll ich's
nicht mehr seh'n?

(impatiently)

Wann werd' ich den Albernen los?

and blinking your eyes –
when shall I finally
see it no more?

Whenever shall I be free of the fool?

MIME

Ich lass' dich schon:
am Quell dort lagr' ich mich.
Steh' du nur hier;
steigt dann die Sonne zur Höh',
merk' auf den Wurm,
aus der Höhle wälzt er sich her:
hier vorbei
biegt er dann,
am Brunnen sich zu tränken.

I'll leave you now
and settle down by the spring.
You just stay here;
when the sun's at its highest
look out for the dragon,
out of the cave it will crawl this way,
then turn
off here
in order to drink at the well.

SIEGFRIED
(laughing)

Mime, weil'st du am Quell,

Mime, if you wait by the spring,

(more animatedly)

dahin lass' ich den Wurm wohl geh'n:
Nothung stoß' ich
ihm erst in die Nieren,
wenn er dich selbst dort
mit 'weg gesoffen!
Darum, hör' meinen Rath,
raste nicht dort am Quell:
kehre dich 'weg,
so weit du kannst,
und komm' nie mehr zu mir!

I think I'll let the beast go there
and not thrust Nothung
into his guts
until he's already
gulped you down there!
Listen, then, to my advice
and don't rest by the spring:
take yourself hence,
as far as you can,
and don't come back to me ever again!

MIME

Nach freislichem Streit
dich zu erfrischen,
wirst du mir wohl nicht wehren?

After the fearful struggle
you surely won't stop me
from bringing refreshment?

(Siegfried waves him away with some vehemence.)

Rufe mich auch,
darb'st du des Rathes –

And call for me, too,
if you're wanting advice –

(He impetuously repeats the gesture.)

oder wenn dir das Fürchten gefällt.

or if you like the feeling of fear.

(He gets to his feet and drives Mime away with angry gestures.) [41]

MIME
(to himself, as he goes)

Fafner und Siegfried –
Siegfried und Fafner –
oh, brächten beide sich um!

Fafner and Siegfried –
Siegfried and Fafner –
if only each might kill the other!

(He disappears into the forest on the left. Siegfried stretches out comfortably beneath the lime-tree and watches Mime go.)

Daß der mein Vater nicht ist,
wie fühl' ich mich drob so froh!
  Nun erst gefällt mir
  der frische Wald;
  nun erst lacht mir
  der lustige Tag,
da der garstige von mir schied,
und ich gar nicht ihn wiederseh'!

That he is not my father –
how happy I feel at that!
  Only now do the fresh
  woods delight me;
  only now does the day
  smile upon me in gladness
now that the loathsome dwarf has left me
and I'll nevermore see him again!

(He falls into a silent rêverie.)

Wie sah mein Vater wohl aus? –
Ha! – gewiß wie ich selbst:
denn wär' wo von Mime ein Sohn, [15]
  müßt' er nicht ganz
  Mime gleichen?
  G'rade so garstig,
  griesig und grau,
  klein und krumm,
  höck'rig und hinkend,
  mit hängenden Ohren,
  triefigen Augen – –
  fort mit dem Alp!
Ich mag ihn nicht mehr seh'n!

What must my father have looked like? –
Ha! – Of course, like me!
If any son of Mime's existed,
  must he not look
  just like Mime?
  Just as filthy,
  fearful and wan,
  short and misshapen,
  hunchbacked and halting,
  with drooping ears
  and rheumy eyes – –
  away with the elf!
I don't care to see him any more!

(He leans further back and looks up through the treetops. Deep silence. Forest murmurs.)

  Aber – wie sah
  meine Mutter wohl aus?
  Das – kann ich
  nun gar nicht mir denken! –
Der Rehhindin gleich
  glänzten gewiß
ihr hell schimmernden Augen, –
  nur noch viel schöner! – –

  But – what must
  my mother have looked like? –
  That I cannot
  conceive of at all! –
Like those of the roe-deer,
  her bright-shining eyes
must surely have glistened –
  only far fairer! – –

(very softly)

Da bang sie mich geboren,
warum aber starb sie da?
Sterben die Menschenmütter
  an ihren Söhnen
  alle dahin?
Traurig wäre das, traun! – –
  Ach! möcht' ich Sohn
  meine Mutter sehen! – –   [42]
  Meine – Mutter! –
  Ein Menschenweib! –

When, in her dismay, she gave me birth,
why did she have to die then?
Do all mortal mothers
  perish
  because of their sons?
Sad that would be, in truth! – –
  Ah, might I, her son,
  see my mother! – –
  My mother –
  a mortal woman! –

(He sighs deeply and leans further back. Deep silence. The forest murmurs increase. Siegfried's attention is finally caught by the song of the forest birds. [47] He listens with growing interest to a woodbird in the branches above him.) [48]

  Du holdes Vög'lein!
  Dich hört' ich noch nie:
bist du im Wald hier daheim? –

  You lovely woodbird!
  I've never heard you before:
is the forest here your home? –

Verstünd' ich sein süßes Stammeln!	Could I only make sense of his [sweet-sounding babble!
Gewiß sagt' es mir 'was, –	He must be telling me something –
vielleicht – von der lieben Mutter? –	perhaps about my dear mother? –

Ein zankender Zwerg	A querulous dwarf
hat mir erzählt,	explained to me once
der Vög'lein Stammeln	that in time
gut zu versteh'n,	one could come to unriddle
dazu könnte man kommen:	the babbling of little birds:
wie das wohl möglich wär'?	but how could that be possible?
Hei! ich versuch's,	Hey! I'll try
sing' ihm nach:	and copy him:
auf dem Rohr tön' ich ihm ähnlich!	I'll sound like him on a reed!
Entrath' ich der Worte,	If I do without words
achte der Weise,	and attend to the tune,
sing' ich so seine Sprache,	I'll sing his language in that way
versteh' ich wohl auch was er [spricht.[108]	and no doubt grasp what he's saying.[108]

(He runs over to the nearby spring, cuts a reed with his sword and rapidly whittles a pipe from it. As he does so, he listens again.)

| Er schweigt und lauscht: – | He stops and listens: – |
| so schwatz' ich denn los! | I'll chatter away then! |

(He blows into the pipe. He removes it from his lips and whittles it down further in order to improve it. Then he blows again. He shakes his head and makes further improvements. He tries again. He grows angry, squeezes the reed in his hand and tries once more. Finally he gives up with a smile.)

Das tönt nicht recht;	That doesn't sound right;
auf dem Rohre taugt	on the reed
die wonnige Weise mir nicht. –	the delightful tune doesn't work. –
Vög'lein, mich dünkt,	I think, little bird,
ich bleibe dumm:	I'll remain a fool:
von dir lernt sich's nicht leicht!	from you it's not easy to learn!

(He hears the woodbird again and looks up at it.) [48]

| Nun schäm' ich mich gar | Now I'm put to shame |
| vor dem schelmischen Lauscher: | by the sharp-eared rogue: |

(very tenderly)

er lugt, und kann nichts erlauschen. –	he looks at me and hears nothing. –
Heida! so höre	Hey there! so listen
nun auf mein Horn;	now to my horn;

(He brandishes the reed, which he then tosses away.)

auf dem dummen Rohre	nothing works
geräth mir nichts. –	on the stupid reed. –
Einer Waldweise,	A woodland tune –
wie ich sie kann,	the blithest I can –
der lustigen sollst du nun lauschen.	you shall lend an ear to now.
Nach lieben Gesellen	With it I tried to lure
lockt' ich mit ihr:	boon companions:
nichts bess'res kam noch	nothing better than wolf
als Wolf und Bär.	or bear has come to me as yet.

Nun lass' mich seh'n,
  wen jetzt sie mir lockt:
ob das mir ein lieber Gesell?

Now let me see
  whom it lures here now:
will it be some boon companion?

(He takes the silver hunting-horn and blows into it. [40, 35] At each sustained note, Siegfried looks expectantly at the bird. Something stirs at the back of the stage. Fafner, in the shape of a huge, lizard-like dragon, has risen from his lair in the cave; he breaks through the undergrowth and drags himself up on to the higher ground until the front part of his body comes to rest, at which point he utters a noise like a loud yawn. Siegfried looks round and fixes his eyes in astonishment on Fafner.) [18]

Haha! Da hätte mein Lied
  mir 'was liebes erblasen!
Du wär'st mir ein saub'rer Gesell!

Ha ha! So my song has produced
  something pretty!
You'd make me a fine companion!

(At the sight of Siegfried, Fafner has paused on the knoll and now remains there.)

FAFNER

Was ist da?[109]

[46]   What's that there?[109]

SIEGFRIED

Ei, bist du ein Thier,
  das zum Sprechen taugt,
wohl ließ' sich von dir 'was lernen?
Hier kennt einer
  das Fürchten nicht:
kann er's von dir erfahren?

Hey, if you're a beast
  that's able to talk,
perhaps I can learn something from you?
There's someone here
  who doesn't know fear:
is he able to learn it from you?

FAFNER

Hast du Übermuth?

Are you so foolhardy?

SIEGFRIED

Muth oder Übermuth –
  was weiß ich!
Doch dir fahr' ich zu Leibe,
lehr'st du das Fürchten mich[110]
  [nicht!

Hardy or foolhardy –
  what do I know!
But I'll lay you low
if you don't teach me fear!

FAFNER
(emitting a noise like laughter)

Trinken wollt' ich:
  nun treff' ich auch Fraß!

I wanted a drink
  but food I find, too!

(He opens his jaws and reveals his teeth.)

SIEGFRIED

Eine zierliche Fresse
  zeig'st du mir da:
  lachende Zähne
  im Leckermaul!
Gut wär' es, den Schlund dir zu
  [schließen;
dein Rachen reckt sich zu weit!

That's an elegant gizzard
  you're showing me there:
  grinning teeth
  in a gourmet's mouth!
Good it would be to stop up your gullet;

your jaws are gaping too wide!

FAFNER

Zu tauben Reden
taugt er schlecht:
dich zu verschlingen
frommt der Schlund.

For empty words
they serve me ill:
my gullet's good
for gulping you down.

SIEGFRIED

Hoho, du grausam
grimmiger Kerl,
von dir verdaut sein
dünkt mich übel:
räthlich und fromm doch scheint's,
du verrecktest hier ohne Frist.

Hoho, you grisly
grim-hearted churl,
I feel no desire
to fill your maw:
but it seems only fit and proper
that you die here without delay.

FAFNER
(roaring)

Pruh! Komm',
prahlendes Kind!

Bah! Come here,
you boastful child!

SIEGFRIED

Hab' Acht, Brüller:
der Prahler naht!

Take care, you roaring beast:
the boastful child draws near!

(He draws his sword, leaps towards Fafner and stands there, challenging him. Fafner drags himself further up the slope and spits at Siegfried through his nostrils. [18] Siegfried avoids the venom, jumps closer and stands to one side of the dragon. [40] Fafner tries to reach him with his tail. Siegfried, whom Fafner has almost reached, jumps over him in a single bound and wounds him in the tail. Fafner roars, draws his tail back violently and raises the front half of his body in order to throw his full weight down on Siegfried; in doing so he exposes his breast to the latter; Siegfried quickly notes the position of the heart and thrusts in his sword as far as the hilt. Fafner rears up even higher in his pain and sinks down on the wound, as Siegfried releases the sword and leaps to one side.)

SIEGFRIED

Da lieg', neidischer Kerl!
Nothung träg'st du im Herzen.

Lie there, you spiteful churl!
Nothung is lodged in your heart.

FAFNER
(in a weaker voice)[111]

Wer bist du, kühner Knabe,
der das Herz mir traf?
Wer reizte des Kindes Muth
zu der mordlichen That?
Dein Hirn brütete nicht,
was du vollbracht.

Who are you, valiant lad,
who has wounded me to the heart?
Who goaded the mettlesome child
to commit this murderous deed?
[19]   Your brain did not brood upon
what you have done.

SIEGFRIED

Viel weiß ich noch nicht,
noch nicht auch wer ich bin:
mit dir mordlich zu ringen
reiztest du selbst meinen Muth.

[35]   There is much that I still don't know:
I still don't know who I am:
to join in murderous fight with you
you goaded me on yourself.

FAFNER

Du helläugiger Knabe,
unkund deiner selbst:
   wen du gemordet
   meld' ich dir.
Der Riesen ragend Geschlecht,
   Fasolt und Fafner,
die Brüder fielen nun beide.
   Um verfluchtes Gold,
   von Göttern vergabt,
traf ich Fasolt zu todt:
   der nun als Wurm
   den Hort bewachte,
Fafner, den letzten Riesen,
fällte ein rosiger Held. –
   Blicke nun hell,
   blühender Knabe;
der dich Blinden reizte zur That,
beräth jetzt des Blühenden Tod.
   Merk', wie's endet: – –
 	
acht' auf mich!
	[46] You bright-eyed boy,
	   unknown to yourself:
	     I'll tell you
	     whom you have murdered.
	   The giants' towering race,
	     Fasolt and Fafner,
	   both brothers now have fallen.
	     For curse-ridden gold,
	     bequeathed by gods,
	   I dealt my brother his deathblow:
	     he who, as dragon,
	     watched over the hoard,
	   Fafner, the last of the giants,
	[23] was felled by a rosy-cheeked hero. –
	     See clearly now,
	     you radiant youth;
	   he who goaded you on in your blindness
	   is plotting the death of the radiant youth.
	[19] Mark how it ends: – –
	(dying)
	     pay heed to me!

SIEGFRIED

Woher ich stamme,
   rathe mir noch;
   weise ja schein'st du
   Wilder im Sterben;
rath' es nach meinem Namen:
Siegfried bin ich genannt.
	Advise me yet
	   on where I have come from;
	     wise you seem,
	     wild beast, in dying;
	[35] divine it from my name:
	   Siegfried am I called.

FAFNER

(sighing deeply)

Siegfried . . . !	Siegfried . . . !

(He rears up and dies.) [46]

SIEGFRIED

Zur Kunde taugt kein Todter. –	The dead can serve as no source of [knowledge. –
So leite mich denn mein lebendes Schwert!	So let my living [23] sword now lead me!

(Fafner, in dying, has rolled over on one side. Siegfried now draws his sword from his breast; as he does so, his hand comes into contact with the dragon's blood: he snatches his hand away.)

Wie Feuer brennt das Blut!	Its blood is burning like fire.

(Involuntarily, he raises his fingers to his mouth in order to suck the blood from them. As he gazes thoughtfully in front of him, his attention is caught increasingly by the song of the forest birds.) [48]

Ist mir doch fast –
als sprächen die Vög'lein zu mir:
   nützte mir das
	It's almost as though
	   the woodbirds were speaking to me:
	     was this brought about

des Blutes Genuß? –
Das selt'ne Vög'lein hier –   [47]
horch! was singt es mir?

by the taste of the blood? –
That strange little bird here –
listen! what is it singing to me?

THE VOICE OF A WOODBIRD[112]
(from the branches of the lime-tree above Siegfried)

Hei! Siegfried gehört   [48]
nun der Niblungen Hort:
o fänd' in der Höhle
den Hort er jetzt!
Wollt' er den Tarnhelm gewinnen,
der taugt' ihm zu wonniger That:
doch wollt' er den Ring sich
[errathen,
der macht' ihn zum Walter der Welt!

Hey! Siegfried now owns
the Nibelung hoard:
o might he now find
the hoard in the cave!
If he wanted to win the tarnhelm,
it would serve him for wondrous deeds:
but could he acquire the ring,
it would make him the lord of the world!

(Siegfried has listened with bated breath and a rapt expression on his face.)

SIEGFRIED
(quietly and with emotion)

Dank, liebes Vög'lein,
für deinen Rath:
gern folg' ich dem Ruf.

My thanks for your counsel,
you dear little bird:
I'll gladly follow your call.

(He turns to the back of the stage and descends into the cave, where he soon disappears from sight.)

SCENE THREE

(Mime creeps back, looking round timidly to convince himself that Fafner is dead; at the same time Alberich emerges from the cleft on the other side; he watches Mime, then rushes forward and bars his way as the latter sets off for the cave.) [3]

ALBERICH

Wohin schleich'st du
eilig und schlau,
schlimmer Gesell?

Where are you sneaking to
swiftly and slyly,
my cunning companion?

MIME

Verfluchter Bruder,
dich brauch' ich hier!
Was bringt dich her?

Accursèd brother,
you're all I need!
What brings you here?

ALBERICH

Geizt es dich Schelm
nach meinem Gold?
Verlang'st du mein Gut?

Are you lusting after
my gold, you rogue?
Are you after my wealth?

MIME

Fort von der Stelle!	Get away from this place!
Die Stätte ist mein:	The field is mine:
was stöberst du hier?	why are you rummaging here?

ALBERICH

Stör' ich dich wohl	I suppose I'm disturbing
im stillen Geschäft,	your shady dealings
wenn du hier stiehl'st?	if it's to steal that you're here!

MIME

Was ich erschwang	What I acquired
mit schwerer Müh',	by arduous toil
soll mir nicht schwinden.	shan't escape me now.

ALBERICH

Hast du dem Rhein	Was it you who robbed the gold
das Gold zum Ringe geraubt?	for the ring from the Rhine?
Erzeugtest du gar	Was it you who cast
den zähen Zauber im Reif?	the tenacious spell on the ring?

MIME

Wer schuf den Tarnhelm,	[16]	Who made the tarnhelm
der die Gestalten tauscht?		that changes men's shapes?
Der sein' bedurfte,		Did he who needed it
erdachtest du ihn wohl?		think it up?

ALBERICH

Was hättest du Stümper	What have *you* ever known
je wohl zu stampfen verstanden?	about beating metals, you bungler?
Der Zauberring	The magic ring
zwang mir den Zwerg erst zur Kunst.	first forced the dwarf to lend me his skill.

MIME

Wo hast du den Ring?	Where's the ring now?
Dir Zagem entrissen ihn Riesen.	It was wrested from you by giants, you [coward.
Was du verlor'st,	What you yourself lost
meine List erlangt' es für mich.	my cunning would gain for me.

ALBERICH

Mit des Knaben That	Would the niggard not share
will der Knicker nun knausern?	the boy's deed with others?
Dir gehört sie gar nicht,	It doesn't belong to you at all:
der Helle ist selbst ihr Herr!	the bright-eyed boy himself is its lord!

MIME

Ich zog ihn auf;		I brought him up;
für die Zucht zahlt er mir nun:		he'll pay me now for rearing him:
für Müh' und Last	[15]	for my pains and all the burdens I've [borne

erlauert' ich lang' meinen Lohn!

I've long lain in wait for my wages!

ALBERICH

Für des Knaben Zucht
will der knick'rige
schäbige Knecht
keck und kühn
wohl gar König nun sein?
Dem räudigsten Hund
wäre der Ring
gerath'ner als dir:
nimmer erring'st
du Rüpel den Herrscherreif!

For rearing the boy
does the niggardly
scurvy slave
boldly and brazenly
want to be king?
To the mangiest cur
were the ring
better suited than you:
you'll never get hold of
the lordly ring, you lout!

MIME
(scratching his head)

Behalt' ihn denn;
und hüt' ihn wohl,
den hellen Reif!
Sei du Herr:
doch mich heiße auch Bruder!
Um meines Tarnhelm's
lustigen Tand
tausch' ich ihn dir:
uns beiden taugt's,
theilen die Beute wir so.

Well, keep it then
and ward
the bright ring well!
You be its lord:
but keep on calling me brother!
I'll give it to you
in return for my tarnhelm's
delightful toy:
it befits us both
that we share the spoils in this way.

(He rubs his hands confidingly.)

ALBERICH
(with mocking laughter)

Theilen mit dir?
und den Tarnhelm gar?
Wie schlau du bist!
Sicher schlief' ich
niemals vor deinen Schlingen!

I? Share with you?
And the tarnhelm, too?
How sly you are!
I'd never sleep
safe from your snares!

MIME
(beside himself)

Selbst nicht tauschen?
Auch nicht theilen?
Leer soll ich geh'n,
ganz ohne Lohn?

Not even exchange it?
And not share either?
I'm to go empty-handed,
quite unrewarded?

(screeching)

Gar nichts willst du mir lassen?

Will you leave me nothing?

ALBERICH

Nichts von allem,
nicht einen Nagel
sollst du mir nehmen!

Nothing at all,
not even a nail
shall you take from me!

(in utmost fury)

Weder Ring noch Tarnhelm	Neither ring nor tarnhelm
soll dir denn taugen!	shall profit you aught!
Nicht theil' ich nun mehr!	I'll share no more,
Gegen dich doch ruf' ich	but Siegfried
Siegfried zu Rath	and his warrior's sword
und des Recken Schwert:	I'll call on to help me against you:
der rasche Held,	the swift-footed hero
der richte, Brüderchen, dich!	will sort you out, dear brother!

(Siegfried appears in the background.)

ALBERICH

Kehre dich um: –	Turn round : –
aus der Höhle kommt er daher. –	he's coming this way from the cave. –

MIME
(turning round)

Kindischen Tand	Children's toys
erkor er gewiß. –	he's doubtless chosen. –

ALBERICH

Den Tarnhelm hält er! –	[6]	He's holding the tarnhelm! –

MIME

Doch auch den Ring! –	But also the ring! –

ALBERICH

Verflucht! – den Ring! –	Damnation! – The ring! –

MIME
(laughing maliciously)

Lass' ihn den Ring dir doch geben!	Get him to give you the ring!
Ich will ihn mir schon gewinnen. –	I still mean to win it myself. –

(With his final words, Mime slips back into the forest.)

ALBERICH

Und doch seinem Herrn		And yet it shall still
soll er allein noch gehören!	[5]	belong to its lord alone!

(He disappears into the cleft. During the foregoing, Siegfried has emerged from the cave, slowly and pensively, with the tarnhelm and ring: sunk in thought, he contemplates his booty and again pauses on the knoll in the middle of the stage.)

SIEGFRIED

Was ihr mir nützt,		What use you are
weiß ich nicht:		I do not know:
doch nahm ich euch	[4]	but I took you
aus des Hort's gehäuftem Gold,		from the heaped-up gold of the hoard
weil guter Rath mir es rieth.		since goodly counsel counselled me
		[to do so.

So taug' eu're Zier
als des Tages Zeuge:
es mahne der Tand,
daß ich kämpfend Fafner erlegt,
doch das Fürchten noch nicht erlernt!

May your trinkets serve
as witness to this day's events:
may the bauble recall
how, fighting, I vanquished Fafner
but still haven't learned the meaning of
[fear!

*(He tucks the tarnhelm under his belt and puts the ring on his finger. Silence. Once again
Siegfried involuntarily becomes aware of the bird.)*

VOICE OF THE WOODBIRD

Hei! Siegfried gehört   [48]
nun der Helm und der Ring!
O traute er Mime
dem treulosen nicht!
Hörte Siegfried nur scharf
auf des Schelmen Heuchlergered':
   wie sein Herz es meint
   kann er Mime versteh'n;
so nützt' ihm des Blutes Genuß.

Hey! Siegfried now owns
the helm and the ring!
Oh let him not trust
the treacherous Mime!
Were Siegfried to listen keenly
to the rogue's hypocritical words,
   he'd be able to understand
   what Mime means in his heart;
thus the taste of the blood was of use to
[him.

*(Siegfried's expression and gestures show that he has understood the meaning of the woodbird's
song. He sees Mime approaching and remains where he is on the knoll, resting motionlessly on
his sword, observant and self-contained, until the end of the following scene. Mime creeps back
and watches Siegfried from the front of the stage.)* [27]

MIME

Er sinnt und erwägt
der Beute Werth: —
weilte wohl hier
ein weiser Wand'rer,
schweifte umher,
beschwatzte das Kind
mit list'ger Runen Rath?[113]
   Zwiefach schlau
   sei nun der Zwerg:
   die listigste Schlinge
   leg' ich jetzt aus,
   daß ich mit traulichem
   Trug-Gerede
bethöre das trotzige Kind![114]

He ponders and broods on
the booty's worth: —
has some wily Wand'rer
been loitering here,
roaming around
and beguiling the child
with his counsel of cunning runes?[113]
   Doubly sly
   the dwarf must be:
   I'll set
   the most cunning snare now
   and fool
   the defiant child
with falsely friendly words![114]

(He comes closer to Siegfried and welcomes him with wheedling gestures.)

Willkommen, Siegfried!   [48]
Sag', du Kühner,
hast du das Fürchten gelernt?

Welcome, Siegfried!
Tell me, brave boy,
have you learned the meaning of fear?

SIEGFRIED

Den Lehrer fand ich noch nicht.

I've not yet found a teacher.

MIME

Doch den Schlangenwurm,

But you've slain

du hast ihn erschlagen:	the snake-like dragon:
das war doch ein schlimmer Gesell?	he must have been a poor companion?

SIEGFRIED

So grimm und tückisch er war,	Grim and spiteful though he was,
sein Tod grämt mich doch schier,	his death yet grieves me deeply
da viel üblere Schächer	since far worse villains
unerschlagen noch leben!	still remain unslain!
Der mich ihn morden hieß,	The man who bade me murder him
den hass' ich mehr als den Wurm.	I hate much more than the dragon.

MIME
(very amiably)

Nur sachte! Nicht lange	But soft! You'll not
sieh'st du mich mehr:	have to see me much longer:

(mawkishly)

zum ew'gen Schlaf	I'll soon lock
schließ' ich dir die Augen bald!	your eyes in lasting sleep!
Wozu ich dich brauchte,	You've done

(as though praising him)

hast du vollbracht;	what I needed you for;
jetzt will ich nur noch	all that I still want to do
die Beute dir abgewinnen: –	is to win from you the booty: –
mich dünkt, das soll mir gelingen;	I think that I ought to succeed in that;
zu bethören bist du ja leicht!	you're easy enough to fool after all!

SIEGFRIED

So sinn'st du auf meinen Schaden?	[27]	So you're planning to do me harm?

MIME
(surprised)

Wie sagt' ich denn das?	[48]	What, did I say that?

(continuing tenderly)

Siegfried, hör' doch, mein Söhnchen!	Siegfried, sonny, listen to me!
Dich und deine Art	You and your kind
haßt' ich immer von Herzen;	I have always hated with all my heart;

(tenderly)

aus Liebe erzog ich	it was not out of love
dich lästigen nicht:	that I brought you up, you [burdensome child:
dem Horte in Fafner's Hut,	my efforts were aimed at the gold,
dem Golde galt meine Müh'.	at the hoard in Fafner's safekeeping.

(as though promising him pretty things)

Giebst du mir das	If you don't give it up
gutwillig nun nicht, –	to me willingly now,

(as though he were ready to lay down his life for him)

Siegfried, mein Sohn,	Siegfried, my son,
das sieh'st du wohl selbst –	you must see for yourself –

(with amiable jocularity)

dein Leben mußt du mir lassen!	[15]	you must yield up your very life to me!

Daß du mich hassest,
hör' ich gern: [48, 27]
doch auch mein Leben muß ich dir
[lassen?

That you hate me
I'm glad to hear:
but must I also yield up my life?

(annoyed)

Das sagt' ich doch nicht?
Du versteh'st mich ja falsch!

Surely I didn't say that?
You've understood me all wrong!

(He produces his flask.)

Sieh', du bist müde
von harter Müh';
brünstig wohl brennt dir der Leib:
dich zu erquicken
mit queckem Trank
säumt' ich Sorgender nicht.
Als dein Schwert du dir branntest,
braut' ich den Sud:
trink'st du nun den,
gewinn' ich dein trautes Schwert,
und mit ihm Helm und Hort.

Look, you are tired
from toilsome exertions;
your body must burn with a raging fire:
anxious as ever, I didn't delay
but came to restore you
with quickening draught.
While you were smelting your sword,
I was brewing this broth:
if you'll drink it now,
I'll win your trusty sword
and with it helmet and hoard.

(sniggering)

SIEGFRIED

So willst du mein Schwert   [48]
und was ich erschwungen,
Ring und Beute mir rauben?

So you'd steal my sword
and all I have won
by way of ring and booty?

MIME
(vehemently)

Was du doch falsch mich versteh'st!
Stamml' ich, fasl' ich wohl gar?
Die größte Mühe
geb' ich mir doch,
mein heimliches Sinnen
heuchelnd zu bergen,
und du dummer Bube
deutest alles doch falsch!
Öffne die Ohren
und vernimm genau:
höre, was Mime meint! –

How you mistake my meaning!
Do I stammer or even talk rubbish?
I'm taking the greatest
pains after all
to hide, by dissembling,
my secret thoughts
and you, stupid boy,
interpret everything wrongly!
Open your ears
and listen closely:
hear what Mime means! –

(very amiable again, making a visible effort)

Hier nimm, und trinke die Labung!
Mein Trank labte dich oft:
that'st du auch unwirsch,
stelltest dich arg:
was ich dir bot –
erbos't auch – nahm'st du's doch
[immer.

Take this, and drink this refreshment!
My drink has often refreshed you:
though you acted morosely,
affecting malice,
you always took
what I offered, even when enraged.

Einen guten Trank
hätt' ich gern:
wie hast du diesen gebrau't?

I'd be glad
of something good to drink:
how did you brew this one here?

(merrily joking, as though describing a pleasantly intoxicated state which the juice would induce)

Hei, so trink' nur:
trau' meiner Kunst!
In Nacht und Nebel
sinken die Sinne dir bald:
ohne Wach' und Wissen
stracks streck'st du die Glieder.
Lieg'st du nun da,
leicht könnt' ich
die Beute nehmen und bergen:
doch erwachtest du je,
nirgends wär' ich
sicher vor dir,
hätt' ich selbst auch den Ring.
D'rum mit dem Schwert,
das so scharf du schuf'st,

Hey, just drink it:
trust in my art!
In darkness and mist
your senses will soon be shrouded:
unwaking, unwitting,
you'll straightway stretch out your limbs.
And once you're lying there,
then I could easily
take the spoils and conceal them:
but if you were ever to waken,
nowhere would I be
safe from you,
though I had the ring itself.
And so with the sword
which you made so sharp

(with a gesture of unrestrained merriment)

hau' ich dem Kind
den Kopf erst ab:
dann hab' ich mir Ruh'
und auch den Ring!

I'll first hack off
the child's head:
then I'll have peace of mind
and the ring as well!

(sniggering)

Im Schlafe willst du mich morden?

You mean to murder me while I'm
[asleep?

(furiously angry)

Was möcht' ich? Sagt' ich denn
[das? –

I mean to do what? Is that what I said? –

(striving to adopt the most tender expression)

Ich will dem Kind

I want only

(with the most meticulous clarity)

nur den Kopf abhau'n.

to hack the child's head off.

(with an expression of sincere concern for Siegfried's health)

Denn haßte ich dich
auch nicht so sehr,
und hätt' ich des Schimpf's
und der schändlichen Mühe
auch nicht so viel zu rächen:

For even if
I hated you less
and hadn't so much
of your hateful abuse
and such shameful toil to avenge,

(gently)

aus dem Wege dich zu räumen

I'd still waste no time

darf ich doch nicht rasten,	in clearing you out of the way

(joking again)

wie käm' ich sonst anders zur Beute,	for how else could I gain the spoils,
da Alberich auch nach ihr lugt? – –	since Alberich covets them, too? – –

(He pours the juice into the drinking-horn and offers it to Siegfried with an insistent gesture.)
[48]

Nun, mein Wälsung!		Now, my Wälsung!
Wolfssohn du!		Son of Wolfe!
Sauf' und würg' dich zu todt:	[15]	Drink and choke yourself to death:
nie thu'st du mehr 'nen Schluck!		you'll never taste another drop!

SIEGFRIED

(raising his sword) [23]

Schmeck' du mein Schwert,	Have a taste of my sword,
ekliger Schwätzer!	you loathsome babbler!

(As though in a paroxysm of violent loathing, he deals Mime a sudden blow; the latter immediately falls to the ground, dead. Alberich's mocking laughter in heard from the cleft. [15] Gazing at the body on the ground, Siegfried calmly replaces his sword.)

Neides-Zoll	Nothung pays
zahlt Nothung:	the wages of spite:
dazu durft' ich ihn schmieden.	for that I had to forge it.

(He snatches up Mime's body and carries it to the knoll outside the mouth of Fafner's cave.)
[19, 15, 40] *(throwing the body down into the cave)*

In der Höhle hier		In the cave here
lieg' auf dem Hort!		lie on the hoard!
Mit zäher List	[19]	With obstinate cunning
erzieltest du ihn:		you tried to win it:
jetzt magst du des wonnigen		the wondrous hoard is now yours to
[walten! –		[command! –
Einen guten Wächter		A goodly watchman
geb' ich dir auch,		I'll give to you, too,
daß er vor Dieben dich deckt.	[46]	to shelter you from thieves.

(With a mighty effort, he rolls the dragon's body over to the mouth of the cave, so that it blocks off the entrance completely.)

Da lieg' auch du,		So lie there, too,
dunkler Wurm!		mysterious beast,
Den gleißenden Hort	[6]	and guard the glistening hoard
hüte zugleich		together with
mit dem beuterührigen Feind:		your booty-grabbing foe:
so fandet beide ihr nun Ruh'!		so both of you have now found rest!

(He gazes down into the cave for a while, thinking, then returns slowly, as though exhausted, to the front of the stage. [15, 46] He wipes his hand across his forehead.) [40]

Heiß ward mir	I'm feeling hot
von der harten Last! –	from the heavy burden! –
Brausend jagt	My raging blood's racing
mein brünst'ges Blut;	fiercely through my veins;
die Hand brennt mir am Haupt. – –	my hand is burned by my brow. – –
Hoch steht schon die Sonne:	The sun's already high in the heavens:
aus lichtem Blau	its eye[115] stares down
blickt ihr Aug'[115]	on the crown of my head

auf den Scheitel steil mir herab. –
  Linde Kühlung
erkies' ich unter der Linde! [47]

(He stretches out beneath the lime-tree and looks up again through the branches.)

Noch einmal, liebes Vög'lein, [42]
  da wir so lang'
  lästig gestört,
lauscht' ich gerne deinem Sange:
  auf dem Zweige seh' ich
  wohlig dich wiegen;
  zwitschernd umschwirren
  dich Brüder und Schwestern,
umschweben dich lustig und lieb!

Doch ich – bin so allein,
hab' nicht Brüder noch Schwestern;
  meine Mutter schwand,
  mein Vater fiel:
nie sah sie der Sohn! –
  Mein einz'ger Gesell [15]
  war ein garstiger Zwerg;

(warmly)

  Güte zwang
  uns nie zu Liebe;
  listige Schlingen
  warf mir der schlaue: –
nun mußt' ich ihn gar erschlagen! –

(He raises his eyes again, in painful emotion, to the branches above him.)

Freundliches Vög'lein,
dich frage ich nun:
  gönntest du mir
  wohl ein gut Gesell?
Willst du mir das rechte rathen?
  Ich lockte so oft
  und erlos't' es mir nie:
  du, mein Trauter,
  träf'st es wohl besser!
So recht ja riethest du schon:

(ever more quietly)

nun sing', ich lausche dem Gesang.

---

from the brilliant blue above. –
  Gentle coolness
I choose beneath the lime!

Once more, my dear little bird,
  since for so long
  we were rudely disturbed,
I'd be glad to hear your song:
  on the branch I can see you
  blissfully swaying;
  twittering, brothers
  and sisters surround you,
fluttering gaily and lovingly round!

But I am so alone,
have no brothers or sisters;
  my mother died,
  my father was slain:
their son never saw them! –
  A loathsome dwarf
  was my only companion;

  kindness never
  led to love;
  he slyly
  set me cunning snares: –
now I've had to slay him! –

My friendly woodbird,
I ask you now:
  would you grant me
  a boon companion?
Will you advise me aright?
  So often I've tried to attract one
  but never yet obtained one:
  you, my dear friend,
  would surely do better!
Already you've given such good advice:

now sing, I'll list to your song.

VOICE OF THE WOODBIRD

Hei! Siegfried erschlug [48, 2]
nun den schlimmen Zwerg!
Jetzt wüßt' ich ihm noch
das herrlichste Weib.
Auf hohem Felsen sie schläft,
Feuer umbrennt ihren Saal:
  durchschritt' er die Brunst,
  weckt' er die Braut, [47]

Hey! Siegfried's now slain
the evil dwarf!
Now I know
the most glorious wife for him.
High on a fell she sleeps,
fire burns round her hall:
  if he passed through the blaze
  and awakened the bride,

Brünnhilde wäre dann sein!   Brünnhilde then would be his!
(Siegfried leaps up impetuously from his sitting position.)

SIEGFRIED

O holder Sang!	O welcome song!
Süßester Hauch!	O sweetest breath!
Wie brennt sein Sinn	Its meaning burns my breast
mir sehrend[116] die Brust!	with searing[116] heat!
Wie zückt er heftig	How it thrills my heart
zündend mein Herz!	with kindling desire!
Was jagt mir so jach	What courses so swiftly
durch Herz und Sinne?	through heart and senses?
Sag' es mir, süßer Freund!	Tell me the answer, sweet friend!

(He listens.)

VOICE OF THE WOODBIRD

Lustig im Leid [47]	Delighting in sorrow,
sing' ich von Liebe;	I sing of love;
wonnig aus Weh'	blissful I weave
web' ich mein Lied:	my lay from woe:
nur Sehnende kennen den Sinn!	lovers alone can know its meaning!

SIEGFRIED

Fort jagt mich's	Exulting, it drives me
jauchzend von hinnen,	away from here,
fort aus dem Wald auf den Fels! −	out of the forest and on to the fell! −
Noch einmal sage mir,	But tell me again,
holder Sänger:	you lovely songster:
werd' ich das Feuer durchbrechen?	shall I break through the fire?
kann ich erwecken die Braut? [35]	Can I awaken the bride?

(Siegfried listens again.) [39]

VOICE OF THE WOODBIRD

Die Braut gewinnt, [47]	He who wins the bride
Brünnhild' erweckt	and awakens Brünnhilde
ein Feiger nie:	shall never be a coward:
nur wer das Fürchten nicht kennt! [48]	only he who knows not fear!

SIEGFRIED
(exultantly)

Der dumme Knab',	The foolish boy
der das Fürchten nicht kennt,	who knows not fear,
mein Vög'lein, der bin ja ich!	my woodbird, that is I!
Noch heute gab ich	This very day
vergebens mir Müh',	I tried in vain
das Fürchten von Fafner zu lernen.	to learn from Fafner what fear may be.
Nun brenn' ich vor Lust,	Now I burn with longing
es von Brünnhild' zu wissen:	to learn it from Brünnhild':
wie find' ich zum Felsen den Weg?	how shall I find my way to the fell?

(The bird flutters up, circles over Siegfried and flies off, hesitantly, ahead of him.)

So wird mir der Weg gewiesen:	Thus shall the way be shown to me:
wohin du flatterst	wherever you flutter,
folg' ich dir nach!	there shall I follow!

(He runs after the bird, which teases him for a time by leading him inconstantly in different directions before finally setting off in a particular direction towards the back of the stage, with Siegfried in pursuit.) [48, 47]

Act Three

PRELUDE AND SCENE ONE

(The curtain rises.[117] *A wild place at the foot of a rocky mountain, which rises abruptly towards the right. Night. A raging storm. Lightning and violent thunder, which latter ceases, while flashes of lightning continue to rend the clouds for some time to come. The Wanderer now enters.*[118] *He strides resolutely to the mouth of a vault-like cavern in a rock at the front of the stage and takes up his position there, leaning on his spear, while calling into the mouth of the cave.)* [30, 20, 32a, 9, 21, 43, 3, 38]

WANDERER

Wache! Wala!		Waken, vala!
Wala, erwach'!	[26a]	Vala, awake!
Aus langem Schlaf		From lengthy sleep
weck' ich dich schlummernde auf.		I awake you, slumberer.
Ich rufe dich auf:		I call upon you:
herauf! herauf!		arise! Arise!
Aus nebliger Gruft,		From mist-clad vault,
aus nächtigem Grunde herauf!		from night-veiled depths arise!
Erda! Erda!	[20]	Erda! Erda!
Ewiges Weib!		Eternal woman!
Aus heimischer Tiefe		From native depths
tauche zur Höh'!		rise up to the heights!
Dein Wecklied sing' ich,		I sing your waking song
daß du erwachest;		that you may waken;
aus sinnendem Schlafe		from brooding sleep
weck' ich dich auf.		I rouse you up.
Allwissende!	[21]	All-knowing!
Urweltweise!		Primevally wise!
Erda! Erda!		Erda! Erda!
Ewiges Weib!		Eternal woman!
Wache, erwache,		Waken, awaken,
du Wala! erwache!	[9]	you vala, awaken!

(The vaulted cave begins to glow with a bluish light, in which Erda is seen rising very slowly from the depths. She appears to be covered in hoar-frost; hair and garments give off a glittering sheen.) [38]

Stark ruft das Lied;		Strong is the call of your lay;
kräftig reizt der Zauber;		mighty the lure of its magic spell;
ich bin erwacht		from knowing sleep
aus wissendem Schlaf:		am I roused:
wer scheucht den Schlummer mir?	[34]	who is it who drives my slumber away?

WANDERER

Der Weckrufer bin ich,	[20]	Your awakener am I,
und Weisen üb' ich,		and strains I sing
daß weithin wache	[21]	that all may wake
was fester Schlaf verschließt.		whom heavy sleep enfolds.
Die Welt durchzog ich,	[43]	I roamed the world
wanderte viel,		and wandered far
Kunde zu werben,		to garner knowledge
urweisen Rath zu gewinnen.		and gain primeval lore.
Kundiger giebt es		None there is
keine als dich:		who is wiser than you:
bekannt ist dir		to you is revealed
was die Tiefe birgt,		what the depths conceal,
was Berg und Thal,		what fills every hill and dale
Luft und Wasser durchwebt.		and moves through air and water.
Wo Wesen sind		Where men have life
wehet dein Athem;		your spirit moves;
wo Hirne sinnen		where brains are brooding
haftet dein Sinn:		your mind remains:
alles, sagt man,		all, it is said,
sei dir bekannt.		is made known to you.
Daß ich nun Kunde gewänne,	[26a]	That I may now gain knowledge,
weck' ich dich aus dem Schlaf.	[9]	I wake you from your sleep.

ERDA

Mein Schlaf ist Träumen,	[38]	My sleep is dreaming,
mein Träumen Sinnen,		my dreaming brooding,
mein Sinnen Walten des Wissens.	[20]	my brooding the exercise of knowledge.
Doch wenn ich schlafe,		But when I sleep,
wachen Nornen:		then Norns keep watch:
sie weben das Seil,	[6]	they weave the rope
und spinnen fromm[120] was ich		and bravely[120] spin whatever I know: –
[weiß: –		
was fräg'st du nicht die Nornen?		why don't you ask the Norns?

WANDERER

Im Zwange der Welt		In thrall to the world
weben die Nornen:		those wise women weave:
sie können nichts wenden noch		naught can they make or mend;
[wandeln;		
doch deiner Weisheit		but I'd thank
dankt' ich den Rath wohl,	[26a]	the store of your wisdom
wie zu hemmen ein rollendes Rad?		to be told how to hold back a rolling
		[wheel.

Männerthaten	[6]	Deeds of men
umdämmern mir den Muth:		becloud my mind:
mich Wissende selbst	[8]	wise though I am,
bezwang ein Waltender einst.		a ruler once tamed me.
Ein Wunschmädchen		A Wish-Maid
gebar ich Wotan:		I bore to Wotan:
der Helden Wal		for him he bade her
hieß für sich er sie küren.		choose slain heroes.
Kühn ist sie	[39]	She is brave
und weise auch:		and wise withal:
was weck'st du mich,	[34]	why waken me
und fräg'st um Kunde		and not seek knowledge
nicht Erda's und Wotan's Kind?		from Erda's and Wotan's child?

WANDERER

Die Walküre mein'st du,	[8, 37]	Do you mean the valkyrie,
Brünnhild', die Maid?		Brünnhild', the maid?
Sie trotzte dem Stürmebezwinger,		She defied the master of storms
wo er am stärksten selbst sich		when, with utmost effort, he mastered
[bezwang:		[himself:
was den Lenker der Schlacht		what the lord of the battle
zu thun verlangte,		longed to do
doch dem er wehrte –		but what he forbade
– zuwider sich selbst –		– in spite of himself –
allzu vertraut		his dissident daughter,
wagte die trotzige		all too conversantly,
das für sich zu vollbringen,	[30]	dared in the heat of that battle
Brünnhild' in brennender Schlacht.		to do for herself.
Streitvater		War-Father
strafte die Maid;		punished the maid;
in ihr Auge drückte er Schlaf;[121]		he closed her eyes in sleep;[121]
auf dem Felsen schläft sie fest:		on yonder fell she's sleeping soundly:
erwachen wird		the hallowed maid
die weihliche nur		will awaken only
um einen Mann zu minnen als Weib.		to love a man as his wife.
Frommten mir Fragen an sie?	[9]	What use would it be to question her?

ERDA

Wirr wird mir,		I've grown confused
seit ich erwacht:		since I was wakened:
wild und kraus		wild and awry
kreis't die Welt!		the world revolves!
Die Walküre,	[38]	The valkyrie,
der Wala Kind,		the vala's child,
büßt' in Banden des Schlaf's,		atones in trammels of sleep
als die wissende Mutter schlief?	[34]	while her knowing mother slept?
Der den Trotz lehrte		Does he who taught defiance
straft den Trotz?		scourge defiance?
Der die That entzündet	[37]	Does he who urged the deed

zürnt um die That?
Der die Rechte wahrt,
der die Eide hütet,
wehret dem Recht,
herrscht durch Meineid? –
Lass' mich wieder hinab:
Schlaf verschließe mein Wissen!

grow wroth when it is done?
Does he who safeguards rights
and helps uphold sworn oaths
gainsay that right
and rule through perjured oath? –
Let me descend once more:
let sleep enfold my knowledge!

WANDERER

Dich Mutter lass' ich nicht zieh'n,   [26a]
da des Zaubers mächtig ich bin. –
  Urwissend
  stachest du einst
  der Sorge Stachel
in Wotan's wagendes Herz:
  mit Furcht vor schmachvoll   [20, 21]
  feindlichem Ende
  füllt' ihn dein Wissen,
daß Bangen band seinen Muth.
  Bist du der Welt   [43]
  weisestes Weib,
  sage mir nun:
wie besiegt die Sorge der Gott?   [9]

Mother, I'll not let you go
while I yet have mastery over the spell. –
  Primevally wise
  you thrust ere now
  the thorn of care
into Wotan's venturous heart:
  with fear of a shamefully
  adverse end
  your knowledge filled him
till dread enmeshed his mind.
  If you are the world's
  wisest woman,
  then tell me now:
how can the god overcome his care?

ERDA

Du bist – nicht
  was du dich nenn'st!
Was kam'st du störrischer Wilder

zu stören der Wala Schlaf?

You are not
  what you say you are!
Stubborn, wild-spirited god, why have
  [you come
to disturb the vala's sleep?

WANDERER

Du bist – nicht   [26a]
  was du dich wähn'st!
Urmütter-Weisheit[122]
  geht zu Ende:
  dein Wissen verweht
  vor meinem Willen.
Weißt du, was Wotan – will?

You are not
  what you think you are!
The wisdom of primeval mothers[122]
  draws towards its end:
  your knowledge wanes
  before my will.
Do you know what Wotan wills?

(Long silence.)

Dir unweisen[123]   [20]
  ruf' ich's in's Ohr,
daß sorglos ewig du nun schläf'st!   [21]

O unwise woman,[123]
  I call on you now
to sleep forever, free from care! –

Um der Götter Ende
  grämt mich die Angst nicht,
seit mein Wunsch es – will!   [26a]
Was in des Zwiespalt's wildem
  [Schmerze
verzweifelnd einst ich beschloß,

Fear of the end of the gods
  no longer consumes me
now that my wish so wills it!
What I once resolved in despair,

in the searing smart of inner turmoil,

froh und freudig		I now perform freely
führe frei ich nun aus:	[49]	in gladness and joy:
weiht' ich in wüthendem Ekel		though once, in furious loathing,
des Niblungen Neid schon die Welt,		I bequeathed the world to the Nibelung's [spite,
dem herrlichsten Wälsung	[35]	to the lordliest Wälsung
weis' ich mein Erbe nun an.	[8]	I leave my heritage now.
Der von mir erkoren,		He whom I chose
doch nie mich gekannt,		but who never knew me,
ein kühnester Knabe,		the bravest of boys,
bar meines Rathes,		though deprived of my counsel,
errang den Niblungenring:	[6, 23]	has won for himself the Nibelung's ring:
liebesfroh,		rejoicing in love,
ledig des Neides,		while free from greed,
erlahmt an dem Edlen		Alberich's curse
Alberich's Fluch;	[35]	is powerless over the noble youth;
denn fremd bleibt ihm die Furcht.		for fear remains unknown to him.
Die du mir gebar'st,	[26a]	Brünnhilde,
Brünnhild'	[26b]	whom you bore to me,
weckt sich hold der Held:		the hero will lovingly waken:
wachend wirkt	[49]	waking,
dein wissendes Kind		your all-wise child
erlösende Weltenthat. –		will work the deed that redeems the [world. –

(somewhat broadly)

D'rum schlafe nun du,		And so, sleep on;
schließe dein Auge;	[38]	close your eyes
träumend erschau' mein Ende!		and, dreaming, behold my end!
Was jene auch wirken –		Whatever they do –
dem ewig Jungen	[49]	to one who's eternally young
weicht in Wonne der Gott. –		the god now yields in gladness. –
Hinab denn, Erda!	[26a]	Descend then, Erda!
Urmütter-Furcht!		Primeval mothers' fear!
Ur-Sorge!		Primeval care!
Hinab! Hinab		Descend! Descend
zu ew'gem Schlaf! –	[38]	to ageless sleep! –

(Having already closed her eyes and begun to descend, Erda now disappears completely; the cave too has now become very dark again. Moonlight casts its pallor over the stage; the storm has abated.)

SCENE TWO

(The Wanderer has moved close up to the cave and he now leans back against it, his face turned towards the stage.)

WANDERER

| Dort seh' ich Siegfried nah'n. – | | Siegfried I see approaching there. – |

(He remains in position by the cave. [48] Siegfried's woodbird flutters downstage. [47] Suddenly the bird stops, flutters to and fro in alarm and disappears quickly towards the back of the stage. Siegfried enters and pauses.)

SIEGFRIED

Mein Vög'lein schwebte mir fort; –	My woodbird's flown away; –
mit flatterndem Flug	with fluttering flight
und süßem Sang	and sweet-sounding song
wies es mich wonnig des Weg's:	it blithely showed me my way:
nun schwand es fern mir davon.	now it has fled far away from me.
Am besten find' ich mir	It's best if I find
selbst nun den Berg:	the rock by myself:
wohin mein Führer mich wies,	I'll follow the path
dahin wandr' ich jetzt fort.	that my guide pointed out.

(He strides upstage.)

WANDERER
(remaining where he is)

Wohin, Knabe,	Whither, my lad,
heißt dich dein Weg?	does your journey lead you?

SIEGFRIED
(stopping and turning round)

Da redet's ja:	There's someone speaking:
wohl räth das mir den Weg. –	perhaps he can tell me the way. –

(He approaches the Wanderer.)

Einen Felsen such' ich,	I'm seeking a rock
von Feuer ist der umwabert:	that's circled by fire:
dort schläft ein Weib,	there sleeps a woman
das ich wecken will.	I mean to wake.

WANDERER

Wer sagt' es dir	Who told you
den Fels zu suchen,	to seek out the rock,
wer nach der Frau dich zu sehnen?	who bade you desire the woman?

SIEGFRIED

Mich wies ein singend	A forest songbird
Waldvög'lein:	directed me:
das gab mir gute Kunde.	it gave me good advice.

WANDERER

Ein Vög'lein schwatzt wohl manches;	A woodbird chatters of many things;
kein Mensch doch kann's versteh'n:	no human can understand it:
wie mochtest du Sinn	how could you make
dem Sang entnehmen?	any sense of its singing?

SIEGFRIED

Das wirkte das Blut	[46]	It was due to the blood
eines wilden Wurm's,		of a fearsome dragon

SIEGFRIED, Act Three   259

der mir vor Neidhöhl' erblaßte:
kaum netzt' es zündend
die Zunge mir,
da verstand ich der Vög'lein
[Gestimm'.

that fell before me at Neidhöhl':
its kindling blood
had scarce wet my tongue
when I understood what the birds were
[saying.

WANDERER

Erschlug'st den Riesen du,
wer reizte dich,
den starken Wurm zu besteh'n?

If you slew the giant,
who urged you on
to defeat the mighty beast?

SIEGFRIED

Mich führte Mime,
ein falscher Zwerg;
das Fürchten wollt' er mich lehren:
zum Schwertstreich aber,
der ihn erstach,
reizte der Wurm mich selbst;
seinen Rachen riß er mir auf.

I was led by Mime,
a false-hearted dwarf;
he wanted to teach me fear:
but the dragon itself
provoked the blow
that proved to be his undoing;
he snapped his jaws at me.

WANDERER

Wer schuf das Schwert
so scharf und hart,
daß der stärkste Feind ihm fiel?

Who made the sword
so sharp and hard
that his fiercest enemy fell before him?

SIEGFRIED

Das schweißt' ich mir selbst,   [40]
da's der Schmied nicht konnte: [15]
schwertlos noch wär' ich wohl sonst.

I forged it myself
since the smith was unable:
I'd otherwise still be swordless.

WANDERER

Doch wer schuf
die starken Stücken,
daraus das Schwert du dir
[geschweißt?

But who made
the mighty fragments
from which you forged the sword?

SIEGFRIED

Was weiß ich davon!
Ich weiß allein,
daß die Stücken mir nichts nützten,
schuf ich das Schwert mir nicht neu.

What do I know of that?
I know only
that the bits were no use
unless I re-made the sword.

WANDERER
(breaking into cheerfully good-natured laughter)
Das – mein' ich wohl auch!   That I can well believe!
(He observes Siegfried, well-pleased.) [27]

SIEGFRIED
(surprised)
Was lach'st du mich aus?   Are you laughing at me?

Alter Frager,	No more of your questions,
hör' einmal auf;	old man;
lass' mich nicht länger hier	don't keep me here talking any longer!
[schwatzen!	
Kannst du den Weg	If you can show me
mir weisen, so rede:	the way, then tell me:
vermag'st du's nicht,	if you're unable,
so halte dein Maul!	then hold your tongue!

WANDERER

Geduld, du Knabe!	Patience, my lad!
Dünk' ich dich alt,	If you think that I'm old,
so sollst du Achtung mir bieten.	you should show me respect.

SIEGFRIED

Das wär' nicht übel!	A fine idea!
So lang' ich lebe	As long as I've lived
stand mir ein Alter	an old man has always
stets im Wege:	stood in my way:
den hab' ich nun fort gefegt.	now I have swept him aside.
Stemm'st du dort länger	If you offer me more
steif dich mir entgegen –	of your stiff opposition,
sieh' dich vor, sag' ich,	take care, I say,

(with an appropriate gesture)

daß du wie Mime nicht fähr'st!	that you don't share Mime's fate!

(He moves even closer to the Wanderer.) [48]

Wie sieh'st du denn aus?	Let me see what you look like!
Was hast du gar	Why are you wearing
für 'nen großen Hut?	so huge a hat?
Warum hängt er dir so in's Gesicht? [27]	Why does it hang down over your face?

WANDERER
(still in the same position)

Das ist so Wand'rers Weise,	[43]	That is the Wanderer's way
wenn dem Wind entgegen er geht.	[8]	when he walks against the wind.

SIEGFRIED
(observing him more closely)

Doch darunter fehlt dir ein Auge!	But under it one of your eyes is missing!
Das schlug dir einer	No doubt someone
gewiß schon aus,	struck it out
dem du zu trotzig	when you stubbornly
den Weg vertrat'st?	stood in his way?
Mach' dich jetzt fort!	Be off with you now!
Sonst könntest du leicht	Or else you could easily
das and're auch noch verlieren.	lose the other one, too.

WANDERER
(very calmly)

Ich seh', mein Sohn,	[8]	I see, my son,

wo du nichts weißt,
da weißt du dir leicht zu helfen.
  Mit dem Auge,
    das als and'res mir fehlt,
erblick'st du selber das eine,
das mir zum Sehen verblieb.[124]

that where you know nothing,
you know how to get your own way.
  With the eye which,
    as my second self, is missing,
you yourself can glimpse the one
that's left for me to see with.[124]

SIEGFRIED
(after listening thoughtfully now bursts out in a peal of spontaneous laughter)

Zum Lachen bist du mir lustig! –
Doch hör', nun schwatz' ich nicht
  [länger;
geschwind zeig' mir den Weg,
deines Weges ziehe dann du!
  Zu nichts and'rem
    acht' ich dich nütz':
d'rum sprich, sonst spreng' ich dich
  [fort!

At least you're good for a laugh! –
But listen, I'll gossip no longer;

quickly, show me the way
and be on your own way, too!
  For nothing else
    do I deem you of use:
so speak or I'll send you packing!

WANDERER
(gently)

Kenntest du mich,   [32a]
  kühner Sproß,
den Schimpf – spartest du mir!
  Dir so vertraut,
trifft mich schmerzlich dein Dräuen.
  Lieb' ich von je
    deine lichte Art, –
  Grauen auch zeugt' ihr
  mein zürnender Grimm.
  Dem ich so hold bin,
    allzu hehrer,
heut' nicht wecke mir Neid, –
er vernichtete dich und mich![125]

If you but knew me,
  brave-hearted youth,
you'd spare me this affront!
  So dear to you,
I'm sorely wounded by your threats.
  Though I've always loved
    your radiant kind,
  my furious rage
  might also cause it dread.
  You to whom I'm well-disposed,
    too glorious by far,
do not arouse my wrath today –
it could ruin both you and me![125]

SIEGFRIED

Bleib'st du mir stumm,
störrischer Wicht?
Weich' von der Stelle!
  Denn dorthin, ich weiß,
führt es zur schlafenden Frau:
  so wies es mein Vög'lein,   [48]
das hier erst flüchtig entfloh.

So you'll still not tell me,
you stubborn wight?
Get out of the way!
  For this slope, I know,
must lead to the sleeping woman:
  so I was shown by my woodbird
that fled from here in flight just now.

(It quickly becomes completely dark again.)

WANDERER
(breaking out in anger and adopting a domineering stance)

Es floh dir zu seinem Heil;   [3]
  den Herrn der Raben
errieth es hier:

It fled from you to save its life;
  it guessed that
the lord of the ravens was here:

weh' ihm, holen sie's ein! –
Den Weg, den es zeigte,
sollst du nicht zieh'n!

[9] woe betide if they overtake it! –
The way that it showed you
you shall not go!

SIEGFRIED
(stepping back in surprise but adopting a defiant attitude)

Hoho! du Verbieter!
Wer bist du denn,
daß du mir wehren willst?

Hoho! You'd forbid me?
Who are you then
who would bar my way?

WANDERER

Fürchte des Felsens Hüter!
Verschlossen hält
meine Macht die schlafende Maid:
wer sie erweckte,
wer sie gewänne,
machtlos macht' er mich ewig! –

Fear the guardian of the fell!
Locked within my power
the sleeping maid is held:
he who awakens her,
he who wins her
would make me powerless for aye! –

Ein Feuermeer
umfluthet die Frau,
glühende Lohe
umleckt den Fels:
wer die Braut begehrt,
dem brennt entgegen die Brunst.

A sea of fire
floods round the woman,
a white-hot blaze
licks round the rock:
he who longs for the bride
will find the fire raging towards him.

(He points his spear at the rocky heights.) [30]

Blick' nach der Höh'!
Erlug'st du das Licht? –
Es wächst der Schein,
es schwillt die Gluth;
sengende Wolken,
wabernde Lohe,
wälzen sich brennend
und prasselnd herab.
Ein Licht-Meer
umleuchtet dein Haupt:

[14a]

Look up to the heights!
Do you see the light? –
The glow is growing,
the heat increasing;
scorching clouds
and flickering flame
roll down the hillside,
burning and crackling.
A sea of light
encircles your head:

(From the top of the rock a flickering glow becomes visible, growing in brightness.)

bald frißt und zehrt dich
zündendes Feuer: –
zurück denn, rasendes Kind!

soon kindling flames
will seize and consume you: –
get back, you foolhardy child!

SIEGFRIED

Zurück, du Prahler, mit dir!
Dort, wo die Brünste brennen,
zu Brünnhilde muß ich dahin!

[35] Get back, you braggart, yourself!
There where the flames are burning,
[39] to Brünnhilde I must go!

(He advances; the Wanderer bars his way.)

WANDERER

Fürchtest das Feuer du nicht,
so sperre mein Speer dir den
[Weg!

If you're not afraid of the fire,
my spear will bar your way for you!

[9, 32a]

SIEGFRIED, Act Three 263

Noch hält meine Hand
der Herrschaft Haft;
das Schwert, das du schwing'st,
zerschlug einst dieser Schaft:
noch einmal denn
zerspring' es am ew'gen Speer!

My hand still holds
the haft of power;
the sword you wield
was shivered ere now by this shaft:
once more let it
splinter upon my eternal spear!

(He stretches out his spear.)

SIEGFRIED
(drawing his sword)

Meines Vaters Feind!
Find' ich dich hier?
Herrlich zur Rache
gerieth mir das!
Schwing' deinen Speer:
in Stücken spalt' ihn mein Schwert! [23]

My father's foe!
Do I find you here?
What a glorious chance
for vengeance is this!
Stretch forth your spear:
my sword shall strike it in splinters!

(With one blow, he strikes the Wanderer's spear in two: a flash of lightning bursts forth from it towards the summit, where the glow, previously somewhat faint, now begins to blaze with ever-increasing fury. The blow is accompanied by a loud clap of thunder, which quickly dies away. The fragments of the spear fall at the Wanderer's feet. He calmly gathers them up.) [9]

WANDERER

Zieh' hin! Ich kann dich nicht
[halten!   [20, 21]

Go on your way! I cannot stop you!

(He suddenly disappears in total darkness.)

SIEGFRIED

Mit zerfocht'ner Waffe   [27]
floh mir der Feige?

Has the coward fled
with vanquished weapon?

(Siegfried's attention is caught by the growing brightness of the clouds of fire that roll down the mountain towards him.)

Ha, wonnige Gluth!   [35]
Leuchtender Glanz!
Strahlend nun offen   [47, 48]
steht mir die Straße. –
Im Feuer mich baden!
Im Feuer zu finden die Braut!
Hoho! hahei!
Jetzt lock' ich ein liebes Gesell!

Ha, rapturous glow!
Radiant gleam!
The pathway lies open,
shining before me. –
To bathe in the fire!
To find the bride in the flames!
Hoho! Hahei!
Now I'll summon some boon
[companion!

(Siegfried raises his horn to his lips and plunges into the billowing fire which, sweeping down from the heights, has now spread to the front of the stage. [40, 14a, 38] No longer visible, Siegfried seems to be moving away towards the summit. [35] The flames reach their brightest intensity. From now on,[126] the glow, having reached its brightest intensity, begins to fade, gradually dissolving into ever finer clouds, which are lit as though by the red light of dawn.) [39]

(The clouds, which have become increasingly fine, have dissolved into a delicate veil of rose-coloured mist and now part in such a way that the haze disperses towards the top of the stage, finally revealing only the cloudless blue sky, while on the edge of the rocky height, which has now become visible (exactly the same scene as in Act III of 'Die Walküre'), a veil of early-morning mist continues to hang, at the same time recalling the magic fire which is still blazing in the valley below. The arrangement of the scene is entirely the same as at the end of 'Die Walküre': in the foreground, beneath the spreading branches of the fir-tree, Brünnhilde lies asleep in full shining armour, her helmet on her head, her long shield covering her. [34] Siegfried reaches the rocky edge of the cliff from the back. At first only the upper part of his body is visible. He remains in this position for a long time, staring round him in astonishment.)

SIEGFRIED
(quietly)

Selige Öde	Blissful wasteland
auf wonniger Höh'!	on wondrous heights!

(He climbs right up and, standing on a rock by the precipice at the back, observes the scene in wonderment. He gazes into the pinewood at the side and moves further downstage.)

Was ruht dort schlummernd		What lies there, in slumber,
im schattigen Tann? –	[30]	within the shade of the pinewood? –
Ein Roß ist's,		A horse I see,
rastend in tiefem Schlaf!		resting in deepest sleep!

(Slowly coming nearer, he stops in astonishment when, still some distance away, he notices Brünnhilde's form.)

Was strahlt mir dort entgegen? –	What beam of light bedazzles my gaze? –
Welch' glänzendes Stahlgeschmeid?	What metalwork wrought in glittering [steel?
Blendet mir noch	Is it the blaze
die Lohe den Blick? –	that still blinds my eye? –
Helle Waffen! –	Shining weapons! –
Heb' ich sie auf?	Shall I remove them?

(He raises the shield and sees Brünnhilde's form, although her face remains largely concealed by her helmet.)

Ha! in Waffen ein Mann: –	Ha! In weapons a man: –
wie mahnt mich wonnig sein Bild! –	how his likeness fills me with wonder! –
Das hehre Haupt	Does his helm perhaps
drückt wohl der Helm?	press on his noble head?
Leichter würd' ihm,	Lighter it were
lös't ich den Schmuck.	if I loosened his headgear.

(He carefully loosens the helmet and removes it from the sleeper; long curling hair breaks free. Siegfried starts.)

(tenderly)

Ach! – wie schön! –	Ah! – how fair! –

(He remains lost in the sight of it.)

Schimmernde Wolken	Shimmering clouds
säumen in Wellen	have fringed a shining
den hellen Himmelssee:	celestial lake with their waves:
leuchtender Sonne	the radiant sunlight's

lachendes Bild	smiling likeness
strahlt durch das Wogengewölk!	shines through a billowing bank of [clouds!

(He bends closer to the sleeping figure.)

Von schwellendem Athem		His breast is heaving
schwingt sich die Brust: –		with swelling breath: –
brech' ich die engende Brünne?	[30]	shall I break the trammelling breastplate [open?

(He tries to loosen the byrnie.)

Komm', mein Schwert,	Come, my sword,
schneide das Eisen!	and cut through the iron!

(Siegfried draws his sword and, with tender care, cuts through the rings of mail on both sides of the armour. [23] He then lifts away the breastplate and greaves, so that Brünnhilde now lies before him in a woman's soft garment. He starts up in shock and astonishment.)

Das ist kein Mann! – –	No man is this! – –

(He stares at the sleeping woman in a state of utter turmoil.)

Brennender Zauber	Burning enchantment
zückt mir in's Herz;	charms my heart;
feurige Angst	fiery terror
faßt meine Augen:	transfixes my eyes:
mir schwankt und schwindelt der [Sinn!	my senses stagger and swoon!

(He is filled with immense apprehension.) [27]

Wen ruf' ich zum Heil,	To save me, whom shall I
daß er mir helfe? –	call on to help me? –
Mutter! Mutter!	Mother! Mother!
Gedenke mein'! –	Remember me! –

(He sinks, as if fainting, on Brünnhilde's breast. He starts up with a sigh.)

Wie weck' ich die Maid,	How shall I waken the maid
daß sie ihr Auge mir öff'ne?	so that she opens her eyes for me?
Das Auge mir öff'nen?	Opens her eyes for me?
Blende mich auch noch der Blick?	What though the sight might yet blind [me!

Wagt' es mein Trotz?		Might my bravery dare it?
Ertrüg' ich das Licht? –		Could I bear their light? –
Mir schwebt und schwankt		Around me everything floats
und schwirrt es umher;		and sways and swims;
sehrendes Sehnen		searing desire
zehrt meine Sinne:		consumes my senses:
am zagenden Herzen		on my quaking heart
zittert die Hand! –	[39]	my hand is trembling! –
Wie ist mir Feigem? –		What is this, coward, that I feel? –
Ist dieß das Fürchten? –		Is this what it is to fear? –
O Mutter! Mutter!		O mother! Mother!
Dein muthiges Kind!		Your mettlesome child!

(very tenderly)

Im Schlafe liegt eine Frau: –	A woman lies asleep: –
die hat ihn das Fürchten gelehrt! –	she has taught him the meaning of fear! –

Wie end' ich die Furcht?	How can I overcome my fear?

Wie fass' ich Muth? –
Daß ich selbst erwache,
muß die Maid ich erwecken! – –

How can I summon up courage? –
That I myself may awaken,
I must waken the maid! – –

(As he approaches the sleeper anew, he is again held enthralled by the sight of her as a result of his more tender feelings. [23] He bends closer.)

Süß erbebt mir
ihr blühender Mund:
wie mild erzitternd
mich zagen er reizt! –
Ach, dieses Athems
wonnig warmes Gedüft'! –

Sweetly quivers
her burgeoning mouth:
gently trembling it lures me on,
faint-hearted that I am! –
Ah, the blissfully warming
fragrance of that breath! –

(as though in despair)

Erwache! erwache!
heiliges Weib! – –

Awake! Awake!
Thrice-hallowed woman! – –

(He gazes at her.) [34]

Sie hört mich nicht. –

She cannot hear me. –

(slowly, with urgent and insistent expression)

So saug' ich mir Leben
aus süßesten Lippen –

So I suck life
from the sweetest of lips –

(relenting)

sollt' ich auch sterbend vergeh'n!

though I should perish and die!

(He sinks, as though dying, on the sleeping woman and, with his eyes closed, presses his lips on her mouth. Brünnhilde opens her eyes. Siegfried starts up and remains standing in front of her. Brünnhilde slowly sits up. She raises her arms and, with solemn gestures, welcomes her return to an awareness of earth and sky.)

BRÜNNHILDE

Heil dir, Sonne!
Heil dir, Licht!
Heil dir, leuchtender Tag!
Lang' war mein Schlaf;   [34]
  ich bin erwacht:
  wer ist der Held,
  der mich erweckt'?

Hail to you, sun!
Hail to you, light!
Hail to you, light-bringing day!
Long was my sleep;
  awakened am I:
  who is the hero
  who woke me?

(Profoundly moved by her appearance and voice, Siegfried stands as though rooted to the spot.)

SIEGFRIED

Durch das Feuer drang ich,   [35]
  das den Fels umbrann;
ich erbrach dir den festen Helm:
  Siegfried bin ich,
  der dich erweckt.

I pressed through the fire
  that burned round the fell;
I broke open your tight-fitting helmet:
  Siegfried am I
  who woke you.

BRÜNNHILDE
(sitting upright)

Heil euch, Götter!
Heil dir, Welt!
Heil dir, prangende Erde!
Zu End' ist nun mein Schlaf;

Hail to you, gods!
Hail to you, world!
Hail to you, splendent earth!
My sleep is at an end now;

erwacht seh' ich:
Siegfried ist es,
der mich erweckt!

awakened, I see
it is Siegfried
who woke me!

SIEGFRIED
(breaking out in the most sublime ecstasy)

O Heil der Mutter,   [50]
die mich gebar;
Heil der Erde,
die mich genährt:
daß ich das Aug' erschaut,
das jetzt mir Seligem lacht!

All hail to the mother
who gave me birth;
hail to the earth
that gave me nurture:
that I saw the eye
that smiles on me now in my bliss!

BRÜNNHILDE

O Heil der Mutter,
die dich gebar;
Heil der Erde,
die dich genährt:
nur dein Blick durfte mich schau'n,
erwachen durft' ich nur dir! –

All hail to the mother
who gave you birth;
hail to the earth
that gave you nurture;
your gaze alone was fated to see me,
to you alone was I fated to wake! –

(Both remain lost in radiant delight as they gaze at one another.) [35]

O Siegfried! Siegfried!   [50]
Seliger Held!
Du Wecker des Lebens,
siegendes Licht!   [51]
O wüßtest du, Lust der Welt,
wie ich dich je geliebt!   [50]
Du war'st mein Sinnen,
mein Sorgen du!
Dich zarten nährt' ich
noch eh' du gezeugt;
noch eh' du geboren
barg dich mein Schild:
so lang' lieb' ich dich, Siegfried!   [49]

O Siegfried! Siegfried!
Thrice-blessed hero!
You waker of life,
all-conquering light!
If only you knew, you joy of the world,
how I have always loved you!
You yourself were all I thought of,
all I ever cared for!
I nurtured you, you tender child,
before you were begotten;
even before you were born,
my shield already sheltered you:
so long have I loved you, Siegfried!

SIEGFRIED
(softly and shyly)

So starb nicht meine Mutter?
Schlief die minnige nur?

So my mother did not die?
Was the lovely woman merely asleep?

(Brünnhilde smiles and stretches out her hand to him in friendly fashion.)

BRÜNNHILDE

Du wonniges Kind,   [51]
deine Mutter kehrt dir nicht wieder.
Du selbst bin ich,[127]
wenn du mich selige lieb'st.
Was du nicht weißt,   [34]
weiß ich für dich:
doch wissend bin ich   [49]
nur – weil ich dich liebe! –

You blithesome child,
your mother won't come back to you.
Your own self am I,[127]
if you but love me in my bliss.
What *you* don't know
I know for you:
and yet I am knowing
only because I love you! –

O Siegfried! Siegfried!	[50]	O Siegfried! Siegfried!
Siegendes Licht!	[51]	Conquering light!
Dich lieb' ich immer:		I loved you always:
denn mir allein		to me alone
erdünkte[128] Wotan's Gedanke.		was Wotan's thought revealed.
Der Gedanke, den ich		The thought which I
nie nennen durfte;		could never name;
den ich nicht dachte,		the thought I did not think
sondern nur fühlte;		but only felt;
für den ich focht,		the thought for which I fought,
kämpfte und stritt;		did battle and have striven;
für den ich trotzte		for which I flouted
dem, der ihn dachte;		him who thought it;
für den ich büßte,		for which I atoned,
Strafe mich band,		incurring chastisement,
weil ich nicht ihn dachte	[37]	because, not thinking,
und nur empfand!		I only felt it!
Denn der Gedanke –	[49]	Because that thought –
dürftest du's lösen! –		could you only guess it! –
mir war er nur Liebe zu dir.	[50]	was but my love for you.

SIEGFRIED

Wie Wunder tönt		Wondrous it sounds
was wonnig du sing'st;		what you blissfully sing;
doch dunkel dünkt mich der Sinn.		yet its meaning seems obscure to me.

(tenderly)

Deines Auges Leuchten		The light of your eye
seh' ich licht;		is clear to see;
deines Athems Wehen		the sigh of your breath
fühl' ich warm;		is warm to feel;
deiner Stimme Singen		the sound of your singing
hör' ich süß:		is sweet to hear:
doch was du singend mir sag'st,		but what you say to me singing,
staunend versteh' ich's nicht.	[34]	stunned, I cannot understand.
Nicht kann ich das Ferne		With my senses I cannot
sinnig erfassen,		grasp far-away things,
wenn alle Sinne		since all these senses
dich nur sehen und fühlen.		can see and feel only you.
Mit banger Furcht		You bind me in fetters
fesselst du mich:		of anxious fear;
du einz'ge hast		you alone have taught
ihre Angst mich gelehrt.		me to dread it.
Den du gebunden		No longer hide
in mächtigen Banden,		that courage of mine
birg meinen Muth mir nicht mehr!		which you bound with powerful bonds!

(He remains in a state of great agitation, gazing at her with an expression of yearning desire. Brünnhilde gently turns her head aside and looks towards the pinewood.) [30]

BRÜNNHILDE

– Dort seh' ich Grane,		– There I see Grane,

mein selig Roß:
wie weidet er munter,
der mit mir schlief!
Mit mir hat ihn Siegfried erweckt.   [50]

my blessed horse:
awake, he grazes
who slept beside me!
Siegfried awoke him with me.

SIEGFRIED
(still in the same position)

Auf wonnigem Munde   [51]
weidet mein Auge:
in brünstigem Durst
doch brennen die Lippen,
daß der Augen Weide sie labe!

My eyes now feast
on your lovely mouth:
yet with keen-edged thirst
my lips are burning,
longing to be regaled by this feast of my
[eyes!

(Brünnhilde points with her hand to her weapons, which she now perceives.) [23a]

BRÜNNHILDE

Dort seh' ich den Schild,
der Helden schirmte;
dort seh' ich den Helm,
der das Haupt mir barg:
er schirmt, er birgt mich nicht mehr!

There I see the shield
that sheltered heroes;
there I see the helmet
that hid my head:
it shields and hides me no more!

SIEGFRIED
(ardently)

Eine selige Maid
versehrte mein Herz;
Wunden dem Haupte
schlug mir ein Weib: –
ich kam ohne Schild und Helm!

A blissful maid
has pierced my heart;
a woman
has wounded my head: –
I came without shield and helmet!

BRÜNNHILDE
(with increased sadness)

Ich sehe der Brünne
prangenden Stahl:
ein scharfes Schwert
schnitt sie entzwei;
von dem maidlichen Leibe
lös't' es die Wehr: –
ich bin ohne Schutz und Schirm,
ohne Trutz ein trauriges Weib!

I see the brinie's
splendent steel:
a keen-edged sword
has cut it in two;
it loosed my maidenly
body's defences: –
I'm stripped of shelter and shield,
a weaponless, sorrowing woman!

SIEGFRIED
(ardently)

Durch brennendes Feuer
fuhr ich zu dir;
nicht Brünne noch Panzer
barg meinen Leib:
nun brach die Lohe
mir in die Brust;
es braus't mein Blut

Through fierce-burning fire
I came to you;
no brinie nor armour
protected my body:
now has the blaze
broken into my breast;
my blood is pounding

in blühender Brunst;
ein zehrendes Feuer
ist mir entzündet:
die Gluth, die Brünnhild's
Felsen umbrann,
die brennt mir nun in der Brust! –
O Weib, jetzt lösche den Brand!
Schweige die schäumende Wuth!

with rampant desire;
consuming fire
is kindled within me:
the flames that raged around
Brünnhilde's fell
are burning now in my breast! –
O woman, quench the fire now!
Quell this chafing rage!

(He has embraced her violently. Brünnhilde leaps up, repulses him with the strength born of fear, and flees to the other side of the stage.)

BRÜNNHILDE

Kein Gott nahte mir je:
der Jungfrau neigten
scheu sich die Helden:
heilig schied sie aus Walhall! –   [8c, 8d]
Wehe! Wehe!
Wehe der Schmach,
der schmählichen Noth!
Verwundet hat mich,
der mich erweckt!
Er erbrach mir Brünne und Helm:
Brünnhilde bin ich nicht mehr!

No god has ever dared draw near me:
in awe the heroes bowed
before the virgin maid:
she left Valhalla inviolate! –
Alas! Alas!
Alas for the shame,
for my ignominious plight!
He who woke me
has wounded me, too!
He broke open my brinie and helmet:
Brünnhilde am I no longer!

SIEGFRIED

Noch bist du mir
die träumende Maid:
Brünnhilde's Schlaf
brach ich noch nicht.
Erwache! Sei mir ein Weib!

To me you are still
the dream-struck maid:
Brünnhilde's sleep
I have not yet disturbed.
Awaken, and be a woman for me!

BRÜNNHILDE
(in a state of confusion)

Mir schwirren die Sinne;
mein Wissen schweigt:
soll mir die Weisheit schwinden?

My senses grow clouded;
my knowledge falls silent:
is my wisdom to forsake me now?

SIEGFRIED

Sang'st du mir nicht,   [49]
dein Wissen sei
das Leuchten der Liebe zu mir?

Did you not sing
that your knowledge stemmed
from the shining light of your love for
[me?

BRÜNNHILDE
(staring ahead of her)

Trauriges Dunkel
trübt meinen Blick;
mein Auge dämmert,   [19]
das Licht verlischt:
Nacht wird's um mich;

Grieving darkness
clouds my gaze;
my eye grows dim,
its light dies out:
night enfolds me;

aus Nebel und Grau'n
windet sich wüthend
ein Angstgewirr!
Schrecken schreitet
und bäumt sich empor!

from mist and dread
a confusion of fear
now writhes in its rage!
Terror stalks
and rears its head!

(Brünnhilde impulsively covers her eyes with her hands.)

SIEGFRIED
(gently removing her hands from her eyes)

Nacht umfängt
gebund'ne Augen;   [49]
mit den Fesseln schwindet
das finst're Grau'n:
tauch' aus dem Dunkel und sieh' –
sonnenhell leuchtet der Tag!

Night encloses
eyes that are bound;
with your fetters
your gloomy dread will fade:
rise from the darkness and see –
bright as the sun shines the day!

BRÜNNHILDE
(in the utmost dismay)

Sonnenhell
leuchtet der Tag meiner Schmach! – [37]
O Siegfried! Siegfried!
Sieh' meine Angst!

Bright as the sun
shines the day of my shame! –
O Siegfried! Siegfried!
Behold my fear!

(Brünnhilde's mien reveals that a delightful image has passed before her mind's eye, at the thought of which she tenderly directs her gaze back to Siegfried.)

Ewig war ich,
ewig bin ich,
ewig in süß
sehnender Wonne –
doch ewig zu deinem Heil!

Ever was I,
ever am I,
ever beset by
sweet-yearning bliss –
but ever working for your own weal!

(ardently, but tenderly)

O Siegfried! Herrlicher!
Hort der Welt!
Leben der Erde!
Lachender Held!
Lass', ach lass'!
Lasse von mir!
Nahe mir nicht
mit der wüthenden Nähe!
Zwinge mich nicht
mit dem brechenden Zwang!
Zertrümm're die Traute dir nicht! –

O Siegfried! Glorious hero!
Hoard of the world!
Life of the earth!
Laughing hero!
Leave, oh leave me!
Leave me be!
Do not draw near
with your raging nearness!
Do not constrain me
with chafing constraint!
Do not destroy a woman who's dear to
[you! –

Sah'st du dein Bild
im klaren Bach?
Hat es dich frohen erfreut?
Rührtest zur Woge
das Wasser du auf;
zerflösse die klare
Fläche des Bach's:

Did you see your face
in the limpid brook?
Did it rejoice you, blithe hero?
If you stirred
the water into a wave,
if the brook's clear
surface dissolved,

dein Bild säh'st du nicht mehr,
nur der Welle schwankend Gewog'.
  So berühre mich nicht,
  trübe mich nicht:
  ewig licht   [39]
  lach'st du selig
dann aus mir dir entgegen,

froh und heiter ein Held! –
  O Siegfried!
  Leuchtender Sproß!
  Liebe – dich,   [34]
  und lasse von mir:
vernichte dein Eigen nicht!

you'd see your own likeness no longer
but only the billow's eddying surge.
  And so do not touch me,
  trouble me not:
  ever bright
  in your bliss
you will smile a smile that passes from
    [me to you,
a hero blithe and happy! –
  O Siegfried!
  Light-bringing youth!
  Love but yourself
  and let me be:
do not destroy what is yours!

SIEGFRIED

Dich – lieb' ich:
o liebtest mich du!
Nicht hab' ich mehr mich:
o hätte ich dich! –
Ein herrlich Gewässer
wogt vor mir;
mit allen Sinnen
seh' ich nur sie,
die wonnig wogende Welle:
  brach sie mein Bild,
  so brenn' ich nun selbst,
  sengende Gluth
  in der Fluth zu kühlen;
  ich selbst, wie ich bin,
  spring' in den Bach: –
  o daß seine Wogen   [39]
  mich selig verschlängen,
mein Sehnen schwänd' in der Fluth! [49]
  Erwache, Brünnhilde!   [50]
  Wache, du Maid!
  Lache und lebe,   [51]
  süßeste Lust!
Sei mein! sei mein! sei mein!

It is you that I love:
if only you loved me!
No longer do I have myself:
would that I might have you! –
A glorious floodtide
billows before me;
with all my senses
I see only it –
the wondrously billowing wave:
  though it shatter my likeness,
  I'm burning myself now
  to cool raging
  passion within the flood;
  I shall leap, as I am,
  straight into the stream: –
  o that its billows
  engulf me in bliss
and my longing be stilled in the flood!
  Awaken, Brünnhilde!
  Waken, you maid!
  Laugh and live,
  sweetest delight!
Be mine! Be mine! Be mine!

BRÜNNHILDE
(very inwardly)

O Siegfried! Dein –
war ich von je!

O Siegfried! Yours
was I aye!

SIEGFRIED
(ardently)

War'st du's von je,
so sei es jetzt!

If you were once,
then be so now!

BRÜNNHILDE

Dein werd' ich	Yours shall I
ewig sein!	be for ever!

SIEGFRIED

Was du sein wirst,   What you will be,
sei es mir heut'!   be today!
Faßt dich mein Arm,   As my arm enfolds you,
umschling' ich dich fest;   I hold you fast;
schlägt meine Brust   as my heart beats wildly
brünstig die deine;   against your own;
zünden die Blicke,   as our glances ignite
zehren die Athem sich;   and breath feeds on breath,
Aug' in Auge,   eye to eye and
Mund an Mund: mouth on mouth,

Was du sein wirst,		What you will be,
sei es mir heut'!		be today!
Faßt dich mein Arm,		As my arm enfolds you,
umschling' ich dich fest;		I hold you fast;
schlägt meine Brust		as my heart beats wildly
brünstig die deine;		against your own;
zünden die Blicke,		as our glances ignite
zehren die Athem sich;		and breath feeds on breath,
Aug' in Auge,		eye to eye and
Mund an Mund:		mouth on mouth,
dann bist du mir	[49]	then, to me, you must be
was bang du mir war'st und wirst!		what, fearful, you were and will be!
Dann brach sich die brennende		Then gone were the burning doubt
[Sorge,		
ob jetzt Brünnhilde mein?		that Brünnhilde might not now be mine.

BRÜNNHILDE

Ob jetzt ich dein? –	[34]	That I'm not yours now? –

Göttliche Ruhe		Godlike composure
ras't mir in Wogen;		rages in billows;
keuschestes Licht		the chastest of light
lodert in Gluthen;		flares up with passion;
himmlisches Wissen		heavenly knowledge
stürmt mir dahin,		floods away,
Jauchzen der Liebe	[50]	love's rejoicing
jagt es davon!		drives it hence!

Ob jetzt ich dein? –		Am I now yours? –

Siegfried! Siegfried!		Siegfried! Siegfried!
Sieh'st du mich nicht?		Can you not see me?
Wie mein Blick dich verzehrt,	[18]	As my gaze consumes you,
erblindest du nicht?		are you not blinded?
Wie mein Arm dich preßt,		As my arm holds you tight,
entbrenn'st du mir nicht?		don't you burn for me?
Wie in Strömen mein Blut		As my blood streams
entgegen dir stürmt,		in torrents towards you,
das wilde Feuer,	[30]	do you not feel
fühl'st du es nicht?		its furious fire?
Fürchtest du, Siegfried,		Do you fear, Siegfried,
fürchtest du nicht		do you not fear
das wild wüthende Weib?	[35]	the wildly raging woman?

(She embraces him passionately.)

SIEGFRIED
(in joyful terror)

Ha! –	Ha! –
Wie des Blutes Ströme sich zünden;	As the blood in our veins ignites,
wie der Blicke Strahlen sich zehren;	as our flashing glances consume one [another,
wie die Arme brünstig sich pressen –	as our arms clasp each other in ardour –
kehrt mir zurück	my courage
mein kühner Muth,	returns
und das Fürchten, ach!	and the fear, ah!
das ich nie gelernt –	the fear that I never learned –
das Fürchten, das du	the fear that you
mich kaum gelehrt:	scarcely taught me:
das Fürchten – mich dünkt – [48]	that fear – I think –
ich Dummer vergaß es nun ganz! [47]	fool that I am, I have quite forgotten it [now!

(At these last words he has involuntarily released Brünnhilde.)

BRÜNNHILDE
(laughing wildly and joyfully)

O kindischer Held! [30]	O childish hero!
O herrlicher Knabe!	O glorious boy!
Du hehrster Thaten	You foolish hoard
thöriger Hort!	of loftiest deeds!
Lachend muß ich dich lieben; [51]	Laughing I must love you;
lachend will ich erblinden;	laughing I must grow blind;
lachend lass' uns verderben –	laughing let us perish –
lachend zu Grunde geh'n!	laughing go to our doom!
Fahr' hin, Walhall's	Be gone, Valhalla's
leuchtende Welt!	light-bringing world!
Zerfall' in Staub	May your proud-standing stronghold
deine stolze Burg!	moulder to dust!
Leb' wohl, prangende	Fare well, resplendent
Götter-Pracht!	pomp of the gods!
End' in Wonne,	End in rapture,
du ewig Geschlecht!	you endless race!
Zerreißt, ihr Nornen,	Rend, you Norns,
das Runenseil!	the rope of runes!
Götter-Dämm'rung,	Dusk of the gods,
dunk'le herauf!	let your darkness arise!
Nacht der Vernichtung,	Night of destruction,
neb'le herein! –	let your mists roll in! –
Mir strahlt zur Stunde	Siegfried's star
Siegfried's Stern;	now shines upon me;
er ist mir ewig,	He's mine forever,
ist mir immer,	always mine,
Erb' und Eigen,	my heritage and own,
ein' und all':	my one and all:
leuchtende Liebe,	light-bringing love

lachender Tod!   [51]   and laughing death!

SIEGFRIED

Lachend erwach'st   [52]   Laughing you wake
du wonnige mir: in gladness to me:
Brünnhilde lebt!   Brünnhilde lives!
Brünnhilde lacht! –   Brünnhilde laughs! –
Heil dem Tage,   [50]   Hail to the day
der uns umleuchtet!   that sheds light all around us!
Heil der Sonne,   Hail to the sun
die uns bescheint!   that shines upon us!
Heil dem Licht,   Hail to the light
das der Nacht enttaucht!   that emerges from night!
Heil der Welt,   Hail to the world
der Brünnhilde lebt!   for which Brünnhilde lives!
Sie wacht! sie lebt!   She wakes! She lives!
Sie lacht mir entgegen!   She smiles upon me!
Prangend strahlt   Brünnhilde's star
mir Brünnhilde's Stern!   shines resplendent upon me!
Sie ist mir ewig,   She's mine forever,
ist mir immer,   always mine,
Erb' und Eigen,   my heritage and own,
ein' und all':   my one and all:
leuchtende Liebe,   light-bringing love
lachender Tod!   [51]   and laughing death!

(Brünnhilde throws herself into Siegfried's arms.) [51, 35, 49]

Götterdämmerung

Twilight of the Gods

Synopsis

Prologue

THE SETTING IS THE VALKYRIE ROCK, as at the end of *Siegfried*. The three Norns, daughters of Erda, are weaving the rope of destiny. Their narrations relate events past, present and future. Their rope breaks and they descend into the earth. Day dawns and Siegfried and Brünnhilde come out of the cave to which they retired at the end of *Siegfried*. Brünnhilde sends Siegfried off on deeds of glory, urging him to remember their love. Siegfried gives her the ring as a token of his faithfulness. The pair sing of their indivisible love and Siegfried embarks on his journey down the Rhine.

Act I

Gunther, the chief of the Gibichungs, sits on a throne in his palace with his sister Gutrune. He is told by his half-brother Hagen that he should find a wife for himself and a husband for Gutrune. Hagen tells of Brünnhilde, how she lies on a rock encircled by fire and how only the hero Siegfried can win her. His plan is for Siegfried, under the influence of a potion which will cause him to forget, to win Brünnhilde for Gunther.

Siegfried's horn is now heard and hospitality is extended to him. He tells of the Nibelung treasure and of the ring which he gave to a 'glorious woman'. Gutrune appears with the drugged potion and Siegfried, in a gesture pregnant with irony, drinks to the memory of Brünnhilde and their love. He is immediately drawn to Gutrune and loses no time in offering himself as her husband.

Siegfried then offers to win Gunther a wife and as he is told about Brünnhilde high on a rock surrounded by fire, it is clear that he has only the faintest memory of her. They swear an oath of blood-brotherhood. Siegfried sets off up the river again, followed by Gunther. The dour Hagen sits guarding the palace, contemplating the satisfactory progress of his scheme to win power.

Back on the Valkyrie Rock, Brünnhilde is visited by her sister Waltraute, who tells how fearfully Wotan and the gods now await the end. She begs Brünnhilde to return the ring to the Rhinedaughters, but Brünnhilde refuses to throw away Siegfried's pledge. Waltraute leaves in agitation and Brünnhilde hears Siegfried's horn. To her horror, she is confronted by a stranger (Siegfried transformed into Gunther by the tarnhelm). He claims her as wife, violently snatches the ring from her finger and forces her into the cave for the night, placing his sword symbolically between them.

Act II

Hagen, sitting outside the Gibichung Hall in a half-sleep, is visited by his father, Alberich. He is urged to acquire the ring and intends to do so, but will swear faithfulness only to himself. Dawn breaks and Siegfried returns, now in his own form once more, having secretly changed places with Gunther.

Hagen summons his vassals to celebrate the wedding. They hail Gunther, who leads Brünnhilde forward, her eyes cast down. He greets Siegfried and hands her over to Gutrune. When Brünnhilde hears Siegfried's name, she reacts in violent amazement. She asks how Siegfried came by the ring on his hand, as it was seized from her by Gunther. Siegfried swears on the point of Hagen's spear that he has kept faith with his 'blood-brother'. The enraged Brünnhilde alleges that Siegfried's sword hung on the wall (not between them) when its master wooed her, and swears that he has perjured himself. Siegfried calls everyone to the wedding-feast and leads Gutrune into the palace.

Brünnhilde, left alone with Gunther and Hagen, laments Siegfried's treachery and falls in with the plan to murder him. Siegfried and Gutrune reappear from the palace and a wedding procession forms.

Act III

The setting is wild woodland and a rocky valley by the bank of the Rhine. The Rhinedaughters sing of the lost gold. They urge Siegfried to return the ring to them; he refuses to succumb to threats. Siegfried rejoins the hunting party and is prevailed upon to tell the story of his life. Hagen gives him another drink which restores his memory. When he reaches the point of his discovery of the sleeping Brünnhilde, whom he awoke with a kiss, Gunther jumps up in alarm at the revelation. Two ravens fly overhead and as Siegfried looks up, Hagen plunges his spear in his back. Siegfried's body is carried off in a solemn funeral procession.

The scene changes to the Hall of the Gibichungs, where Gutrune is anxiously awaiting Siegfried's return. His corpse is brought in and Gunther blames the death on Hagen. Hagen steps forward to seize the ring and when Gunther stands in his way, he is murdered by Hagen. Hagen tries again to take the ring, but as he approaches Siegfried, the dead man's arm rises into the air, to the horror of all.

Brünnhilde enters, now calm, and tells how Siegfried swore her an eternal oath. She orders a funeral pyre for the hero, and addressing Wotan in Valhalla, she says that Siegfried's death has atoned for his guilt and brought her enlightenment through sorrow. She takes Siegfried's ring, promising that it will be returned to the Rhinedaughters. She ignites the pyre and, mounting her horse Grane, rides into the flames. The whole building catches fire and the Rhine bursts its banks. Hagen is dragged into the depths by the Rhinedaughters, who hold up the ring in triumph. The gods and heroes are seen assembled in Valhalla, before it too is engulfed in flames. The long-awaited end of the gods has come to pass.

Götterdämmerung

Third Day of the Stage Festival 'The Ring of the Nibelung'

First performed at the Bayreuth Festspielhaus, 17 August 1876

Siegfried (tenor)	Georg Unger
Gunther (bass–baritone)	Eugen Gura
Alberich (bass–baritone)	Karl Hill
Hagen (bass)	Gustav Siehr
Brünnhilde (soprano)	Amalie Materna
Gutrune (soprano)	Mathilde Weckerlin
Waltraute (mezzo-soprano)	Luise Jaide
First Norn (contralto)	Johanna Jachmann-Wagner
Second Norn (mezzo-soprano)	Josephine Schefsky
Third Norn (soprano)	Friederike Sadler-Grün
Woglinde (soprano)	Lilli Lehmann
Wellgunde (soprano)	Marie Lehmann
Flosshilde (mezzo-soprano)	Minna Lammert
Vassals, women	

Prologue.   On the valkyries' rock
Act I.   Gunther's royal palace on the Rhine
           The valkyries' rock
Act II.   Outside Gunther's hall
Act III. Wooded area on the banks of the Rhine
           Gunther's hall

First UK performance: Her Majesty's Theatre, London, 9 May 1882

First US performance: Metropolitan Opera, New York, 25 January 1888

Götterdämmerung

PROLOGUE

(The curtain opens slowly.[129] The scene is the same as at the end of the second day, on the valkyries' rock. Night. A fiery glow is visible at the very back of the stage. The three Norns, tall female figures in long, dark veil-like garments. The First (the oldest) is lying at the front of the stage on the left, beneath the spreading pine-tree; the Second (younger) is reclining on a stone terrace in front of the rocky chamber; the Third (youngest) is sitting on a rocky outcrop of the mountain ridge in the centre at the back of the stage. Sombre silence and absence of any movement.) [20]

FIRST NORN

Welch' Licht leuchtet dort?   What light is gleaming yonder?

SECOND NORN

Dämmert der Tag schon auf?   Is day already dawning?

THIRD NORN

Loge's Heer[130]   Loge's host[130]
lodert feurig um den Fels.   burns brightly round the fell.
Noch ist's Nacht: Night still reigns:
was spinnen und singen wir nicht?   why don't we spin and sing?

SECOND NORN
(to the First)

Wollen wir spinnen und singen,   If we're to spin and sing,
woran spann'st du das Seil?   on what will you stretch the rope?

FIRST NORN
(unwinding a golden rope from around herself and attaching one end of it to a branch of the pine-tree.)
So gut und schlimm es geh',   For good or ill,
schling' ich das Seil, und singe. –   I wind the rope and sing. –

    An der Welt-Esche[131]   [53]   At the world-ash[131]
    wob ich einst,   once I wove
    da groß und stark   when, tall and strong,
    dem Stamm entgrünte   a forest of sacred branches

weihlicher Äste Wald;
  im kühlen Schatten   [8e]
rauscht' ein Quell,
Weisheit raunend
rann sein Gewell':
da sang ich heil'gen Sinn. –

Ein kühner Gott
trat zum Trunk an den Quell;
  seiner Augen eines   [8]
zahlt' er als ewigen Zoll:
  von der Welt-Esche
brach da Wotan einen Ast;[132]
  eines Speeres Schaft   [9]
entschnitt der Starke dem Stamm. –

In langer Zeiten Lauf
zehrte die Wunde den Wald;
falb fielen die Blätter,
dürr darbte der Baum:
  traurig versiegte
  des Quelles Trank;
  trüben Sinnes
  ward mein Gesang.   [53]
  Doch web' ich heut'
an der Welt-Esche nicht mehr,
  muß mir die Tanne
taugen zu fesseln das Seil: –
  singe, Schwester, –
  – dir werf' ich's zu –
weißt du wie das wird?   [33]

blossomed from its bole;
  in its cooling shade
there plashed a spring,
whispering wisdom,
its ripples ran:
I sang then of sacred things. –

A dauntless god
came to drink at the spring;
  one of his eyes
he paid as toll for all time:
  from the world-ash
Wotan broke off a branch;[132]
  the shaft of a spear
the mighty god cut from its trunk. –

In the span of many seasons
the wound consumed the wood;
fallow fell the leaves,
barren, the tree grew rotten:
  sadly the well-spring's
  drink ran dry;
  the sense of my singing
  grew troubled.
  But if I no longer
weave by the world-ash today,
  the fir must serve
to fasten the rope: –
  sing, my sister, –
  – I cast it to you –
do you know what will become of it?

SECOND NORN

(winding the rope that has been thrown to her around a projecting rock at the entrance to the chamber.)

  Treu berath'ner
  Verträge Runen
  schnitt Wotan   [54]
  in des Speeres Schaft: [9]
den hielt er als Halt der Welt.
  Ein kühner Held
zerhieb im Kampfe den Speer;
  in Trümmer sprang
der Verträge heiliger Haft. –
  Da hieß Wotan
  Walhall's Helden,
  der Welt-Esche
  welkes Geäst
mit dem Stamm in Stücke zu fällen:
  die Esche sank;
ewig versiegte der Quell! –   [53]

  The runes of trustily
  counselled treaties
  Wotan carved
  on the shaft of the spear:
he held it as his grip on the world.
  A dauntless hero
shattered the spear in combat;
  the contracts' hallowed haft
was smashed to whirling splinters. –
  Then Wotan bade
  Valhalla's heroes
  hew into pieces
  the world-ash's
withered boughs and bole:
  the ash-tree fell;
the spring ran dry for ever! –

Fess'le ich heut'	If I tether the rope
an den scharfen Fels das Seil:	to the jagged rock today,
singe, Schwester,	sing, my sister,
– dir werf' ich's zu –	– I cast it to you –
weißt du wie das wird? [33]	do you know what will become of it?

THIRD NORN

(catching the rope and throwing the end behind her)

Es ragt die Burg,	Built by giants,
von Riesen gebaut:	the stronghold towers aloft;
mit der Götter und Helden	with the hallowed kin
heiliger Sippe	of gods and heroes
sitzt dort Wotan im Saal. [21]	Wotan sits there within the hall.
Gehau'ner Scheite [54]	A rearing pile
hohe Schicht	of rough-hewn logs
ragt zu Hauf'	towers on high
rings um die Halle: [35]	around the hall:
die Welt-Esche war dieß einst! [53]	this was once the world ash-tree! –
Brennt das Holz	When the timber blazes
heilig brünstig und hell,	brightly in sacred fire,
sengt die Gluth	when its embers singe
sehrend den glänzenden Saal:	the glittering hall with their searing [heat,
der ewigen Götter Ende [21]	the downfall of the immortal gods
dämmert ewig da auf. –	will dawn for all eternity. –
Wisset ihr noch, [34]	If you know yet more,
so windet von neuem das Seil;	then coil the rope anew;
von Norden wieder	from the north I cast it
werf' ich's dir nach:	back to you:

(She throws the rope to the Second Norn; the latter tosses it to the First, who unties it from the branch and attaches it to another bough.)

spinne, Schwester, und singe!	spin, my sister, and sing!

FIRST NORN

(looking behind her as she busies herself with the rope)

Dämmert der Tag?	Is daylight dawning?
oder leuchtet die Lohe?	Or is it the light of the fire?
Getrübt trügt sich mein Blick;	Clouded, my sight plays tricks on me;
nicht hell eracht' ich	I cannot see clearly
das heilig Alte,	the hallowed past,
da Loge einst	when Loge once
brannte in lichter Gluth: – [14b]	flared up in white-hot flame: –
weißt du was aus ihm ward? [33]	do you know what became of him?

SECOND NORN

(once again winding the rope that has been thrown to her round the rock)

Durch des Speeres Zauber [54]	By the spell of his spear
zähmte ihn Wotan;	Wotan tamed him;
Räthe raunt' er dem Gott:	he whispered wisdom to the god:

an des Schaftes Runen,		to work himself free
frei sich zu rathen,		he gnawed and destroyed
nagte zehrend sein Zahn.		the runes on the shaft.
Da mit des Speeres		Then with the spear's
zwingender Spitze		all-powerful point
bannte ihn Wotan,		Wotan cast a spell on him,
Brünnhilde's Fels zu umbrennen: −		bidding him blaze round Brünnhilde's [rock: −

(She throws the rope to the Third Norn, who once again throws it behind her.)

weißt du was aus ihm wird?	[33]	do you know what will come of him?

THIRD NORN

Des zerschlag'nen Speeres	[54]	The shattered spear's
stechende Splitter		sharp-pointed splinters
taucht einst Wotan		Wotan will one day bury
dem Brünstigen tief in die Brust:		deep in the fire-god's breast:
zehrender Brand		a ravening fire
zündet da auf;		will then flame forth,
den wirft der Gott		which the god will hurl
in der Welt-Esche	[53]	on the world-ash's
zu Hauf' geschichtete Scheite.	[8b]	heaped-up logs. −

(She throws back the rope; the Second Norn coils it and throws it back to the First.) [38]

Wollt ihr wissen	[34]	If you want to know
wann was wird,		when that will be,
schwinget, Schwestern, das Seil! −		sisters, wind the rope! −

FIRST NORN
(fastening the rope again)

Die Nacht weicht;		Night is waning;
nichts mehr gewahr' ich:		I see no more:
des Seiles Fäden		the strands of the rope
find' ich nicht mehr;		I can find no longer;
verflochten ist das Geflecht.	[6]	the threads have become entangled.
Ein wüstes Gesicht		A desolate vision
wirrt mir wüthend den Sinn: −		maddingly throws my mind into [turmoil: −
das Rheingold	[4, 5]	Alberich once
raubte Alberich einst: −		stole the Rhinegold: −
weißt du was aus ihm ward?	[6]	do you know what became of him?

SECOND NORN
(winding the rope with effortful haste round the jagged rock outside the chamber)

Des Steines Schärfe		The stone's sharp edge
schnitt in das Seil;		is cutting the rope;
nicht fest spannt mehr		the web of its strands
der Fäden Gespinnst:		is no longer stretched taut:
verwirrt ist das Geweb'.		the woven skein is ravelled.
Aus Noth und Neid		From need and spite
ragt mir des Niblungen Ring: −		the Nibelung's ring stands proud: −
ein rächender Fluch	[3]	an avenging curse

nagt meiner Fäden Geflecht: gnaws at the tangle of threads:

(throwing the rope to the Third Norn)

weißt du was daraus wird?   [23]   do you know what will come of that?

THIRD NORN

(hastily seizing the rope that has been thrown to her)

Zu locker das Seil!	The rope's too slack!
Mir langt es nicht:	It doesn't reach me:
soll ich nach Norden [40]	if I'm to draw
neigen das Ende,	the end to the north,
straffer sei es gestreckt!	tauter let it be stretched!

(She pulls hard on the rope, which breaks.)

Es riß![133]   [19]   It's snapped![133]

SECOND NORN

Es riß!   It's snapped!

FIRST NORN

Es riß!   It's snapped!

(They gather up the pieces of broken rope and bind themselves together with them.)

THE THREE NORNS

Zu End' ewiges Wissen!	An end to eternal wisdom!
Der Welt melden	Wise women no longer
Weise nichts mehr.	tell the world their tidings.

THIRD NORN

Hinab!   [38]   Descend!

SECOND NORN

Zur Mutter!   To our mother!

FIRST NORN

Hinab!   [34]   Descend!

(They disappear.)

(Dawn. The sky begins to brighten and the fiery glow at the back of the stage grows increasingly faint. [55, 56] Sunrise. Broad daylight. Siegfried and Brünnhilde emerge from the rocky chamber. He is fully armed; she leads her horse by the bridle.) [55, 30]

BRÜNNHILDE

Zu neuen Thaten, [56]	To new adventures,
theurer Helde,	beloved hero,
wie liebt' ich dich –	what would my love be worth
ließ' ich dich nicht?	if I did not let you go forth?
Ein einzig Sorgen	A single worry
läßt mich säumen:	makes me falter –
daß dir zu wenig [57]	that my merit
mein Werth gewann!	has brought you too little gain!

Was Götter mich wiesen,	What gods have taught me

gab ich dir:
heiliger Runen
reichen Hort;
doch meiner Stärke
magdlichen Stamm[134]
nahm mir der Held,   [50]
dem ich nun mich neige.

I gave to you:
a bountiful store
of hallowed runes;
but the maidenly source
of all my strength[134]
was taken away by the hero
to whom I now bow my head.

Des Wissens bar –
doch des Wunsches voll;
an Liebe reich –
doch ledig der Kraft:
mög'st du die Arme
nicht verachten,
die dir nur gönnen –
nicht geben mehr kann!   [55]

Bereft of wisdom
but filled with desire;
rich in love
yet void of strength,
I beg you not to despise
the poor woman
who grudges you naught
but can give you no more!

SIEGFRIED

Mehr gab'st du, Wunderfrau,
als ich zu wahren weiß: [57]
nicht zürne, wenn dein Lehren [56]
mich unbelehret ließ!
Ein Wissen doch wahr' ich wohl:

You gave me more, o wondrous woman,
than I know how to cherish:
chide me not if your teaching
has left me untaught!
One lore I cherish yet:

(ardently)

daß mir Brünnhilde lebt;
eine Lehre lernt' ich leicht:
Brünnhilde's zu gedenken!

that Brünnhilde lives for me;
one lesson I learned with ease:
to be ever mindful of Brünnhild'!

BRÜNNHILDE

Willst du mir Minne schenken, [55]
gedenke deiner nur,[135]
gedenke deiner Thaten!
Gedenk' des wilden Feuers,
das furchtlos du durchschrittest, [35]
da den Fels es rings umbrann –

If you'd bestow your love on me,
be mindful only of yourself,[135]
be mindful of your exploits!
Recall the raging fire
through which you fearlessly passed,
when it burned around the fell –

SIEGFRIED

Brünnhilde zu gewinnen!   [57, 30, 55]   in order to win Brünnhilde!

BRÜNNHILDE

Gedenk' der beschildeten Frau,
die in tiefem Schlaf du fandest, [34]
der den festen Helm du erbrach'st – [35]

Recall the shield-clad woman
whom you found there deep in sleep
and whose close-fitting helmet you
    [loosed –

SIEGFRIED

Brünnhilde zu erwecken!   in order to waken Brünnhild'!

BRÜNNHILDE

Gedenk' der Eide,   [56]   Recall the oaths

die uns einen;
gedenk' der Treue,
die wir tragen;
gedenk' der Liebe, [57]
der wir leben:
Brünnhilde brennt dann ewig
heilig dir in der Brust! –

that unite us;
recall the trust
that we place in each other;
recall the love
for which we live:
Brünnhilde then will burn for aye
with holy fire in your breast! –

(She embraces Siegfried.) [49]

SIEGFRIED

Lass' ich, Liebste, dich hier [55]
in der Lohe heiliger Hut,

If, my dearest, I leave you here
in the fire's hallowed guard,

(He has removed Alberich's ring from his finger and now hands it to Brünnhilde.)

zum Tausche deiner Runen
reich' ich dir diesen Ring.
Was der Thaten je ich schuf, [35]
dess' Tugend schließt er ein;
ich erschlug einen wilden Wurm, [18]
der grimmig lang' ihn bewacht.
Nun wahre du seine Kraft
als Weihe-Gruß meiner Treu'!

in return for all your runes
I hand this ring to you.
Whatever deeds I have done,
their virtue it enfolds;
I slew a savage dragon
that long had guarded it grimly.
Now keep its power safe
in solemn token of my troth.

BRÜNNHILDE

(rapturously putting on the ring)

Ihn geiz' ich als einziges Gut: [6]
für den Ring nimm nun auch mein
[Roß! [4]
 Ging sein Lauf mit mir [30]
 einst kühn durch die Lüfte –
 mit mir [38]
verlor es die mächt'ge Art;
 über Wolken hin
 auf blitzenden Wettern
 nicht mehr
schwingt es sich muthig des Weg's.
 Doch wohin du ihn führ'st
 – sei es durch's Feuer –
grauenlos folgt dir Grane; [55]
 denn dir, o Helde,
 soll er gehorchen!
 Du hüt' ihn wohl;
 er hört dein Wort: –
o bringe Grane [26b]
oft Brünnhilde's Gruß![136]

I covet it as my only wealth:
for the ring now take my horse!

 As once, with me, he boldly
 clove the air in flight,
 with me
he's lost that mighty power;
 over the clouds,
 through lightning-rent storms,
 no more
will he bravely soar on his way.
 But wherever you lead him
 – be it through fire –
Grane will fearlessly follow;
 for you, o hero,
 he shall obey!
 Guard him well;
 he'll heed your word: –
 oh, often give Grane
 Brünnhilde's greeting![136]

SIEGFRIED

Durch deine Tugend allein [57, 30]
soll so ich Thaten noch wirken?
Meine Kämpfe kiesest du,
meine Siege kehren zu dir?

Through your virtue alone
shall I still undertake adventures?
Is it you who'll choose my battles,
you to whom all my victories redound?

Auf deines Rosses Rücken,		Upon your stallion's back,
in deines Schildes Schirm,		within the shelter of your shield,
nicht Siegfried acht' ich mich	[58]	no more do I think of myself as
[mehr:		[Siegfried,
ich bin nur Brünnhilde's Arm!		I am Brünnhilde's arm alone!

BRÜNNHILDE

O wäre Brünnhild' deine Seele! If only Brünnhilde were your soul!

SIEGFRIED

Durch sie entbrennt mir der Muth. Through her my courage is kindled.

BRÜNNHILDE

So war'st du Siegfried und So you yourself would be Siegfried and
[Brünnhild'? [Brünnhild'?

SIEGFRIED

Wo ich bin, bergen sich beide. Wherever I am, both will be safe.

BRÜNNHILDE
(animatedly)

So verödet mein Felsensaal? So my mountain hall is deserted?

SIEGFRIED

Vereint faßt er uns zwei. United, it holds us both.

BRÜNNHILDE
(with great emotion)

O heilige Götter,	[56]	O holy gods,
hehre Geschlechter!		hallowed kinsmen!
Weidet eu'r Aug'		Feast your eyes
an dem weihvollen Paar!		on this blessed pair!
Getrennt – wer will uns scheiden?	[58]	Parted – who would divide us?
Geschieden – trennt es sich nie!	[57]	Divided – they'll never part!

SIEGFRIED

Heil dir, Brünnhilde, Hail to you, Brünnhilde,
prangender Stern! glittering star!
Heil, strahlende Liebe! Hail, lightening love!

BRÜNNHILDE

Heil dir, Siegfried, Hail to you, Siegfried,
siegendes Licht! conquering light!
Heil, strahlendes Leben! Hail, lightening life!

BOTH

Heil! Heil!	[57, 30]	Hail! Hail!
Heil! Heil!		Hail! Hail!

(Siegfried leads the horse quickly to the rocky slope, while Brünnhilde follows. [55, 58] *During the previous three bars[137] Siegfried disappears with his horse down behind the rocky*

promontory, so that the audience can no longer see him; Brünnhilde thus stands suddenly alone at the top of the slope, gazing after Siegfried as he descends. [56] Brünnhilde's gesture shows that Siegfried has now disappeared from sight. Siegfried's horn is heard from below. [40] Brünnhilde listens. [56] She steps further out on to the slope. She now catches sight of Siegfried again far below her: she waves to him with a gesture of delight. Her joyful smile indicates that she can see the hero as he merrily goes on his way. [26a] At this point[138] *the curtain must be quickly lowered.)* [40, 14b, 1b, 4, 6, 3]

Act One

(During the last four bars[139] *the curtain has been raised again.)*

SCENE ONE

The Hall of the Gibichungs on the Rhine. The hall is entirely open at the back. The back of the stage itself is occupied by an open shore extending as far as the river; rocky outcrops border the shore.
(Gunther and Gutrune sit enthroned to one side, with a table bearing drinking vessels in front of them; Hagen is seated in front of the table.) [59]

GUNTHER

Nun hör', Hagen!
  Sage mir, Held: [60]
sitz' ich herrlich am Rhein,
Gunther zu Gibich's Ruhm?

Now hearken, Hagen!
  Tell me, hero:
do I sit here in splendour by the Rhine,
Gunther, worthy of Gibich's fame?

HAGEN

Dich ächt genannten
  acht' ich zu neiden:
die beid' uns Brüder gebar,
Frau Grimhild' ließ mich's begreifen.

You who are said to be true-born
  I deem to be worthy of envy:
she who bore us brothers both,
the Lady Grimhild', gave me to know
  [the reason why.

GUNTHER

Dich neide ich:
  nicht neide mich du!
Erbt' ich Erstlingsart,
Weisheit ward dir allein:
  Halbbrüder-Zwist
  bezwang sich nie besser;
deinem Rath nur red' ich Lob,
frag' ich dich nach meinem Ruhm.

I envy you:
  don't envy me!
If I fell heir to the first-born's ways,
wisdom was yours alone:
  half-brothers' strife
  was never better settled;
I merely praise your sound advice
when I ask you about my fame.

HAGEN

So schelt' ich den Rath,
  da schlecht noch dein Ruhm:
denn hohe Güter weiß ich,

Then I blame my advice,
  since your fame is still poor:
for worthy goods I know of

die der Gibichung noch nicht
[gewann.

that the Gibichung's not yet won.

GUNTHER

Verschwieg'st du sie,
so schelt' auch ich.

If you keep them hidden,
I too shall chide.

HAGEN

In sommerlich reifer Stärke
seh' ich Gibich's Stamm,
dich, Gunther, unbeweibt,
dich, Gutrun', ohne Mann.

In summer's ripe strength
I see Gibich's line,
you, Gunther, unwed,
you, Gutrun', without a husband.

(Gunther and Gutrune are lost in silent thought.)

GUNTHER

Wen räth'st du nun zu frei'n,
daß uns'rem Ruhm es fromm'?

Whom would you have me woo
that it should serve our fame?

HAGEN

Ein Weib weiß ich, [30]
das herrlichste der Welt: –
auf Felsen hoch ihr Sitz; [14a]
ein Feuer umbrennt ihren Saal: [47]
nur wer durch das Feuer bricht,
darf Brünnhilde's Freier sein.

I know of a woman,
the noblest in the world: –
high on a fell her home;
a fire burns round her hall:
only he who breaks through the fire
may sue for Brünnhilde's love.

GUNTHER

Vermag das mein Muth zu besteh'n?

Is my courage equal to that?

HAGEN

Einem Stärk'ren noch ist's nur
[bestimmt.

A man yet stronger is fated to win her.

GUNTHER

Wer ist der streitlichste Mann?

Who's that most stalwart of men?

HAGEN

Siegfried, der Wälsungen Sproß:
der ist der stärkste Held.
Ein Zwillingspaar, [29]
von Liebe bezwungen,
Siegmund und Sieglinde
zeugten den ächtesten Sohn:
der im Walde mächtig erwuchs, [40]
den wünsch' ich Gutrun' zum Mann.

Siegfried, the Wälsungs' offspring –
he is the strongest of heroes.
A twin-born pair,
impelled by love,
Siegmund and Sieglinde
bore the truest of sons:
he who waxed mightily in the
[wildwood –
him would I have as Gutrune's husband.

GUTRUNE
(beginning shyly)

Welche That schuf er so tapfer,

What was the feat he performed so
[bravely

daß als herrlichster Held er genannt?   that he is called the most glorious hero?

HAGEN

Vor Neidhöhle   [18]   Outside Neidhöhl'
  den Niblungenhort   the Nibelung hoard
bewachte ein riesiger Wurm: was guarded by a giant dragon:
  Siegfried schloß ihm   Siegfried closed
  den freislichen Schlund,   its fearsome maw,
erschlug ihn mit siegendem Schwert.   slew the beast with conquering sword.
Solch' ungeheurer That   [35]   From such a tremendous feat
enttagte des Helden Ruhm.   [40]   the hero's fame has sprung.

GUNTHER
(pensively)

Vom Niblungenhort vernahm ich: [6]   I've heard of the Nibelung hoard:
er birgt den neidlichsten Schatz?   does it not hide the most coveted
                                        [treasure?

HAGEN

Wer wohl ihn zu nützen wüßt',   He who knew how to use it
dem neigte sich wahrlich die Welt. [4] could bend the world, in truth, to his [will.

GUNTHER

Und Siegfried hat ihn erkämpft?   And Siegfried won it in fair fight?

HAGEN

Knecht sind die Niblungen ihm.[140] [3] The Nibelungs are now his slaves.[140]

GUNTHER

Und Brünnhild' gewänne nur er?   And he alone could win Brünnhilde?

HAGEN

Keinem and'ren wiche die Brunst. [30]   Only to him would the fire yield.

GUNTHER
(rising angrily from his seat)

Was weck'st du Zweifel und Zwist!   Why waken doubt and dissent!
Was ich nicht zwingen soll,   Why make me
  danach zu verlangen   long for
  mach'st du mir Lust?   what I can't gain by force?
*(He paces up and down the hall in agitation. [60] Without leaving his seat, Hagen stops him
with a mysterious gesture as he approaches him again.)* [16]

HAGEN

Brächte Siegfried   If Siegfried brought
  die Braut dir heim,   the bride back home,
wär' dann nicht Brünnhilde dein?   wouldn't Brünnhilde then be yours?

GUNTHER
(turning away again in doubt and anger)

Was zwänge den frohen Mann	What would force the carefree man
für mich die Braut zu frei'n?	to woo the bride for me?

HAGEN
(as before)

Ihn zwänge bald deine Bitte,	Your entreaty would quickly force him
bänd' ihn Gutrun' zuvor.	if Gutrune bound him first.

GUTRUNE

Du Spötter, böser Hagen!	You mock me, wicked Hagen!
Wie sollt' ich Siegfried binden?	How should I ever bind Siegfried?
Ist er der herrlichste	If he's the world's
Held der Welt,	most glorious hero,
der Erde holdeste Frauen	the loveliest women on earth
friedeten[141] längst ihn schon.	would have wooed[141] him long ago.

HAGEN
(leaning closer towards Gutrune, confidentially)

Gedenk' des Trankes im Schrein;	Recall the potion in the chest;

(more secretively)

vertraue mir, der ihn gewann:	trust in me who obtained it:
den Helden, dess' du verlang'st,	it will bind to you in love
bindet er liebend an dich.	the hero for whom you long.

(Gunther has returned to the table and, leaning on it, listens attentively.)

Träte nun Siegfried ein,		If Siegfried were to enter now
genöss' er des würzigen Trank's,		and taste the herbal drink,
daß vor dir ein Weib er ersah,	[16]	he'd be forced to forget
daß je ein Weib ihm genaht –		that he'd seen a woman before you,
vergessen müßt' er dess' ganz. –		that a woman had ever come near him. –
Nun redet: –		Now tell me: –
wie dünkt euch Hagen's Rath?		what think you of Hagen's advice?

GUNTHER
(starting up, animatedly)

Gepriesen sei Grimhild',	[60]	Praise be to Grimhild',
die uns den Bruder gab!		who gave us our brother!

GUTRUNE

Möcht' ich Siegfried je ersch'n!	Might I only set eyes on Siegfried!

GUNTHER

Wie fänden ihn wir auf?	[19]	How could we find where he is?

(An off-stage horn is heard from the back on the right. [40] Hagen listens. He turns to Gunther.)

HAGEN

Jagt er auf Thaten	When he rides out gaily
wonnig umher,	in search of adventure,
zum engen Tann	the world becomes
wird ihm die Welt:	a narrow pinewood:
wohl stürmt er in rastloser Jagd	in restless chase he'll surely ride

auch zu Gibich's Strand an den [Rhein.

to Gibich's shores along the Rhine.

GUNTHER

Willkommen hieß' ich ihn gern.
(Horn closer, but still in the distance. [40] *Both men listen. Hagen hurries down to the shore.)*
Vom Rhein her tönt das Horn.

I'd gladly bid him welcome.

The horn rings forth from the Rhine.

HAGEN
(looking downstream and calling back)

In einem Nachen Held und Roß:
der bläs't so munter das Horn. –

Hero and stallion on board a skiff:
It is he who is blowing the horn so [blithely. –

(Gunther goes half way towards him, but then holds back, listening.)
(as before) [5]

Ein gemächlicher Schlag
wie von müssiger Hand
treibt jach den Kahn
wider den Strom;
so rüstiger Kraft
in des Ruders Schwung
rühmt sich nur der,   [23]
der den Wurm erschlug: –
Siegfried ist es, sicher kein and'rer!

A leisurely stroke,
as of idle hand,
drives the boat headlong
against the stream;
only he who slew
the dragon can boast
such doughty strength
in the sweep of the oar: –
Siegfried it is: no other, surely!

GUNTHER

Jagt er vorbei?

Is he sweeping past?

HAGEN
(calling towards the river through cupped hands)

Hoiho! Wohin,
du heit'rer Held?

Hoiho! Whither bound,
you blithe-spirited hero?

SIEGFRIED
(from the distance)

Zu Gibich's starkem Sohne.   [60]

To Gibich's stalwart son.

HAGEN

Zu seiner Halle entbiet' ich dich:
(Siegfried appears on the shore in a small boat.)
hieher! hier lege an!

I bid you welcome to his hall:

this way! Put in to shore here!

SCENE TWO

(Siegfried brings his boat ashore. Hagen makes it fast with a chain. Siegfried leaps down on to the beach with his horse.)

HAGEN

Heil Siegfried! theurer Held!   [19]   Hail! Siegfried, much-loved hero!

(Gunther has joined Hagen on the shore. From the throne Gutrune looks at Siegfried in astonished admiration. Gunther prepares to offer a friendly greeting. All remain fixed in silent mutual contemplation.)

SIEGFRIED

(leaning on his horse and standing quietly by his boat)

Wer ist Gibich's Sohn?	[35]	Which of you is Gibich's son?

GUNTHER

Gunther, ich, den du such'st.	[60]	Gunther, I, whom you seek.

SIEGFRIED

Dich hört' ich rühmen	I heard you praised
weit am Rhein:	far along the Rhine:
nun ficht mit mir,	now fight with me,
oder sei mein Freund![142]	or be my friend![142]

GUNTHER

Lass' den Kampf:	Think not of fighting:
sei willkommen!	be welcome here!

SIEGFRIED

(looking round calmly)

Wo berg' ich mein Roß?	Where shall I shelter my horse?

HAGEN

Ich biet' ihm Rast.	I'll offer him rest.

SIEGFRIED

(turning to Hagen)

Du rief'st mich Siegfried:	[19]	You called me Siegfried:
sah'st du mich schon?		have you seen me before?

HAGEN

Ich kannte dich nur	[35]	I knew you only
an deiner Kraft.		by your strength.

SIEGFRIED

(handing over the horse to Hagen)

Wohl hüte mir Grane!	[56]	Take good care of Grane!
Du hieltest nie		You never held
von edlerer Zucht	[57]	the bridle
am Zaume ein Roß.	[30]	of a horse of nobler breed.

(Hagen leads the horse away. While Siegfried gazes thoughtfully after him, the latter, unnoticed by Siegfried, gestures to Gutrune, who withdraws to her chamber through a door on the right. At Gunther's invitation, Siegfried advances into the hall.) [59]

GUNTHER

Begrüße froh, o Held,	Greet gladly, o hero,
die Halle meines Vaters;	my father's hall;
wohin du schreitest,	wherever you tread,

was du ersieh'st,
das achte nun dein Eigen:
  dein ist mein Erbe,
  Land und Leut' –
hilf, mein Leib, meinem Eide! –
mich selbst geb' ich zum Mann.[144]

whatever you see,
now treat it as your own:
  yours are my birthright,
  lands and men –
by my body I swear this oath![143] –
Myself I give you as liegeman![144]

SIEGFRIED

Nicht Land noch Leute biete ich,
noch Vaters Haus und Hof:
  einzig erbt' ich   [29]
  den eig'nen Leib;
lebend zehr' ich den auf.   [51]
  Nur ein Schwert hab' ich,
  selbst geschmiedet –   [23]
hilf, mein Schwert, meinem Eide! –
das biet' ich mit mir zum Bund.

I can offer you neither lands nor men,
nor a father's house and court:
  I inherited only
  this body of mine;
living, I waste it away.
  I've only a sword,
  which I forged myself –
by that sword I swear this oath! –
With myself I present it as part of the
  [bond.

HAGEN
(having returned, now standing behind Siegfried)

Doch des Niblungen-Hortes   [15]
nennt die Märe dich Herrn?

But the tale names you lord
of the Nibelung hoard.

SIEGFRIED
(turning to Hagen)

Des Schatzes vergaß ich fast:
so schätz' ich sein müss'ges Gut!
In einer Höhle ließ ich's liegen,   [18]
wo ein Wurm es einst bewacht.

I'd almost forgotten the treasure,
so little I treasure its barren worth.
I left it lying inside a cave,
where a dragon used to guard it.

HAGEN

Und nichts entnahm'st du ihm?

And did you take nothing from it?

SIEGFRIED

Dieß Gewirk, unkund seiner Kraft.

This metalwork piece, not knowing its
  [power.

HAGEN

Den Tarnhelm kenn' ich,
der Niblungen künstliches Werk:
er taugt, bedeckt er dein Haupt,   [16]
dir zu tauschen jede Gestalt;
verlangt dich's an fernsten Ort,
er entführt flugs dich dahin. –
Sonst nichts entnahm'st du dem
  [Hort?

I recognize the tarnhelm,
the Nibelungs' artful device:
when it covers your head, it serves
to change you to any shape;
if you want to go to the farthest spot,
it transports you there in a trice. –
You took nothing else from the hoard?

SIEGFRIED

Einen Ring.   [6]

A ring.

Den hütest du wohl?   [57]   You're keeping it safe?

SIEGFRIED
(tenderly)

Den hütet ein hehres Weib.   A glorious woman is keeping it safe.

HAGEN
(aside)

Brünnhild'! . . .   Brünnhild'!

GUNTHER

Nicht, Siegfried, sollst du mir   I want nothing, Siegfried, by way of
[tauschen: [exchange;
Tand gäb' ich für dein Geschmeid',   I would give mere dross for your jewels
nähm'st all' mein Gut du dafür!   if you took all my wealth in return!
Ohn' Entgelt dien' ich dir gern.   I serve you gladly without reward.

(Hagen has gone over to Gutrune's door and now opens it. Gutrune comes out, carrying a filled drinking-horn, which she takes over to Siegfried.) [61]

GUTRUNE

Willkommen, Gast,   Welcome, guest,
in Gibich's Haus!   to Gibich's home!
Seine Tochter reicht dir den Trank.   His daughter brings you this drink.

(Siegfried bows to her in friendly fashion and takes the horn. He holds it thoughtfully in front of him.)

SIEGFRIED
(quietly, but with extreme determination)

Vergäß' ich alles   Were all forgotten
was du mir gab'st,   that you gave me,
von einer Lehre   one lesson alone
lass' ich doch nie: –   I'll never neglect: –
den ersten Trunk   [49]   this first drink
zu treuer Minne,[145]   to true remembrance,[145]
Brünnhilde, bring' ich dir!   Brünnhild', I drink to you!

(He raises the horn to his lips and takes a long draught. [16] He returns the horn to Gutrune who, ashamed and confused, stares at the ground. Siegfried fixes his gaze on her with suddenly inflamed passion.) [61]

Die so mit dem Blitz   You who sear my sight
den Blick du mir seng'st,   with your flashing glance,
was senk'st du dein Auge vor mir?   why lower your eyes before me?

(Blushing, Gutrune raises her eyes to his face.)
(passionately)

Ha, schönstes Weib!   Ha, fairest of women!
Schließe den Blick!   Close your eyes!
Das Herz in der Brust   The heart in my breast
brennt mir sein Strahl: is burned by their beam;
zu feurigen Strömen fühl' ich   in fiery streams I feel it
ihn zehrend zünden mein Blut! – consume and kindle my blood! –

(with trembling voice)

Gunther – wie heißt deine
[Schwester?

(with trembling voice)
Gunther, what is your sister's name?

GUNTHER

Gutrune.

Gutrune.

SIEGFRIED
(quietly)

Sind's gute Runen,
die ihrem Aug' ich entrathe? –

Are they goodly runes
that I read in her eyes? –

(He seizes Gutrune ardently by the hand.)

Deinem Bruder bot ich mich zum
[Mann;
der stolze schlug mich aus: –
trüg'st du, wie er, mir Übermuth,
böt' ich mich dir zum Bund?

I offered myself as your brother's
[liegeman;
the proud man turned me down: –
would you treat me as brashly as he did
if I offered myself as your husband?

(Gutrune involuntarily catches Hagen's eye; she bows her head in humility and, with a gesture indicating that she feels unworthy of him, leaves the hall with faltering steps. Watched closely by Hagen and Gunther, Siegfried gazes after Gutrune as though bewitched.) [19]

(without turning round)

Hast du, Gunther, ein Weib?

Gunther, have you a wife?

GUNTHER

Nicht freit' ich noch,
und einer Frau
soll ich mich schwerlich freu'n!
Auf eine setzt' ich den Sinn,
die kein Rath mir je gewinnt. [60]

I've not yet wooed
nor shall lightly
have joy of a woman!
On one have I set my mind
whom no shift can ever win me.

SIEGFRIED
(turning animatedly to Gunther)

Was wär' dir versagt,
steh' ich zu dir?

What would be denied to you
were *I* to stand beside you?

GUNTHER

Auf Felsen hoch ihr Sitz – [14a] High on a fell her home –

SIEGFRIED
(breaking in with astonished haste)

»Auf Felsen hoch ihr Sitz?«

'High on a fell her home?'

GUNTHER

ein Feuer umbrennt den Saal. – a fire burns round the hall. –

SIEGFRIED

»Ein Feuer umbrennt den Saal?«

'A fire burns round the hall?'

GUNTHER

Nur wer durch das Feuer bricht – [47] Only he who breaks through the fire –

SIEGFRIED

(with an immense effort to recall some forgotten memory)

»Nur wer durch das Feuer   'Only he who breaks through the fire?'
  [bricht« . . ?

GUNTHER

– darf Brünnhilde's Freier sein.   [48]   – may sue for Brünnhilde's love.
(Siegfried's gesture at the mention of Brünnhilde's name shows that all memory of her has faded completely.)

Nun darf ich den Fels nicht   Now I may not climb that fell;
  [erklimmen;
das Feuer verglimmt mir nie!   the fire will never die down for me!

SIEGFRIED

(returning to his senses from his dream-like state and turning to Gunther with high-spirited animation)

Ich – fürchte kein Feuer: I'm not afraid of any fire:
für dich frei' ich die Frau;   for you I'll woo the woman;
  denn dein Mann bin ich,   for your liegeman am I
  und mein Muth ist dein –   and my courage is yours, –
gewinn' ich mir Gutrun' zum Weib.   if *I* can win Gutrun' as wife.

GUNTHER

Gutrune gönn' ich dir gerne.   I grant you Gutrune gladly.

SIEGFRIED

Brünnhilde bring' ich dir.   I'll bring back Brünnhilde for you.

GUNTHER

Wie willst du sie täuschen?   How do you plan to deceive her?

SIEGFRIED

Durch des Tarnhelm's Trug   Through the tarnhelm's disguise
tausch' ich mir deine Gestalt.   I'll change my shape with yours.

GUNTHER

So stelle Eide zum Schwur!   Swear oaths, then, as a vow!

SIEGFRIED

Blut–Brüderschaft[146]   [62]   Let an oath be swown
  schwöre ein Eid!   [19]   to blood-brotherhood.[146]
(Hagen fills a drinking-horn with new wine and offers it to Siegfried and Gunther, who scratch their arms with their swords and hold them for a moment over the top of the horn. Both men place two fingers on the horn, which Hagen continues to hold between them.) [9]

SIEGFRIED

Blühenden Lebens   [63]   The freshening blood
  labendes Blut   of flowering life
träufelt' ich in den Trank.   I let trickle into the drink.

Bruder-brünstig
muthig gemischt,
blüh' im Trank unser Blut.

Bravely blended
in brotherly love,
may our lifeblood bloom in the drink!

BOTH

Treue trink' ich dem Freund:
froh und frei
entblühe dem Bund
Blut-Brüderschaft heut'!

Faith I drink to my friend:
happy and free
may blood-brotherhood
spring from our bond today!

GUNTHER

Bricht ein Bruder den Bund, –

[6] If a brother breaks the bond –

SIEGFRIED

Trügt den Treuen der Freund: –

If a friend betrays his faithful friend –

BOTH

Was in Tropfen heut'
hold wir tranken,
in Strahlen ström' es dahin,
fromme[147] Sühne dem Freund!

What we drank today
in drops of sweetness
shall stream in rivers,
in righteous atonement of a friend.[147]

GUNTHER
(drinking and then offering the horn to Siegfried) [19, 9]

So – biet' ich den Bund!

Thus do I swear the oath!

SIEGFRIED

So –

Thus –

(He drinks and hands the empty drinking-horn to Hagen.)

trink' ich dir Treu'!   [23b]   do I pledge my faith to you!

(Hagen strikes the horn in two with his sword. [9] Gunther and Siegfried join hands. Siegfried watches Hagen, who has stood behind him during the oath.)

SIEGFRIED

Was nahm'st du am Eide nicht Theil?   Why did you take no part in the oath?

HAGEN

Mein Blut verdürb' euch den Trank! [6]
Nicht fließt mir's ächt
und edel wie euch;
störrisch und kalt
stockt's in mir;
nicht will's die Wange mir röthen.
D'rum bleib' ich fern
vom feurigen Bund.

My blood would mar your drink!
It doesn't flow truly
and nobly like yours;
stubborn and cold
it curdles within me,
refusing to redden my cheek.
So I keep well away
from your fiery bond.

GUNTHER
(to Siegfried)

Lass' den unfrohen Mann!

Leave the cheerless man alone!

SIEGFRIED

(putting on his shield again)

Frisch auf die Fahrt!	Quick, let's be off!
Dort liegt mein Schiff;	There lies my boat;
schnell führt es zum Felsen: [14b]	to the fell it will bring us swiftly:

(He draws closer to Gunther to explain his meaning.)

eine Nacht am Ufer	one night on the shore
harr'st du im Nachen:	you'll wait in the skiff:
die Frau fähr'st du dann heim.	you'll then bring the woman home.

(He turns to go and beckons Gunther to follow him.)

GUNTHER

Rastest du nicht zuvor?	Won't you rest beforehand?

SIEGFRIED

Um die Rückkehr ist's mir jach.	I'm longing to return.

(He goes down to the shore in order to untie the boat.)

GUNTHER

Du Hagen, bewache die Halle!	You, Hagen! Guard the hall!

(He follows Siegfried to the shore. Having placed their weapons in the boat, Siegfried and Gunther hoist the sail and prepare to leave, during which time Hagen takes up his spear and shield. Gutrune appears at the door of her chamber at the very moment[148] that Siegfried pushes the boat out into the middle of the river.)

GUTRUNE

Wohin eilen die Schnellen?[149]	Where are the heroes[149] hurrying?

HAGEN

(seating himself comfortably in front of the hall with his shield and spear)

Zu Schiff, Brünnhild' zu frei'n.	To the boat, to woo Brünnhild' as wife.

GUTRUNE

Siegfried?	Siegfried?

HAGEN

Sieh', wie's ihn treibt	See how he hastens
zum Weib dich zu gewinnen!	to win you as wife!

GUTRUNE

Siegfried – mein!	Siegfried – mine!

(She returns to her chamber in lively agitation. Siegfried has seized the oar and with its strokes drives the boat downstream, so that it is soon lost completely from view.)

HAGEN

(sitting motionless, his back resting against the doorpost of the hall)

Hier sitz' ich zur Wacht,	I sit here on watch,
wahre den Hof,	guarding the garth,
wehre die Halle dem Feind: –	defending the hall from the foe: –
Gibich's Sohne	the wind wafts

wehet der Wind;	Gibich's son away,
auf Werben fährt er dahin.	awooing he is going.
Ihm führt das Steuer [35]	His helm is held
ein starker Held,	by a doughty hero,
Gefahr ihm will er besteh'n:	who'll face every danger for him:
die eig'ne Braut	his very own bride
ihm bringt er zum Rhein;	he'll bring to the Rhine;
mir aber bringt er – den Ring. – [4]	to me, though, he'll bring the ring. –
Ihr freien Söhne,	You freeborn sons,
frohe Gesellen,	carefree companions,
segelt nur lustig dahin!	merrily sail on your way!
Dünkt er euch niedrig,	Though you think him lowly,
ihr dient ihm doch –	you'll serve him yet,
des Niblungen Sohn'.	the Nibelung's son.

(A curtain downstage of the hall is closed, cutting off the stage from the audience.) [6, 35, 9, 56, 19]

SCENE THREE

The curtain opens again.
The rocky height, as in the Prelude.
(Brünnhilde is seated at the entrance to the stone chamber in silent contemplation of Siegfried's ring. Overcome by joyful memories, she covers the ring with kisses. Distant thunder is heard; she looks up and listens. [30] She turns back to the ring. A distant flash of lightning. Brünnhilde listens again and peers into the distance, from where a dark thundercloud can be seen approaching the edge of the rock.)

BRÜNNHILDE

Altgewohntes Geräusch	Old-familiar sounds
raunt meinem Ohr die Ferne: –	steal to my ear from afar: –
ein Luftroß jagt	a winged horse is sweeping
im Laufe daher;	this way at full gallop;
auf der Wolke fährt es	midst thunder and lightning
wetternd zum Fels! –	it flies on the cloud to the fell! –
Wer fand mich einsame auf?	Who's sought me out in my solitude?

WALTRAUTE'S VOICE
(in the distance)

Brünnhilde! Schwester! [31]	Brünnhilde! Sister!
Schläf'st oder wach'st du?	Are you asleep or awake?

BRÜNNHILDE
(leaping to her feet)

Waltraute's Ruf,	Waltraute's call,
so wonnig mir kund! –	so blissfully dear! –

(calling offstage)

Komm'st du, Schwester,	Are you coming, sister,

schwing'st dich kühn zu mir her? | and boldly flying hither to me?

(She hurries to the edge of the rock.)

Dort im Tann | There in the pinewood –
– dir noch vertraut – | – known to you yet –
steige vom Roß | dismount from your horse,
und stell' den Renner zur Rast! – | and leave the courser to rest! –

(She plunges into the pinewood, from where a loud noise, like a clap of thunder, can be heard. Brünnhilde returns, violently agitated, with Waltraute and remains in a state of joyful excitement, failing to notice Waltraute's anxious fear.)

Komm'st du zu mir? | Are you coming to me?
Bist du so kühn? | Are you so bold?
Mag'st ohne Grauen | Can you offer your greeting
Brünnhild' bieten den Gruß? | to Brünnhild' without feeling dread?

WALTRAUTE

Einzig dir nur | For you alone
galt meine Eil'. | I hurried here.

BRÜNNHILDE

So wagtest du, Brünnhild' zu lieb, | So, for Brünnhilde's sake, you've dared
Walvater's Bann zu brechen? | to break War-Father's ban?
Oder wie? o sag'! | Or what else? O say!
wär' wider mich | Might Wotan's heart
Wotan's Sinn erweicht? – | have relented towards me? –
Als dem Gott entgegen | When I shielded Siegmund
Siegmund ich schützte, | against the god,
fehlend – ich weiß es – | erring – I know –
erfüllt' ich doch seinen Wunsch: | I fulfilled his wish none the less:
daß sein Zorn sich verzogen, | that his anger had passed
weiß ich auch; | I also know;
denn verschloß er mich gleich in | for, although he locked me in sleep at
[Schlaf, | [once,
fesselt' er mich auf dem Fels, | fettered me to the fell
wies er dem Mann mich zur Magd, | and left me, as maid, to the man
der am Weg' mich fänd' und | who chanced to find and awake me,
[erweckt' –
meiner bangen Bitte | he granted
doch gab er Gunst: | my timid entreaty:
mit zehrendem Feuer | with ravening fire
umzog er den Fels, | he girdled the fell
dem Zagen zu wehren den Weg. | to bar the faint-heart's way.
So zur Seligsten [37] | So his punishment
schuf mich die Strafe: | made me thrice-blessed:
der herrlichste Held [35] | the most glorious of heroes
gewann mich zum Weib; | won me as wife;
in seiner Liebe | in his love
leucht' und lach' ich heut' auf. – | I exult and glory today. –

(She embraces Waltraute with passionate demonstrations of joy, which the latter attempts to ward off with timid impatience.)

Lockte dich Schwester mein Loos? | Were you lured here, sister, by my lot?

An meiner Wonne
willst du dich weiden,
theilen, was mich betraf?

Do you want to
feast on my joy
and share in the fate that befell me?

WALTRAUTE
(vehemently)

Theilen den Taumel,
der dich Thörin erfaßt? –
Ein and'res bewog mich in Angst
zu brechen Wotan's Gebot.

Share in the frenzy
that's seized you, you fool? –
Something else drove me in dread
to break Wotan's behest.

(Only now, to her surprise, does Brünnhilde notice Waltraute's wild agitation.)

BRÜNNHILDE

Angst und Furcht
fesseln dich Arme?
So verzieh der Strenge noch nicht?

Poor sister, you're fettered
by dread and fear?
So the hard-hearted god hasn't
[pardoned me yet?

Du zag'st vor des Strafenden Zorn?

You quail at my punisher's wrath?

WALTRAUTE
(sombrely)

Dürft' ich ihn fürchten,   [32a]
meiner Angst fänd' ich ein End'!

If only I feared it,
my dread would be over!

BRÜNNHILDE

Staunend versteh' ich dich nicht!

Stunned, I don't understand you!

WALTRAUTE

Wehre der Wallung:
achtsam höre mich an!
Nach Walhall wieder
treibt mich die Angst,
die von Walhall hieher mich trieb.

Come to your senses,
mark me closely!
Back to Valhalla
the same dread drives me
that drove me here from Valhalla.

BRÜNNHILDE
(alarmed)

Was ist's mit den ewigen Göttern?

What ails the immortal gods?

WALTRAUTE

Höre mit Sinn was ich dir sage! –
Seit er von dir geschieden,
  zur Schlacht nicht mehr
  schickte uns Wotan;
  irr und rathlos
ritten wir ängstlich zu Heer.
Walhall's muthige Helden
  mied Walvater:
  einsam zu Roß   [20]
  ohne Ruh' noch Rast,
durchschweift' er als Wand'rer die
  [Welt.

Hear and reflect on what I now tell you. –
Since he and you were parted,
  Wotan has sent us
  no more into battle;
  lost and helpless
we anxiously rode to the field.
The Lord of the Slain avoided
  Valhalla's valiant heroes:
  alone on his horse,
  without rest or repose,
he roamed the world as the Wanderer.

Jüngst kehrte er heim;		He came home of late;
in der Hand hielt er	[9]	in his hand he was holding
seines Speeres Splitter:		his spear's splintered shards:
die hatte ein Held ihm geschlagen.		they'd been shattered by a hero.
Mit stummem Wink		With a silent sign
Walhall's Edle		he sent Valhalla's warriors
wies er zum Forst,		into the forest
die Welt-Esche zu fällen;		to fell the world ash-tree;
des Stammes Scheite		he bade them pile up
hieß er sie schichten		the logs from its trunk
zu ragendem Hauf'		in a towering heap
rings um der Seligen Saal.		round the hall of the blessed immortals.
Der Götter Rath	[8]	He convened
ließ er berufen;		the council of gods;
den Hochsitz nahm		his high seat
heilig er ein:		he solemnly took
ihm zu Seiten		and on either side
hieß er die bangen sich setzen,		bade the anxious gods be seated,
in Ring und Reih'		inviting the heroes to fill
die Hall' erfüllen die Helden.		the hall in their circles and rows.
So – sitzt er,		So he sits,
sagt kein Wort,	[34]	says not a word,
auf hehrem Sitze		silent and grave
stumm und ernst,		on his hallowed seat,
des Speeres Splitter		with the splintered spear
fest in der Faust;		held tight in his hand;
Holda's Äpfel	[13]	Holda's apples
rührt er nicht an:		he does not touch:
Staunen und Bangen	[8]	wonder and fear
binden starr die Götter. –		hold the gods in thrall. –
Seine Raben beide		Both his ravens
sandt' er auf Reise:		he sent on their travels:
kehrten die einst		if ever they come
mit guter Kunde zurück,		back again with good tidings,
dann noch einmal	[5]	then once again
– zum letzten Mal –		– for one last time –
lächelte ewig der Gott. –		the god would smile for ever. –
Seine Knie' umwindend	[32a]	Clasping his knees
liegen wir Walküren:		we valkyries lie:
blind bleibt er		he is blind
den flehenden Blicken;		to our pleading glances;
uns alle verzehrt		we are all consumed
Zagen und endlose Angst.		by dismay and infinite dread.
An seine Brust		To his breast
preßt' ich mich weinend:		I pressed myself, weeping:
	(hesitating)	
da brach sich sein Blick –		his glance grew less harsh;
er gedachte, Brünnhilde, dein'!		he was thinking, Brünnhild', of you!
Tief seufzt' er auf,		Sighing deeply,
schloß das Auge,		he closed his eye

und wie im Traume [5]
raunt' er das Wort: –
»des tiefen Rheines Töchtern [6]
gäbe den Ring sie wieder zurück,
   von des Fluches Last [19]
erlös't wär' Gott und Welt!« –
   Da sann ich nach:
   von seiner Seite [32a, 64]
durch stumme Reihen
stahl ich mich fort;
in heimlicher Hast
bestieg ich mein Roß,
und ritt im Sturme zu dir. [30]
   Dich, o Schwester,
beschwör' ich nun:
was du vermag'st,
vollend' es dein Muth!
Ende der Ewigen Qual!

and, as in a dream,
   whispered the words:
'If she gave back the ring
to the deep Rhine's daughters,
   from the weight of the curse
both god and world would be freed.' [5]
   I weighed his words:
from his side,
through silent ranks,
I stole away;
in secret haste
I mounted my horse
and rode to you like the wind.
   You, o sister,
I now entreat:
whatever you can,
have courage to do it!
End the immortals' torment!

(She has thrown herself at Brünnhilde's feet.)

BRÜNNHILDE
(calmly)

Welch' banger Träume Mären
meldest du traurige mir!
   Der Götter heiligem
   Himmels-Nebel
bin ich Thörin enttaucht:
nicht fass' ich, was ich erfahre.
   Wirr und wüst
scheint mir dein Sinn; [64]
in deinem Aug'
– so übermüde –
glänzt flackernde Gluth:
   mit blasser Wange
   du bleiche Schwester,
was willst du wilde von mir?

What tales of fearful dreams
are you telling me, sad sister?
   Poor fool that I am,
   I have risen above
the mists of the gods' hallowed heaven:
I do not grasp what I hear.
   Your meaning seems
   wild and confused;
in your eye
– so over-weary –
fitful fire gleams:
   with pallid cheek,
   wan sister,
what would you have me do in your
   [wildness?

WALTRAUTE
(vehemently)

An deiner Hand der Ring –
er ist's: hör' meinen Rath!
für Wotan wirf ihn von dir!

Upon your hand, the ring –
that's it: o heed my counsel!
For Wotan, cast it away from you!

BRÜNNHILDE

Den Ring – von mir?

The ring – from me?

WALTRAUTE

Den Rheintöchtern gieb ihn zurück!   Give it back to the Rhinedaughters!

BRÜNNHILDE

Den Rheintöchtern – ich – den Ring?	To the Rhinedaughters – I – the ring?
Siegfried's Liebespfand? –	Siegfried's pledge of love? –
Bist du von Sinnen?	Are you out of your mind?

WALTRAUTE

Hör' mich! hör' meine Angst!	Hear me, hear of my fears!
Der Welt Unheil	The world's ill fate
haftet sicher an ihm: –	surely hangs upon it: –
wirf ihn von dir	cast it away,
fort in die Welle!	into the waves!
Walhall's Elend zu enden,	To end Valhalla's distress,
den verfluchten wirf in die Fluth!	cast the accursèd ring in the river.

BRÜNNHILDE

Ha! weißt du, was er mir ist?		Ha! Do you know what it means to me?
Wie kannst du's fassen,		How can you grasp it,
fühllose Maid! –		you unfeeling child! –
Mehr als Walhall's Wonne,		More than Valhalla's bliss,
mehr als der Ewigen Ruhm –		more than the glory of the immortals
ist mir der Ring:		the ring is to me:
ein Blick auf sein helles Gold,		one glance at its bright-shining gold,
ein Blitz aus dem hehren Glanz –		one flash of its noble fire
gilt mir werther		is worth far more
als aller Götter		than all the gods'
ewig währendes Glück!		eternal joy!
Denn selig aus ihm	[49]	For Siegfried's love
leuchtet mir Siegfried's Liebe:		shines blissfully forth from it!
Siegfried's Liebe		Siegfried's love –
– o ließ' sich die Wonne dir sagen! –	[56]	if only my rapture could speak to you! –
sie – wahrt mir der[150] Reif.	[50]	That love the ring embodies for me.

Geh' hin zu der Götter	[64]	Go hence to the gods'
heiligem Rath;		hallowed council;
von meinem Ringe		of my ring
raune ihnen zu:		tell them only this:
die Liebe ließe ich nie,	[7]	I shall never relinquish love,
mir nähmen nie sie die Liebe –		they'll never take love from me,
stürzt' auch in Trümmern		though Valhalla's glittering pomp
Walhall's strahlende Pracht![151]		should moulder into dust![151]

WALTRAUTE

		Is this your loyalty?
Dieß deine Treue?	[19]	So, in grief,
So in Trauer		would you lovelessly send your sister
entlässest du lieblos die Schwester?		[away?

BRÜNNHILDE

Schwinge dich fort;	Betake yourself hence;
fliege zu Roß:	fly off on your horse:

den Reif entführ'st du mir nie!   you'll never take the ring from me!

WALTRAUTE

Wehe! Wehe!   Alas! Alas!
Weh' dir, Schwester!   Woe betide you, sister!
Walhall's Göttern Weh'!   Woe betide Valhalla's gods!
(She rushes away. A stormcloud can soon be seen rising from the pinewood.)

BRÜNNHILDE
(watching the brightly lit stormcloud disappear into the distance)
Blitzend Gewölk,   Flashing stormclouds,
vom Wind getragen,   borne by the wind,
stürme dahin: rush on your way:
zu mir nie steu're mehr her! –   never again head back to me here! –
*(It is evening. From below, the glow of the fire gradually increases in brightness. Brünnhilde
looks out calmly over the landscape.)* [14a]
Abendlich Dämmern   Evening twilight
deckt den Himmel: shrouds the heavens:
heller leuchtet   more brightly shines
die hütende Lohe herauf. –   the sheltering blaze below. –
*(The glowing fire moves up the mountainside. Tongues of flame, glowing ever brighter, dart up
over the edge of the cliff.)*
Was leckt so wüthend   Why does the blazing billow
die lodernde Welle zum Wall?   lick at the bulwark in such wild fury?
Zur Felsenspitze   The fiery tide is rolling
wälzt sich der feurige Schwall. –   towards the top of the fell. –
(On-stage horn in the distance. Brünnhilde starts up in delight.) [35]
Siegfried! . . .   [40]   Siegfried!
Siegfried zurück!   Siegfried is back!
Seinen Ruf sendet er her! . . .   Hither he sends his call!
Auf! – Auf, ihm entgegen!   Up! Up! To meet him!
In meines Gottes Arm!   Into the arms of my god!
*(She hurries to the edge of the cliff in the utmost joy. Flames shoot up from below: Siegfried
leaps from them and lands on a rocky promontory, whereupon the flames immediately recede
and can soon be seen playing on only the lower slopes once more. On his head Siegfried wears
the tarnhelm, which covers half his face, leaving only his eyes free. He appears in Gunther's
form.)*

BRÜNNHILDE
Verrath! –   Betrayal! –
*(Brünnhilde shrinks back in terror, fleeing to the front of the stage, from where she fixes her
gaze on Siegfried in speechless astonishment.)*
Wer drang zu mir?   [16]   Who forced his way here?
*(Siegfried remains on the rock at the back, observing Brünnhilde and resting motionlessly on his
shield. Long silence.)* [60]

SIEGFRIED
(with a disguised – rougher – voice)
Brünnhild'! Ein Freier kam,   [16]   Brünnhild'! A suitor has come,
der dein Feuer nicht geschreckt.   whom your fire did not frighten.

Dich werb' ich nun zum Weib;
du folge willig mir!

I woo you as my wife;
follow me of your own will!

BRÜNNHILDE
(trembling violently)

Wer ist der Mann,
der das vermochte,
was dem stärksten nur bestimmt?

Who is the man
who has done
what only the strongest was fated to do?

SIEGFRIED
(motionless, as before)

Ein Helde, der dich zähmt –
bezwingt Gewalt dich nur.

A hero who'll tame you,
if force alone can constrain you.

BRÜNNHILDE
(seized with horror)

Ein Unhold schwang sich
auf jenen Stein; –
ein Aar kam geflogen
mich zu zerfleischen![152] –
Wer bist du, Schrecklicher?

A demon has leaped
on to yonder stone; –
an eagle came flying
to tear at my flesh![152] –
Who are you, dread creature?

(Long silence.)

Stamm'st du von Menschen?
Komm'st du von Hella's
nächtlichem Heer?

Are you of human kind?
Are you from Hella's
night-dwelling host?

SIEGFRIED
(as before, beginning with a somewhat quavering voice but continuing with increasing confidence)

Ein Gibichung bin ich,
und Gunther heißt der Held,
dem, Frau, du folgen soll'st.

A Gibichung am I,
and Gunther's the name of the hero
whom, woman, you must follow.

BRÜNNHILDE
(breaking out in despair)

Wotan, ergrimmter,
grausamer Gott!
Weh'! Nun erseh' ich
der Strafe Sinn:
zu Hohn und Jammer
jag'st du mich hin!

[64]

Wotan, grim-hearted,
pitiless god!
Alas! Now I see
the sense of my sentence:
to scorn and sorrow
you hound me hence!

SIEGFRIED
(leaping down from the rock and stepping nearer)

Die Nacht bricht an:
in deinem Gemach
mußt du dich mir vermählen.

Night draws on:
within your chamber
you'll have to wed me.

BRÜNNHILDE
(threateningly stretching out the finger on which she wears Siegfried's ring)

Bleib' fern! Fürchte dieß Zeichen!
Zur Schande zwing'st du mich nicht,
so lang' der Ring mich beschützt.

Keep away! Fear this token!
You'll never force me into shame
as long as this ring protects me.

SIEGFRIED

Mannesrecht gebe er Gunther:
durch den Ring sei ihm vermählt!

Let it give Gunther a husband's rights:
be wedded to him with the ring!

BRÜNNHILDE

Zurück, du Räuber!
Frevelnder Dieb!   [6]
Erfreche dich nicht mir zu nah'n!
Stärker als Stahl
macht mich der Ring:
nie – raub'st du ihn mir!

Away, you robber!
Impious thief!
Make not so bold as to near me!
The ring makes me
stronger than steel:
you'll never steal it from me!

SIEGFRIED

Von dir ihn zu lösen   [19]
lehr'st du mich nun.[153]

To wrest it from you
you teach me now.[153]

(He makes to attack her. They struggle. Brünnhilde breaks free, runs away and then turns to defend herself. [30] Siegfried seizes her again. She escapes; he catches her. They wrestle violently with each other. He seizes her by the hand and tears the ring from her finger. Brünnhilde screams violently. As she sinks down in his arms, as though broken, her gaze unconsciously meets Siegfried's. [16, 56] He lowers her fainting body on to the stone terrace outside the rocky chamber.)

Jetzt bist du mein!
Brünnhilde, Gunther's Braut –
gönne mir nun dein Gemach!

Now you are mine!
Brünnhilde, Gunther's bride,
allow me to enter your chamber!

BRÜNNHILDE
(staring impotently ahead of her, weakly)

Was könntest du wehren,
elendes Weib!

How could you stop him,
woman most wretched!

(Siegfried drives her away with a gesture of command. Trembling and with faltering steps, she returns to the chamber. [64] Siegfried draws his sword.) [23]

SIEGFRIED
(in his natural voice)

Nun, Nothung, zeuge du,   [62]
daß ich in Züchten warb:
die Treue wahrend dem Bruder,   [61]
trenne mich von seiner Braut!   [23]

Now, Nothung, attest
that I wooed her chastely:
keeping faith with my brother,
keep me apart from his bride!

(He follows Brünnhilde. [16, 56] The curtain falls.)

Act Two

Prelude and Scene One

(The curtain rises.[154] *An open space on the shore in front of the Gibichung Hall: to the left is the open entrance to the hall; on the right, the bank of the Rhine, from which ascends a rocky height cut by several mountain paths as it rises diagonally towards the upstage left-hand corner. An altar-stone can be seen there, dedicated to Fricka; a larger one for Wotan is visible higher up the slope, with a similar one dedicated to Donner to one side of it. It is night. Hagen, his spear on his arm, his shield at his side, is sitting asleep, leaning against one of the doorposts of the hall. At this point*[155] *the moon suddenly appears from behind a cloud and casts its harsh light on Hagen and his immediate surroundings: Alberich can be seen crouching in front of Hagen, his arms resting on the latter's knees.)*

ALBERICH
(softly)

Schläf'st du, Hagen, mein Sohn? –	Are you sleeping, Hagen, my son?
Du schläf'st, und hör'st mich nicht,	You're asleep and do not hear me
den Ruh' und Schlaf verrieth?	whom rest and sleep bewrayed.

HAGEN
(softly, without moving, so that he still seems to be asleep, even though there is a glassy stare in his permanently open eyes)

Ich höre dich, schlimmer Albe:	I hear you, evil elf:
was hast du meinem Schlaf zu sagen?	What do you have to tell my sleep?

ALBERICH

Gemahnt sei der Macht,	Be mindful of the power
der du gebietest,	that you'll command
bist du so muthig,	if you're as mettlesome
wie die Mutter dich mir gebar.	as the mother who gave you birth.

HAGEN
(as before)

Gab mir die Mutter Muth,	Though my mother gave me mettle,
nicht mag ich ihr[156] doch danken,	I've no reason to be thankful
daß deiner List sie erlag:	that she yielded to your cunning:
frühalt, fahl und bleich,	old too early, pale and wan,
hass' ich die Frohen,	I hate the happy,
freue mich nie!	am never glad!

ALBERICH
(as before)

Hagen, mein Sohn,	Hagen, my son,
hasse die Frohen!	hate the happy!
Mich lust-freien,	But me, the mirthless,
leid-belasteten,	much-wronged dwarf,

lieb'st du so wie du soll'st!   you love just as you ought!

   Bist du kräftig,   If you're stalwart,

   kühn und klug: bold and clever,

   die wir bekämpfen   those whom we fight

   mit nächtigem Krieg,   in nightly feud

schon giebt ihnen Noth unser Neid.   already suffer our spite.

Der einst den Ring mir entriß,   [6]   He who once wrenched the ring from me,

Wotan, der wüthende Räuber,   Wotan, that furious robber,

   vom eig'nen Geschlechte   was worsted

   ward er geschlagen: by his own kind:

   an den Wälsung verlor er   to the Wälsung he forfeited

   Macht und Gewalt: power and might:

mit der Götter ganzer Sippe   in company with the whole kindred of
[gods

in Angst ersieht er sein Ende.   he awaits his end in dread.

Nicht ihn fürcht' ich mehr: Him do I fear no more:

fallen muß er mit allen! –   he must fall with all the rest! –

Schläf'st du, Hagen, mein Sohn?   Are you sleeping, Hagen, my son?

HAGEN
(remaining motionless, as before)

Der Ewigen Macht,   The immortals' power –

wer erbte sie?   who would inherit it?

ALBERICH

Ich – und du: [65]   I – and you:

wir erben die Welt,   we'll inherit the world

trüg' ich mich nicht   if I'm not deceived

in deiner Treu',   in my trust in you,

theil'st du meinen Gram und   if you share my grief and rage. –
[Grimm. –

Wotan's Speer   [23]   Wotan's spear

zerspellte der Wälsung,   was split by the Wälsung

der Fafner, den Wurm,   [46]   who felled the dragon,

im Kampfe gefällt,   Fafner, in combat

und kindisch den Reif sich errang: and, child that he is, won the ring for
[himself:

jede Gewalt   [6]   every power

hat er gewonnen;   he has gained;

Walhall und Nibelheim   Valhalla and Nibelheim

neigen sich ihm;   bow down before him;

(with a continuing air of secrecy)

an dem furchtlosen Helden   even my curse grows feeble

erlahmt selbst mein Fluch:[157]   in face of the fearless hero:[157]

denn nicht kennt er   for he does not know

des Ringes Werth,   what the ring is worth,

zu nichts nützt er   he makes no use

die neidliche Macht;   of its coveted power;

lachend in liebender Brunst   [40]   laughing, in loving desire,

brennt er lebend dahin.
Ihn zu verderben
taugt uns nun einzig ...

he burns his life away.
To destroy him alone
avails us now.

Schläf'st du, Hagen, mein Sohn?

Are you sleeping, Hagen, my son?

HAGEN
(as before)

Zu seinem Verderben
dient er mir schon.

To his own destruction
he serves me even now.

ALBERICH

Den gold'nen Ring,   [65]
den Reif gilt's zu erringen!
Ein weises Weib
lebt dem Wälsung zu Lieb':
rieth' es ihm je
des Rheines Töchtern   [2]
— die in Wassers Tiefen
einst mich bethört! —   [6]
zurück zu geben den Ring:
verloren ging' mir das Gold,
keine List erlangte es je.
D'rum ohne Zögern
ziel' auf den Reif!
Dich zaglosen
zeugt' ich mir ja,
daß wider Helden
hart du mir hieltest.
Zwar stark nicht genug
den Wurm zu besteh'n
— was allein dem Wälsung bestimmt —

The golden ring,
the circlet, must be gained!
A wise woman
lives for the Wälsung alone:
were she ever to urge him
to give back the ring
to the deep Rhine's daughters
who once befooled me
in watery depths,
the gold would be lost to me then,
no cunning could ever reclaim it.
So strive for the ring
without delay!
Fearless Hagen,
I fathered you
to take a firm stand
against heroes.
Though not strong enough
to defeat the dragon
— which the Wälsung alone was fated to
[do —

zu zähem Haß   [65]
doch erzog ich Hagen:
der soll mich nun rächen,
den Ring gewinnen,
dem Wälsung und Wotan zum Hohn.
Schwör'st du mir's, Hagen, mein
[Sohn?   [8]

I brought up Hagen
to feel stubborn hatred:
now he'll avenge me
and win the ring
in contempt of the Wälsung and Wotan.
Do you swear to it, Hagen, my son?

*(From this point onwards an increasingly dark shadow starts to envelop Alberich again. At the
same time, the first streaks of light begin to appear in the sky.)*

HAGEN
(as before)

Den Ring soll ich haben:
harre in Ruh'!

The ring I shall have:
only be patient!

ALBERICH

Schwör'st du mir's, Hagen, mein
[Held?

Do you swear to it, Hagen, my hero?

Mir selbst schwör' ich's: To myself I swear it:
  schweige die Sorge!   [19]   silence your care!

(During the following Alberich's form gradually disappears from sight, while his voice grows more and more inaudible.)

ALBERICH

Sei treu, Hagen, mein Sohn!   Be true, Hagen, my son!
Trauter Helde, sei treu!   Beloved hero – be true!
  Sei treu! – treu!   Be true! True!

(Alberich has disappeared completely. Hagen, who has remained in the same position, stares motionlessly and fixedly at the Rhine, over which the light of dawn is already beginning to spread.) [66]

SCENE TWO

(From this point onwards[158] the Rhine begins to glow with the deepening red of dawn. Hagen starts. [16] Siegfried suddenly appears from behind a bush close to the shore.) [40]

SIEGFRIED

Hoiho! Hagen!   Hoiho! Hagen!
Müder Mann!   Weary man!
Sieh'st du mich kommen?   Did you see me coming?

(Hagen rises slowly to his feet. Siegfried is restored to his own shape, though he still wears the tarnhelm on his head; he now removes it and, stepping forward, hangs it from his belt.)

HAGEN

Hei! Siegfried!   [66]   Hey! Siegfried!
Geschwinder Helde!   Fleet-footed hero!
Wo brausest du her?   From where have you sped?

SIEGFRIED

Vom Brünnhildenstein;   [14b]   From Brünnhilde's rock;
dort sog ich den Athem ein,   it was there that I drew the breath
  mit dem ich dich rief: with which I called your name:
so schnell war meine Fahrt!   so quick was my journey here!
Langsamer folgt mir ein Paar: Two others follow more slowly:
zu Schiff gelangt das her.   they're coming here by boat.

HAGEN

So zwang'st du Brünnhild'?   So you overpowered Brünnhild'?

SIEGFRIED

Wacht Gutrune?   Is Gutrun' awake?

HAGEN
(calling into the hall)

Hoiho! Gutrune!
Komm' heraus!
Siegfried ist da:
was säum'st du drin?

[67]

Hoiho! Gutrune!
Come on out!
Siegfried is here:
why linger within?

SIEGFRIED
(turning to the hall)

Euch beiden meld' ich,
wie ich Brünnhild' band.[159]

I'll tell you both
how I bound[159] Brünnhilde.

(Gutrune comes from the hall to meet him.)[160] [61]

Heiß' mich willkommen,
Gibichskind!
Ein guter Bote bin ich dir.

Bid me welcome,
Gibich's child!
A goodly herald I am for you.

GUTRUNE

Freia grüße dich
zu aller Frauen Ehre!

May Freia give you greeting
in honour of all women!

SIEGFRIED

Frei und hold
sei nun mir frohem:
zum Weib gewann ich dich heut'.

Be open-handed and well-disposed
to me in my happy state:
today I won you as my wife.

GUTRUNE

So folgt Brünnhild' meinem Bruder?

So Brünnhilde's following my brother?

SIEGFRIED

Leicht ward die Frau ihm[161] gefreit.

The woman was easily wooed.[161]

GUTRUNE

Sengte das Feuer ihn nicht?

Didn't the fire singe him?

SIEGFRIED

Ihn hätt' es auch nicht versehrt;
doch ich durchschritt es für ihn,
da dich ich wollt' erwerben.

It wouldn't have harmed him either;
but I myself passed through it for him,
because I wanted to win you.

GUTRUNE

Doch dich hat es verschont?

But you came through it unscathed?

SIEGFRIED

Mich freute die schwebende Brunst.

The flickering flames refreshed me.

GUTRUNE

Hielt Brünnhild' dich für Gunther?

Did Brünnhilde take you for my brother?

SIEGFRIED

Ihm glich ich auf ein Haar:
der Tarnhelm wirkte das,
wie Hagen tüchtig es wies.

I resembled him to a hair:
the tarnhelm brought that about,
as Hagen wisely said it would.

HAGEN

Dir gab ich guten Rath.   I gave you good advice.

GUTRUNE

So zwang'st du das kühne Weib?   So you overcame the intrepid woman?

SIEGFRIED

Sie wich – Gunther's Kraft.   [60]   She yielded – to Gunther's strength.

GUTRUNE

Und vermählte sie sich dir?   And yet she was wed to you?

SIEGFRIED

Ihrem Mann gehorchte Brünnhild'   Brünnhild' obeyed her husband
eine volle bräutliche Nacht.   for the whole of the bridal night.

GUTRUNE

Als ihr Mann doch galtest du?   But you yourself were deemed her
                             [husband?

SIEGFRIED

Bei Gutrune weilte Siegfried.   Siegfried stayed with Gutrun'.

GUTRUNE

Doch zur Seite war ihm Brünnhild'?   But Brünnhild' was at his side?

SIEGFRIED

Zwischen Ost und West der Nord: Twixt east and west – the north:
       (pointing to his sword)
so nah' – war Brünnhild' ihm fern.   so close was the distance between them.

GUTRUNE

Wie empfing Gunther sie nun von   How did Gunther receive her from you?
   [dir?

SIEGFRIED

Durch des Feuers verlöschende Lohe   Down through the fire's dying embers
im Frühnebel vom Felsen   she followed me in the morning mist
folgte sie mir zu Thal;   from the fell to the valley below;
   dem Strande nah',   close to the shoreline
   flugs die Stelle   Gunther and I
tauschte Gunther mit mir: changed places in a trice:
durch des Geschmeides Tugend   through the trinket's magic virtue
wünscht' ich mich schnell hieher.   I wished myself straight back here.
Ein starker Wind nun treibt   [40]   A strong wind's now driving
die Trauten den Rhein herauf: the lovers back up the Rhine:
d'rum rüstet jetzt den Empfang!   and so make ready their welcome!

GUTRUNE

Siegfried, mächtigster Mann: Siegfried, mightiest of men:

wie faßt mich Furcht vor dir!	how fear of you grips me fast!

HAGEN

(calling from the shore)

In der Ferne seh' ich ein Segel.	I can see a sail in the distance.

SIEGFRIED

So sagt dem Boten Dank!	Then give the messenger thanks!

GUTRUNE

Lasset uns sie hold empfangen,	Let's welcome her fondly
daß heiter sie und gern hier weile!	that, carefree, she's glad to stay here!
Du Hagen! Minnig	You, Hagen, lovingly
rufe die Männer	call the menfolk
nach Gibich's Hof zur Hochzeit!	to Gibich's garth for the wedding!
Frohe Frauen [61]	Happy women
ruf' ich zum Fest:	I'll call to the feast:
der freudigen folgen sie gern.	they'll be glad to follow me in my joy.

(walking towards the hall and turning round once more)

Rastest du, schlimmer Held?	Won't you rest, you wicked hero?

SIEGFRIED

Dir zu helfen ruh' ich aus.	Helping you is rest enough.

(He offers her his hand and returns to the hall with her. Hagen has mounted a rock high at the back of the stage: here he raises his cowhorn to his lips and begins to blow.) [66]

SCENE THREE

HAGEN

Hoiho! Hoiho hoho! [3]	Hoiho! Hoiho hoho!
Ihr Gibichs-Mannen,	You men of Gibich,
machet euch auf!	bestir yourselves!
Wehe! Wehe!	Woe! Woe!
Waffen! Waffen!	To arms! To arms!
Waffen durch's Land! [67]	To arms throughout the land!
Gute Waffen!	Goodly weapons!
Starke Waffen,	Sturdy weapons,
scharf zum Streit!	sharp for the fray!
Noth ist da!	Danger is here!
Noth! Wehe! Wehe!	Danger! Woe! Woe!
Hoiho! Hoiho hoho!	Hoiho! Hoiho hoho!

(Hagen remains in the same position on the rock. Armed vassals enter hurriedly over the various hillpaths, running in singly, then in increasing numbers, before assembling on the shore outside the hall.)

THE VASSALS

Was tos't das Horn?	Why does the horn ring out?

was ruft es zu Heer?	Why does it call us to battle?
Wir kommen mit Wehr,	We come in arms,
wir kommen mit Waffen.	we come with weapons.
Hagen! Hagen!	Hagen! Hagen!
Hoiho! Hoiho!	Hoiho! Hoiho!
Welche Noth ist da?	What danger is here?
Welcher Feind ist nah'?	What foe is near?
Wer giebt uns Streit?	Who bids us fight?
Ist Gunther in Noth?	Is Gunther in danger?
Wir kommen mit Waffen,	We come with weapons,
mit scharfer Wehr,	with sharp-edged weapons,
mit schneidiger Wehr!	with keen-edged weapons!
Hoiho! Ho! Hagen!	Hoiho! Ho! Hagen!

HAGEN

(still in his former position on the raised ground at the back)

Rüstet euch wohl	Arm yourselves well
und rastet nicht!	and do not rest!
Gunther sollt ihr empfah'n:	Gunther you must welcome:
ein Weib hat der gefreit.	he's wooed a wife for himself.

THE VASSALS

Drohet ihm Noth?	Does danger threaten him?
Drängt ihn der Feind?	Is the enemy at his heels?

HAGEN

Ein freisliches Weib	A fearsome woman
führet er heim.	he's bringing home.

THE VASSALS

Ihm folgen der Magen	Is he being pursued
feindliche Mannen?	by her kinsmen's hostile vassals?

HAGEN

Einsam fährt er:	He's coming alone:
keiner folgt.	no one's following.

THE VASSALS

So bestand er die Noth?	So he triumphed over the danger?
So bestand er den Kampf?	So he triumphed in the fray?
Sag' es an!	Tell us!

HAGEN

Der Wurmtödter	The dragon-killer
wehrte der Noth:	averted the danger:
Siegfried, der Held,	Siegfried the hero
der schuf ihm Heil.	made sure he was safe.

ONE VASSAL

Was soll ihm das Heer nun noch [helfen?	What can the army still do to help him?

NINE OTHERS

| Was hilft ihm nun das Heer? | What help can the army now offer? |

HAGEN

Starke Stiere	Stout-limbed steers
sollt ihr schlachten:	you're to slaughter:
am Weihstein fließe	on the altar-stone let
Wotan ihr Blut.	their blood flow for Wotan.

ONE VASSAL

| Was, Hagen, was heißest du uns | What, Hagen, would you have us do |
| [dann? | [then? |

EIGHT VASSALS

| Was heißest du uns dann? | What would you have us do then? |

HAGEN

Einen Eber fällen	Bring down
sollt ihr für Froh;	a boar for Froh;
einen stämmigen Bock	a sturdy goat
stechen für Donner:	slay for Donner:
Schafe aber	for Fricka, though,
schlachtet für Fricka,	you must slaughter sheep,
daß gute Ehe sie gebe!	so that she gives a goodly marriage!

THE VASSALS
(with ever-increasing hilarity)

| Schlugen wir Thiere, | When we've slaughtered the beasts, |
| was schaffen wir dann? | what then should we do? |

HAGEN

Das Trinkhorn nehmt,	Take up the drinking-horn
von trauten Frau'n	blissfully filled
mit Meth und Wein	by your sweethearts
wonnig gefüllt.	with mead and with wine.

THE VASSALS

| Das Trinkhorn zur Hand, | With horn in hand, |
| wie halten wir es dann? | how should we then behave? |

HAGEN

Rüstig gezecht,	Quaff all you can,
bis der Rausch euch zähmt:	till drunkenness tames you –
alles den Göttern zu Ehren,	and all to honour the gods,
daß gute Ehe sie geben!	that they give a goodly marriage!

THE VASSALS
(breaking into ringing laughter)

| Groß Glück und Heil | Fair fortune and good |
| lacht nun dem Rhein, | now smile on the Rhine, |

da Hagen, der grimme,
so lustig mag sein!
Der Hage-Dorn[162]
sticht nun nicht mehr:
zum Hochzeitsrufer   [67]
ward er bestellt.

since Hagen the grim
can make so merry!
The hawthorn bush[162]
no longer pricks:
he's been installed
as bridal herald.

(Having remained entirely serious, Hagen now descends from his position at the back of the stage and joins the vassals.)

HAGEN

Nun laßt das Lachen,
  muth'ge Mannen!
Empfangt Gunther's Braut:
Brünnhilde naht dort mit ihm.

Now leave off laughing,
  valiant vassals!
Receive Gunther's bride:
Brünnhilde's coming here with him.

(He points towards the Rhine: some of the vassals run up the slope at the back, while others line up on the shore in order to see the new arrivals.)

(approaching some of the vassals)

Hold seid der Herrin,
helfet ihr treu:
traf sie ein Leid,
rasch seid zur Rache!

To your lady be loyal,
serve her truly:
if wrong should befall her,
be swift to vengeance!

(He turns slowly aside towards the back of the stage. During the following, the boat bearing Gunther and Brünnhilde appears on the Rhine.)

THE VASSALS

Heil! Heil!

Hail! Hail!

(The vassals who had been standing on the slope descend to the riverbank.)

Willkommen! Willkommen!

Welcome! Welcome!

(Some of the vassals leap into the water and draw the boat ashore. They all press closer to the shore.)

Willkommen, Gunther!
Heil! Heil!

Welcome, Gunther!
Hail! Hail!

SCENE FOUR

(Gunther steps out of the boat with Brünnhilde: the vassals line up respectfully to receive them. Throughout the following, Gunther leads Brünnhilde solemnly by the hand.)

THE VASSALS

Heil dir, Gunther!
Heil dir, und deiner Braut!
Willkommen!

Hail to you, Gunther!
Hail to you, and to your bride!
Welcome!

(They strike their weapons noisily together.)

GUNTHER

(presenting Brünnhilde, who follows him pale-faced and with downcast eyes, to the vassals)
[30]

Brünnhild', die hehrste Frau,	Brünnhild', most hallowed of women,
bring' ich euch her zum Rhein:	I bring to you here on the Rhine:
ein edleres Weib	a nobler wife
ward nie gewonnen!	was never won!
Der Gibichungen Geschlecht,	The gods have favoured
gaben die Götter ihm Gunst,	the Gibichung race;
zum höchsten Ruhm	now let it rise
rag' es nun auf!	to the highest renown!

THE VASSALS

(ceremoniously clashing their weapons)

Heil dir,	Hail to you,
glücklicher Gibichung!	happy Gibichung!

(Gunther leads Brünnhilde, who never once raises her eyes, to the hall, from which Siegfried and Gutrune emerge, attended by womenfolk.) [30, 64, 61]

GUNTHER

(pausing outside the hall)

Gegrüßt sei, theurer Held!	Be welcome, dear hero!
Gegrüßt, holde Schwester!	Be welcome, fair sister!
Dich seh' ich froh ihm zur Seite,	I see you happy beside him
der dich zum Weib gewann.	who won you as his wife.
Zwei sel'ge Paare	Two blissful couples
seh' ich hier prangen:	I see here resplendent:

(He draws Brünnhilde closer towards them.)

Brünnhild' – und Gunther,	Brünnhild' – and Gunther,
Gutrun' – und Siegfried!	Gutrun' – and Siegfried!

(Brünnhilde raises her eyes in alarm and sees Siegfried; her gaze remains fixed on him in amazement. Gunther has released her violently trembling hand and, like the others, shows genuine perplexity at her behaviour.)

SOME VASSALS

Was ist ihr?	[34, 16]	What ails her?
Ist sie entrückt?		Is she distraught?

(Brünnhilde begins to tremble.)

SIEGFRIED

(taking a few steps towards Brünnhilde)

Was müht Brünnhilden's Blick? ·	What troubles Brünnhilde's features?

BRÜNNHILDE

(scarcely able to control herself)

Siegfried . . . hier . .! Gutrune . .?	[61]	Siegfried . . . here! . . Gutrune . .?

SIEGFRIED

Gunther's milde Schwester:	Gunther's gentle sister:
mir vermählt,	wedded to me,
wie Gunther du.	as you are to Gunther.

BRÜNNHILDE
(with terrible vehemence)

Ich ... Gunther ..? du lüg'st! –   I ... Gunther ..? You lie! –

(She sways and appears about to collapse; Siegfried supports her.)

Mir schwindet das Licht ...   The light is fading from my eyes ...

(In his arms, looking weakly up at him.)

Siegfried ... kennt mich nicht? ... [56]   Siegfried ... knows me not! ...

SIEGFRIED

Gunther, deinem Weib ist übel!   Gunther, your wife's unwell!

(Gunther joins them.)

Erwache, Frau!   Wake up, woman!

Hier steht dein Gatte.   Here stands your husband!

(Brünnhilde sees the ring on Siegfried's outstretched finger and starts up with terrible violence.)

BRÜNNHILDE

Ha! – der Ring ...   Ha! ... the ring ...

an seiner Hand!   upon his hand!

Er ... Siegfried?   [19]   He ... Siegfried?

SOME VASSALS

Was ist? Was ist?   What is it? What is it?

HAGEN
(emerging from the back and advancing among the vassals)

Jetzt merket klug,   Mark closely now

was die Frau euch klagt!   what the woman discloses!

BRÜNNHILDE
(trying to regain her composure, while forcibly restraining the most terrible agitation)

Einen Ring sah ich   A ring I saw

an deiner Hand: –   upon your hand: –

nicht dir gehört er,   it belongs not to you

ihn entriß mir   but was wrested from me

(pointing to Gunther)

– dieser Mann!   – by this man here!

Wie mochtest von ihm   How could you have

den Ring du empfah'n?   got the ring from him?

SIEGFRIED
(examining the ring on his finger)

Den Ring empfing ich   I did not get

nicht von ihm.   [4]   the ring from him.

BRÜNNHILDE
(to Gunther)

Nahm'st du von mir den Ring, If you took from me the ring

durch den ich dir vermählt; by which I was wed to you,

so melde ihm dein Recht,   then tell him of your right to it,

ford're zurück das Pfand!   demand the token back!

GUNTHER
(in great confusion)

Den Ring? – Ich gab ihm keinen: –   The ring? – I gave him none: –
doch kenn'st du ihn auch gut?   but are you sure that it's the same?

BRÜNNHILDE

Wo bärgest du den Ring,   Where are you hiding the ring
den du von mir erbeutet?   that you carried off as your prize?
  (Thoroughly perplexed, Gunther says nothing. [16] *Brünnhilde flares up in her rage.)*
Ha! – Dieser war es,   Ha! He it was
der mir den Ring entriß: who wrested the ring away from me:
Siegfried, der trugvolle Dieb!   [6]   Siegfried, the treacherous thief!
(All look expectantly at Siegfried, who is completely lost in contemplation of the ring.) [64]

SIEGFRIED

Von keinem Weib   It was not from a woman
kam mir der Reif;   the ring came to me,
noch war's ein Weib,   nor was it a woman
dem ich ihn abgewann: from whom I took it:
  genau erkenn' ich   I recognize clearly
  des Kampfes Lohn,   [5]   the spoils from the fight
den vor Neidhöhl' einst[163] ich   which I once[163] won at Neidhöhl'
  [bestand,
als den starken Wurm ich   when slaying the mighty dragon.
  [erschlug.   [46, 4]

HAGEN
(stepping between them)

Brünnhild', kühne Frau!   Brünnhild', intrepid woman!
Kenn'st du genau den Ring?   Do you recognize the ring?
Ist's der, den du Gunther'n gab'st,   If it's the one that you gave to Gunther,
  so ist er sein, –   then it is his alone
und Siegfried gewann ihn durch   and Siegfried won it by fraud,
  [Trug,   [35]
den der Treulose büßen sollt'!   for which the traitor must pay!

BRÜNNHILDE
(crying out in the most terrible anguish)

Betrug! Betrug!   Deceit! Deceit!
Schändlichster Betrug!   Most shameful deceit!
Verrath! Verrath –   Betrayal! Betrayal –
wie noch nie er gerächt!   [64, 3]   as never before avenged!

GUTRUNE

Verrath? An wem?   Betrayal? Of whom?

WOMEN AND VASSALS

Verrath? An wem?   Betrayal? Of whom?

BRÜNNHILDE

Heil'ge Götter!   [8]   Hallowed gods!
Himmlische Lenker!   Heavenly rulers!
Rauntet ihr dieß   [64]   Was this what you whispered
in eurem Rath?   within your council?
Lehrt ihr mich Leiden   Would you teach me suffering
wie keiner sie litt?   as none yet suffered?
Schuf't ihr mir Schmach   Have you caused me shame
wie nie sie geschmerzt?   more painful than any yet felt?
Rathet nun Rache   Now teach me revenge
wie nie sie geras't!   as never yet raged!
Zündet mir Zorn   Kindle such wrath
wie noch nie er gezähmt!   as has never been tamed!
Heißet Brünnhild'   Bid Brünnhilde
ihr Herz zu zerbrechen,   break her heart in twain
den zu zertrümmern,   to destroy the man
der sie betrog!   who betrayed her!

GUNTHER

Brünnhild', Gemahlin!   Brünnhilde, wife!
Mäß'ge dich!   Control yourself!

BRÜNNHILDE

Weich' fern, Verräther!   [64]   Keep away, betrayer!
selbst verrath'ner! –   Self-betrayed! –
Wisset denn alle: Know then, all of you:
nicht – ihm, –   not to him,
dem Manne dort   but to that man there
bin ich vermählt.   am I wed.

WOMEN

Siegfried? Gutrun's Gemahl?   Siegfried? Gutrune's husband?

VASSALS

Gutrun's Gemahl?   Gutrune's husband?

BRÜNNHILDE

Er zwang mir Lust   He forced delight
und Liebe ab.   from me, and love.

SIEGFRIED

Achtest du so   Are you so careless
der eig'nen Ehre?   of your own honour?
Die Zunge, die sie lästert,   The tongue that defames it,
muß ich der Lüge sie zeihen? –   must I accuse it of lying? –
Hört, ob ich Treue brach!   Listen whether I broke my faith!
Blutbrüderschaft   [62]   Blood-brotherhood
hab' ich Gunther geschworen!   have I sworn to Gunther.
Nothung, das werthe Schwert, [9, 23]   Nothung, my worthy sword,
wahrte der Treue Eid;   defended the oath of loyalty;

mich trennte seine Schärfe
von diesem traur'gen Weib.

its sharp edge sundered me
from this unhappy woman.

BRÜNNHILDE

Du listiger Held,
sieh' wie du lüg'st, —
wie auf dein Schwert
du schlecht dich beruf'st!
Wohl kenn' ich seine Schärfe, [23]
doch kenn' auch die Scheide, [57]
darin so wonnig
ruht' an der Wand
Nothung, der treue Freund,
als die Traute sein Herr sich
[gewann.[164]

You cunning hero,
look how you're lying,
just as you're wrong
to appeal to your sword!
Well do I know its sharp-set edge,
but I also know the scabbard
in which your true friend,
Nothung, rested
serenely against the wall
while its master won him his
[sweetheart.[164]

(The vassals and women gather together in lively indignation.)

THE VASSALS

Wie? brach er die Treue?
Trübte er Gunther's Ehre?

What? Has he broken faith?
Has he tarnished Gunther's honour?

THE WOMEN

Brach er die Treue?

Has he broken faith?

GUNTHER
(to Siegfried)

Geschändet wär' ich,
schmählich bewahrt,
gäb'st du die Rede
nicht ihr zurück!

I'll be disgraced
and held in shame,
if you don't refute
the words she utters.

GUTRUNE

Treulos, Siegfried,
sannest du Trug?
Bezeuge, daß jene
falsch dich zeiht!

Faithlessly, Siegfried,
you plotted deception?
Bear witness that she
accuses you falsely!

THE VASSALS

Reinige dich,
bist du im Recht:
schweige die Klage,
schwöre den Eid!

Clear yourself
if you're in the right:
silence the charge,
swear an oath!

SIEGFRIED

Schweig' ich die Klage,
schwör' ich den Eid:
wer von euch wagt
seine Waffe daran?

If I silence the charge
and swear an oath:
which of you'll venture
his weapon upon it?

HAGEN

Meines Speeres Spitze [64] The point of my spear
wag' ich daran: I'll venture upon it:
sie wahr' in Ehren den Eid. let it honour the oath.

(The vassals form a circle round Siegfried and Hagen. [6] Hagen holds out his spear; Siegfried places two fingers of his right hand on the point of the spear.)

SIEGFRIED

Helle Wehr! Shining steel!
Heilige Waffe! Hallowed weapon!
Hilf meinem ewigen Eide! – Assist my eternal oath! –
Bei des Speeres Spitze By the point of this spear
sprech' ich den Eid: I swear the oath:
Spitze, achte des Spruch's! – spear-point, mark what I say! –
Wo Scharfes mich schneide, [65] Where blade may bleed me,
schneide du mich; be it you that bleeds me;
wo der Tod mich soll treffen where death may strike,
treffe du mich: be it you that strikes
klagte das Weib dort wahr, if that woman's charge is true,
brach ich dem Bruder den Eid! if I broke my vow to my brother!

BRÜNNHILDE

(striding furiously into the circle, tearing Siegfried's hand away from the spear and seizing the tip of it with her own hand) [30, 31]
Helle Wehr! Shining steel!
Heilige Waffe! Hallowed weapon!
Hilf meinem ewigen Eide! – Assist my eternal oath! –
Bei des Speeres Spitze [64] By the point of this spear
sprech' ich den Eid: I swear the oath:
Spitze, achte des Spruch's! – spear-point, mark what I say! –
Ich weihe deine Wucht, [65] I hallow your thrust
daß sie ihn werfe! that it overthrow him!
Seine Schärfe segne ich, I bless your blade
daß sie ihn schneide: that it bleed him:
denn brach seine Eide er all', for, just as he broke every oath he swore,
schwur Meineid jetzt dieser Mann! this man has now forsworn himself!

THE VASSALS
(in utter turmoil)

Hilf, Donner! Help, Donner!
Tose dein Wetter, Let your tempest roar
zu schweigen die wüthende to silence this raging disgrace!
[Schmach! [57]

SIEGFRIED

Gunther, wehr' deinem Weibe, Gunther! Stop your wife
das schamlos Schande dir lügt! – from shamelessly bringing dishonour
[upon you! –
Gönnt ihr Weil' und Ruh', Grant the wild mountain woman
der wilden Felsen-Frau, a moment's respite and rest

daß ihre freche Wuth sich lege,	[26b]	that her brazen rage may abate,
die eines Unhold's		which a demon's
arge List		cunning craft
wider uns alle erregt! –		has roused against us all! –
Ihr Mannen, kehret euch ab,		You vassals, withdraw
laßt das Weiber-Gekeif'!		and leave this women's wrangling!
Als Zage weichen wir gern,		Like cowards we gladly give ground
gilt es mit Zungen dem Streit.		when it comes to a battle of tongues.

(He goes right up to Gunther.)

Glaub', mehr zürnt es mich als		Believe me, it angers me more than you
[dich,	[14b, 16]	
daß schlecht ich sie getäuscht:		that I took her in so badly:
der Tarnhelm, dünkt mich fast,		I almost think that the tarnhelm
hat halb mich nur gehehlt.		must have only half concealed me.
Doch Frauengroll	[6]	But women's resentment
friedet sich bald:		quickly passes:
daß ich dir es gewann,		that I won her for you
dankt dir gewiß noch das Weib.	[57]	the woman will surely be thankful yet.

(He turns to the vassals.)

Munter, ihr Mannen!		Cheer up, you vassals!
Folgt mir zum Mahl! –		Follow me to the feast! –

(to the women)

Froh zur Hochzeit		Be happy to help
helfet, ihr Frauen! –		at the wedding, you women! –
Wonnige Lust		May blissful delight
lache nun auf:		now laugh out aloud!
in Hof und Hain	[61]	In garth and grove
heiter vor allen		you shall see me
sollt ihr heute mich seh'n.		gladdest of all today.
Wen die Minne freut,		He whom love delights,
meinem frohen Muthe		let the lucky man
thu' es der Glückliche gleich!	[67]	share in my happy frame of mind!

(Siegfried throws his arm around Gutrune in exuberant high spirits and draws her away with him into the hall. The vassals and womenfolk, carried away by his example, follow him. The stage has emptied. Only Brünnhilde, Gunther and Hagen remain behind. His face covered, Gunther has sat down to one side in deep shame and terrible dejection. Brünnhilde remains standing at the front of the stage, gazing in her anguish at the disappearing forms of Siegfried and Gutrune, before lowering her head.) [19, 57]

SCENE FIVE

BRÜNNHILDE
(wholly absorbed in her thoughts)

Welches Unhold's List	[64]	What demon's art
liegt hier verhohlen?		lies hidden here?
Welches Zaubers Rath[165]		What store[165] of magic
regte dieß auf?	[34]	stirred this up?

Wo ist nun mein Wissen		Where now is my wisdom
gegen dieß Wirrsal?		against this bewilderment?
Wo sind meine Runen		Where are my runes
gegen dieß Räthsel?		against this riddle?
Ach Jammer! Jammer!		Ah, sorrow! Sorrow!
Weh'! ach Wehe!		Woe, ah woe!
All' mein Wissen	[49]	All my wisdom
wies ich ihm zu:	[57]	I gave to him:
in seiner Macht		in his power
hält er die Magd;		he holds the maid;
in seinen Banden		in his bonds
hält er die Beute,		he holds the booty
die, jammernd ob ihrer Schmach,		which, sorrowing for her shame,
jauchzend der reiche verschenkt! –	[65]	the rich man exultantly gave away. –

Wer bietet mir nun das Schwert,	[64, 3]	Who'll offer me now the sword
mit dem ich die Bande zerschnitt'?		with which to sever those bonds?

HAGEN
(drawing closer to Brünnhilde)

Vertraue mir,	Have trust in me,
betrog'ne Frau!	deserted wife!
Wer dich verrieth,	Whoever betrayed you,
das räche ich.	I shall avenge it.

BRÜNNHILDE
(looking round, weakly)

An wem?	On whom?

HAGEN

An Siegfried, der dich betrog.	On Siegfried, who deceived you.

BRÜNNHILDE

An Siegfried? .. du?	On Siegfried? .. You?

(smiling bitterly)

Ein einz'ger Blick	A single glance
seines blitzenden Auges	from his flashing eye –
– das selbst durch die Lügengestalt	which, even through his false disguise,
leuchtend strahlte zu mir –	brightly lighted upon me –
deinen besten Muth	would make
machte er bangen!	your greatest courage quail!

HAGEN

Doch meinem Speere	Would not his false oath
spart' ihn sein Meineid?	mark him out for my spear?

BRÜNNHILDE

Eid und Meineid –	Oaths true or false –
müssige Acht!	an idle concern!
Nach stärk'rem späh',	Seek stronger means

deinen Speer zu waffnen,
willst du den stärksten besteh'n!

to arm your spear
if you'd best the strongest of men!

HAGEN

Wohl kenn' ich Siegfried's
siegende Kraft,
wie schwer im Kampf er zu fällen:

How well do I know Siegfried's
conquering strength,
how hard it would be to kill him in
[battle:

d'rum raune nun du
mir guten Rath,
wie doch der Recke mir wich'?

so whisper me
sound advice and say
how the hero may yield to my might.

BRÜNNHILDE

O Undank! schändlichster Lohn!
Nicht eine Kunst
war mir bekannt,
die zum Heil nicht half seinem Leib'! [51]
Unwissend zähmt' ihn
mein Zauberspiel,
das ihn vor Wunden nun gewahrt.

O rank ingratitude! Shameful reward!
Not a single art
was known to me
that did not help to keep his body safe!
Unknown to him, he was tamed
by my magic spells
which ward him now against wounds.

HAGEN

So kann keine Wehr ihm schaden?

And so no weapon can harm him?

BRÜNNHILDE

Im Kampfe nicht: – doch –
träf'st du im Rücken ihn.
Niemals – das wußt' ich –
wich' er dem Feind, [35]
nie reicht' er fliehend ihm den
[Rücken: [23]
an ihm d'rum spart' ich den
[Segen.[166]

In battle, no! But –
if you struck him in the back.
Never, I knew,
would he yield to a foe,
never, fleeing, present his back;

so I spared it the spell's protection.[166]

HAGEN

Und dort trifft ihn mein Speer! [64] And there my spear shall strike him!
(He turns quickly away from Brünnhilde and towards Gunther.)

Auf, Gunther,
edler Gibichung!
Hier steht dein starkes Weib: [6]
was häng'st du dort in Harm?

Up, Gunther,
noble Gibichung!
Here stands your stalwart wife:
why hang your head in grief?

GUNTHER
(with an impassioned outburst)

O Schmach!
O Schande!
Wehe mir,
dem jammervollsten Manne!

O shame!
O disgrace!
Woe is me,
most sorrowful of men!

HAGEN

In Schande lieg'st du –   You're beset by disgrace,
läugn' ich das?   can I deny it?

BRÜNNHILDE
(to Gunther)

O feiger Mann!   O craven man!
Falscher Genoß!   False companion!
Hinter dem Helden   Behind the hero
hehltest du dich,   you hid yourself,
daß Preise des Ruhmes   that the harvest of fame
er dir erränge!   he might reap for you!
Tief wohl sank   The much-loved race
das theure Geschlecht,   has sunk far indeed
das solche Zagen gezeugt!   that fathers such faint-hearts as you!

GUNTHER
(beside himself)

Betrüger ich – und betrogen!   Deceiver I – and deceived!
Verräther ich – und verrathen! – Betrayer I – and betrayed!
Zermalmt mir das Mark,   Crush my bones,[167]
zerbrecht mir die Brust!   break my breast!
  Hilf, Hagen!   Help, Hagen!
  Hilf meiner Ehre!   Help my honour!
  Hilf deiner Mutter,   Help your mother,
die mich[168] – auch ja gebar!   who bore me too in truth!

HAGEN

  Dir hilft kein Hirn,   [64]   No brain can help you,
  dir hilft keine Hand: no hand can help you,
dir hilft nur – Siegfried's Tod! [3]   only Siegfried's death can help you!

GUNTHER
(seized with horror)

Siegfried's Tod!   Siegfried's death!

HAGEN

Nur der sühnt deine Schmach.   That alone can purge your shame.

GUNTHER
(staring ahead of him)

Blutbrüderschaft   [63]   Blood-brotherhood
schwuren wir uns!   we swore to one another!

HAGEN

Des Bundes Bruch   May blood now atone
sühne nun Blut!   for the broken bond!

GUNTHER

Brach er den Bund?   Did he break the bond?

HAGEN

Da er dich verrieth.   When he betrayed you!

GUNTHER

Verrieth er mich?   Did he betray me?

BRÜNNHILDE

Dich verrieth er,   You he betrayed,
und mich verriethet ihr alle!   and me have you all betrayed!
Wär' ich gerecht,   If I had my due,
alles Blut der Welt   all the blood in the world
büßte mir nicht eure Schuld!   could never make good your guilt!
Doch des Einen Tod   But one man's death
taugt mir für alle: [56]   will serve me for all:
Siegfried falle –   may Siegfried fall
zur Sühne für sich und euch!   to atone for himself and you!

HAGEN
(turning to Gunther)
Er falle –   May he fall –
(secretively)
        dir zum Heil!   for your good!
Ungeheure Macht wird dir,   [6]   Tremendous power will then be yours
gewinn'st von ihm du den Ring,   if you win from him the ring
den der Tod ihm wohl nur entreißt.   that death alone would wrest from him.

GUNTHER
(softly)
Brünnhilde's Ring?   Brünnhilde's ring?

HAGEN

Des Nibelungen Reif.   The Niblung's band.

GUNTHER
(sighing deeply)
So wär' es Siegfried's Ende!   [64, 3]   Must this be Siegfried's end?

HAGEN

Uns allen frommt sein Tod.   His death will serve us all.

GUNTHER

Doch Gutrune, ach!   [61]   But Gutrune, ah!
der ich ihn gönnte: whom I didn't begrudge him:
straften den Gatten wir so,   if we punished her husband so,
wie bestünden wir vor ihr?   how would we stand in her sight?

BRÜNNHILDE
(flaring up in her rage)
Was rieth mir mein Wissen?   What did my wisdom tell me?
Was wiesen mich Runen?   What did my runes have to teach me?
Im hilflosen Elend   In my helpless distress

achtet mir's hell:
Gutrune heißt der Zauber,
der den Gatten[169] mir entzückt!
Angst treffe sie!

it dawns on me now:
Gutrun's the name of the spell
that spirited away my husband![169]
May she be struck by dread!

HAGEN
(to Gunther)

Muß sein Tod sie betrüben,
verhehlt sei ihr die That.
Auf munt'res Jagen
ziehen wir morgen:
der Edle braus't uns voran –
ein Eber bracht' ihn da um.

Since his death is bound to afflict her,
then let the deed be hid from her.
Tomorrow let's merrily
go a-hunting:
the noble hero will rush on ahead –
a boar might bring him down.

GUNTHER AND BRÜNNHILDE

So soll es sein!
Siegfried falle:
sühn' er die Schmach,
die er mir schuf!
Des Eides Treue
hat er getrogen:
mit seinem Blut
büß' er die Schuld!

So shall it be!
May Siegfried fall:
let him purge the shame
that he caused me!
The oath of loyalty
he has betrayed:
with his blood
let him cleanse his guilt!

Allrauner![170]
Rächender Gott!
Schwurwissender
Eideshort!
Wotan!
Wende dich her!
Weise die schrecklich
heilige Schaar,
hieher zu horchen
dem Racheschwur!

All-wise,[170]
avenging god!
Oath-knowing
guardian of vows!
Wotan!
Turn this way!
Bid your awesomely
hallowed host
come hither to hear
this oath of vengeance!

[67]

HAGEN

Sterb' er dahin,
der strahlende Held!
Mein ist der Hort,
mir muß er gehören:
d'rum sei der Reif
ihm entrissen!

So let him die,
the radiant hero!
Mine is the hoard,
it must be mine:
so let the ring
be wrested from him!

Alben-Vater!
Gefall'ner Fürst!
Nacht-Hüter!
Niblungen-Herr!
Alberich!
Achte auf mich!
Weise von neuem

Elfen father,
fallen prince!
Guardian of night!
Nibelung lord!
Alberich!
Heed me!
Bid the

der Niblungen Schaar,
dir zu gehorchen,
des Reifes Herrn!

Nibelung host
obey you anew,
the lord of the ring!

(As Gunther turns impetuously to the hall with Brünnhilde, they are met by the bridal procession on its way out. Boys and girls, waving flowers, dance merrily at its head. Siegfried is carried on a shield by the men, Gutrune on a chair. On the slope at the back servants and maidservants bring sacrificial implements and animals over the various mountain paths to the altar-stones, which they decorate with flowers. Siegfried and the menfolk sound the wedding-call on their horns. The women invite Brünnhilde to walk alongside Gutrune with them. Brünnhilde stares blankly at Gutrune, who beckons her with a friendly smile. Brünnhilde is on the point of withdrawing impetuously, when Hagen quickly intervenes and pushes her towards Gunther, who seizes her hand once again and leads her over to the women. He then invites the menfolk to raise him on a shield. [64] After this brief interruption, the procession quickly resumes its progress towards the slope at the back, as the curtain falls.) [3]

Act Three

Prelude and Scene One

([40, 3, 67, 1a, 5, 4] The curtain rises.[171] A wild, wooded and rocky valley along the Rhine, which flows past a steep cliff at the back of the stage. The three Rhinedaughters (Woglinde, Wellgunde and Flosshilde), swim to the surface and swim round in a circle, as though performing a dance.)

THE THREE RHINEDAUGHTERS
(pausing briefly in their swimming)

Frau Sonne[172]	The sun-goddess[172]
sendet lichte Strahlen;	sends her bright-shining beams;
Nacht liegt in der Tiefe: [4]	night lies in the depths:
einst war sie hell,	once it was light
da heil und hehr	when, safe and hallowed,
des Vaters Gold noch in ihr glänzte!	our father's gold still gleamed there.
Rhein-Gold,	Rhinegold,
klares Gold!	radiant gold!
Wie hell du einsten strahltest,	How brightly you used to shine,
hehrer Stern der Tiefe!	you hallowed star of the deep.

(They resume their aquatic dance.)

Weialala leia,	Weialala leia,
wallala leialala!	wallala leialala!

(Distant horn call. They listen, then beat the water in jubilation.)

Frau Sonne,	O sun-goddess,
sende uns den Helden,	send us the hero
der das Gold uns wieder gebe!	who may give us back the gold!
Ließ' er es uns,	If he left it with us,
dein lichtes Auge	your bright-shining eye
neideten dann wir nicht länger!	we'd then need envy no longer!

Rhein-Gold,
klares Gold!
Wie froh du dann strahltest,
freier Stern der Tiefe!

Rhinegold,
radiant gold!
How happily then you would shine,
you free-spirited star of the deep!

(Siegfried's horn call is heard, closer than before.)

WOGLINDE

Ich höre sein Horn.

I can hear his horn.

WOGLINDE

Der Helde naht.

The hero's approaching.

FLOSSHILDE

Laßt uns berathen!

Let us take counsel!

(All three plunge beneath the waves. Siegfried appears on the cliff, fully armed.)

SIEGFRIED

Ein Albe führte mich irr',
daß ich die Fährte verlor: –
He Schelm! In welchem Berge
barg'st du so schnell mir das Wild?

An elf has led me astray,
so that I lost the trail: –
Hey, rogue! In which hill
have you hidden the game so swiftly?

THE THREE RHINEDAUGHTERS
(resurfacing and resuming their dance)

Siegfried!

Siegfried!

FLOSSHILDE

Was schilt'st du so in den Grund?

Why are you grumbling at the ground?

WELLGUNDE

Welchem Alben bist du gram?

With whatever elf are you angry?

WOGLINDE

Hat dich ein Nicker geneckt?

Has a nixie been teasing you?

ALL THREE

Sag' es, Siegfried, sag' es uns!

Tell us, Siegfried, tell us!

SIEGFRIED
(observing them with a smile)

Entzücktet ihr zu euch
den zottigen Gesellen,
der mir verschwand?
Ist's euer Friedel,
euch lustigen Frauen
lass' ich ihn gern.

Did you spirit away
the shaggy-haired fellow
who disappeared from my sight?
If he's your lover,
I gladly leave him to you,
you light-hearted women.

(The Rhinedaughters laugh.)

WOGLINDE

Siegfried, was giebst du uns,

Siegfried, what will you give us,

wenn wir das Wild dir gönnen?	if we grant you your game?

SIEGFRIED

Noch bin ich beutelos:	I'm still without a catch,
so bittet, was ihr begehrt.	so ask what you desire.

WELLGUNDE

Ein gold'ner Ring	A golden ring
glänzt dir am Finger –	glints upon your finger –

ALL THREE

Den gieb uns!	Give that to us!

SIEGFRIED

Einen Riesenwurm	A giant dragon
erschlug ich um den Reif:	I slew for the sake of this ring;
für eines schlechten Bären Tatzen	should I offer it now
böt' ich ihn nun zum Tausch?	in return for a mangy bear-skin?

WOGLINDE

Bist du so karg?	Are you so mean?

WELLGUNDE

So geizig beim Kauf?	So miserly in your dealings?

FLOSSHILDE

Freigebig	You ought to be
solltest Frauen du sein.	open-handed with women.

SIEGFRIED

Verzehrt' ich an euch mein Gut,	If I wasted my wealth on you,
dess' zürnte mir wohl mein Weib.	my wife would surely chide me.

FLOSSHILDE

Sie ist wohl schlimm?	I expect she's strict.

WELLGUNDE

Sie schlägt dich wohl?	I expect she beats you.

WOGLINDE

Ihre Hand fühlt schon der Held!	The hero's already felt her hand!

(They laugh immoderately.)

SIEGFRIED

Nun lacht nur lustig zu!	Laugh as much as you like!
In Harm lass' ich euch doch:	I'll still leave you to your sorrow:
denn giert ihr nach dem Ring,	for though you desire the ring,
euch Neckern geb' ich ihn nie.	I'll never give it to you, you teasers.

(The Rhinedaughters have resumed their dance.)

FLOSSHILDE

So schön!   So handsome!

WELLGUNDE

So stark!   So strong!

WOGLINDE

So gehrenswerth!   And so desirable!

ALL THREE

Wie schade, daß er geizig ist!   What a pity that he's stingy!
(They laugh and dive beneath the waves.)

SIEGFRIED
(descending further into the valley)

Wie leid' ich doch   Why should I brook
das karge Lob?   such meagre praise?
Lass' ich so mich schmäh'n? –   Shall I let myself be so reviled? –
Kämen sie wieder   If they came back
zum Wasserrand,   to the water's edge,
den Ring könnten sie haben. –   the ring would be theirs for the asking. –
(calling out)

He! Hehe! Ihr munt'ren   Hey! Hey there! You merry
Wasserminnen!   water-maids!
Kommt rasch: ich schenk' euch den   Come quickly! I'll give you the ring!
[Ring!
(He has removed the ring from his finger and holds it up. The Rhinedaughters return to the surface. They adopt a serious, solemn stance.)

FLOSSHILDE

Behalt' ihn, Held,   [4]   Hold on to it, hero,
und wahr' ihn wohl,   and ward it well,
bis du das Unheil erräth'st,   [6]   until you divine the evil,

WOGLINDE AND WELLGUNDE

das in dem Ring du heg'st.   that you harbour within the ring.

ALL THREE

Froh fühl'st du dich dann,   You'll then feel glad
befrei'n wir dich von dem Fluch.   that we freed you from its curse.

SIEGFRIED
(calmly replacing the ring on his finger)

So singet was ihr wiss't!   Then sing of what you know!

THE RHINEDAUGHTERS

Siegfried! Siegfried! Siegfried!   Siegfried! Siegfried! Siegfried!
Schlimmes wissen wir dir.   Evil we know lies in store for you.

WELLGUNDE

Zu deinem Unheil   To your own undoing
wahr'st du den Ring!   you keep the ring!

ALL THREE

Aus des Rheines Gold   [4]   From the gold of the Rhine
ist der Ring geglüht: the ring was annealed:

WELLGUNDE

der ihn listig geschmiedet   he who cunningly wrought it

WOGLINDE

und schmählich verlor,   and shamefully lost it

ALL THREE

der verfluchte ihn,   laid a curse upon it,
in fernster Zeit   [19]   until the end of time
zu zeugen den Tod   to bring about the death
dem, der ihn trüg'.   of him who wears it.

FLOSSHILDE

Wie den Wurm du fälltest,   Just as you felled the dragon,

WELLGUNDE AND FLOSSHILDE

so fäll'st auch du,   so you too shall fall

ALL THREE

und heute noch   this very day
− so heißen wir's dir: −   [3]   − this fate we foretell −
tauschest den Ring du uns nicht, [5, 15] if you don't hand over the ring to us

WELLGUNDE AND FLOSSHILDE

im tiefen Rhein ihn zu bergen.   to be hidden away in the deep-flowing
                                         [Rhine.

ALL THREE

Nur seine Fluth   Its floodtide alone
sühnet den Fluch.   [1b]   can atone for the curse.

SIEGFRIED

Ihr listigen Frauen,   You crafty women,
lass't das sein!   have done!
Traut' ich kaum eurem Schmeicheln,   Since I scarcely believed your flattering
                                         [tongues,
euer Drohen schreckt mich noch   your threats can alarm me still less.
[minder.

THE RHINEDAUGHTERS

Siegfried! Siegfried!   Siegfried! Siegfried!
Wir weisen dich wahr: We're telling the truth:

weiche, weiche dem Fluch!
  Ihn flochten nächtlich
  webende Nornen
in des Urgesetzes Seil!

[6] avoid, avoid the curse!
  Night-spinning Norns
  have woven it
into the rope of primeval law.

SIEGFRIED

Mein Schwert zerschwang einen
  [Speer: –
  des Urgesetzes
  ewiges Seil,
  flochten sie wilde
  Flüche hinein,
Nothung zerhaut es den Nornen!

My sword once splintered a spear:

  primeval law's
  eternal rope
  – though they wove
  wild curses into its strands –
Nothung will hew from the hands of the
  [Norns!

  Wohl warnte mich einst
  vor dem Fluch' ein Wurm,
doch das Fürchten lehrt' er mich
  [nicht; –

[46] A dragon once warned me
  against the curse,
but it did not teach me fear; –

(He looks at the ring.) [5]

  der Welt Erbe
  gewänne mir ein Ring:
  für der Minne Gunst
  miss' ich ihn gern;
ich geb' ihn euch, gönnt ihr mir
  [Gunst.
Doch bedroht ihr mir Leben und
  [Leib:
  faßte er nicht
  eines Fingers Werth –
den Reif entringt ihr mir nicht!
  Denn Leben und Leib –
  seht! – so

[8a, 8b] though the ring were to win me
  the world's inheritance,
  for the sake of love's favours
  I gladly forgo it;
I'll give it to you if you grant me your
  [favours.
But since you threaten both life and limb

  – though it were worth
  not a whit –
[3] the ring you'll never wrest from me!
  For life and limb –
[6] lo: thus

(He picks up a clod of earth from the ground, holds it above his head and with the final words throws it behind him.)

werf' ich sie weit von mir![173]

do I fling them far away from me![173]

THE RHINEDAUGHTERS

Kommt, Schwestern!
Schwindet dem Thoren!
So weise und stark
  verwähnt sich der Held,
als gebunden und blind er doch ist.

Come, sisters!
Flee from the fool!
Wise and strong
  as he weens himself,
the hero is hoppled and blind.

(In wild agitation they swim close to the shore in widening circles.)

Eide schwur er –
und achtet sie nicht;

Oaths he swore
and doesn't heed them;

(More violent movement.)

Runen weiß er –
und räth sie nicht.

runes he knows
and cannot read them.

Ein hehrstes Gut	[56]	A most hallowed gift
ward ihm gegönnt –		was granted to him –

ALL THREE

daß er's verworfen   that he's cast it away
weiß er nicht: he doesn't know:

FLOSSHILDE

nur den Ring,   the ring alone,

WELLGUNDE

der zum Tod ihm taugt –   which will deal him death –

ALL THREE

den Reif nur will er sich wahren!   the circlet alone he wishes to keep!

Leb' wohl, Siegfried!   Fare well, Siegfried!
Ein stolzes Weib   A proud-hearted woman
wird noch heut' dich argen beerben: will be your heir today, you wretch:
sie beut uns bess'res Gehör.   she'll give us a fairer hearing.
Zu ihr! Zu ihr! Zu ihr!   To her! To her! To her!

(They quickly resume their dance and swim away, at a leisurely pace, towards the back of the stage. Siegfried watches them go with a smile, one leg resting on a rocky outcrop on the shore, while supporting his chin with his hand.)

Weialala leia,   Weialala leia,
Wallala leialala.   Wallala leialala.

SIEGFRIED

Im Wasser wie am Lande   In water as on land
lernte nun ich Weiberart: I've learned the ways of women now:
wer nicht ihrem Schmeicheln traut,   the man who's not taken in by their
                            [wheedling,
den schrecken sie mit Drohen;   they frighten with their threats;
wer dem nun kühnlich trotzt,   he who dares to defy them

(By now the Rhinedaughters have disappeared completely.)

dem kommt dann ihr Keifen dran. –   then has to suffer their scolding tongues. –
Und doch –   And yet –

(The Rhinedaughters can be heard in the farther distance.)

trüg' ich nicht Gutrun' Treu',   were I not true to Gutrun',
der zieren Frauen eine   one of these winsome women
hätt' ich mir frisch gezähmt!   I'd have wasted no time in taming!

(He continues to watch after them. Hunting horns can be heard approaching over the heights at the back of the stage.) [19]

HAGEN'S VOICE
(from afar)

Hoiho!   [3]   Hoiho!

(Siegfried starts up from his dreamy rêverie and answers the call with his horn.) [40]

Scene Two

VASSALS' VOICES
(offstage)

Hoiho! Hoiho!   Hoiho! Hoiho!

SIEGFRIED
(answering)

Hoiho! Hoiho! Hoihe!   Hoiho! Hoiho! Hoihey!

(Hagen appears on the cliff top, followed by Gunther.)

HAGEN
(catching sight of Siegfried)

Finden wir endlich   At last have we found
wohin du flogest?   where you fled?

SIEGFRIED

Kommt herab! Hier ist frisch und   Come below! It's cool and refreshing
  [kühl!   [here!

(The vassals all arrive on the cliff top and, together with Hagen and Gunther, descend into the valley.)

HAGEN

Hier rasten wir   Let's rest here
und rüsten das Mahl.   and prepare the meal.

(The spoils of the hunt are placed in a pile.)

Laßt ruh'n die Beute   Put down the bag
und bietet die Schläuche!   and hand round the wineskins!

(Wineskins and drinking-horns are produced. All settle down.)

Der uns das Wild verscheuchte,   He who scared away our game,
nun sollt ihr Wunder hören   you'll now hear wondrous things
was Siegfried sich erjagt.[174]   of all that Siegfried hunted down.[174]

SIEGFRIED

Schlimm steht es um mein Mahl: I'm ill provided for my meal:
  von eurer Beute   some of your spoils
  bitte ich für mich.   I must beg for myself.

HAGEN

Du beutelos?   You're empty-handed?

SIEGFRIED

Auf Waldjagd zog ich aus,   I set out in search of wood-game
doch Wasserwild zeigte sich nur: but only waterfowl showed itself:
war ich dazu recht berathen,   had I been better equipped,
drei wilde Wasservögel   I might have caught for you
hätt' ich euch wohl gefangen,   three wild waterbirds,
die dort auf dem Rhein mir sangen,   who sang to me there on the Rhine
erschlagen würd' ich noch heut'. [3]   that I would be slain today.

(Gunther starts and looks darkly at Hagen. Siegfried settles down between Gunther and Hagen.) [64]

HAGEN
(giving instructions to one of the vassals to fill a drinking-horn for Siegfried, which he then offers the latter)

Das wäre üb'le Jagd,	It would be an ill-fated hunt
wenn den beutelosen selbst	if the luckless hunter himself
ein lauernd Wild erlegte!	were brought down by a lurking head of [game!

SIEGFRIED

Mich dürstet!	I'm thirsty!

HAGEN

Ich hörte sagen, Siegfried,		Siegfried, I've heard it said
der Vögel Sanges-Sprache	[47a]	you can understand
verstündest du wohl:		the language of birdsong:
so wäre das wahr?	[47b]	can it be true?

SIEGFRIED

Seit lange acht' ich	It's long since
des Lallens nicht mehr.	I've heeded their warbling.

(He seizes the drinking-horn and turns to Gunther with it. He drinks and offers the horn to Gunther.) [67]

Trink', Gunther, trink'!	Drink, Gunther, drink!
Dein Bruder bringt es dir.	To you your brother brings it.

(Gunther looks into the horn with horror.)

GUNTHER
(dully)

Du mischtest matt und bleich: −	You've mixed it insipid and pale:

(even more subdued)

dein Blut allein darin!	[64]	your blood alone is in it!

SIEGFRIED
(laughing)

So misch' es mit dem deinen!	So mix it with your own!

(He pours wine from Gunther's horn into his own so that it overflows.) [67]

Nun floß gemischt es über:	Mixed, it's overflowed:
der Mutter Erde	to Mother Earth
lass' das ein Labsal sein!	let it bring refreshment!

GUNTHER
(with a deep sigh)

Du überfroher Held!	You overjoyous hero!

SIEGFRIED
(quietly to Hagen)

Ihm macht Brünnhilde Müh'?	Is Brünnhilde making him brood?

HAGEN

(quietly to Siegfried)

Verstünd' er sie so gut,   If only he understood her
wie du der Vögel Sang!   as you do the singing of birds!

SIEGFRIED

Seit Frauen ich singen hörte, [47b, 48] Since I've heard women singing,
vergaß ich der Vög'lein ganz.   I've quite forgotten those songsters.

HAGEN

Doch einst vernahm'st du sie?   Yet once you knew what they said?

SIEGFRIED

(turning animatedly to Gunther)

Hei! Gunther!   Hey! Gunther,
Grämlicher Mann!   woebegone man!
Dank'st du es mir,   If you'll thank me for it,
so sing' ich dir Mären   I'll sing you tales
aus meinen jungen Tagen.[175] about my boyhood days.[175]

GUNTHER

Die hör' ich gern.   I'd like to hear them.

(All settle down close to Siegfried, who is the only one to sit upright, while the others lie outstretched further downstage.) [47a, 47b, 48]

HAGEN

So singe, Held!   Sing on then, hero!

SIEGFRIED

Mime hieß   [15] In thrall to greed,
ein mürrischer Zwerg; a surly dwarf
in des Neides Zwang by the name of Mime
zog er mich auf,   brought me up,
daß einst das Kind, so that, when the child
wann kühn es erwuchs, was bigger and bolder,
einen Wurm ihm fäll' im Wald, he'd fell a dragon in the forest
der lang' dort hütet' einen Hort. that long had guarded a hoard there.
Er lehrte mich schmieden He taught me forging
und Erze schmelzen: and smelting ores:
doch was der Künstler but what the artist
selber nicht konnt', himself could not do,
des Lehrlings Muthe the prentice's courage
mußt' es gelingen – was bound to achieve –
eines zerschlag'nen Stahles Stücken to weld together into a sword
neu zu schweißen zum Schwert. [23] the fragments of a shattered blade.
Des Vaters Wehr   My father's weapon
fügt' ich mir neu;   I fit together;
nagelfest   as hard as nails
schuf ich mir Nothung; I fashioned Nothung;
tüchtig zum Kampf it seemed to the dwarf

dünkt' er dem Zwerg:		to be fit for the fight:
der führte mich nun zum Wald; [8]		so he led me into the wildwood
dort fällt' ich Fafner, den Wurm.		and there I felled Fafner, the dragon.

Jetzt aber merkt
  wohl auf die Mär':
Wunder muß ich euch melden. [27]
  Von des Wurmes Blut
  mir brannten die Finger;
sie führt' ich kühlend zum Mund:

But now listen
  closely to the tale:
wondrous things I must tell you.
  The dragon's blood
  burned my fingers;
to cool them, I raised them up to my
  [mouth:

  kaum netzt' ein wenig
  die Zunge das Naß, –
was da die Vög'lein sangen,
das konnt' ich flugs versteh'n.
Auf den Ästen saß es und sang: –
»Hei, Siegfried gehört nun [48]
  der Niblungen Hort:
  o fänd' in der Höhle
  den Hort er jetzt!
Wollt' er den Tarnhelm gewinnen,
der taugt' ihm zu wonniger That!
doch wollt' er den Ring sich errathen,
der macht' ihn zum Walter der
  [Welt!«

  the gore had scarcely
  wet my tongue
when all at once I understood
what the little birds were singing.
On the boughs one sat and sang: –
'Hey! Siegfried now owns
  the Nibelung hoard:
  o might he now find
  the hoard in the cave!
If he wanted to win the tarnhelm,
it would serve him for wondrous deeds!
But could he acquire the ring,
it would make him the lord of the
  [world!'

HAGEN

Ring und Tarnhelm	[27]	Ring and tarnhelm
trug'st du nun fort?		you bore away?

A VASSAL

Das Vög'lein hörtest du wieder?	Did you hear the woodbird again?

SIEGFRIED

Ring und Tarnhelm
hatt' ich gerafft;
  da lauscht' ich wieder
  dem wonnigen Laller;
der saß im Wipfel und sang: –
»Hei, Siegfried gehört nun [48]
  der Helm und der Ring:
  o traute er Mime,
  dem treulosen, nicht!
Ihm sollt' er den Hort nur erheben;
nun lauert er listig am Weg:
nach dem Leben trachtet er
  [Siegfried –
o traute Siegfried nicht Mime!« [27]

Ring and tarnhelm
I'd gathered up;
  then I listened again
  to the wonderful warbler;
it sat in the treetop and sang: –
'Hey, Siegfried now owns
  the helm and the ring:
  oh let him not trust
  the treacherous Mime!
He only wants him to win him the hoard;
now he's craftily lying in wait
and seeking to take Siegfried's life –
oh let him not trust Mime!'

HAGEN

Es mahnte dich gut?   Did he warn you well?

FOUR VASSALS

Vergaltest du Mime?   You rewarded Mime?

SIEGFRIED

Mit tödtlichem Tranke   With deadly drink
trat er zu mir;   he came over to me;
bang und stotternd   timid and stuttering
gestand er mir Böses: he confessed evil thoughts:
Nothung streckte den Strolch.   Nothung laid the rogue low.

HAGEN
(laughing harshly)

Was nicht er geschmiedet   [15]   What he hadn't forged
schmeckte doch Mime!   Mime felt all the same!

(Hagen has the drinking-horn refilled and squeezes the juice of a herb into it.)

TWO VASSALS

Was wies das Vög'lein dich wieder?   What else did the bird have to tell you?

HAGEN

Trink' erst, Held,   Drink first, hero,
aus meinem Horn: from my horn:
ich würzte dir holden Trank,   I've seasoned a sweet-tasting drink
die Erinnerung hell dir zu wecken, [16]   to stir your memory afresh
(He hands Siegfried the horn.)
das Fernes nicht dir entfalle!   so that distant things don't escape you!

SIEGFRIED
(gazing thoughtfully into the horn and then drinking slowly from it) [57, 56]
In Leid zu dem Wipfel   In sadness I raised
lauscht' ich hinauf;   an ear to the treetop:
da saß es noch und sang: –   it sat there still and sang: –
»Hei, Siegfried erschlug nun   [48]   'Hey! Siegfried's now slain
den schlimmen Zwerg!   the evil dwarf!
Jetzt wüßt' ich ihm noch   Now I know
das herrlichste Weib: –   the most glorious wife for him: –
auf hohem Felsen sie schläft,   [47b]   high on a fell she sleeps,
Feuer umbrennt ihren Saal;   fire burns round her hall;
durchschritt' er die Brunst,   if he passed through the blaze
weckt' er die Braut,   [47a]   and awakened the bride,
Brünnhilde wäre dann sein!«   Brünnhilde then would be his!'

HAGEN

Und folgtest du   And did you follow
des Vög'leins Rathe?   the bird's advice?

SIEGFRIED

Rasch ohne Zögern zog ich nun aus,	Without delay I set out at once

(Gunther listens with increasing astonishment.)

bis den feurigen Fels ich traf; die Lohe durchschritt ich, und fand zum Lohn –	till I came to the fiery fell; I passed through the flames and found as reward

(with mounting ecstasy)

schlafend ein wonniges Weib [39] in lichter Waffen Gewand. Den Helm löst' ich der herrlichen Maid; mein Kuß erweckte sie kühn: – o wie mich brünstig da umschlang [49] der schönen Brünnhilde Arm!	a wondrous woman asleep in a suit of shining armour. I loosed the glorious woman's helmet; emboldened, my kiss awoke her: – oh! how the fair Brünnhilde's arm clasped me in its ardour!

GUNTHER
(leaping up in utter horror)

Was hör' ich?	[14b]	What's that I hear?

(Two ravens fly up out of a bush, circle over Siegfried and then fly off in the direction of the Rhine.)

HAGEN

Erräth'st du auch dieser Raben Geraun'?	Can you also guess what those ravens whispered?

(Siegfried starts up suddenly and, turning his back on Hagen, watches the ravens fly away.)
[3, 19]

Rache riethen sie mir!	To me they counselled vengeance!

(Hagen thrusts his spear into Siegfried's back. Gunther and the vassals throw themselves at Hagen. Siegfried raises his shield in both hands in order to throw it at Hagen: his strength fails him; the shield falls to the ground behind him and he himself collapses on top of it.) [35]

FOUR VASSALS
(having tried in vain to restrain Hagen)

Hagen! was thu'st du?	Hagen, what are you doing?

TWO OTHERS

Was thatest du?	What have you done?

GUNTHER

Hagen, – was thatest du?	[34]	Hagen, – what have you done?

HAGEN

Meineid rächt' ich!	A false oath I avenged!

(Hagen turns away calmly and disappears over the cliff top, where he can be seen walking away slowly through the gathering gloom. Griefstricken, Gunther bends down beside Siegfried. In a gesture of sympathy, the vassals form a circle round the dying man.)

SIEGFRIED
(supported in a sitting position by two men, opens his eyes radiantly)

Brünnhilde –	Brünnhilde –
heilige Braut –	hallowed bride –
wach' auf! öff'ne dein Auge! –	awaken! Unclose your eyes! –
Wer verschloß dich	Who locked you
wieder in Schlaf?	in sleep once again?
Wer band dich in Schlummer so	Who bound you in slumber's dread
[bang? – –	[bonds? – –
Der Wecker kam;	One came to wake you;
er küßt dich wach, [35]	his kiss awakes you
und aber der Braut	and once again he breaks
bricht er die Bande: –	the bride's bonds: –
da lacht ihm Brünnhilde's Lust! –	and Brünnhilde's joy laughs upon him. –
Ach, dieses Auge, [50]	Ah! Those eyes –
ewig nun offen! –	now open for ever! –
Ach, dieses Athems	Ah, this breath's
wonniges Wehen! – [51]	enchanted sighing!
Süßes Vergehen –	Sweet extinction, –
seliges Grauen – :	blissful terror – :
Brünnhild' bietet mir – Gruß! –	Brünnhild' gives me her greeting! –

(Siegfried sinks back and dies. Motionless grief on the part of those around him. [27] Night has fallen. At Gunther's silent command, the vassals lift up Siegfried's body and, during the following, carry it away slowly in solemn procession over the cliff top. [29] The moon breaks through the clouds and casts an increasingly bright light on the funeral procession which has now reached the top of the cliff. [26b] Mists have risen from the Rhine and gradually fill the whole of the stage, on which the funeral procession has already become invisible, so that it remains completely hidden throughout the musical interlude. [27, 23, 35, 55] From this point onwards[176] the mists begin to divide again, until finally the Hall of the Gibichungs can be made out once more, as in the opening act.) [56]

SCENE THREE

(It is night. Moonlight is mirrored in the surface of the Rhine. [19, 55] Gutrune enters the hall from her chamber.) [61]

GUTRUNE

War das sein Horn? [40]	Was that his horn?
	(She listens.)
Nein! – Noch	No! He's still
kehrt' er nicht heim. –	not come home. –
Schlimme Träume	Troubled dreams
störten mir den Schlaf! –	disturbed my sleep! –
Wild wieherte sein Roß: –	His horse was neighing wildly: –
Lachen Brünnhilde's[177]	Brünnhilde's laughter[177]
weckte mich auf. – –	woke me up. – –
Wer war das Weib,	Who was the woman
das ich zum Ufer schreiten sah? – [5]	I saw going down to the shore? –
Ich fürchte Brünnhild'! –	I'm afraid of Brünnhild'! –

| Ist sie daheim? [34] | Is she within? |

(She listens at the door on the left and calls out.)

| Brünnhild'! Brünnhild'! | Brünnhild'! Brünnhild'! |
| Bist du wach? – | Are you awake? – |

(She opens the door timidly and looks into the inner chamber.) [56]

Leer das Gemach! – –	The chamber's empty! – –
So war es sie,	So it was she
die ich zum Rheine schreiten sah? –	whom I saw going down to the Rhine? –
War das sein Horn? – [67]	Was that his horn? –
Nein! –	No! –
Öd' alles! – –	Everywhere desolate! – –

(Anxiously she looks outside.) [64]

| Säh' ich Siegfried nur bald! | Might I only see Siegfried soon! |

HAGEN'S VOICE
(approaching from outside)

| Hoiho! hoiho! [3] | Hoiho! Hoiho! |

(Hearing Hagen's voice, Gutrune stops and, stricken with fear, remains motionless for a moment.)

Wacht auf! wacht auf!	Wake up! Wake up!
Lichte! Lichte!	Torches! Torches!
Helle Brände!	Lighted firebrands!
Jagdbeute	The spoils of the chase
bringen wir heim.	we're bringing home.
Hoiho! hoiho!	Hoiho! Hoiho!

(The light from the torches increases outside. Hagen enters the hall.) [67]

Auf! Gutrun'!	Up, Gutrun'!
Begrüße Siegfried!	Welcome Siegfried!
Der starke Held,	The doughty hero
er kehrt heim. [55]	is coming home.

GUTRUNE
(in great fear)

| Was geschah, Hagen? [64] | What's happened? Hagen! |
| Nicht hört' ich sein Horn! | I didn't hear his horn! |

(The procession of vassals returning with Siegfried's body is accompanied by a great confusion of men and women carrying torches and firebrands.)

HAGEN

Der bleiche Held,	The bloodless hero
nicht bläs't er es mehr;	will blow it no more;
nicht stürmt er zur Jagd,	no more will he storm
zum Streite nicht mehr,	to hunt or to battle
noch wirbt er um wonnige Frauen!	nor sue for the hand of fair women!

GUTRUNE
(with mounting terror)

| Was bringen die? | What are they bringing? |

(The procession reaches the middle of the hall and the vassals set down the body on a rapidly prepared mound.) [35]

Eines wilden Ebers Beute:
Siegfried, deinen todten Mann!

A wild boar's prey:
Siegfried, your dead husband!

(Gutrune cries out and throws herself on the body. General dismay and grief; Gunther looks to his swooning sister.)

GUNTHER

Gutrun', holde Schwester!
  Hebe dein Auge!
  Schweige mir nicht!

Gutrun', sweet sister,
  raise your eyes!
  Speak to me!

GUTRUNE
(recovering consciousness)

Siegfried! – Siegfried erschlagen!

Siegfried! Siegfried slain!

(She pushes Gunther violently away.)

Fort, treuloser Bruder!
Du Mörder meines Mannes!
  O Hilfe! Hilfe!
  Wehe! Wehe!
Sie haben Siegfried erschlagen!

Away, faithless brother,
my husband's murderer!
  Oh help me! Help me!
  Woe! Ah woe!
They've slaughtered Siegfried!

GUNTHER

Nicht klage wider mich!
Dort klage wider Hagen:
er ist der verfluchte Eber,
der diesen Edlen zerfleischt'.

Hold me not to blame!
Blame Hagen there:
he's the accursèd boar
that rent the noble hero's flesh.

HAGEN

Bist du mir gram darum?

Do you hate me for that?

GUNTHER

Angst und Unheil
greife dich immer!

[65] May fear and misfortune
hound you for ever!

HAGEN
(stepping forward with terrible defiance)

Ja denn! Ich hab' ihn erschlagen:
  ich – Hagen –
  schlug ihn zu todt!
Meinem Speer war er gespart,
bei dem er Meineid sprach.
Heiliges Beute-Recht
hab' ich mir nun errungen:
d'rum fordr' ich hier diesen Ring.

Yes, then! I slew him:
  I – Hagen –
  I struck him dead!
He was marked out by my spear
by which he'd falsely sworn.
I've now acquired
the sacred right of conquest:
and so I demand this ring.

[6]

GUNTHER

Zurück! Was mir verfiel
sollst nimmer du empfah'n.

Get back! What has fallen to me
you'll never receive as your own.

HAGEN

Ihr Mannen, richtet mein Recht!   You vassals, judge my right!

GUNTHER

Rühr'st du an Gutrune's Erbe,   How dare you touch Gutrun's
                                                  [inheritance,

schamloser Albensohn?   shameless son of an elf!

HAGEN
(drawing his sword)

Des Alben Erbe   [19]   The elf's inheritance
fordert so – sein Sohn!   his son now demands!

(He rushes upon Gunther; the latter defends himself; they fight. The vassals throw themselves between them. Hagen strikes Gunther dead.)

Her den Ring!   Give me the ring!

(He reaches towards Siegfried's hand, which raises itself threateningly.[178] Gutrune has cried out in terror as Gunther falls. All remain transfixed with horror. [23] Brünnhilde steps forward from the back of the stage and, firmly and solemnly, moves downstage.) [21]

BRÜNNHILDE
(still at the back of the stage)

Schweigt eures Jammers   [20]   Silence your grief's
jauchzenden Schwall!   exultant clamour!
Das ihr alle verriethet,   His wife, whom you all betrayed,
zur Rache schreitet sein Weib.   [34]   comes in quest of revenge.
(advancing calmly)
Kinder hört' ich   I heard children
greinen nach der Mutter,   whimpering for their mother
da süße Milch sie verschüttet: since they'd spilt some fresh milk:
doch nicht erklang mir   but no sound I heard
würdige Klage,   of a worthy lament
des höchsten Helden werth.   [33]   befitting the greatest of heroes.

GUTRUNE
(raising herself impetuously from the ground)

Brünnhilde! Neid-erbos'te!   Brünnhilde! Grieved by your grudge!
Du brachtest uns diese Noth!   You brought this harm upon us!
Die du die Männer ihm verhetztest,   You who goaded the men against him,
weh', daß du dem Haus genah't!   alas, that you ever came near this house!

BRÜNNHILDE

Armsel'ge, schweig'!   Wretched woman, peace!
Sein Eheweib war'st du nie: You were never his lawful wife:
als Buhlerin   as wanton alone
bandest du ihn.   you bound him.
Sein Mannes-Gemahl bin ich,   [49]   His rightful wife am I,
der ewige Eide er schwur,   to whom he swore eternal vows
eh' Siegfried je dich ersah.   ere Siegfried ever saw you.

GUTRUNE

(breaking out in sudden despair)

Verfluchter Hagen!	Accursèd Hagen!
Daß du das Gift mir riethest,	That you counselled the poison
das ihr den Gatten entrückt!	that robbed her of her husband!
Ach, Jammer!	Ah, sorrow!
Wie jäh nun weiß ich's:	How swiftly I see it now:
Brünnhild' war die Traute,	Brünnhild' was his one true love,
die durch den Trank er vergaß!	whom the philtre made him forget.

(Filled with shame, she turns away from Siegfried and, dying, bends over Gunther's body, where she remains motionless until the end. Leaning defiantly on his spear, Hagen stands deep in sombre thought at the other side of the stage. [34] Brünnhilde is alone in the centre; after remaining lost for some time in contemplation of Siegfried, she now turns to the men and women in a mood of solemn exaltation.) [54]

BRÜNNHILDE

(to the vassals)

Starke Scheite		Heavy logs
schichtet mir dort		heap up for me here
am Rande des Rhein's zu Hauf':		in a pile at the edge of the Rhine:
hoch und hell		high and bright
lod're die Gluth,	[14a]	let the flames flare up
die den edlen Leib		and consume the noble limbs
des hehrsten Helden verzehrt! –	[35]	of the most exalted hero! –
Sein Roß führet daher,		Lead his stallion hither:
daß mit mir dem Recken es folge:		let it follow the warrior with me:
denn des Helden heiligste	[35]	for my own body yearns
Ehre zu theilen		to share in the hero's
verlangt mein eigener Leib. –	[54]	holiest honour. –
Vollbringt Brünnhilde's Wort!		Do as Brünnhilde bids!

(During the following, the young men raise a huge funeral pyre outside the hall, near to the bank of the Rhine: women cover it with rugs over which they strew herbs and flowers. Once again Brünnhilde becomes lost in contemplation of Siegfried's face. Her features grow increasingly transfigured.) [50]

Wie Sonne lauter		Purer than sunlight
strahlt mir sein Licht:		streams the light from his eyes:
der Reinste war er,		the purest of men it was
der mich verrieth!		who betrayed me!
Die Gattin trügend		False to his wife
– treu dem Freunde –		– true to his friend –
vor der eig'nen Trauten		from her who was faithful
– einzig ihm theuer –		– she alone who was loyal –
schied er sich durch sein Schwert. –	[23]	he sundered himself with his sword. –
Ächter als er		Never were oaths
schwur keiner Eide;		more nobly sworn;
treuer als er		never were treaties
hielt keiner Verträge;		kept more truly;
laut'rer als er		never did any man
liebte kein and'rer:		love more loyally:
und doch alle Eide,		and yet every oath,

alle Verträge,
die treueste Liebe –
trog keiner wie er! –

every treaty,
the truest love –
no one betrayed as he did!

Wiss't ihr wie das ward? – [33]
(looking upward)

Do you know why that was so? –

O ihr, der Eide [8]
ewige Hüter!
Lenkt eu'ren Blick
auf mein blühendes Leid:
erschaut eu're ewige Schuld!
Meine Klage hör', [37]
du hehrster Gott! [34]
Durch seine tapferste That,
dir so tauglich erwünscht,
weihtest du den,
der sie gewirkt,
dem Fluche, dem du verfielest: –

mich – mußte
der Reinste verrathen,
daß wissend würde ein Weib! – [34]

Oh you, eternal
guardians of oaths!
Direct your gaze
on my burgeoning grief:
behold your eternal guilt!
Hear my lament,
most mighty of gods!
By the bravest of deeds,
which you dearly desired,
you doomed him
who wrought it to suffer
the curse to which you in turn
[succumbed: –
it was I whom the purest man
had to betray,
that a woman might grow wise. –

Weiß ich nun was dir frommt? –

Do I now know what you need? –

Alles! Alles!
Alles weiß ich:
alles ward mir nun frei!
Auch deine Raben
hör' ich rauschen:
mit bang ersehnter Botschaft
send' ich die beiden nun heim. [19]
Ruhe! Ruhe, du Gott! – [5, 8d, 54, 8e]

All things, all things,
all things I know,
all is clear to me now!
I hear the rustle
of your ravens' wings:
with anxiously longed-for tidings
I send the two of them home.
Rest now, rest now, you god! –

(She signals to the vassals to bear Siegfried's body to the funeral pyre; at the same time she draws the ring from his finger and gazes at it thoughtfully.) [54, 21, 1b]

Mein Erbe nun
nehm' ich zu eigen. – [6]

My inheritance now
I take as my own. –

Verfluchter Reif!
Furchtbarer Ring!
Dein Gold fass' ich,
und geb' es nun fort.
Der Wassertiefe
weise Schwestern,
des Rheines schwimmende Töchter, [2]
euch dank' ich redlichen Rath!
Was ihr begehrt,
ich geb' es euch:
aus meiner Asche [4]
nehmt es zu eigen!

Accursèd band!
Fear-ridden ring!
I grasp your gold
and give it away.
Wise sisters
of the watery deep,
you daughters who swim in the Rhine,
I thank you for your sound advice!
I give you
what you covet:
from my ashes
take it as your own!

Das Feuer, das mich verbrennt,		Let the fire that consumes me	
rein'ge vom Fluche den Ring:		cleanse the ring of its curse:	
ihr in der Fluth		in the floodwaters	
löset ihn auf,		let it dissolve,	
und lauter bewahrt	[5]	and safely guard	
das lichte Gold,	[6]	the shining gold	
das euch zum Unheil geraubt. –	[19]	that was stolen to your undoing. –	

(She has placed the ring on her finger and now turns to the pile of logs on which Siegfried's body lies outstretched. She seizes a great firebrand from one of the vassals, brandishes it aloft and points to the back of the stage.) [9]

Fliegt heim, ihr Raben!	[14a]	Fly home, you ravens!	
Raunt es eurem Herren,		Whisper to your lord	
was hier am Rhein ihr gehört!		what you heard here by the Rhine!	
An Brünnhilde's Felsen	[14b]	Make your way	
fahrt vorbei:		past Brünnhilde's rock:	
der dort noch lodert,		tell Loge, who burns there,	
weiset Loge nach Walhall!	[21]	to haste to Valhalla!	
Denn der Götter Ende	[1b]	For the end of the gods	
dämmert nun auf:		is dawning now:	
so – werf' ich den Brand		thus do I hurl the torch	
in Walhall's prangende Burg.		into Valhalla's proud-standing [stronghold.	

(She hurls the firebrand on to the pile of wood, which quickly ignites. Two ravens have flown up from the rock on the riverbank and disappear into the background.[179] *She catches sight of her horse, which two men have just led in.)* [31, 30]

Grane, mein Roß,		Grane, my horse,	
sei mir gegrüßt!		take this my greeting!	

(She has leapt towards it. Taking it, she quickly removes its bridle and leans towards it, confidingly.)

Weißt du auch, mein Freund,		Do you know, my friend,	
wohin ich dich führe?		where I'm taking you now?	
Im Feuer leuchtend	[36, 35]	Lit by the fire,	
liegt dort dein Herr,		your lord lies there,	
Siegfried, mein seliger Held.		Siegfried, my blessed hero.	
Dem Freunde zu folgen,	[30]	You whinny with joy	
wieherst du freudig?		to follow your friend?	
Lockt dich zu ihm	[31]	Does the laughing fire	
die lachende Lohe? –	[14a]	lure you to him? –	
Fühl' meine Brust auch,	[36]	Feel how the flames	
wie sie entbrennt,		burn in my breast,	
helles Feuer		effulgent fires	
das Herz mir erfaßt:		seize hold of my heart:	
ihn zu umschlingen,		to clasp him to me	
umschlossen von ihm,		while held in my arms	
in mächtigster Minne		and in mightiest love	
vermählt ihm zu sein! –		to be wedded to him! –	
Heiajaho! Grane!	[31]	Heiayoho! Grane!	
Grüß' deinen Herren!		Greet your master!	
Siegfried! Siegfried! Sieh'!	[35]	Siegfried! Siegfried! See!	

(She has leapt on to the horse and raises it to jump.)

Selig grüßt dich dein Weib!   In bliss your wife bids you welcome!
*(With a single bound she urges the horse into the blazing pyre. [31, 30] The flames
immediately flare up so that the fire fills the entire space in front of the hall and appears to seize
on the building itself. [14a] Horrified, the men and women press to the very front of the stage.
When the whole stage seems to be engulfed in flames [38], the glow suddenly subsides, so that
soon all that remains is a cloud of smoke which drifts away to the back of the stage, settling on
the horizon as a layer of dark cloud. At the same time the Rhine overflows its banks in a
mighty flood, surging over the conflagration. The three Rhinedaughters are borne along on its
waves and now appear over the scene of the fire. Hagen, who since the incident with the ring,
has been watching Brünnhilde with increasing concern, is seized with extreme alarm at the sight
of the Rhinedaughters. He hastily throws aside his spear, shield and helmet and plunges into the
floodwaters like a man possessed, shouting the words:* Get back from the ring! *[19] Woglinde
and Wellgunde twine their arms around his neck and, swimming away, draw him with them
into the depths. Flosshilde leads the way as they swim towards the back of the stage, holding the
regained ring aloft in a gesture of jubilation. [2] A red glow breaks out with increasing
brightness from the cloudbank that had settled on the horizon. By its light, the three
Rhinedaughters can be seen swimming in circles and merrily playing with the ring on the calmer
waters of the Rhine, which has little by little returned to its bed. [8, 2, 36] From the ruins of
the fallen hall, the men and women watch moved to the very depths of their being,[180] as the
glow from the fire grows in the sky. As it finally reaches its greatest intensity, the hall of
Valhalla comes into view, with the gods and heroes assembled as in Waltraute's description in
Act I. [8, 54, 35] Bright flames seem to flare up in the hall of the gods [21], finally hiding
them from sight completely. The curtain falls.) [36]*

Appendix: rejected versions

1. *Die Walküre*, Act II, Scene 1 (see p. 141)

FRICKA

Von dir nun heisch' ich	Of you I now demand
harte Buße	harsh punishment
an Sieglinde und Siegmund.	for Sieglinde and Siegmund.

WOTAN

Was so schlimmes	What was so wrong
schuf das Paar,	that was done by the couple
das liebend einte der Lenz?	whom spring united in love?
Der Minne Zauber	Love's magic spell
entzückte sie:	beguiled them:
wer büßt mir der Minne Macht?	who'll make me amends for the power of [love?

FRICKA

Wie thörig und taub du dich [stell'st,	How foolish and deaf you feign to be,
als wüßtest fürwahr du nicht	as though in truth you did not know
an welchen Frevel	of the crime
Fricka dich mahnt,	of which Fricka accuses you
was im Herzen sie härmt.	and the grief she feels in her heart.

WOTAN

Du sieh'st nur das Eine;	You see but one thing alone;
das And're seh' ich,	what I see is something else
das Jenes mir jagt aus dem Blick.	that drives the former out of my sight.

FRICKA

Das Eine nur seh' ich,	I see but one thing alone –
was ewig ich hüte,	that which I uphold for ever,
der Ehe heiligen Eid:	wedlock's hallowed vow:
meine Seele kränkt,	he who breaks it
wer ihn versehrt,	wounds my soul,
wer ihn trübt, trifft mir das Herz.	he who transgresses it strikes at my [heart.

WOTAN

So zweifellos sprichst du von Ehe,	Can you speak so lightly of wedlock,

wo nur Zwang der Liebe ich seh'?
  Unheilig
  acht' ich den Eid,
der Unliebende eint.
  Wahrlich, leicht
  wiegt dir das Weib,
weihest du selbst die Gewalt,
die für Hunding freite Frau!

when I see only love's constraints?
  Unholy
  I deem the vow
that binds unloving hearts.
  Truly, woman
  weighs little with you
if you even sanction the force
by which Hunding wooed a wife!

FRICKA

Wenn blinde Gewalt
  trotzig und wild
rings zertrümmert die Welt,
  wer trägt einzig
  des Unheil's Schuld,
als Wotan, Wüthender, du?
Schwache beschirm'st du nie,
Starken steh'st du nur bei:
  der Männer Rasen
  in rauhem Muth,
  Mord und Raub
  ist dein mächtig Werk;
das meine doch ist es allein,
daß Eines noch heilig und hehr.

When purblind force,
  defiant and wild,
destroys the world about us,
  who alone bears
  the blame for such evil
save Wotan, you madman, you?
You never shield the weak
but only help the strong:
  men's raging madness
  and savage moods,
  murder and theft
  are your mighty achievements;
mine alone is to see
that one thing yet remains hallowed and
  [holy.

Wo nach Ruhe
  der Rauhe sich sehnt,
  wo des Wechsels
  sehrender Wuth
wehre sanft ein Besitz, –
dort steh' ich lauschend still.
  Der zerrissenen Sitte
  lenkendes Seil
bind' ich neu zum Band:
  wo Alles verloren,
  lab' ich mich so
an der Hoffnung heiligem Thau. –
  Übte Hunding
  einstens Gewalt,
was ich Schwache nicht wehren
  [konnte,
du ließest es kühn gewähren:
  sühnte er dann
  des Frevels Schuld,
Freundin ward ihm da Fricka
durch heiliger Ehe Eid:
  so vergess' ich
  was je er beging,
  mit meinem Schutze
  schirm' ich sein Recht.

  When the ruffian
  yearns for rest,
  where possessions
  may gently oppose
the chafing fury of change,
there do I stand and listen in silence.
  Cloven custom's
  guiding rope
I bind anew to create a bond:
  where all is lost,
  I seek relief
in the hallowed dew of hope. –
  When Hunding once
  used force
– which, weak as I am, I couldn't
  [prevent –
you brazenly let him have his way:
  when he then atoned
  for the guilt of his outrage,
Fricka became his friend
through holy wedlock's vow:
  thus I forget
  whatever his fault
  and raise my shield
  to shelter his rights.

Der nicht seinem Frevel gesteuert,
meinen Frieden stör' er nun nicht!

Let him who failed to hinder his outrage
refrain from disturbing my peace of
[mind!

WOTAN

Stört' ich dich je
in deinem Walten?
Gewähren ließ ich dich stets.
Knüpfe du bindender
Knoten Band,
fess'le was nicht sich fügt;
heuch'le Frieden,
und freue dich hehr
ob gelog'ner Liebe Eid:
doch mir, wahrlich,
muthe nicht zu,
daß mit Zwang ich halte
was dir nicht haftet;
denn wo kühn Kräfte sich regen,
da gewähr' ich offen dem Krieg.

Have I ever disturbed you
in your dominion?
I always let you have your way.
Tie the bonds
of binding ties,
fetter what doesn't fit;
dissemble peace
and proudly rejoice
in the vows of pretended love:
but you cannot in truth
expect me now
to bind by force
what won't be bound by you;
wherever forces are boldly stirring
I openly counsel war.

FRICKA

Achtest du rühmlich
der Ehe Bruch,
so prahle nun weiter
und preis' es heilig,
daß Blutschande entblüht
dem Bund eines Zwillingspaar's.
Mir schaudert das Herz,
es schwindelt mein Hirn:
bräutlich umfing
die Schwester der Bruder!
Wann – ward es erlebt,
daß leiblich Geschwister sich liebten?

If you think breach
of wedlock worthy of praise,
then go on boasting
and deem it holy
that incest springs
from the bond of a twin-born pair.
My heart is quaking,
my brain is reeling:
a brother embraced
his sister as bride!
When was it known
for natural siblings to love one another?

WOTAN

Heut' – hast du's erlebt:
erfahre so
was von selbst sich fügt,
sei zuvor auch nie es gescheh'n.

Today you have seen it happen:
learn thus that a thing
might befall of itself
though it never happened before.

FRICKA

So frechen Hohn
nur weckt dir mein Harm?
Deinen Spott nur erzielt
mein brennender Zorn?
Verlach'st du die Würde,
die selbst du verlieh'n?
Zertritt'st du die Ehre
des eig'nen Weibes?

Such brazen contempt
does my grief arouse?
Does my burning anger
meet only with scorn?
Do you ridicule the dignity
which you yourself bestowed?
Do you trample upon
your own wife's honour?

Wohin renn'st du,
    rasender Gott,
reißest die Schöpfung du ein,
der selbst das Gesetz du gab'st?

Where are you heading,
    you headstrong god,
destroying the world you created,
a world whose laws you made yourself?

WOTAN

WOTAN

Des Urgesetzes
    walt' ich vor Allem:
wo Kräfte zeugen und kreisen,
zieh' ich meines Wirkens Kreis;
    wohin er läuft
    leit' ich den Strom,
    den Quell hüt' ich
    aus dem er quillt:
wo Leibes- und Liebeskraft,

One primal law
    I obey above all others:
wherever forces stir and strive,
I circumscribe my sphere of action;
    I guide the flood
    wherever it flows
    and guard the well-spring
    from which it wells:
where strength of limb and of love is
[found,

da wahrt' ich mir Lebensmacht.
    Das Zwillingspaar
    zwang meine Macht:
    Minne nährt' es
    im Mutterschooß;
unbewußt lag es einst dort,
unbewußt liebt' es sich jetzt.
    Soll süßer Lohn
    deinem Segen entblüh'n,
    so seg'ne mit göttlich
    heiliger Gunst
Siegmund's und Sieglinde's Bund.

I've exercised power over life.
    That power
    the twin-born pair has felt:
    love nurtured them
    within their mother's womb;
unwittingly, they lay there once,
unwittingly, they love each other now.
    If sweet reward
    is to spring from your blessing,
    then bless with divinely
    hallowed grace
Siegmund's and Sieglinde's bond.

2. *Siegfried*, Act I, Scene 1 (see p. 207)

MIME

Halte! halte! Wohin?
höre mich, Siegfried, hör'!
Er stürmt mir fort! – he! Siegfried! –
Wie halt' ich das kind mir fest?
(He calls after him with the greatest effort.)
Nicht alles ward dir schon kund –
von der mutter mußt du noch hören!

verschmähst du der mutter rath?

Stop! Stop! Where are you going?
Listen, Siegfried, listen to me!
Away he storms! – Hey! Siegfried! –
How can I hold the child with me here?

Not everything's known to you yet –
you've still got to hear about your
[mother!

Would you scorn your mother's advice?

SIEGFRIED
(returning)

von der mutter? – rede heraus!

About my mother? – Out with it, tell me!

MIME

So tritt nur ein,

Then step inside,

traue dem alten:　　　　　　　　　　trust your old man:
wichtiges mußt du noch wissen!　　　matters of moment you still have to
　　　　　　　　　　　　　　　　　　[learn!

SIEGFRIED
(reentering)

Ich bin ja da: –　　　　　　　　　　Here I am then: –
was bargst du mir noch?　　　　　　　what are you still concealing from me?

MIME
(embarrassed)

Ja, das ist bald nicht gesagt! –　　　Well, that's not so easily said! –
　　　　　　　　　　　　　　　　　(coughing)
Doch hör', ich hab's　　　　　　　　But listen, there's something
was du hören mußt! –　　　　　　　　I've got to tell you! –
Du willst aus dem wald　　　　　　　Do you want to leave the forest
fort in die welt? –　　　　　　　　　and go out into the world? –
Hör', was deine mutter　　　　　　　Then hear what your mother
Mime vertraut! –　　　　　　　　　　confided in Mime! –
Mime, sprach sie,　　　　　　　　　　Mime, she said,
kluger mann!　　　　　　　　　　　　you clever man:
Wenn einst mein kind erwächst,　　　one day, when my child grows up,
hüte den kühnen im wald!　　　　　　don't let the lad leave the forest!
Die welt ist tückisch und falsch,　　　The world is artful and false,
dem thör'gen stellt sie fallen:　　　　it sets cunning traps for the foolish:
nur wer das fürchten gelernt,　　　　only he who has learned what fear is
mag dort sich leidlich behüten.　　　may keep himself fairly safe there.

SIEGFRIED

Das hat dir die mutter gemeldet?　　　Is that what my mother told you?

MIME

glaube, ich rede ihr gleich!　　　　　Believe me, those were her very words!

SIEGFRIED

das fürchten möcht' ich lernen!　　　I'd like to learn what fear is!

MIME

ein kluger kann es leicht,　　　　　　A clever man can do so easily,
dumme lernen es schwer.　　　　　　foolish ones find it harder to learn.
Der kluge spürt　　　　　　　　　　The clever man sniffs
und späht umher　　　　　　　　　　and snivels around
ob gefahr ihn wohl befiel'!　　　　　to see whether danger threatens!
naht der feind,　　　　　　　　　　If his enemy's near
neigt er sich fein,　　　　　　　　　he ducks down smartly
daß ihn nicht der dräuende trifft!　　so that the threat doesn't strike him!

SIEGFRIED

das, Mime, wäre das fürchten?　　　　Is that what fear is, Mime?

MIME

die list ist es
die furcht uns lehrt:
sie ist des fürchtens frucht!

It is cunning
that teaches us fear:
that is the fruit of fear!

SIEGFRIED

Listen kenn' ich,
sie lernt' ich vom fuchs.
Wer aber lehrt mich das fürchten?

Cunning I know already,
I've learned it from the fox.
But who will teach me what fear is?

MIME

Wie dumm du noch bist
das nicht zu wissen!
so wolltest du in die welt?
Im walde bist du vertraut,
in der welt trügt dich der blick
dein auge lugt
es lauscht dein ohr,
wie gefahr dich auch umlauert,
du erlugst und erlauschest nichts,
zeigt dir die furcht
nicht die gefahr,
daß mit list du dich gegen sie legst.

How stupid you are
not to know that!
And you wanted to go off into the world?
You're at home in the forest,
in the world your eyes will deceive you:
your eye keeps watch,
your ear is cocked
to find out if danger is lying in wait:
not a thing will you see and hear
if fear doesn't
show you the danger
so you may meet it with cunning.

SIEGFRIED

Das fürchten muß ich drum lernen.

And so I'll have to learn what fear is.

MIME

Wenn dein auge nicht hell mehr
[sieht,
wenn dein ohr nur träumend noch
[hört;
wenn dir's dann schwirrend
näher schwebt,
verschwimmend die sinne dir
[schwinden,
die glieder dir schwankend versagen,
im busen bang
das herz dir erbebt –
dann hast du das fürchten gelernt.

When your eye no longer sees clearly,

when your ear hears only as though in
[a dream;
when whirling noises
float towards you,
your senses swim and desert you,

your limbs grow weak and give way
and your heart quakes
anxiously in your breast –
then you'll have learned the meaning of
[fear.

SIEGFRIED

Nun fühl' ich, das lernt' ich noch
[nicht.

I can feel that I still haven't learned it.

MIME

O thöriger knabe,
dummes kind!
bleibe im walde

O foolish boy,
you stupid child!
Stay in the woods

laß die welt!
Für deine mutter
mahn' ich dich:
laß' es der mutter zu lieb!
fühltest du noch
das fürchten nicht:
in der list'gen welt
verlierst du dich;
wo dein vater fiel,
fällst auch du:
dich warne der mutter weh!
Wem die furcht die sinne
neu nicht schuf,
in der welt erblindet
dem der blick:
Wo nichts du siehst
wirst du versehrt:
wo nichts du hörst
trifft es dein herz.
Nicht schneidet der stahl
eh die gluth ihn nicht schmolz:
wem die furcht die sinne
nicht scharf gefegt –
blind und taub in der welt
schlingt ihn die welle hinab!

drum achte des alten wort:
bleib, du dummer, im wald!

and let the world be!
For your mother's sake
I warn you:
for love of your mother forsake it!
If even now
you have felt no fear,
in the cunning world
you will lose your way;
where your father fell,
you too will fall:
let your mother's grief be a warning!
He whose senses are not
newly stirred by fear
will blink in the blinding
light of the world:
where you see nothing
you'll suffer harm;
where you hear nothing
your heart will be hurt.
The steel will not cut
ere the heat has annealed it:
he whose senses are not
made keen by fear –
blind and deaf in the world
he'll be swallowed up by the surging
[wave!
so heed your old man's words:
remain in the forest, you fool!

SIEGFRIED

Das fürchten mag
und muß ich lernen!
durch deinen witz
gewinn' ich's nie!
Drum aus dem wald
fort in die welt:
sie lehrt mich das fürchten allein!
Bei dir versäß' ich
säumig den tag:
ich bliebe dumm,
taub und blind.
Und lern' ich das fürchten,
lern' ich es nicht:
wo man's lernt, da will ich doch sein!
Drum rath' ich dir jetzt,
rüste das schwert
schweiße die starken
stücken zu ganz!
täusche mich nicht
mit schlechtem tand:

I want to learn fear
and have to learn it!
I'll never acquire it
through your wit!
So forth from the forest
and into the world!
The world alone will teach me fear!
With you I'd idle
the day away:
I'd still be stupid,
deaf and blind.
And whether or not
I learn what fear is,
I want to be where people learn it!
And so I advise you now:
make ready the sword
and make the mighty
pieces whole!
Don't try to trick me
with worthless trinkets:

den trümmern allein	in those shards alone
trau' ich 'was zu!	do I place any trust!
Find' ich dich faul,	If I find you idle
gefällt mir es nicht,	or if I don't like it,
machst du mir flausen	if you offer excuses
und flickst du schlecht:	and fit them badly,
ich such' einen neuen gesellen,	I'll look for some new companion
mit dem seh' ich dir nach:	with whom I'll seek you out:
scheid' ich das fürchten zu lernen,	when I set off to learn the meaning of [fear,
dich lehr' ich das fegen zuvor!	I'll teach you all about tanning first!

(He runs away, laughing, into the forest.)

MIME
(alone)

Nun sitz' ich da,	Here I sit
hab' zur schande	and suffer disgrace
noch den schimpf!	on top of my shame!
Zur alten noth	To my age-old plight
die neue noch:	I can now add a new one:
vernagelt bin ich nun ganz!	I'm well and truly trapped!
Gräulicher geiz	Loathsome lust
verfluchte gier	and accursèd greed
nach des reifes gold!	for the gold of the ring!
nun duld' ich wahrlich	Now I have to endure
schönen dank,	truly splendid thanks,
ich alter, dummer narr!	stupid old fool that I am!
das kind erzog ich	I brought up the child
mit zäher müh:	with obstinate effort
daß mir zu lieb	that the deed might redound
ihm die that geläng':	to my own advantage:
an mir einz'gem sollt' er hängen,	on me alone he was meant to depend
und mich einz'gen haßt er nun!	and me alone he now despises!
verfluchte brut	Accursèd brat,
aus der menschen brunst,	born of human lust,
mischten sich götter noch drein!	in which gods have also meddled!
Was ich nun rathe	All I advise
geräth mir zum übel:	turns out amiss:
in jeder schlinge	in every snare
verschling' ich mich selbst:	I ensnare myself:
mit dem fürchten wollt' ich ihn [fangen,	I wanted to trap him with fear,
mit dem fürchten fängt er nun mich!	but with fear he now entraps me!
Wie halt' ich ihn jetzt	How can I hold him
in meinem haus,	now in my house
daß er den dienst mir thu'?	so that he does my wishes?

(He broods – Fafner's motif in the music.)

Das fürchten will er lernen:	He wants to learn the meaning of fear:
geläng's ihn damit zu fesseln?	might I manage to bind him with that?
zum lehrer erbiet' ich mich,	I'll offer myself as his mentor

führe den buben
  zu Fafners nest!
So hätt' ich den huien gefangen,
zum hort hülf' er mir noch! –
  doch ach! das schwert! –
  mir schwindelt's wieder! –
  wie schweiß' ich die stücken
  des tück'schen stahls?
  der zwerge kunst
  kann's nicht zwingen:
  wie oft vergebens
  gab ich mir müh'!
  Müßige noth,
  nutzlose pein!
  mach' ich umsonst
  an die sorge mich?
  die stücken glühen
  mir nicht in der gluth:
  die harten zwingt
  mein hammer nicht!
das schwert, das mir einzig nützt,
erschweißen kann ich's nicht!

and lead the lad
  to Fafner's lair!
And so I'd have caught the hothead,
he'd help me to win the hoard! –
  But ah! The sword! –
  My head is reeling once more! –
  How can I forge the shards
  of insidious steel?
  No dwarfish art
  can subdue them:
  how often have I
  laboured in vain!
  Idle effort,
  useless torment!
  Should I incur
  such cares for nothing?
  The shards won't fire
  for me in the furnace:
  my hammer won't subdue
  their stubborn strength!
The sword that alone would serve me –
that sword I cannot weld!

(In his despair he crumples up on the stool in front of the anvil.)

3. Brünnhilde's peroration (see p. 348) caused Wagner a great deal of difficulty and was recast several times in the light of his current thinking before achieving the form familiar from *Götterdämmerung*.

3a. *Siegfried's Tod*, Act III, Scene 3 (completed on 28 November 1848)

BRÜNNHILDE

Du übermuthiger Held,
  wie hieltest du mich gebannt!
All' meiner Weisheit   mußt' ich
  [entrathen,
denn all' mein Wissen   verrieth ich
  [dir:
was du mir nahmst,   nütztest du
  [nicht, –
deinem muthigen Trotz   vertrautest
  [du nur!
Nun du, gefriedet,   frei es mir
  [gabst,
  kehrt mir mein Wissen wieder,
  erkenn' ich des Ringes Runen.
Der Nornen Rath   vernehm' ich nun
  [auch,

You overweening hero,
  how you held me in thrall!
All my wisdom   I had to forgo,

for all my knowledge   I gave to you:

what you took   you did not use, –

in your bold defiance   you trusted alone!

Now that, appeased,   you gave it me
  [freely,
  my knowledge returns once more
  and I read the runes of the ring.
The Norns' ancient lore   I can also hear

darf ihren Spruch jetzt deuten:
des kühnsten Mannes   mächtigste
[That,
mein Wissen taugt sie zu weih'n. –

Ihr Nibelungen,   vernehmt mein
[Wort!
eure Knechtschaft künd' ich auf:
der den Ring geschmiedet,   euch
[Rührige band, –
nicht soll er ihn wieder
[empfah'n, –
doch frei sei er, wie ihr!
Denn dieses Gold   gebe ich euch,
weise Schwestern   der Wassertiefe!
    Das Feuer, das mich verbrennt,
    rein'ge den Ring vom Fluch:
ihr löset ihn auf   und lauter
[bewahrt
    das strahlende Gold des Rhein's,
    das zum Unheil euch geraubt! –
    [Nur Einer herrsche:
    Allvater! Herrlicher du!
Freue dich   des freiesten Helden!
    Siegfried führ' ich dir zu:
    biet' ihm minnlichen Gruß,
    dem Bürgen ewiger Macht!]

the bravest of men's   most mighty
[deed
must now be blessed by my
[knowledge. –
You Nibelungs,   heed my words!

Your thraldom now I end:
he who forged the ring   and enthralled
[you restless spirits, –
he shall not regain it. –

But let him be free, like you!
For I give   this gold unto you,
wise sisters   of the watery deep!
    Let the fire that now consumes me
    cleanse the ring of its curse:
    you will melt it down   and safely
[guard
    the glistening gold of the Rhine,
    that was stolen to your undoing! –
    [One alone shall rule:
    All-Father! Glorious god!
Rejoice   in the freest of heroes!
    Siegfried I bring to you now:
    grant him a loving greeting,
    the bondsman of boundless might!]

(The funeral pyre has already been set alight; Brünnhilde's horse is brought in: she seizes it by the reins, kisses it and whispers softly in its ear:)

Freue dich, Grane: bald sind wir
[frei!

Rejoice, Grane: soon we'll be free!

(At her bidding the vassals bear Siegfried's body in a solemn procession to the pile of wood: Brünnhilde follows initially on foot, leading the horse by the reins; behind the body she then mounts the funeral pyre with it.)

3b.   The words in square brackets in 3a were deleted (probably before 18 December 1848) and replaced by

Selige Sühnung
ersah ich den hehren
heilig ewigen
einigen Göttern!
Freuet euch
des freiesten Helden!
Göttlichem Brudergruß
führt seine Braut ihn zu!

Machtlos scheidet

Blessed atonement
I saw for the holy,
sacredly ageless
and only gods!
Rejoice
in the freest of heroes!
To the greeting of his brotherly gods
his bride is bringing him now!

Depart without power

die die Schuld nun meidet.

Eurer Schuld entsproß   der
    [froheste Held
dessen freie That   sie getilgt:
erspart ist euch   der bange Kampf
    um eure endende Macht:
Erbleichet in Wonne   vor des
    [Menschen That,
vor dem Helden,   den ach ihr
    [gezeugt!
    Aus eurer bangen Furcht
verkünd' ich euch   selige
    [Todeserlösung!

whom guilt now shuns.

From your guilt has sprung   the
    [blithest of heroes
whose unwilled deed   has expunged it:
you're spared   the anxious struggle
    to save your waning power:
fade away in bliss   before man's deed,

before the hero   whom, alas, you
    [created!
    In the midst of your anxious fear
I proclaim to you   blessed redemption
    [in death!

3c. By December 1852 *Siegfried's Tod* had largely assumed the form in which it is reproduced in the main body of the text above. The following lines were included in Brünnhilde's peroration between the lines 'in Walhall's prangende Burg' and 'Grane, mein Roß' and are usually described as the 'Feuerbach ending':

Ihr, blühenden Lebens
bleibend Geschlecht:
was ich nun euch melde,
merket es wohl! –
Sah't ihr vom zündenden Brand

Siegfried und Brünnhild' verzehrt;
sah't ihr des Rheines Töchter

zur Tiefe entführen den Ring:
    nach Norden dann
    blickt durch die Nacht:
    erglänzt dort am Himmel
    ein heiliges Glühen,
    so wisset all' –
daß ihr Walhall's Ende gewahrt! –

Verging wie Hauch
    der Götter Geschlecht,
    lass' ohne Walter
    die Welt ich zurück:
meines heiligsten Wissens Hort
weis' ich der Welt nun zu. –
    Nicht Gut, nicht Gold,
    noch göttliche Pracht;
    nicht Haus, nicht Hof,
    noch herrischer Prunk;
    nicht trüber Verträge

You, blossoming life's
enduring race:
heed well
what I tell you now! –
For when you've seen Siegfried and
    [Brünnhild'
consumed by the kindling blaze;
and when you've seen the Rhine's
    [daughters
return the ring to its depths,
    to the north then
    look through the night:
    when a sacred glow
    starts to gleam in the sky,
    then shall you know
that you've witnessed Valhalla's end! –

Though the race of gods
    passed away like a breath,
    though I leave behind me
    a world without rulers,
I now bequeath to that world
my most sacred wisdom's hoard. –
    Not wealth, not gold,
    nor godly pomp;
    not house, not garth,
    nor lordly splendour;
    not troubled treaties'

trügender Bund,
nicht heuchelnder Sitte
hartes Gesetz:
selig in Lust und Leid
läßt – die Liebe nur sein. –

treacherous bonds,
not smooth-tongued custom's
stern decree:
blessed in joy and sorrow
love alone can be. –

3d. In May 1856 Wagner decided to replace the foregoing lines with the following 'Schopenhauer ending' (the versification probably dates from 1871 or 1872):

Führ' ich nun nicht mehr
nach Walhall's Feste,
wiss't ihr, wohin ich fahre?
Aus Wunschheim zieh' ich fort,
Wahnheim flieh' ich auf immer;
  des ew'gen Werdens
  off'ne Thore
schließ' ich hinter mir zu:
  nach dem wunsch- und wahnlos
  heiligstem Wahlland,
der Welt-Wanderung Ziel,
von Wiedergeburt erlös't,
zieht nun die Wissende hin.
  Alles Ew'gen
  sel'ges Ende,
wiss't ihr, wie ich's gewann?
  Trauernder Liebe
  tiefstes Leiden
schloß die Augen mir auf:
enden sah ich die Welt. –

Were I no more to fare
  to Valhalla's fortress,
do you know whither I fare?
I depart from the home of desire,
I flee forever the home of delusion;
  the open gates
  of eternal becoming
I close behind me now:
  to the holiest chosen land,
  free from desire and delusion,
the goal of the world's migration,
redeemed from reincarnation,
the enlightened woman now goes.
  The blessed end
  of all things eternal,
do you know how I attained it?
  Grieving love's
  profoundest suffering
opened my eyes for me:
I saw the world end. –

Notes on the translation

1 According to the full score, the curtain rises at bar 126, eleven bars before Woglinde's entry.

2 In his open letter to Friedrich Nietzsche of 12 June 1872 Wagner explained that Woglinde's opening gambit is based on OHG *heilawâc* (= water drawn from a river or well at some divinely appointed hour), recast by analogy with the *eia popeia* (= hushabye) of children's nursery rhymes (GS IX,300; PW V,297).

3 In conversation with Cosima, Wagner described this passage as 'the world's lullaby' (CT, 17 July 1869), a reading already suggested by *Opera and Drama*, where the composer imputes the birth of language to a melodic vocalization (GS IV,91–2; PW II,224–5). At the same time, the round dance of the three sisters is adumbrated in *The Art-Work of the Future* (GS III,67–8; PW I,95–6), where the three 'primeval sisters', Dance, Music and Poetry, form a single unity before being wrenched apart in the later development of art. As Tibor Kneif has argued (Kneif 1969), there is an alliterative analogy between Woglinde, Wellgunde and Flosshilde and *Tanzkunst, Tonkunst* and *Dichtkunst*, the three arts which will be drawn together again in the artwork of the future, a unity illustrated in the opening and closing bars of the *Ring* as a whole.

4 The alternative reading *die Fliehende* (your fleeing sister) has no authority.

5 Although the etymology of the word Nibelheim is uncertain, most 19th-century writers derived it from OHG *nebel* and ON *nifl*, meaning 'mist'. The 1848 prose draft of the *Ring* begins: 'From the womb of night & death there sprang forth a race which dwells in Nibelheim (land of mists), i.e., in gloomy subterranean clefts & caverns: they are called Nibelungs, in inconstant, restless activity they burrow their way through the bowels of the earth (like vermin in a dead body): they heat, refine & forge brittle metals' (GS II,156; PW VII,301).

6 MHG *vrîdel* = lover.

7 It is not clear whether Wagner draws a semantic distinction between *Liebe* and *Minne*, both of which mean 'love'. During the classical MHG period (1050–1400) *Minne* was the standard word for love in all its multiplicity of meanings. From the fifteenth century onwards,

it assumed more obviously sexual connotations but, under the influence of the early 19th-century Romantics, came to assume increasingly ethical overtones. There is some suggestion, within the context of the *Ring*, that *Minne* is more overtly sexual than *Liebe*.

8 A play on words: *grätig* means not only 'full of fish bones' but also 'surly'.

9 For an interpretation of this scene as a parody of Meyerbeerian grand opera, see Nattiez 1993: 60–68.

10 For the anti-Semitic connotations of screeching declamation, see Millington 1991: 256–7.

11 *weihlich* is Wagner's own coinage, glossed by Grimm (XXVIII,706) as 'inspiring a feeling of solemn awe at the sight of something mysterious'.

12 There may be a reminiscence here of Book XIV of the *Iliad* in which 'the gracious earth' sends up a bed of grass and flowers for Zeus and Hera to lie on; see Müller and Panagl 1990: III,21; English trans., p. 49. For a fuller treatment of the Greek influence on the *Ring*, see Ewans 1982; Lloyd-Jones 1982; and Müller and Panagl 1990.

13 On the importance of contract law in the *Ring*, see White 1988.

14 There is no contradiction here with the First Norn's account in the prologue to *Götterdämmerung*, where it is said that Wotan sacrificed an eye at the Well of Wisdom. It is clear from the 1852 prose draft that, having forfeited one eye, Wotan offered to stake his remaining one in order to win Fricka. There is nothing in the Norse sources to substantiate this offer, which was presumably introduced by Wagner to indicate the strength of Wotan's youthful love for Fricka.

15 Strictly speaking, *Schwäher* means 'brother-in-law', but Wagner appears to use it here in the more general sense of 'kinsman'; see Panagl 1988: 55–6; English trans., p. 120.

16 MHG *nît* has a much wider semantic field than modern German *Neid* (envy) and covers such meanings as hostility, grudge, spite and violence; see also notes 22 and 48.

17 According to Jacob Grimm (1875–8: 248–

56), Freia was the goddess of love and fertility but not identical with Frau Holde, a figure of contemporary folk belief. Wagner has assimilated the two. See Magee 1990: 190–92.

18 According to Snorri Sturluson (1987: 96–7), Odin's spear (Gungnir) was crafted by dwarfs but had no ethical associations. The idea that it is carved with the runes of legally binding contracts may have been suggested to Wagner by Ludwig Feuerbach who, in *The Essence of Christianity*, equates Odin with 'the primeval or most ancient law' (1903: 26).

19 Perhaps used here in the sense of *Einfriedigung*, i.e., an enclosed space.

20 According to the 1852 prose draft, the giants decide to take Freia at this point to punish the gods for their arrogance. The sin of *superbia* figures prominently in Herbert Huber's theologically inspired interpretation of the *Ring*.

21 Although SW prefers 'Fordert andern Sold!', the version in GS, 'Sinnt auf andern Sold' (Think of some other payment), makes more sense alliteratively.

22 MHG *nîtspil* = hostility or conflict. The hostility between dwarfs and giants seems to have been taken over from Ernst Raupach's 1834 stage play, *Der Nibelungen-Hort*; see Magee 1990: 75–6.

23 MHG *wilte* means not only 'wild' but also 'strange, unfamiliar'.

24 The *Nibelungenlied* contains reference to a *tarnkappe* (a cloak of invisibility), which Sîvrit (Siegfried) wrests from the dwarf Alberich and which he later wears when deflowering Prünhilt. Its dwarfish origins and ability to transport its wearer to distant places are Wagner's additions, based on his reading of Grimm's *Teutonic Mythology* (1875–8: 383).

25 According to Jacob Grimm (1875–8: 368), dwarfs and black elves are synonymous. Wagner himself equates gods and light elves.

26 A wingless dragon. Committed, as he is, to Germanic linguistic roots, Wagner uses the word *Wurm* to describe the beast, rather than the more familiar, Greek-based, *Drache*. According to Grimm (1875–8: 573), ON *ormr*, OE *vyrm* and OHG *wurm* all refer to a serpent-like creature with or without wings. The compound *Lindwurm* (from OHG *lint* = glittering) is used in *Siegfried* to describe Fafner's transmogrification into the monster despatched by the hero. Here Wagner was insistent that the creature should be wingless (see CT, 3 April 1878).

27 Strictly speaking, *knebeln* means 'to gag'.

28 GS has the alliteratively more attractive 'find' ich euch *faul*.

29 The reading in GS, 'die List, es zu schmieden, erlangt', is preferable from an alliterative point of view.

30 On the role of Hegelian necessity in the *Ring*, see Corse 1990.

31 The opposition between love and fear, which will play such an important role in *Siegfried*, is already prefigured here; see Corse 1990.

32 As August Röckel pointed out in his letter to Wagner of October 1853, there appears to be an inconsistency here inasmuch as the gods are destroyed in spite of the fact that Wotan gives up the ring. However, it is clear from the 1852 prose draft that this inconsistency is merely apparent. The relevant passage reads: 'It bodes no good that the gods are deceitful in their treaties; far worse is in store if you retain the ring; your end draws slowly nearer, yet it will overwhelm you with precipitate suddenness if you refuse to relinquish the ring' (Strobel 1930: 227).

33 According to 19th-century mythographers, the sun was Wotan's missing eye; see Magee 1990: 139–40.

34 MHG *blöde* = foolish, craven, feeble.

35 MHG *veige* = doomed to die, cf. English 'fey'. This reading makes more sense of the final lines than the traditional translation, 'cowardly'.

36 i.e., at bar 112.

37 GS contains a rather more elaborate description of the tree 'whose prominently raised roots extend a considerable distance before disappearing into the ground. The top of the tree is cut off by a timber roof with holes let into it in such a way that the bole of the tree and the boughs which branch out from it pass through the holes, which fit them exactly. We are to imagine that the leafy top of the tree spreads out above this roof' (GS VI,2). In the *Volsunga saga* the tree is described as an *eik*, which von der Hagen (1815: 11) translates as 'oak'. The tree may originally have been an apple-tree and, as such, a remnant of an ancient fertility cult (see Finch 1965: 4–5). Wagner may have changed it to an ash-tree in order to draw a parallel with the World Ash, Yggdrasill (see notes 131 and 132). According to Snorri (1987: 13), the first human beings were created from logs of ash wood. There is no doubt that the irruption of the human world into the gods' decaying cosmos is an essential part of the Hegelian process at work in the *Ring*. Other 19th-century writers – notably Carl Wilhelm Göttling in his *Nibelungen und Gibelinen* – saw a similar development from gods to heroes and finally human beings.

38 As Magee has pointed out (Magee 1990: 175–8), one of Wotan's names is ON Oski, MHG Wunsch; hence the description of the valkyries as *Wunschmädchen* or 'daughters of Wunsch/Wotan'; and hence, too, the present lines which, to quote Magee, 'have their own special pathos within the context of the drama and the twins' eventual fate'.

39 The sign of the serpent or dragon indicates Wälsung blood; see Magee 1990: 156.

40 In the *Volsunga saga*, Sigmund and his son, Sinfjötli, discover a couple of wolfskins, which they proceed to try on, with the result that, for a time, they are forced to live as marauding werewolves in the forest, a curse from which they finally escape. Wagner has transferred the episode to Siegmund and *his* father, Wälse, whom the composer equates with Wotan. For an explanation of the names adopted by Siegmund, see the glossary on pp. 373–75.

41 MHG *harst* has survived in Swiss and Hessian dialects with the meaning 'crowd, pack or host'. Wagner uses it in the sense of 'fray'; see Panagl 1990: 43; English trans., p. 112.

42 Wagner seems to be adopting MHG usage here, in which *lîp* may have a merely circumlocutory force: *mîn selbes lîp = ich*.

43 'The Wild Huntsman of popular superstition was, as Grimm portrays him, Wotan's most dangerous surviving manifestation. Grimm has much to say and many reports to record of the Wild Huntsman and his "wütendes Heer", riding eerily through forest and sky at night with tremendous din of baying hounds and hunting calls'; Magee 1990: 180. Wotan is clearly attempting to influence his son's actions and engineer his arrival at Hunding's hut. Indeed, in the 1852 prose draft, the god was present at the meeting and coupling of his semi-divine offspring.

44 German *Heil* is ambiguous, its meaning extending from physical safety and well-being to eschatological salvation. For Wagner it seems to have been associated additionally with that sense of 'wholeness' which comes through mutual recognition. The following scene and, in particular, Sieglinde's speech beginning 'You are the Spring' resonate with Hegelian ideas of self-recognition; see Corse 1990: 116–19.

45 In GS Wotan's cloak is blue, an error probably due to von der Hagen's mistranslation of ON *blár* in his version of the *Volsunga saga* (1815: 54). In the *Volsunga saga* the god appears dressed variously in grey or black.

46 The brother/sister imagery works more naturally in German, where *der Lenz* (Spring) is masculine and *die Liebe* (Love) feminine. For the present, the language remains metaphorical. Not until the end of the act do Siegmund and Sieglinde recognize each other as siblings and reenact the imagery in an incestuous relationship prefigured and, hence, sanctioned by Nature herself. Wagner's own views on incest are spelt out in *Opera and Drama*: 'Did Oedipus sin against human nature when he married his mother? Most certainly not. Otherwise Nature, violated, would surely have revealed the fact by allowing no children to issue from this marriage. But Nature, in fact, showed herself entirely willing. Jocasta and Oedipus, who had met as two strangers, loved each other and were only disturbed in their love from the moment when it was made known to them from outside that they were mother and son. Oedipus and Jocasta did not *know* in what social relationship they stood to one another: they had acted unconsciously, according to the natural instinct of the purely human individual' (GS IV,56–7; PW II,182). In other words, the spontaneity of authentic feeling is more important than the incestuous relationship.

47 The epiphany of the 'wonder' was an important element in Wagner's thinking at this time: see GS IV,81–91; PW II,212–23; see also Borchmeyer 1991: 148 and 339–40; and Corse 1990: 127.

48 MHG *nîtlich* = hostile, fearsome. The appearance of the Renunciation motif at this point in the score has been explained in various ways; see, for example, Newman 1949: 536–7; Donington 1963: 139–40; Millington 1983: 21–2; Lévi-Strauss 1985: 236; and Nattiez 1993: 335.

49 i.e., at bar 72.

50 The word 'valkyrie' derives from two Norse words, *valr* = the slain and *kjósa* (cognate with German *kiesen*) = to choose. As Magee makes clear (1990: 172–5), the element of choice that was left to the individual valkyrie varies from source to source. Unable to accept such an ill-defined situation, 19th-century scholars posited a development from dependence to free will, a development which Brünnhilde herself embodies in her evolution from the 'blindly elective tool of Wotan's will' to the free-thinking humanity of her later manifestations.

51 For an expanded version of this scene – not set to music by Wagner – see p. 352.

52 GS and the Breitkopf & Härtel vocal score prefer the reading 'der', turning Siegmund into the subject of the verb. However, both the Schott and Peters full scores treat Sieglinde as the subject, thereby giving her a more dynamic role in the relationship which may well reflect Wagner's view of women in the early 1850s: see, for example, his letter to August Röckel of 24 August 1851.

53 See note 38.

54 Wagner's use of the word *Muth* covers a much wider semantic field than its standard NHG translation of 'courage'. In keeping with its etymology, it can also mean 'mind' or 'mood' and appears to be used here in the sense of 'independence of mind', a Hegelian reading suggested by the importance of the master/slave relationship in Wagner's thinking at this time; see Corse 1990: 119–21.

55 Nattiez 1993: 256 quotes a remarkable Saint-Simonian parallel to this passage in the writings of Pierre-Simon Ballanche: humankind's lost unity will be regained 'when woman, as the embodiment of the male will, ceases to be man's slave'.

56 For an account of the role of narrative and the function of the repetitions in the *Ring*, see Abbate 1991: 156–205.

57 In spite of the awkwardness of the repetition, both full scores prefer *empfing* to the *barg* (hid) of GS and the various vocal scores.

58 Although the 1874 full score has *seines* (his), this appears to be a misreading and has not been adopted by later editions.

59 The 1874 full score has the definite article *der*, an alternative ignored by later editions.

60 The 1874 reading, *heiliger*, has not been taken up by later editions.

61 The 1874 reading, *nicht*, has been ignored by later editors.

62 The 1874 reading, *Feind*, although alliteratively viable, has been ignored by later editors.

63 The 1874 reading, *sollt'*, appears to be an aberration.

64 The 1874 reading, *doch*, has not been followed by later editors.

65 Although the majority of English translators have read this as *Wal* – which they have then proceeded to translate as 'battle' – this reading seems to be ruled out on two counts: not only is *Wahl* common to all the full and vocal scores, but Wagner never uses *Wal* in the sense of 'battlefield', but only as 'the slain'. Although the passage remains obscure, 'choice' seems to be the only possible translation here.

66 Although later editions generally prefer *Forst* (forest), the 1874 full score's alliteratively more acceptable *Wald* has been favoured here.

67 i.e., at bar 36.

68 "'Sintolt the Hegeling" gets his name from a court official in the *Nibelungenlied* and his patronymic from a leading tribe in *Kudrun*. "Wittig the Irming" is a concoction from the late medieval German epics where a Witege is the minion of a King Ermenrich'; Gillespie 1983: 34.

69 The 1874 full score's dittographical reading, *Haß*, has not been followed by later editors.

70 The colour of Sigmund's complexion is not mentioned by the compiler of the *Volsunga saga*, but of Sigurð (Siegfried) it is said: 'His hair, which fell in long locks, was brown and handsome to look on' (Finch 1965: 41).

71 Wotan's eight-legged horse, Sleipnir, was fathered by Loki in an attempt to extricate the gods from their promise to pay a giant for building them a fortification; the sources do not state whether the animal could fly.

72 See note 43.

73 This claim is shown to be untrue in Act II of *Siegfried*, where Wotan, ever anxious to stage-manage the course of events, confronts first Alberich and then Fafner.

74 The 1874 full score reads *herschenden* [*sic*] but later editors have preferred the GS reading, *herrischen*.

75 The 1874 full score reads *vor Scham*.

76 The 1874 full score reads *gelegt* (lodged).

77 The 1874 full score reads *gewähren* (grant).

78 The 1874 full score reads *friedlichen* (peaceful).

79 The 1874 full score prefers the present tense, *liebe*.

80 i.e., at bar 113.

81 Nattiez (1993: 69–73) points out that Wagner draws a critical distinction between Mime as the embodiment of the 19th-century artist, whose art is sterile and unproductive, and the spontaneous skill of the naturally gifted Siegfried. The word *Kunst* is repeatedly applied to Mime, and always with negative overtones.

82 Although Nattiez (1993: 71) is right to remark that Mime is obsessed with the idea of payment or reward, this in itself is insufficient evidence to read the character as an anti-Semitic caricature, since the word *Lohn* (reward) is regularly used by other figures, too. For a fuller treatment of the character of Mime, see Newman (1933: II,346–7); Adorno (1952: 23–7); Rose (1992: 71) and Nattiez (1993: 69–76).

83 See note 42.

84 Although the 1875 edition of the full score reads 'Ein Schwert nur', the later amendment, placing the semantic stress on 'ein', has been preferred here.

85 There is an ambiguity in the German: the line could conceivably be translated 'she who gave you into my care'.

86 It is not clear why Mime lies here: it emerges from his riddle scene with the Wanderer that he knows far more details about Siegfried's past than he is now prepared to divulge.

87 Literally, 'Stop that eternal starling's song'.

88 There is an untranslatable pun in the German: *fegen* means both 'to burnish or polish metal' and also 'to beat or thrash'. Siegfried's psychotic treatment not only of Mime but also of Fafner and the Wanderer is prefigured in Wagner's medieval and modern sources; see Magee 1990: 107–18.

89 For a fuller version of this dialogue, see appendix on p. 355.

90 Such expressions of gnomic wisdom are typical of the *Hávamál*, one of the Eddic poems which became available to Wagner through Simrock's translation in the spring of 1851; the sources for this scene are discussed in Golther 1902, Müller and Panagl 1988 and Magee 1990.

91 For an anthropological study of this battle of wits, see Vajda 1988; for a musical analysis, see Brinkmann 1972.

92 Although Wagner's use of the verb *tagen* is probably conditioned by purely alliterative constraints, it may be significant, none the less, that its meanings include 'to meet in order to transact business', a reading entirely consonant with Wagner's interpretation of the Nibelungs as a thriving business community. In this context it is worth recalling Wagner's reaction to London's docklands in 1877: 'This is Alberich's dream come true – Nibelheim, world dominion, activity, work, everywhere the oppressive feeling of steam and fog' (CT, 25 May 1877).

93 See note 25.

94 According to Snorri Sturluson (1987: 11–12), the world was created from various parts of the body of the giant Ymir. Although Snorri makes it clear that Niflheim (i.e., Wagner's Nibelheim) existed 'ages before the earth was created', Snorri's metaphorical language has clearly left its mark on Wagner's imagery here.

95 The 1875 full score has *Herz* instead of *Heer*, but this is evidently an aberration.

96 As Magee (1990: 138–9) points out, dwarfs traditionally lost their native wit when exposed to the rays of Wotan's eye which, as mentioned in note 33, is synonymous with the sun. It is not clear whether Mime identifies his visitor here or later.

97 See note 38.

98 Literally, 'Cave of Spite'. According to the *Poetic Edda*, Fafnir dwelt on Gnítaheiðr, which Otto Höfler identifies as the Knetterheide between Minden and Paderborn. This hypothesis rests on the assumption that the figure of Siegfried is based on the historical figure of Arminius and that the defeat of the dragon Fafner is a literary reflex of Arminius's defeat of the Roman army in AD 9; see Höfler 1961. For more on the historical background, see Wais 1953; Finch 1965: xxxii–xxxvi; and Dronke 1969: 29–38.

99 The 1875 full score reading, *Dann*, has not been followed by later editors.

100 NHG prefers the form *Pappe*, but Wagner's Saxon dialect does not distinguish between voiced and voiceless plosives.

101 See note 22.

102 This anvil-splitting motif is shared by the *Volsunga saga* and the Grimms' 'Tale of the Lad Who Set Out to Learn Fear' (1858: 13–24) and may have been one of the factors which persuaded Wagner to expand the *Ring* to include an account of Siegfried's youthful adventures.

103 i.e., at bar 96.

104 Although the 1875 full score reads *zahlte* (paid), the repetition is awkward and the GS reading of *lohnte* (rewarded) seems preferable.

105 Another case of dittography: the full score has *stark* (strong), whereas GS reads *stolz* (proud).

106 The Proudhonesque implications of the dragon's inert enjoyment of the hoard are briefly discussed by Kreckel (1986: 101–8 and 154–64), but most interpretations of this episode concentrate on the Jungian aspect of Siegfried's encounter with the 'Great Mother'; see, for example, Jung 1956: 363–4 and Donington 1963: 193–6.

107 The 1875 reading of *leicht* (light, i.e., not heavy) has not been adopted by later editors.

108 Nattiez (1993: 73–4) points out that this attempt on Siegfried's part to understand the language of the woodbird is foredoomed to failure, since it ignores the primacy of words central to Wagner's programme of reform.

109 A note in the full score reads: 'The body of the giant serpent is represented by a camouflaged machine; when it reaches the top of the mound, a trapdoor is opened through which the singer sings the following using a speaking-trumpet let into the jaws of the monster from within.'

110 The 1875 reading of *mir* is grammatically impossible.

111 A note in the full score reads: 'The machine representing the serpent has been moved somewhat further downstage during the fight; a new trapdoor is now opened underneath it and from it the singer sings through a weaker speaking-trumpet.'

112 Although the 1875 full score specifies 'to be sung by a boy treble', this solution has rarely been adopted. As a matter of ornithological interest, it may be mentioned that the *Poetic Edda* and *Volsunga saga* refer to a whole flock of birds described in ON as *igður*, variously translated as 'quails' (von der Hagen), 'hen eagles' (Simrock), 'tits' (Neckel/Kuhn), 'woodpeckers' (Morris) and 'nuthatches' (Finch and Byock).

113 In the *Volsunga saga*, Oðin frequently and opportunely intervenes in Sigurð's life, helping him choose a horse, advising him how to kill Fafnir and so on.

114 In the *Volsunga saga*, Sigurð kills his foster-father on the mere hearsay of one of the nuthatches. According to Newman (1933: II,406), Wagner altered his source in the light of Friedrich Hopp's *Dr. Fausts Hauskäppchen*, a 19th-century farce in which the eponymous cap allows its wearer to compel people to answer questions truthfully. It no doubt gratified Wagner to admit to this borrowing in a letter of 10 August 1874, since it helped to underline the popular nature of the work, a point he had been keen to emphasize from the outset: see, for example, his letters to Julie Ritter of 6 May 1857 and Otto Wesendonck of 28 August 1859; see also CT, 25 June 1876: 'The children liked the first act of *Siegfried* best of all – which pleases R., for it supplies proof of its folk character, whereas all the artists have up to now treated this first act as if it were quite incomprehensible.'

115 Wotan is literally keeping an eye on the situation: see notes 33 and 113.

116 Although the 1875 full score reads *sehnend* (yearning), the GS reading of *sehrend* (searing) has been preferred here.

117 i.e., at bar 55.

118 i.e., at bar 66.

119 As Magee (1990: 130–31) points out, the *Siegfried* Erda predates her *Rheingold* counterpart. Whereas the latter is based on the all-knowing vala or prophetess of the Eddic *Völuspá*, the former is clearly influenced by the relatively ineffectual grave-dwelling vala of the *Vegtamsqvið*, with its scene of recognition and mutual acrimony. Perhaps Wagner retained the inconsistency of characterization in order to emphasize his belief that godly wisdom has already been supplanted in the Hegelian world-process as the race of mortal heroes supersedes the gods' redundant rule.

120 MHG *vrum* meant 'brave' and assumed connotations of Christian piety only under Luther's influence.

121 Literally, 'into her eye he pressed sleep', an image drawn from the Eddic *Sigrdrífumál*, where we read of Sigurð's awakening of the sleeping Sigrdrífa: 'Her name was Sigrdrífa, meaning Victory-Granter, and she was a valkyrie. She said that two kings had fought. One was named Helm-Gunnar; he had grown old but was still the greatest of warriors, and to him Odin had decreed victory. The other was Agnar, Hauda's brother, who never had hopes of being favoured. Victory-Granter felled Helm-Gunnar in battle. In revenge Odin pricked her with a sleep-thorn and said that she should never thereafter fight for victory but should be married. "But", she said to him, "I in my turn bind myself by a vow to marry no man except one who knows no fear"' (Auden and Taylor 1981: 86). From this bald narrative Wagner developed the events of Act II of *Die Walküre*.

122 The 'primeval mothers' referred to here are presumably other valas. Wagner may have been influenced by the closing section of the *Vegtamskviða*, with its reference to 'þriggia þursa móðir' (the mother of three giants), and perhaps also by Goethe's allusion to the enigmatic 'Mütter' in *Faust* part II (ll. 6216–24).

123 Although the 1875 full score reads *Urweisen* (primevally wise), later editors have preferred the GS reading of *unweisen* (unwise).

124 As Magee (1990: 141–3) points out, Wotan's missing eye is the sun, which is embodied in turn in the figure of Siegfried. The encounter between the god and his grandson thereby assumes cosmological significance.

125 There appears to be an inconsistency here between Wotan's aggressive stance towards his grandson and his resolve, espoused only moments earlier, to 'yield in delight to the eternally young'. August Röckel first drew attention to the contradiction and, in doing so, provoked Wagner's famous proto-Schopenhauerian interpretation of the *Ring* in his long letter of 25/26 January 1854: 'Faced with the prospect of his own annihilation, [Wotan] finally becomes so instinctively human that – in spite of his supreme resolve – his ancient pride is once more stirred, provoked moreover (mark this well!) by – his jealousy of Brünnhilde.' As the present writer has pointed out (Spencer 1981: 98–102), an examination of the sketches and drafts makes this line of argument seem an oversimplification: the Wanderer would appear to be motivated, rather, by a desire to prove to himself that Siegfried is the free and fearless hero who will redeem both gods and world from their guilty existence. Only by provoking Siegfried into brushing him aside and allowing his spear to be shattered by his grandson's sword can he prove to himself that Siegfried is a free agent. This interpretation receives support from a conversation which the wife of the Russian composer and critic Alexander Nikolayevich Serov recorded with Wagner in 1869: 'In this confrontation the god sees standing before him one of his successors. Fate has decreed that dominion over the earth will pass to him, now that the dwellers in the sky have lost their powers and begun to fade away. Siegfried's childlike ways affect Wotan profoundly and, although he is certain of the imminent downfall of the gods, he still yearns to witness an act which is a genuine expression of free will and completely independent of divine intervention' (Serova 1991: 22).

126 i.e., at bar 799.

127 For an androgynous interpretation of this love duet, see Nattiez 1993: 76–84; for a Hegelian interpretation, see Corse 1990: 157–61; for a Jungian interpretation, see Jung 1956: 387–9 and Donington 1963: 207–16; for a feminist interpretation, see Zurmühl 1984; for the importance of solar myth, see Magee 1990: 143–52.

128 *hapax legomenon*; generally Wagner suppresses initial syllables for archaizing effect (*gehren* for *begehren*, *hehlen* for *verhehlen*, *kiesen* for *erkiesen*, and so on) but the prefix *er-* seems to have been added here for purely metrical reasons.

129 i.e., at bar 19.

130 According to the *Völuspá*, Loki will be freed from his bonds at *ragnarök*, when he will lead an army of giants into the final battle with the gods. The Third Norn's reference to 'Loge's host' suggests that the end of the gods is at hand.

131 The world-ash, or Yggdrasill, bestrode the earth and heavens alike. Of its three roots, one passed into the land of the gods, a second into that of the frost-giants and the third into the kingdom of the dead. Beneath the root in giant-land was Mimir's Well, whose waters vouchsafed wisdom. A second spring, the Well of Urðr (Fate), was located in the land of the gods, and it was here that the three Norns dwelt. Wagner has conflated the two wells.

132 See note 18. Although the world-ash was never a very healthy tree (it was constantly gnawed by the animals living in its shade), there is nothing in the mythological sources to foreshadow Wagner's original and significant claim that Wotan's spear was hewn from one of its branches and that this rape of Nature led to the devastation of the surrounding area.

133 The fraying of the Norns' rope and the supersession of divine wisdom are Wagner's invention.

134 In the *Nibelungenlied*, Prünhilt owes her Amazonian strength to her virginity, the loss of which reduces her to a cipher. In the case of the 13th-century epic, however, she loses it involuntarily when Sîvrit, disguised as Gunther, rapes her.

135 The remainder of this scene illustrates the Hegelian importance of mutual recognition in love; see Corse 1990: 167–70.

136 Since 'Grane' could conceivably be the subject of the optative 'bringe', rather than the dative object of the imperative, these lines might be rendered alternatively as 'O may Grane often / bring Brünnhilde's greeting'.

137 i.e., at bars 647–9.

138 i.e., at bar 717.

139 i.e., at bars 889–92.

140 In the *Nibelungenlied*, Sîvrit comes upon two princes, Schilbunc and Niblunc, quarrelling over their treasure and, for no good reason, kills them. As a result he falls heir to their wealth and acquires a retinue of human followers, the Nibelungs. These appear not to be the same as the Nibelung dwarfs of the Scandinavian tradition, although Wagner has assumed that they are. His reasons for introducing this blind motif are unclear, unless it be to indicate that Siegfried is indifferent to the power which he wields.

141 A Wagnerian coinage, based on MHG *vrîdel* = sweetheart, although there may also be a play on the verb *frieden* = to confine or prevent from running wild.

142 This unexpectedly belligerent greeting derives from the comparable episode in the *Nibelungenlied*, where it has often been interpreted as a sign of the arrogance for which the hero is later punished. A similar – theologically inspired – interpretation has been advanced more recently by Huber (1988: 288). However, as Panzer (1955) has pointed out, Siegfried's greeting is the traditional way of asserting territorial rights and has precedents in English and Scandinavian history.

143 Literally, 'assist, my body, this oath of mine'.

144 In the *Nibelungenlied*, Sîvrit pretends to be Gunther's vassal in order to win Kriemhilt for himself and Prünhilt for his prospective brother-in-law. Whereas the deceit has disastrous consequences in the medieval epic, leading directly to

the quarrel between the two queens and thereafter to Sîvrit's death, the motif is not elaborated in the *Ring*.

145 As Magee points out (1990: 94), Wagner's use of the word *Minne* here clearly reflects his reading of Grimm's *Teutonic Mythology* (1875–8: 48–51), where *minnetrinken* is glossed as a drink in memory of absent friends, *minne* being used in the ON sense of 'memory'. ON poets refer to the potion as *óminnisveig* or 'draught of oblivion'.

146 In spite of the apparently authentic details of this scene, Wagner's account of the blood-brotherhood ceremony owes more to his own imagination than to any historical source; see Magee 1990: 95–6.

147 'fromme' (righteous) could be an adjective qualifying 'Sühne' (expiation), or it could be the optative of the verb 'frommen': 'may expiation serve the friend'.

148 i.e., at bar 828.

149 There may be a suggestion here of MHG *snel* = bold, warriorlike.

150 The reading in SW ('Sie wahrt mir den Reif') is evidently incorrect.

151 It is striking that love encourages Brünnhilde to reject Waltraute's pleas and to condemn the gods and the world to destruction. Although the *Ring* had originally been intended, *inter alia*, as a paean to love, Wagner's views changed following his reading of Schopenhauer in the autumn of 1854 and he now came to see love as a 'fundamentally devastating force' (letter to August Röckel of 23 August 1856); for the medieval inspiration behind this theme, see Spencer 1992: 165–6.

152 There is almost certainly a reminiscence here of Aeschylus's *Prometheus Bound*, in which Zeus's eagle tears daily at Prometheus's liver as the latter lies chained to a rock; see Müller and Panagl 1990: V,21; English trans., p. 55.

153 Once again the ring proves ineffectual. Donington (1963: 228) argues that 'the total needs of the situation, as opposed to the needs of any of the individual characters seen in isolation,' require Brünnhilde to forfeit the ring at this juncture. Huber (1988: 292) claims, somewhat ingeniously, that, because Siegfried and Brünnhilde are one, he is merely helping himself to what is already his. Sabor (1991) suggests, with some plausibility, that the power of the ring is effective only over those who are afraid of its power. Certainly, both the Wanderer (in *Siegfried* III,1) and Alberich (in *Götterdämmerung* II,1) make the specific point that the latter's curse leaves Siegfried unscathed because he has never learned the meaning of fear.

154 i.e., at bar 30.

155 i.e., at bar 39.

156 Although SW reads 'dir', GS, the 1876 full score, and the Breitkopf vocal score all prefer 'ihr' (I do not care to thank *her*). In the *Thidreks saga* (Wagner's source for this episode) the queen is raped by an unnamed elf while in a drunken stupor.

157 Alberich is mistaken, as Siegfried will learn to his cost in Act III. It remains unclear, however, whether Wagner wishes us to believe that Siegfried dies because he has learned the meaning of fear in his encounter with Brünnhilde (an assumption called into question by the fact that Siegfried is able to return to Brünnhilde's rock at the end of Act I only because he has *not* learned what it is to feel fear) or whether he dies simply because Hagen has inveigled him into swearing a perjured oath. Siegfried's death had always been central to Wagner's thinking. Initially the hero had died in order to bolster up the gods' decaying rule, but as soon as the gods themselves were consigned to oblivion, Siegfried's death lost its ethical justification. By the 1870s Wagner was reluctant to accord Siegfried any tragic grandeur: 'Which is the greater, Wotan or Siegfried? Wotan the more tragic, since he recognizes the guilt of existence and is atoning for the error of creation' (CT, 2 July 1872); 'after lunch conversation about Siegfried and Brünnhilde, the former not a tragic figure, since he does not become conscious of his position' (CT, 4 July 1873).

158 i.e., at bar 205.

159 In the *Nibelungenlied* Sîvrit tames Prünhilt by binding her and hanging her from a peg in Gunther's bedchamber. There is no suggestion that bondage played any part in the events which end Act I of *Götterdämmerung*.

160 For an interpretation of this bantering exchange between Siegfried and Gutrune as a parody of Auber's *La Muette de Portici* and the French *opéra comique* style, see Nattiez 1993: 84–90.

161 The dative pronoun 'ihm' is intentionally ambiguous and could mean either 'for him' or 'by him'; Gutrune seizes on the former alternative, although she knows of the plan to introduce Siegfried into Brünnhilde's bedchamber in Gunther's disguise. Since a translation of the pronoun would necessarily remove the ambiguity, it has been omitted here.

162 The pun on Hagen and Hagedorn (hawthorn) defies translation. In the 10th-century Latin *Waltharius* (which Wagner reread in July/August 1871), Hagen is described as *spinosus* (thorny).

163 The use of 'einst' (normally used of events some distance away in time) raises questions about the chronology of the work. It is far from clear how long Siegfried and Brünnhilde spent together in her mountain cave and whether, on descending from her rock, Siegfried went straight to the Gibichung court (where his fame had already preceded him). In Act III of

Götterdämmerung Siegfried describes the events of Acts II and III of *Siegfried* and says that they took place 'in meinen jungen Tagen' (in the days of my youth) – which suggests that some considerable time may have elapsed between the end of *Siegfried* and the prologue to *Götterdämmerung*, or, alternatively, between the prologue and opening act of *Götterdämmerung*. Perhaps – as Donington (1963: 222) and others have remarked – questions of time are irrelevant in a mythological context.

164 Wapnewski (1984) argues that Brünnhilde is wilfully disingenuous in her accusation, deliberately confusing Siegfried's two visits to her cave.

165 *Rath* is used in the MHG sense of 'supply, expedient, help', although its similarity to the NHG word for 'advice' has misled the editor of the Schott vocal score into misreading *Zaubers Rath* (store of magic) as *Zaubrers Rath* (sorcerer's counsel).

166 In the *Nibelungenlied* Sîvrit acquires his invulnerability by bathing in the blood of a (nameless) dragon; a linden leaf falls between his shoulder-blades, leaving him vulnerable only at that point. This motif raised too many practical and ethical problems for Wagner, and so he replaced it with one borrowed from the ON *Sigrdrífumál*, in which the wakened valkyrie confers on the hero her runic lore. The idea that she omitted to protect his back because she saw no need to do so is Wagner's own addition and one which, as Magee points out (1990: 103), 'has the merit of paying full tribute to Siegfried's bravery'.

167 Literally, 'crush my marrow', but the horticultural ambiguity of the term seemed to suggest the need for a less literal translation.

168 Although Schott's 1876 full score and vocal score both have *dich* (you), SW prefers the GS reading, *mich* (me).

169 It is odd that Wagner should allow Brünnhilde to describe Siegfried as her husband within earshot of Gunther.

170 A Wagnerian allonym for Wotan based on the elements *All* (universe) and *raunen* (to whisper runic lore).

171 i.e., at bar 50.

172 In his *Teutonic Mythology* (1875–8: 587), Jacob Grimm points out medieval instances of the expression *Frau Sonne* and, in his dictionary (IV,72), argues that *Frau* originally meant 'goddess'. The mythological resonances of this scene are enhanced by the fact that the sun is Wotan's missing eye and that this appeal to the sun-goddess conjures up the sun-god himself in the shape of Siegfried.

173 See Grimm's *Teutonic Mythology* (1875–8: 535): 'Our 16th-century mercenaries still threw a clod of earth on going into battle [...] as a sign of their complete detachment from life.' GS includes four extra lines for Siegfried at this point: 'Denn Leben und Leib / – sollt' ohne Lieb' / in der Furcht Bande / bang ich sie fesseln – / Leben und Leib – / seht! – so / werf' ich sie weit von mir!' (For life and body – if, without love, I'm to bind them, anxious, within the bonds of fear – life and body – lo! thus do I throw them far away from me!). Although these lines (for all their convoluted syntax) express the Hegelian opposition between love and fear, Wagner evidently decided to suppress them because they presuppose a level of consciousness on Siegfried's part which he never achieves elsewhere.

174   This *apo koinou* construction is typical of the *Nibelungenlied*, on whose narrative the events surrounding Siegfried's death are closely based. Indeed, there even seems to be a verbal reminiscence here of the opening strophe of the medieval poem: 'Uns ist in alten mæren wunders vil geseit / von helden lobebæren, von grôzer arebeit, / von fröuden, hôchgezîten, von weinen und von klagen, / von küener recken strîten muget ir nu wunder hœren sagen' (We have been told in ancient tales many marvels of famous heroes, of mighty toil, joys, and high festivities, of weeping and wailing, and the fighting of bold warriors – of these you can now hear marvels told).

175   See note 35.

176   i.e., at bar 977.

177   Brünnhilde's laughter is a prominent feature of several ON sources; the question of whether it has any moral implications in Wagner's version is discussed in detail in Abbate 1991: 206–49.

178   In the *Nibelungenlied* Sîvrit's wounds begin to bleed afresh when Hagen approaches the corpse, thus confirming his identity as Sîvrit's assassin. Practicalities of staging the work presumably obliged Wagner to make this rather melodramatic change. For a more charitable explanation of the 'numinous' nature of the incident, see Wintle 1988.

179   For the variant endings of the work, see the appendix on p. 360.

180   It is difficult to know whether to read any significance into the wording of this stage direction. In GS the men and women watch these eschatological events unfold *in sprachloser Erschütterung* (in speechless dismay); in the full score, by contrast, they react *in höchster Ergriffenheit* (moved to the very depths of their being). Perhaps the end of the world is now a consummation devoutly to be wished: the bystanders accept that 'breaking of the will' which, according to Wagner (CT, 4 October 1873), is the ethical theme of the *Ring*. For further interpretations of the end of the cycle, see Shaw 1898; Ellis 1903/4; Donington 1963; Dahlhaus 1971; Hollinrake 1976; Spencer 1981; Darcy 1986; and Deathridge 1988.

Glossary of names

The names of many of the characters in the *Ring* *mean* something and an understanding of that meaning is often necessary for an appreciation of the symbolism involved. All the names, including that of the eponymous *Walküre*, are stressed on the first syllable in German.

Alberich　A dwarf who acquires dominion over his fellow Nibelungs by renouncing love and forging an all-powerful ring. The name may mean 'king of the elves'. Wagner's Alberich is a composite character based, *inter alia*, on the whip-wielding, treasure-guarding Alberich of the MHG *Nibelungenlied*, the aquatic Andvari of the Eddic tradition and the thieving Alfrek of the *Thidreks saga*. Alberich's curse on the ring derives from the Scandinavian tradition, but his curse on love is Wagner's own invention.

Brünnhilde　The dissident daughter of Wotan and Erda derives her name from MHG *brünne* = brinie or coat of mail and MHG *hilt* = battle. Her evolution from hoydenish shield-maid to jealous wife represents a masterful piece of psychologizing on Wagner's part, involving, as it does, a successful attempt to make sense of the schizophrenic figure of the *Volsunga saga* in the light of the scholarly writings of Ludwig Frauer and Jacob Grimm. Her cosmological contribution to the final moments of the *Ring* is Wagner's own invention.

Donner　The Teutonic god of thunder was the son of Oðin and the earth goddess, Iorð, and the hero of many tales of knock-about humour in Scandinavian mythology, where his importance equals and sometimes surpasses that of Oðin. For Wagner, he is a blusteringly ineffectual character, ripe for supersession in the Hegelian world-process.

Erda　Wagner's earth-goddess is a composite figure based upon the prophetic vala of the ON *Völuspá*, the ineffectual grave-dweller of the ON *Vegtamsqviða* and perhaps also the Greek earth-goddess, Gaia. In Wagner's cosmogony, she is the mother of Brünnhilde and the three Norns. Her wisdom is finite.

Fafner　One of two giants who murders his brother and gains possession of the Nibelung hoard, which he guards in the shape of a dragon. The character and his function are fleshed out from events narrated in several Scandinavian sources.

Fasolt　Fafner's brother and the first victim of the curse on Alberich's ring. Like that of Fafner, the figure of Fasolt is largely inspired by the events surrounding the theft of Andvari's ring in the Eddas and *Volsunga saga*, as well as by an episode in which an unnamed mountain-giant is tricked out of his reward for building a fortification (not Valhalla) for the gods. The name is taken from the 13th-century MHG *Ecken Ausfahrt*. The characterization, generally held to be Wagner's own, probably derives from Wilhelm Müller's *Altdeutsche Religion*.

Flosshilde　One of three Rhinedaughters. These figures are largely Wagner's own invention, based on a passing reference to two prophetic *merewîbe* (mermaids) in the *Nibelungenlied* and an iconographical description in Jacob Grimm's *Teutonic Mythology*. Like the *Wasserminnen* of the Grimms' *Deutsche Sagen*, they traditionally lure men to their ruin. In the 1848 scenario they are conceived as 'three maidens with swans' wings'; the number three was suggested by Julius Schnorr von Carolsfeld's and Eugen Neureuther's woodcuts accompanying Gustav Pfizer's 1843 edition of the *Nibelungenlied*. The initial element of Flosshilde's name derives from the verb *fließen* = to flow, while the second element derives from MHG *hilt* = battle. For the symbolic importance of the Rhinedaughters' names, see note 3 above. Their 'father', referred to on several occasions, is presumably the River Rhine.

Freia　Freyja was the sister of Freyr and a Scandinavian fertility goddess, although, according to Snorri, the apples of eternal youth were tended not by her but by Iðunn.

Fricka　In the *Ring*, Fricka is Wotan's wife and guardian of wedlock. Wagner follows Jacob

Grimm in allocating this divine charge to her. In the Scandinavian sources, Frigg is notorious, rather, for her infidelities.

Friedmund One of the names which Siegmund wishes he might adopt: NHG *Friede* = peace but derives from MHG *vride*, which has the additional meaning of security or protection; *-munt* is a suffix meaning guardianship and survives in NHG *Bevormundung*; the name might be translated 'Guardian of Peace'.

Froh Froh is based on Freyr, the Norse god of plenty and sister of Freyja, but he remains a largely undifferentiated figure in *Das Rheingold*.

Frohwalt Another of the names which Siegmund longs to assume: MHG *vrô* = joyful, while *-walt* derives from the verb *walten* = to rule or be in charge of; 'Purveyor of Joy' would be a possible translation.

Gerhilde MHG *gêr* = spear; MHG *hilt* = battle. All the valkyries have warlike names and, with the exception of Brünnhilde and Siegrune, are Wagner's own invention. Their role, attested by many medieval sources and codified by such 19th-century scholars as Grimm, Ettmüller and Frauer, involved summoning doomed warriors to Valhalla to assist Wotan in his final battle against the forces of evil. Grimm suggested the number nine. Their parentage is unclear both in the sources and in the *Ring* itself, although a reference in Cosima Wagner's Diaries (CT, 8 May 1874) seems to indicate that only Brünnhilde was fathered on Erda and that her sister valkyries are the result of what Fricka terms Wotan's 'wanton' affairs with other women.

Grimgerde A valkyrie; MHG *grim* = fury; MHG *gerte* = staff.

Grimhilde The mother of Gunther, Gutrune and Hagen derives her name from the Scandinavian tradition.

Gunther Prince of the Gibichungs, sister of Gutrune and (in Wagner's version) half-brother of Hagen. The somewhat weak characterization of this figure (who is based ultimately on a 5th-century Burgundian king) derives from the early sections of the *Nibelungenlied*.

Gutrune Gunther's sister, Gutrune is a relatively insubstantial figure in *Götterdämmerung*, her role and characterization being largely circumscribed by the mechanics of the plot. She is based on the Gudrún of the Scandinavian sources and the Kriemhilt of the *Nibelungenlied*.

Hagen Son of the Nibelung Alberich and half-brother of Gunther and Gutrune, Hagen combines features from the MHG *Nibelungenlied* and ON Eddas and *Thidreks saga*, although his motivation, for the most part, is Wagner's own.

Hella The Norse underworld, inhabited by those who die of disease or old age and presided over by Loki's daughter, Hel.

Helmwige A valkyrie; MHG *helm* = helmet; MHG *wîc* = battle.

Hunding ON *hundr* = dog; Wagner's Hunding combines the name of Sigmund's enemy in the *Volsunga saga* with the role played in the same saga by Siggeir, the king of Gautland and husband of Sigmund's sister, Signy.

Loge Wagner's fire god is based on the Scandinavian Loki, an ambivalent figure who appears as both the gods' ally and – in the final battle – as their arch-opponent. Wagner's characterization may also owe something to that anarchical arsonist, Mikhail Bakunin.

Mime Alberich's brother and a master-craftsman uniquely capable of forging the tarnhelm. His prototype is the Mimir of the *Thidreks saga*, although the characterization is largely Wagner's own.

Neiding The Wälsungs' enemies in the *Ring* derive their name from MHG *nît* = hatred, grudge or greed. Wagner had originally used the name in his *Wieland* sketch of 1849/50.

Norns The Norse Fates; although they vary in number in the Scandinavian sources, Wagner has settled on three on the basis of a passage in Snorri's Edda, which describes three Norns – Urðr, Verðandi and Skuld – dwelling by a well beneath one of the roots of the world ash-tree. According to Grimm's *Teutonic Mythology*, these three Norns were responsible, respectively, for past, present and future. From Grimm, too, came the motif of spinning.

Nothung The *Not(h)* element is intentionally ambiguous and derives from MHG *nôt* = affliction, plight, extreme necessity and need. In the MHG *Nibelungenlied* Sîvrit's sword is called Balmunc, in the ON *Volsunga saga* it is Gramr. Wagner adopted the name Nothung only when he versified the drama in June 1852.

Ortlinde A valkyrie; MHG *ort* = point, especially of a weapon; MHG *lint* = dragon.

Rossweisse A valkyrie; NHG *Roß* = stallion; *weiße* = white; called Rosswilde in the 1852 prose draft.

Schwertleite A valkyrie; NHG *Schwert* = sword; the verb *leiten* = to lead or bear; the MHG compound *swertleite* was used to mean 'investiture'.

Siegfried Son of the incestuous union of Siegmund and Sieglinde; *Sieg* = victory; *Friede* peace or protection. In the 1848 scenario Wagner glosses the name as 'der durch Sieg Friede bringen soll' (he who shall bring peace through victory); in the 1852 versification this became 'Siegfried erfreu' sich des Siegs' (may Siegfried joy in victory). Wagner always intended Siegfried to be a popular hero. It is perhaps inevitable that, for a generation familiar with Brecht's 'Unhappy the land that has need of heroes', the character of Siegfried should become problematical and that attempts should be made to deflate the hero by dressing him in a romper-suit in order to ensure that his behaviour, far from being heroic, appears simply infantile.

Sieglinde Daughter of Wotan and an unnamed mortal, twin sister of Siegmund, wife of Hunding and mother of Siegfried; *Sieg* = victory, while *linde* = gentle, mild and, independently, the linden tree whose heart-shaped leaves traditionally symbolize love. Wagner's Sieglinde combines the name of Sîvrit's mother from the *Nibelungenlied* with the role of Signy in the *Volsunga saga*; her sylvan *accouchement* comes from the *Thidreks saga*. In the 1848 scenario the twins' father is an unnamed hero; not until 1852 did Wotan, masquerading as Wälse, usurp this role.

Siegmund Son of Wotan, twin brother of Sieglinde and father of Siegfried; also known as Wehwalt; *Sieg* = victory, MHG *-munt* = guardianship.

Siegrune A valkyrie; *Sieg* = victory; MHG *rûne* = rune, secret or spell.

Valhalla Although Grimm glosses the name as *aula optionis* (Hall of the Chosen), Wagner follows other authorities in deriving the initial element from ON *valr* = the slain. According to ON sources, Valhalla was a hall in which warriors who had fallen in battle, together with men and women who had been sacrificed to Oðin, would foregather to await the final battle, when they would sally forth to confront the forces of evil. Wagner has conflated this myth with another in which a single, unnamed giant is duped into building a fortress for the gods in return for the empty promise of the goddess Freyja.

Wälse The name which Wotan assumes in fathering the Wälsung twins on a mortal woman. The ON form would be Volsi, but no such character appears in the *Volsunga saga*. Wagner borrowed details from Karl Lachmann and, in an inspired move of his own, equated Lachmann's Wälse with Wotan: not only did this move add to the poignancy of the relationship between Wotan and his semi-divine son, it also enmeshed him further in the toils of his tragic dilemma.

Waltraute A valkyrie; ON *valr* = slain warriors; MHG *traut* = devoted.

Wehwalt Siegmund's assumed name in *Die Walküre*; *Weh* = woe or affliction, MHG *-walt* = bringer of.

Wellgunde One of the three Rhinedaughters; *Welle* = wave; the second element frequently occurs in women's names and may be cognate with ON *gunnr* = battle.

Woglinde One of the three Rhinedaughters; the verb *wogen* = to billow or welter, while MHG *linde* = gentle, mild.

Wotan According to Jacob Grimm and Wagner, Oðin/Wotan was the chief of the Teutonic gods. (Onomastic studies suggest that Thor may have been more widely revered.) Grimm derived the name from the word meaning 'rage' or 'fury' (NHG *Wut*) and saw the figure first and foremost as the god of battle commanding the Wild Hunt (see note 43), but also as a creative force, the god of poetry and fruitfulness. Among his other names were *valföðr* (Father of the Slain) and *herjaföðr* (Father of Hosts). One of his more benign manifestations was ON Osci / NHG Wunsch, a name reflected in the *Wunschmädchen* or Wish-Maids who wait on fallen heroes in Valhalla. As Gangleri (= the Wanderer), he roams the earth, interfering in the lives of humans. Typically, he wears a dark cloak and a broad-brimmed hat pulled low over his face to conceal his missing eye (see notes 13 and 33). His attributes are the spear Gungnir, two wolves and two ravens, Huginn and Muninn (Thought and Memory). In the *Ring*, Wotan is guilty of the first wrong in despoiling Nature and, from the outset, was conceived as a hubristic figure whose power was based upon 'force and cunning'. As the *Ring* developed, Wagner grew more sympathetic towards Wotan's dilemma. Interpretations of the character have veered between these extremes. Whereas one early reviewer had no hesitation in describing Wotan as an 'assassin, adulterer, swindler, thief, and liar', later generations of singers placed greater emphasis on the 'noble' aspects of the character. Since the 1970s, Wotan has once again come to be seen as a manipulative figure on a moral par with a used-car salesman.

Bibliography

The following bibliography contains only those books and articles which are mentioned in the annotation to the present volume or which may provide the reader with further information on particular aspects of the *Ring*. A fuller bibliography may be found under 'Wagner' in *The New Grove Dictionary of Opera*, ed. Stanley Sadie, 4 vols (London, 1992).

Abbate, Carolyn: 'Opera as Symphony, a Wagnerian Myth', *Analyzing Opera: Verdi and Wagner*, ed. Carolyn Abbate and Roger Parker (Berkeley, 1989), 92–124
————: *Unsung Voices: Opera and Musical Narration in the Nineteenth Century* (Princeton, 1991)
Aberbach, Alan David: *The Ideas of Richard Wagner: An Examination and Analysis of his Major Aesthetic, Political, Economic, Social, and Religious Thoughts*, 2nd edn (Lanham, MD, 1988)
Adorno, Theodor W.: *Versuch über Wagner* (Frankfurt am Main, 1952); trans. Rodney Livingstone as *In Search of Wagner* (London, 1981)
Andersson, Theodore M.: *The Legend of Brynhild* (Ithaca and London, 1980)
Appia, Adolphe: *La Mise en scène du drame wagnérien* (Paris, 1895); trans. Peter Loeffler as *Staging Wagnerian Drama* (Basel, 1962)
Arblaster, Anthony: 'Wagner's politics and Wagner's music', *Wagner*, viii (1987), 82–92
————: *'Viva la libertà': Politics and Opera* (London, 1992)
Ashman, Mike: 'Producing Wagner', *Wagner in Performance*, ed. Barry Millington and Stewart Spencer (New Haven, 1992), 29–47
Bailey, Robert: 'Wagner's Musical Sketches for "Siegfrieds Tod"', *Studies in Music History: Essays for Oliver Strunk* (Princeton, 1968), 459–94
————: 'The Structure of the *Ring* and Its Evolution', *19th Century Music*, i (1977), 48–61
Barth, Herbert, ed.: *Bayreuther Dramaturgie: Der Ring des Nibelungen* (Stuttgart and Zurich, 1980)
Barth, Herbert, Mack, Dietrich and Voss, Egon: *Wagner: Sein Leben, sein Werk und seine Welt in zeitgenössischen Bildern und Texten* (Vienna, 1975); trans. P.R.J. Ford and Mary Whittall as *Wagner: A Documentary Study* (London, 1975)
Bauer, Oswald Georg: *Richard Wagner: Die Bühnenwerke von der Uraufführung bis heute* (Frankfurt am Main, 1982); trans. Stewart Spencer as *Richard Wagner: The Stage Designs and Productions from the Premières to the Present* (New York, 1983)
Bermbach, Udo, ed.: *In den Trümmern der eignen Welt: Richard Wagners 'Der Ring des Nibelungen'* (Berlin and Hamburg, 1989)
Borchmeyer, Dieter: *Das Theater Richard Wagners: Idee – Dichtung – Wirkung* (Stuttgart, 1982); trans. Stewart Spencer as *Richard Wagner: Theory and Theatre* (Oxford, 1991)
————, ed.: *Wege des Mythos in der Moderne: Richard Wagner, 'Der Ring des Nibelungen'* (Munich, 1987)
Boulez, Pierre and others: *Histoire d'un 'Ring'* (Paris, 1980)
Breig, Werner: 'Der "Rheintöchtergesang" in Wagners "Rheingold"', *Archiv für Musikwissenschaft*, xxxvii (1980), 241–63
Breig, Werner and Fladt, Hartmut, eds.: *Dokumente zur Entstehungsgeschichte des Bühnenfestspiels Der Ring des Nibelungen*, vol 29/I of *Richard Wagner: Sämtliche Werke* (Mainz, 1976)
Brink, Louise: *Women Characters in Richard Wagner: A Study in 'The Ring of the Nibelung'* (New York, 1924)
Brinkmann, Reinhold: '"Drei der Fragen stell' ich mir frei": Zur Wanderer-Szene im 1. Akt von Wagners "Siegfried"', *Jahrbuch des Staatlichen Instituts für Musikforschung Preußischer Kulturbesitz* (Berlin, 1972), 120–62
————: 'Mythos – Geschichte – Natur: Zeitkonstellationen im *Ring*', *Richard Wagner: Von der Oper zum Musikdrama*, ed. Stefan Kunze (Berne and Munich, 1978), 61–77
Brown, Hilda Meldrum: *Leitmotiv and Drama: Wagner, Brecht, and the Limits of 'Epic' Theatre* (Oxford, 1991)
Carnegy, Patrick: 'Designing Wagner: Deeds of Music Made Visible?', *Wagner in Performance*, ed. Barry Millington and Stewart Spencer (New Haven, 1992), 48–74

Chapman, Graham and others: *Monty Python's Second Film: A First Draft* (London, 1977)

Clément, Catherine: *Opera, or the Undoing of Women*, trans. Betsy Wing (Minneapolis, 1988)

Conrad, Peter: *Romantic Opera and Literary Form* (Berkeley and Los Angeles, 1977)

Cooke, Deryck: *I Saw the World End: A Study of Wagner's 'Ring'* (Oxford, 1979)

Coren, Daniel: 'The Texts of Wagner's "Der junge Siegfried" and "Siegfried"', *19th Century Music*, vi (1982/83), 17–30

Corse, Sandra: *Wagner and the New Consciousness: Language and Love in the 'Ring'* (Rutherford, 1990)

Culshaw, John: *Ring Resounding: The Recording in Stereo of 'Der Ring des Nibelungen'* (London, 1967)

————: *Reflections on Wagner's 'Ring'* (London, 1976)

Dahlhaus, Carl: 'Wagners Begriff der "dichterisch-musikalischen Periode"', *Beiträge zur Geschichte der Musikanschauung im 19. Jahrhundert*, ed. Walter Salmen (Regensburg, 1965), 179–87

————: 'Formprinzipien in Wagners "Ring des Nibelungen"', *Beiträge zur Geschichte der Oper*, ed. Heinz Becker (Regensburg, 1969), 95–129

————: 'Zur Geschichte der Leitmotivtechnik bei Wagner', *Das Drama Richard Wagners als musikalisches Kunstwerk*, ed. Carl Dahlhaus (Regensburg, 1970), 17–36

————: 'Über den Schluß der *Götterdämmerung*', *Richard Wagner: Werk und Wirkung*, ed. Carl Dahlhaus (Regensburg, 1971a), 97–115

————: *Richard Wagners Musikdramen* (Velber, 1971b); trans. Mary Whittall as *Richard Wagner's Music Dramas* (Cambridge, 1979)

————: 'Tonalität und Form in Wagners "Ring des Nibelungen"', *Archiv für Musikwissenschaft*, xl (1983), 165–73

————: 'Entfremdung und Erinnerung: Zu Wagners *Götterdämmerung*', *Bericht über den internationalen musikwissenschaftlichen Kongreß Bayreuth 1981*, ed. Christoph-Helmut Mahling and Siegrid Wiesmann (Kassel, 1984), 419–20

————: 'What is a Musical Drama?', *Cambridge Opera Journal*, i (1989), 95–111

Darcy, Warren: 'The Pessimism of the *Ring*', *The Opera Quarterly*, 4/2 (Summer 1986), 24–48

————: 'Redeemed from Rebirth: The Evolving Meaning of Wagner's *Ring*', *Wagner in Retrospect*, ed. Leroy R. Shaw, Nancy R. Cirillo and Marion S. Miller (Amsterdam, 1987), 50–61

————: '"Alles was ist, endet!" Erda's Prophecy of World Destruction', *Die Programmhefte der Bayreuther Festspiele 1988: II – 'Das Rheingold'*, pp. 67–92

————: 'Creatio ex nihilo: The Genesis, Structure, and Meaning of the *Rheingold* Prelude', *19th Century Music*, xiii (1989), 79–100

————: *Wagner's 'Das Rheingold': Its Genesis and Structure* (Oxford, 1993)

Deathridge, John: 'Wagner's Sketches for the "Ring"', *Musical Times*, cxviii (1977), 383–9

————: 'The Ring: An Introduction', essay in booklet accompanying James Levine's DG recording of *Die Walküre* (Hamburg, 1988), 41–58

————: '*Götterdämmerung*: Finishing the End', Royal Opera House programme for new production of the *Ring* (October 1991), 59–62

Deathridge, John, Geck, Martin, and Voss, Egon: *Wagner Werk-Verzeichnis (WWV): Verzeichnis der musikalischen Werke Richard Wagners und ihrer Quellen* (Mainz, 1986)

DiGaetani, John, ed.: *Penetrating Wagner's Ring: An Anthology* (Rutherford, NJ, 1978, R/1991)

Donington, Robert: *Wagner's 'Ring' and its Symbols* (London, 1963)

Dronke, Ursula: *The Poetic Edda: Heroic Poems* (Oxford, 1969)

Edda *See* Poetic Edda *and* Snorri Sturluson

Ellis, William Ashton: 'Die verschiedenen Fassungen von "Siegfrieds Tod"', *Die Musik*, iii (1903/4), 239–51 and 315–31

————: 'Schopenhauer's Private Copy of the Ring-Poem', *The Life of Richard Wagner*, 6 vols (London, 1900–08), IV, 440–61

Ellis Davidson, Hilda Roderick: *Gods and Myths of Northern Europe* (Harmondsworth, 1964)

Ettmüller, Ludwig: *Die Lieder der Edda von den Nibelungen* (Zurich, 1837)

Ewans, Michael: *Wagner and Aeschylus: The 'Ring' and the 'Oresteia'* (London, 1982)

Fay, Stephen, and Wood, Roger: *The Ring: Anatomy of an Opera* (London, 1984)

Feuerbach, Ludwig: *Das Wesen des Christenthums*, ed. Wilhelm Bolin and Friedrich Jodl (Stuttgart, 1903); trans. George Eliot [Marian Evans] (London, 1853, R/1957)

————: 'Grundsätze der Philosophie der Zukunft', *Werke in sechs Bänden*, ed. Erich Thies (Frankfurt am Main, 1975), III, 247–322; trans. Manfred Vogel as *Principles of the Philosophy of the Future* (Indianapolis, 1986)

Field, Geoffrey G.: *Evangelist of Race: The Germanic Vision of Houston Stewart Chamberlain* (New York, 1981)

Fouqué, Friedrich de la Motte: *Der Held des Nordens* (Berlin, 1810)

Fox, Malcolm: 'Siegfried's Death', *Wagner*, x (1989), 127–40

Franke, Rainer: *Richard Wagners Zürcher Kunstschriften: Politische und ästhetische Entwürfe auf seinem Wege zum 'Ring des Nibelungen'* (Hamburg, 1983)

Frauer, Ludwig: *Die Walkyrien der skandinavisch-germanischen Götter- und Heldensage* (Weimar, 1846)

Fricke, Richard: *Bayreuth vor dreissig Jahren* (Dresden, 1906); trans. Stewart Spencer as 'Bayreuth in 1876', *Wagner*, xi (1990), 93–109, 134–50 and *Wagner*, xii (1991), 25–44

Furness, Raymond: *Wagner and Literature* (Manchester, 1982)

Gardiner, Patrick: *Schopenhauer* (London, 1969)

Gillespie, George: 'New Myths for Old', *The Valkyrie*, ed. Nicholas John (London, 1983), 27–34

Gillespie, Iris: 'Richard Wagner and the heroic mystique', *Wagner*, xii (1991), 99–115

Glass, Frank W.: *The Fertilizing Seed: Wagner's Concept of the Poetic Intent* (Ann Arbor, 1983)

Gollancz, Victor: *The Ring at Bayreuth: And Some Thoughts on Operatic Production* (London, 1966)

Golther, Wolfgang: *Die sagengeschichtlichen Grundlagen der Ring-Dichtung Richard Wagners* (Charlottenburg, 1902)

Göttling, Carl Wilhelm: *Nibelungen und Gibelinen* (Rudolstadt, 1816)

Grimm, Jacob: *Deutsche Mythologie*, 4th edn, 3 vols (Gütersloh, 1875–8); trans. J.S. Stallybrass as *Jacob Grimm's Teutonic Mythology* (London, 1883–8, R/1966)

Grimm, Jacob and Wilhelm: *Deutsches Wörterbuch*, 33 vols (Leipzig, 1854–1971, R/1984)

————: 'Märchen von einem, der auszog das Fürchten zu lernen', *Kinder- und Hausmärchen*, 10th edn (Berlin, 1858), 13–24; trans. Stewart Spencer as 'Tale of the youth who left home to learn fear', *Wagner*, iii (1982), 48–53

Gutman, Robert W.: *Richard Wagner: The Man, His Mind, and His Music* (London, 1968)

Hartford, Robert, ed.: *Bayreuth: The Early Years* (London, 1980)

————: 'The first London "Ring"', *Wagner*, iv (1983), 127–32

Hauptmann, Gerhart: *Das gesammelte Werk*, 17 vols (Berlin, 1942)

Hegel, Georg Wilhelm Friedrich: *Hegel's Philosophy of History*, trans. J. Sibree (New York, 1956)

Höfler, Otto: *Siegfried, Arminius und die Symbolik* (Heidelberg, 1961)

Hollingdale, R.G.: *Nietzsche: The Man and his Philosophy* (London, 1965)

Hollinrake, Roger: 'Carl Dahlhaus and the *Ring*', *Wagner 1976*, ed. Stewart Spencer (London, 1976), 68–82

————: *Nietzsche, Wagner, and the Philosophy of Pessimism* (London, 1982)

Huber, Herbert: *Richard Wagner: Der Ring des Nibelungen nach seinem mythologischen, theologischen und philosophischen Gehalt Vers für Vers erklärt* (Weinheim, 1988)

Hübscher, Arthur: 'Schopenhauer und Wagner', *Schopenhauer-Jahrbuch*, xxxvi (1956), 26–31

Ingenschay-Goch, Dagmar: *Richard Wagners neu erfundener Mythos: Zur Rezeption und Reproduktion des germanischen Mythos in seinen Operntexten* (Bonn, 1982)

Jacobs, Robert L.: 'A Freudian View of *The Ring*', *Music Review*, xxvi (1965), 201–19

————: 'The Shakespearean element in the "Ring"', *Wagner*, iv (1983), 2–9

John, Nicholas, ed.: *The Valkyrie*, English National Opera Guide 21 (London, 1983) (contains essays by Geoffrey Skelton, Barry Millington, George Gillespie and Andrew Porter)

————, ed.: *Siegfried*, English National Opera Guide 28 (London, 1984) (contains essays by Ulrich Weisstein, Anthony Newcomb and Derrick Puffett)

————, ed.: *Twilight of the Gods*, English National Opera Guide 31 (London, 1985) (contains essays by Michael Tanner, Robin Holloway and Christopher Wintle)

————: ed. *The Rhinegold*, English National Opera Guide 35 (London, 1985) (contains essays by John Deathridge, Roger North and Stewart Spencer)

Jung, Carl Gustav: *Symbole der Wandlung* (Zurich, 1952); trans. R.F.C. Hull as *Symbols of Transformation* (London, 1956)

Just, Klaus Günther: 'Richard Wagner – ein Dichter? Marginalien zum Opernlibretto des 19. Jahrhunderts', *Richard Wagner: Von der Oper zum Musikdrama*, ed. Stefan Kunze (Berne and Munich, 1978), 79–94

Kamenka, Eugene: *The Philosophy of Ludwig Feuerbach* (New York, 1970)

Karbaum, Michael: *Studien zur Geschichte der Bayreuther Festspiele* (Regensburg, 1976)

Kelly, Aileen: *Mikhail Bakunin* (New Haven and London, 1987)

Kester, Sally: *An Examination of the Themes of Love, Power and Salvation in Richard Wagner's 'The Ring of the Nibelung': The Study of a Failed Individuation Process* (diss. Univ. Western Australia, 1984)

Kinderman, William: 'Dramatic Recapitulation in Wagner's *Götterdämmerung*', *19th Century Music*, iv (1980/81), 101–12

Kneif, Tibor: 'Zur Deutung der Rheintöchter in Wagners "Ring"', *Archiv für Musikwissenschaft*, xxvi (1969), 297–306; trans. Stewart Spencer as 'On the meaning of the Rhinemaidens in Wagner's "Ring"', *Wagner*, x (1989), 21–8

Kreckel, Manfred: *Richard Wagner und die französischen Frühsozialisten: Die Bedeutung der Kunst und des Künstlers für eine neue Gesellschaft* (Frankfurt am Main, 1986)

Kropfinger, Klaus: *Wagner und Beethoven*

(Regensburg, 1974); trans. Peter Palmer as *Wagner and Beethoven: Richard Wagner's Reception of Beethoven* (Cambridge, 1991)

Kunze, Stefan: 'Über Melodiebegriff und musikalischen Bau in Wagners Musikdrama dargestellt an Beispielen aus *Holländer* und *Ring*', *Das Drama Richard Wagners als musikalisches Kunstwerk*, ed. Carl Dahlhaus (Regensburg, 1970), 111–44

Lachmann, Karl: *Zu den Nibelungen und zur Klage* (Berlin, 1836)

Large, David C.: 'The Political Background of the Foundation of the Bayreuth Festival, 1876', *Central European History*, xi (1978), 162–72

Lee, M. Owen: *Wagner's 'Ring': Turning the Sky Round* (New York, 1990)

Levin, Irving: 'Some Psychoanalytic Concepts in Richard Wagner's "The Ring of the Niblung"', *Archives of Criminal Psychodynamics*, iii (1959), 260–316

Lévi-Strauss, Claude: *Le Regard éloigné* (Paris, 1983); trans. Joachim Neugroschel and Phoebe Hoss as *The View from Afar* (Oxford, 1985)

Lévy, Albert: *La Philosophie de Feuerbach et son influence sur la littérature allemande* (Paris, 1904)

Lied vom Hürnen Seyfrid, Das, ed. K.C. King (Manchester, 1958)

Liszt, Franz: 'Richard Wagner's Rheingold', *Sämtliche Schriften*, 9 vols, ed. Detlef Altenburg (Wiesbaden, 1989), V,115–17

Lloyd-Jones, Hugh: 'Wagner', *Blood for the Ghosts: Classical Influences in the Nineteenth and Twentieth Centuries* (London, 1982), 126–42

Lorenz, Alfred: *Das Geheimnis der Form bei Richard Wagner: I. Band · Der musikalische Aufbau des Bühnenfestspieles Der Ring des Nibelungen* (Berlin, 1924)

Löwith, Karl: *Von Hegel bis Nietzsche* (Zurich, 1941); trans. David Green as *From Hegel to Nietzsche: The Revolution in 19th Century Thought* (London, 1965)

Lunen, Wilhelm: 'Der Ring des Nibelungen', *Dinge der Zeit*, i (1947), 60–104; English trans. in *Contemporary Issues*, v (1954), 156–99

McClatchie, Stephen: 'The warrior foil'd', *Wagner*, xi (1990), 3–12

McCreless, Patrick: *Wagner's 'Siegfried': Its Drama, History, and Music* (Ann Arbor, 1982)

———: 'Schenker and the Norns', *Analyzing Opera: Verdi and Wagner*, ed. Carolyn Abbate and Roger Parker (Berkeley, 1989), 276–97

Mack, Dietrich: *Der Bayreuther Inszenierungsstil* (Munich, 1976)

Magee, Bryan: *Aspects of Wagner*, 2nd edn (Oxford, 1988)

———: *The Philosophy of Schopenhauer* (Oxford, 1983)

Magee, Elizabeth: 'Wagner's "Wibelungen" and the Royal Library at Dresden', *Wagner*, x (1989), 2–6

———: *Richard Wagner and the Nibelungs* (Oxford, 1990)

Mann, Thomas: *Wagner und unsere Zeit*, ed. Erika Mann (Frankfurt am Main, 1963); trans. Allan Blunden as *Pro and contra Wagner* (London, 1985)

Millington, Barry: 'An Introduction to the Music of "The Valkyrie"', *The Valkyrie*, ed. Nicholas John (London, 1983), 17–26

———: 'Nuremberg Trial: Is there anti-semitism in *Die Meistersinger*?', *Cambridge Opera Journal*, iii (1991), 247–60

———: *Wagner*, 2nd edn (London, 1992)

———, ed.: *The Wagner Compendium* (London, 1992)

Millington, Barry, and Spencer, Stewart, eds.: *Wagner in Performance* (London and New Haven, 1992)

Müller, Ulrich, and Panagl, Oswald: 'Die mittelalterlichen Quellen zu Richard Wagners "Ring"-Dichtung', *Die Programmhefte der Bayreuther Festspiele 1988: II – 'Das Rheingold'*, 15–66; English trans., 123–51; *III – 'Die Walküre'*, 67–99; English trans., 147–68

———: 'Literatur und Mythologie der Griechen in Richard Wagners "Ring"-Dichtung: Eine kommentierte Dokumentation', *Die Programmhefte der Bayreuther Festspiele 1990: III – 'Das Rheingold'*, 17–31; English trans., 45–59; *IV – 'Die Walküre'*, 13–18; English trans., 26–31; *V – 'Siegfried'*, 10–30; English trans., 39–63; *VI – 'Götterdämmerung'*, 26–35; English trans., 57–64

Müller, Ulrich and Wapnewski, Peter, eds.: *Richard-Wagner-Handbuch* (Stuttgart, 1986); English trans., ed. John Deathridge (Cambridge, MA, 1992)

Müller, Wilhelm: *Geschichte und System der altdeutschen Religion* (Göttingen, 1844)

Nattiez, Jean-Jacques: *Tétralogies – Wagner, Boulez, Chéreau: Essai sur l'infidélité* (Paris, 1983)

———: '"Fidelity" to Wagner: Reflections on the Centenary *Ring*', *Wagner in Performance*, ed. Barry Millington and Stewart Spencer (London and New Haven, 1992), 75–98

———: *Wagner androgyne* (Paris, 1990); trans. Stewart Spencer as *Wagner Androgyne* (Princeton, NJ, 1993)

Neumann, Angelo: *Erinnerungen an Richard Wagner*, 3rd edn (Leipzig, 1907); trans. Edith Livermore as *Personal Recollections of Wagner* (London, 1909)

Newcomb, Anthony: 'The Birth of Music out of the Spirit of Drama: An Essay in Wagnerian Formal Analysis', *19th Century Music*, v (1981/2), 38–66

Newman, Ernest: *The Life of Richard Wagner*, 4 vols (London, 1933–47, R/1976)

———: *Wagner Nights* (London, 1949) [as *The Wagner Operas* (New York, 1949)]

Nibelungenlied, Das, ed. Karl Bartsch and Helmut de Boor, 21st edn (Wiesbaden, 1979); trans. Arthur T. Hatto as The Nibelungenlied (Harmondsworth, 1969)

Nietzsche, Friedrich: Der Fall Wagner, ed. Dieter Borchmeyer (Frankfurt am Main, 1983); Walter Kaufmann's translation of 'The Case of Wagner' may be found in Basic Writings of Nietzsche (New York, 1968), 601–48

Noon, Ray: '"Know you what Wotan wills?"', Wagner, viii (1987), 122–42

Osborne, Charles: The Complete Operas of Richard Wagner (London, 1990)

Panagl, Oswald: '"Vermählen wollte der Magen Sippe dem Mann ohne Minne die Maid": Archaisches und Archaisierendes in der Sprache von Wagners Ring', Die Programmhefte der Bayreuther Festspiele 1988 – IV: 'Siegfried', 37–65; English trans., 108–29

Panzer, Friedrich: Das Nibelungenlied: Entstehung und Gestalt (Stuttgart, 1955)

Petersen, Peter: 'Die dichterisch-musikalische Periode: Ein verkannter Begriff Richard Wagners', Hamburger Jahrbuch für Musikwissenschaft, ii (1977), 105–23

Petsch, Robert: 'Der "Ring des Nibelungen" in seinen Beziehungen zur griechischen Tragödie und zur zeitgenössischen Philosophie', Richard Wagner-Jahrbuch 2, ed. Ludwig Frankenstein (Berlin, 1907), 284–330

Poetic Edda. Edda: Die Lieder des Codex Regius, ed. Gustav Neckel and Hans Kuhn, 2 vols (Heidelberg, 1962–8); English translations by Henry Adams Bellows (New York, 1968) and W.H. Auden and Paul B. Taylor (London, 1981)

Porges, Heinrich: Die Bühnenproben zu den Bayreuther Festspielen des Jahres 1876 (Chemnitz and Leipzig 1881–96); trans. Robert L. Jacobs as Wagner Rehearsing the 'Ring' (Cambridge, 1983)

Preetorius, Emil: Richard Wagner: Bild und Vision (Berlin, 1942); trans. Stewart Spencer as 'Richard Wagner: Stage Picture and Vision', Wagner, xii (1991), 75–86

Rather, L.J.: The Dream of Self-Destruction: Wagner's 'Ring' and the Modern World (Louisiana, 1981)

Rose, Paul Lawrence: Wagner: Race and Revolution (London, 1992)

Sabor, Rudolph, trans.: Richard Wagner: Rheingold (London, 1991)

Saga of Thidrek of Bern, The, trans. Edward R. Haymes (New York and London, 1988)

Sans, Édouard: Richard Wagner et la pensée schopenhauerienne (Paris, 1969)

Schadewaldt, Wolfgang: 'Richard Wagner und die Griechen: Drei Bayreuther Vorträge', Hellas und Hesperien, 2 vols (Zurich, 1970), II,341–405

Schopenhauer, Arthur: Die Welt als Wille und Vorstellung, ed. Arthur Hübscher, 2 vols (Wiesbaden, 1988); trans. E.F.J. Payne as The World as Will and Representation, 2 vols (New York, 1969)

Serova, Valentina: 'Richard Wagner: An extract from my memoirs', Teatral'nïy i muzikal'nïy zhurnal Artist, xii (1891), 64–72; trans. Roland Matthews, Wagner, xii (1991), 13–24

Shaw, George Bernard: The Perfect Wagnerite: A Commentary on the Ring of the Niblungs (London, 1898); reprinted in Shaw's Music, ed. Dan H. Laurence, 3 vols (London, 1989), III, 408–545

Simrock, Karl: Die Edda, die ältere und jüngere, nebst den mythischen Erzählungen der Skalda (Stuttgart, 1851)

Skelton, Geoffrey: Wagner at Bayreuth: Experiment and Tradition, 2nd edn (London, 1976)
———: Wagner in Thought and Practice (London, 1991)

Snorri Sturluson: Heimskringla: Sagas of the Norse Kings, trans. Samuel Laing, rev. Peter Foote (London, 1961)
———: Edda, trans. Anthony Faulkes (London, 1987)

Spencer, Stewart: '"Zieh hin! Ich kann dich nicht halten!"', Wagner, ii (1981), 98–120
———: 'Who were the Nibelungs?', Wagner, x (1989), 14–21
———: 'Wagner's Middle Ages', The Wagner Compendium, ed. Barry Millington (London, 1992), 164–7

Srocke, Martina: Richard Wagner als Regisseur (Munich and Salzburg, 1988)

Stein, Jack Madison: Richard Wagner & the Synthesis of the Arts (Detroit, 1960)

Stephan, Rudolf: 'Gibt es ein Geheimnis der Form bei Richard Wagner?', Das Drama Richard Wagners als musikalisches Kunstwerk, ed. Carl Dahlhaus (Regensburg, 1970), 9–16

Stern, J.P.: Nietzsche (Glasgow, 1978)

Strobel, Otto, ed.: Richard Wagner: Skizzen und Entwürfe zur Ring-Dichtung (Munich, 1930); English translations of the prose sketches and drafts of the preliminary stages of the Ring appear in Bayreuth Festival programmes for the Ring for 1984 and 1985
———: 'Zur Entstehungsgeschichte der Götterdämmerung', Die Musik, iv (1933), 336–41

Suneson, Carl: Richard Wagner och den indiska tankevärlden (Stockholm, 1985); Ger. trans. 1989

Tanner, Michael: 'The Total Work of Art', The Wagner Companion, ed. Peter Burbidge and Richard Sutton (London, 1979), 140–224

Tarasti, Eero: Myth and Music (Helsinki, 1978)

Thorp, Mary: The Study of the Nibelungenlied: Being the History of the Study of the Epic and Legend from 1755 to 1937 (Oxford, 1940)

Vaget, Hans Rudolf: 'Strategies for Redemption: Der Ring des Nibelungen and Faust',

Wagner in Retrospect, ed. Leroy R. Shaw, Nancy R. Cirillo and Marion S. Miller (Amsterdam, 1987), 91–104

Vajda, László: 'Weisheitskampf und Lebenswette', *Die Programmhefte der Bayreuther Festspiele 1988: IV – 'Siegfried'*, 16–35; English trans., 97–107

Volsunga saga, trans. Friedrich Heinrich von der Hagen (Breslau, 1815); English translations by Eiríkr Magnússon and William Morris (London, 1870), R.G. Finch (London, 1965) and Jesse L. Byock (Berkeley, 1990)

Voss, Egon: *Studien zur Instrumentation Richard Wagners* (Regensburg, 1970)

————: 'Noch einmal: Das Geheimnis der Form bei Richard Wagner', *Theaterarbeit an Wagners Ring*, ed. Dietrich Mack (Munich, 1978), 251–67; trans. Stewart Spencer as 'Once again: the secret of form in Wagner's works', *Wagner*, iv (1983), 66–79

Wagner, Cosima: *Die Tagebücher*, ed. Martin Gregor-Dellin and Dietrich Mack, 2 vols (Munich and Zurich, 1976–77); trans. Geoffrey Skelton as *Cosima Wagner's Diaries*, 2 vols (London and New York, 1978–80)

Wagner, Richard: *The Nibelung's Ring*, trans. Alfred Forman (London, 1877)

————: *Gesammelte Schriften und Dichtungen*, 10 vols, 2nd edn (Leipzig, 1887–88); trans. William Ashton Ellis as *Richard Wagner's Prose Works*, 8 vols (London 1892–99)

————: *Mein Leben*, ed. Martin Gregor-Dellin (Munich, 1976); trans. Andrew Gray as *My Life* (Cambridge, 1983)

————: *The Ring of the Nibelung*, trans. Andrew Porter (London, 1977)

————: *Selected Letters of Richard Wagner*, ed. Stewart Spencer and Barry Millington (London, 1987)

Wais, Kurt: *Frühe Epik und die Vorgeschichte des Nibelungenliedes* (Tübingen, 1953)

Wapnewski, Peter: 'Der Ring und sein Kreislauf: Überlegungen zum Textverständnis der "Götterdämmerung"', *Die Programmhefte der Bayreuther Festspiele 1984: VI – 'Götterdämmerung'*, 25–50; English trans., 74–98

Westernhagen, Curt von: *Richard Wagners Dresdener Bibliothek 1842 bis 1849* (Wiesbaden, 1966)

————: *Die Entstehung des 'Ring'* (Zurich, 1973); trans. Arnold and Mary Whittall as *The Forging of the 'Ring': Richard Wagner's Composition Sketches for 'Der Ring des Nibelungen'* (Cambridge, 1976)

Weston, Jessie Laidlay: *The Legends of the Wagner Drama: Studies in Mythology and Romance* (London, 1896, R/1976)

White, David A.: *The Turning Wheel: A Study of Contracts and Oaths in Wagner's 'Ring'* (Selinsgrove, London and Toronto, 1988)

Whittall, Arnold: 'Wagner's Great Transition? From *Lohengrin* to *Das Rheingold*', *Music Analysis*, ii (1983), 269–80

————: 'Analytic Voices: The Musical Narratives of Carolyn Abbate', *Music Analysis*, xi (1992), 95–107

Wiessner, Hermann: *Der Stabreimvers in Richard Wagners 'Ring des Nibelungen'* (Berlin, 1924, R/1967)

Windell, George C.: 'Hegel, Feuerbach, and Wagner's *Ring*', *Central European History*, ix (1976), 27–57

Winkler, Franz: *For Freedom Destined: Mysteries of Man's Evolution in the Mythology of Wagner's Ring Operas and Parsifal* (New York, 1974)

Winterbourne, A.T.: 'Wagner's *Ring* and the Nature of Freedom: Some Kantian Speculations', *British Journal of Aesthetics*, xxviii (1988), 341–52

Wintle, Christopher: 'The Numinous in *Götterdämmerung*', *Reading Opera*, ed. Arthur Groos and Roger Parker (Princeton, NJ, 1988), 200–234

Wolzogen, Hans von: *Thematischer Leitfaden durch die Musik von R. Wagner's Festspiel 'Der Ring des Nibelungen'* (Leipzig, 1876); trans. Nathan Haskell Dole as *Guide to the Music of Richard Wagner's Tetralogy 'The Ring of the Nibelung'* (New York, 1880)

Zurmühl, Sabine: *Leuchtende Liebe, lachender Tod: Zum Tochter-Mythos Brünnhilde* (Munich, 1984)

The 'Ring' on compact disc and video

Compact disc

Potential purchasers of a set of the *Ring* on compact disc have never had a wider range of choice in all price categories. Two rival full-price sets, both with superbly recorded sound, have been issued opera by opera, almost in parallel by **Deutsche Grammophon** and **EMI**. The respective conductors are **James Levine**, with the Metropolitan Opera Orchestra and Chorus, and **Bernard Haitink**, with the Bavarian Radio Symphony Orchestra and Chorus. Much of the playing and singing in the Levine set is magnificent: from beginning to end the ear is ravished. But for all the meticulous pointing up of detail in the score, the tetralogy is all too rarely projected as a compelling drama. Haitink's set lacks the super-refinement and glossiness of Levine's but conveys a better sense of the score's visceral quality, the ruggedness of primeval myth.

The drawback to the EMI set is the Brünnhilde of Eva Marton, whose singing lacks the vibrant presence of her rival Hildegard Behrens on DG. The Siegfried of Reiner Goldberg for DG, on the other hand, is markedly inferior to that of Siegfried Jerusalem for EMI. James Morris is the reliable, authoritative Wotan on both sets.

The first complete *Ring* to be made in the studio was that by **Georg Solti** for **Decca** (1959–66), and the sense of immediacy and drama projected in this set make it far more than simply a historical document. Hans Hotter was the greatest Wotan of his day, even if he was past his prime by the sixties. The set additionally boasts the gloriously incisive Brünnhilde of Birgit Nilsson and the heroic but intelligent Siegfried of Wolfgang Windgassen.

Nilsson and Windgassen also feature on the set recorded by **Karl Böhm** at Bayreuth in 1966–7 (**Philips**). The dynamism and nervous energy of Böhm's live performance in the Festspielhaus are well captured on this set.

Altogether more refined – arguably too refined – is the intimate, chamber approach of **Herbert von Karajan** (**DG**), also from the late sixties, with the less predictable casting of Régine Crespin and Helga Dernesch as Brünnhilde, Jess

Thomas and Helge Brilioth as Siegfried and Dietrich Fischer-Dieskau and Thomas Stewart as Wotan. A second Karajan set, derived from live performances at Salzburg (1967–9), is available on **Hunt**.

Karajan's 'lyrical cosmos' is a far cry from the grand edifices of sound carved out by **Reginald Goodall** on his set recorded by **EMI** live at performances given by the English National Opera in 1973–7. Goodall's spacious tempi may sacrifice something in terms of dramatic immediacy, but his interpretation is notable both for its utterly convincing grasp of the overall structure and for the beauty of its incidental detail. This *Ring* was meticulously prepared over a long period of time, during which the greatest care was given to instrumental balances and vocal nuances. Rita Hunter, Alberto Remedios and Norman Bailey head a cast singing in the English translation of Andrew Porter. Two further modern recordings should be mentioned: that of **Pierre Boulez** on **Philips**, a reading that ideally complemented Patrice Chéreau's demythologized staging of the cycle at Bayreuth (1979–80), and the studio recording of **Marek Janowski** on **Eurodisc**; both are strongly cast.

Of older recordings, there are two classic ones by **Wilhelm Furtwängler**, for many the greatest Wagner conductor of them all. The first, made live at La Scala, Milan, in 1950, has the radiant Brünnhilde of Kirsten Flagstad among its merits and two rather unsatisfactory Siegfrieds (Set Svanholm and Max Lorenz) among its demerits. Furtwängler's incandescent, superbly paced reading makes the set an attractive proposition at bargain price. The other recording by this conductor comes from an RAI broadcast made in 1953. The interpretation is a more majestic one and features the fine Siegfried of Ludwig Suthaus, as well as the Brünnhilde of Martha Mödl. The sound, in the CD set digitally remastered by **EMI**, is acceptable.

Another classic performance released even more recently is that of **Clemens Krauss** (**Foyer**), made at Bayreuth in 1953. The set is notable not only for Krauss's authoritative reading, but also for the admirable performances of Astrid Varnay, Wolfgang Windgassen and Hans Hotter as Brünnhilde, Siegfried and Wotan respectively. A pair of recordings made at Bayreuth in 1957 and 1958 by the great Wagnerian **Hans Knappertsbusch** have been released. The latter, on **Hunt**, again with Varnay, Windgassen and Hotter, is the safer recommendation.

Video and laserdisc

The Bayreuth centenary production by **Patrice Chéreau** (see p. 27) is available on video and laserdisc from **Philips**, as is the one from Munich by **Nikolaus Lehnhoff** (conducted by Wolfgang Sawallisch) from **EMI**. Recordings of the productions by **Harry Kupfer** (Bayreuth) and **Otto Schenk** (Metropolitan, New York) are also in preparation.

Sources of Illustrations

Bayreuth: Copyright Bayreuther Festspiele GmbH 4, 6, (photo Siegfried Lauterwasser) 8, 11, 12, (photo Rauh) 13; Nationalarchiv der Richard-Wagner-Stiftung / Richard-Wagner-Gedenkstätte 2, 3, 7; photo Mara Eggert 14; New York: Metropolitan Opera Association Inc. (photo Winnie Klotz) 15; Private Collection 1; photo Stuart Robinson 9; Seattle Opera 16; photo Helga Wallmüller 10.

The Contributors

WARREN DARCY is Professor of Music Theory at Oberlin College, Ohio. Among his many publications is *Wagner's 'Das Rheingold': Its Genesis and Structure* (1993).

ROGER HOLLINRAKE studied at Cambridge, Harvard, Oxford and Heidelberg Universities and at the Royal College of Music. He has made a study of music and philosophy and written widely on Wagner and Nietzsche.

ELIZABETH MAGEE is the author of *Richard Wagner and the Nibelungs* (1990) and a regular contributor to *Wagner*. Dr Magee studied in Vienna.

BARRY MILLINGTON is the author of the Master Musicians *Wagner* (1984), editor of *The Wagner Compendium* (1992) and co-editor of *Selected Letters of Richard Wagner* (1987) and *Wagner in Performance* (1992). He writes regularly for *The Guardian* and contributed the Wagner article to the second edition of *New Grove*.

STEWART SPENCER taught medieval German language and literature at London University before retiring to devote himself to writing and translating. He is co-editor, with Barry Millington, of *Selected Letters of Richard Wagner* (1987) and *Wagner in Performance* (1992). He is the author of *Wagner Remembered* (2000).